FRANZ ROSENZWEIG: HIS LIFE AND THOUGHT

Franz Rosenzweig:

HIS LIFE AND THOUGHT

PRESENTED BY NAHUM N. GLATZER

SCHOCKEN BOOKS · NEW YORK

SECOND, REVISED, EDITION

Second Printing, 1967

Library of Congress Catalog Card No. 53-656

Manufactured in the United States of America

PREFACE TO THE SECOND EDITION

Eight years ago, when the first edition of this volume appeared, the name of Franz Rosenzweig was barely known in the English-speaking countries. Since then, however, the small group of those who took note of Rosenzweig's work has greatly expanded and today includes a variety of thinking people everywhere. Increasingly, he is being ranked among the outstanding contemporary Jewish philosophers and religious thinkers in general. His work is studied in universities and theological schools and is the basis for a number of dissertations. Rather than soliciting consent, his thinking inspires a critical re-evaluation of the reader's intellectual position: it opens a dialogue with the reader. Rosenzweig's heroic life (related in the first part of the present work) adds to the interest in his philosophical and religious discourse; but ultimately, it is the discourse that counts.

The ground is prepared for an English rendition of the complete works of Rosenzweig. Preparations are under way for English editions first of the *Notes* on the poetry of Judah ha-Levi, then of the *Star of Redemption*.

For the new edition of the present volume the text was revised in several places and printing errors corrected; the selected bibliography has been brought up to date.

NAHUM N. GLATZER

May 1961.

CONTENTS

INTRODUCTION

INTRODUCTION

1

When, after the end of the First World War, Franz Rosenzweig took residence in Frankfort on the Main and assumed the leadership of the Freies Jüdisches Lehrhaus, he said in one of his first lectures: "You will always understand what I say; but you will probably always be vexed by what I say . . . because I intend to shatter ideas that have become very dear to you."

Thus did he make his appearance in bourgeois, well-to-do, traditionalist, and rather stolid Frankfort. He came ready to fight for the soul of his audience, unwilling to compromise, and not at all afraid to become an enigma. An enigma, indeed, he remained to many. His personal life was full of unusual, unanticipated turns; his writings a challenge; his teachings contrary to expectation.

The course of Rosenzweig's life and the contents of his work are in a paradoxical relation to each other. Where an incident in his biography would suggest that one could find a sentimental or, anyway, an irrational reflection in his work, we find a most rigid and sober formulation. Where the perfect architectonic of a book would lead one to imagine a scholar working under the most comfortable conditions, we find the author a soldier in the trenches, writing out his manuscript of several hundred pages on army post cards which are dispatched home one by one. An outsider looking on at the observance of the Sabbath in Franz Rosenzweig's home—with prayer, benedictions, song, and a scru-

pulous abstinence from all proscribed manner of work—
would expect to find a strictly Orthodox Jew. He would
discover that this man was one of the most undogmatic
thinkers of his time.

Those who knew only the believing Jew Rosenzweig, at-
tentively studying the Talmud and its commentaries, could
not have guessed this man to be the author of such a philosophic work as *Hegel und der Staat* ("Hegel and the State").
The German academicians, on the other hand, would have
found it strange had they known that one of them was
translating medieval Hebrew poetry and writing theological
treatises on the Bible.

And to cap the paradox: Where the reader of a brilliant,
audacious essay brimming with exuberant humor would
imagine its writer to be a happy and healthy warrior of the
mind, a man in his prime, the biography would instead reveal another man, one paralyzed for many years, and without the faculty of speech—dependent on his wife for help
in the transmission of each and every syllable.

When Sigmund Freud heard how Rosenzweig had tran-
scended his terrible affliction and managed to live the life of
an active scholar and prolific essayist and critic, he said:
"The man had no other choice!"[1] The founder of psycho-
analysis, in this instance, looked for no complexes, no secret
causes, but simply accepted the extraordinary mould of this
life as its normal shape. Here he was certainly right. For
all the outward contradictions in the life and work of Franz
Rosenzweig cohere to form a singular drama, a personal
history that is unique, yet exemplary.

2

The story of Franz Rosenzweig is the story of a redis-
covery of Judaism. A European intellectual and assimilation-

[1] Robert Waelder, *The Living Thoughts of Freud*, 1941, p. 17.

ist breaks with his personal past and becomes a Jew by conviction, rediscovers his people's existence, and becomes the modern interpreter of this existence.

A West European intellectual, he was a proud heir of the nineteenth century. This was the bourgeois world of faith in progress, a faith assured by the steady development of science; the evolution of man and of society appeared inevitable. The belief in "the infinite perfectibility of the human race," as Rousseau put it, made for an air of optimism that pervaded the universities, academies of art, and other institutions of scholarship and *Bildung*. The man of action was not alone in considering himself the master of all he surveyed; he shared the field with the thinker who, following Hegel, believed in the omnipotence of thought, for whom thought was "not an impotent thing that is found, so to speak, in our heads, and may or may not be transformed into realities according to our own whims. Thought itself is action; thought itself is reality" (Hegel). The young Rosenzweig identified himself with this *Weltanschauung* of progress and faith in reason.

Emancipation had opened the windows of the self-contained Jewish communities toward this new world of the spirit. Jewish separation, as expressed in the traditional synagogue and home rituals, seemed obsolete and meaningless. As for the messianic universalist ideas proclaimed by the prophets and preserved in rabbinic doctrine and prayer—they, it was felt, had found their fulfilment, or at least were in the process of realization, in European humanity.

It happened that a member of Rosenzweig's family had taken an active part in the process of freeing Jewish existence from the separateness that had largely characterized it up to the nineteenth century. The fact of his family's involvement in this development made a strong impression on Rosenzweig, evident before and after his conversion. Repeatedly, in his writings, we find reference to the family actor in this particular turn of Jewish history—Samuel Meir Ehrenberg, Rosenzweig's great-grandfather.

S. M. Ehrenberg (1773-1853) was an instructor, later the superintendent, of the Jewish Free School in Wolfenbüttel (Duchy of Brunswick). He counted among his pupils the historians Isaac Marcus Jost and Leopold Zunz, who laid the foundations of the *Wissenschaft des Judentums* ("Science of Judaism"), a movement that propagated an objective and scholarly—one might almost say clinical—approach to the culture and history of the Jews on the assumption that no further living growth and development could be expected of Judaism.

Zunz (who once asked a Russian Jew, introduced to him as a Hebrew poet: "When did you live?") described the life of S. M. Ehrenberg and his institution in a little volume, privately printed in 1854. He quite properly characterized the school as "the institution that was originally a Talmudic school in which a few general disciplines were tolerated, later a scholarly institution in which Talmud was tolerated and finally a high school without Talmud instruction." Thus the impact of Enlightenment and Emancipation made itself felt; Ehrenberg, aware of the demand of the hour, put it this way: "I show my students the path we must take if we wish to be more highly esteemed among the nations." The aim of the school became to "transform ignorant, ill-bred *bahurim*, crude in speach and ideas, into well-bred, polished young men." Traditional learning was replaced by an introduction to universal ethics. Special courses undertook to "define those fundamental moral ideas which form the cornerstone of all moral and theological doctrine." A printed manual was used for the "details of religion." The Pentateuch was read in Mendelssohn's translation, done into the best German of the day. Classical commentaries of the Bible were no longer studied; all necessary explanations were given orally. In 1848, fired by revolutionary hopes,

Ehrenberg advocated that from that year on the phrase, "this year we are slaves, next year we shall be free men," be omitted from the Passover Haggadah.

Ehrenberg, and the majority of Jewish modernists with him, felt that the step from Jewish seclusion into the European world was a mere matter of necessary adjustment, the result of which would be a compromise or a synthesis between inherited Judaism and the modern spirit. But, generations later, to Franz Rosenzweig the process of whole-hearted adjustment and integration necessarily demanded baptism. The other great-grandsons of S. M. Ehrenberg—Rosenzweig's close friends, Hans and Rudolf Ehrenberg—became and remained faithful Christians, a fact which made an early and powerful impression on Rosenzweig; it demonstrated an honest conclusion, once the premise was accepted.

3

An examination of the intellectual movements prevailing at the beginning of the century led Rosenzweig and his friends (all in their early twenties) to a critical attitude toward German idealism, Hegel's "religious intellectualism," and the overemphasis on a history in which God supposedly reveals himself. Against Hegel's theodicy of history that stamped the individual person's life as merely subjective, as a "passion" irrelevant to the whole, Rosenzweig and his friends felt that God must redeem man not indirectly, through history, but individually, through religious practice. In his "Diaries," Rosenzweig notes: "The battle against history in the nineteenth-century sense becomes for us the battle for religion in the twentieth-century sense."

More and more Rosenzweig moved away from academic philosophy as taught in the German universities of the day, more and more he felt himself drawn toward the "existential" philosophy that took its starting point in the situation of the concrete individual person. Religion seemed to hold the key. Yet Rosenzweig, trained in the sciences, in logical criticism, and in methods of modern historical research, could not conceive of a Western scholar "accepting religion," after all.

In Eugen Rosenstock, a Christian of Jewish descent, jurist and historian by profession, Rosenzweig possessed a friend who, against the formal, timeless, abstract truths of logic, spoke of a truth that is revealed in the relationship of man with God, and with his fellow man. In contrast to the logos of philosophy that has the nature of a monologue, Rosenstock reinterpreted the biblical "word" as a part of a dialogue. His philosophical position, rooted in religious faith, was secure, while Rosenzweig, though outspoken in his criticism of contemporary philosophy, had not yet broken through to a positive solution. In the frequent discussions between the two men, in which Rudolf Ehrenberg sometimes made a third—the time was the spring of 1913— Rosenzweig found himself, contrary to his instincts, defending a belief in autonomous scholarship and the relativist position of philosophy against Rosenstock's faith based on revelation.

Yet Rosenzweig came gradually to realize, more and more, that his friend's thinking was sounder than his own. Rosenzweig could not counter the faith of the Christian with the faith of a Jew, for Judaism as understood by Rosenzweig appeared then to be an anachronism. Rosenstock regarded his friend's superficial Judaism as merely "a personal idiosyncrasy, or at best a pious romantic relic" that could not address itself to a modern man in search of orientation in the Western world. Rosenzweig himself felt that a Jewish intellectual had only two choices: Zionism, if he wanted to affirm his Judaism, or baptism, if he turned to religion as a Western European.

In the course of a conversation between the two friends, the problem was brought up of the man in *The Miracles of Antichrist* by Selma Lagerlöf. Rosenzweig asked: What would you do when all answers fail? Rosenstock replied, with the simplicity of faith: I would go to the next church, kneel and try to pray. These simple words did more than all the previous discussions concerning reason and faith, history and revelation, Hegel and Nietzsche, to convince Rosenzweig that Christianity was a living power in the world. That a man like Rosenstock, not a naive believer and not a romantic, but a scholar and thinker, was able to accept religion as his personal answer, showed Rosenzweig that a union of mind and faith was indeed possible. He came to see, with the clarity of conviction, that an intellectual's attitude toward the world and history can be one of religious faith. He had thought that faith existed, but not for the objective scholar. Now he learned differently.

Rosenzweig then proceeded to assert that philosophy, historically speaking, had until the eighteenth century represented the pagan element in thought and had operated in opposition to religion, but that in modern times it had been transformed and absorbed by the church. The modern (Protestant) church makes room for the thinker. Rosenzweig noted that Descartes and Leibniz "no longer regard themselves as pagans outside the church, but as active, more or less vocal, heretics *within it*."[2] The next step is the return of the heretics into the bosom of the church, as evidenced by Kant, Fichte, Schelling, and Hegel. From now on "the destiny of philosophical speculation is bound up with the church. Philosophy has renounced its autonomy as far as the contents of thought are concerned. 'Philosopher' no longer means 'free thinker' as it did with some justice up to

[2] *Letters*, p. 81.

the eighteenth century. The philosopher is no longer the *discipulus Graeciae* whom Tertullian distinguished from *discipulus coeli,* but simply, without reservations, a Christian. Hegel can be considered the 'last philosopher' in the old sense of the word—Hegel himself realized that—and the first of the new church fathers, a fact which Hegel did not realize."[3] The new leaders of the church, Rosenzweig continued, do not sit on bishops' thrones in the principal cities of the *oekumene;* they are to be found on the most advanced frontiers of thought and culture. Scholarship, which as the heritage of the Greeks existed before the establishment of the church, came, in 1500, into the possession of the church; in 1800 it became part and parcel of the church. The nineteenth century finds scholarship, science, philosophy *within* the church.

It would be an easy task to show how only partially correct this interpretation of the history of philosophy was, and how an entirely different reading could be given of the relation of philosophy and the church in the nineteenth century. Nevertheless, for a young scholar with a strong tendency toward a religious orientation within the world, such an interpretation of modern Protestantism afforded a forthright solution that could do justice alike to scholarship and faith, reason and revelation. Indeed, it appeared to be the only practical way out of Rosenzweig's personal dilemma, accepting as he did the historical position of German Protestantism and the historical development and structure of the Western world as final, as metaphysically necessary.

4

Rosenzweig decided to become a Christian. Systematically minded and history-conscious, he made only one pro-

[3] *Ibid.*

vision, a procedural one: He wished to enter Christianity as did its founders, as a Jew, not as a "pagan." Rosenzweig attended the synagogue services of the New Year's Days and the Day of Atonement *in preparation* for the church. Here was a Jew who did not wish to "break off," but who deliberately aimed to "go through" Judaism to Christianity.

He was stopped on his way and called back into Judaism. This event came about with that suddenness and in that spirit of absolute finality reported in great conversions. Rosenzweig's biography indicates that it happened during the service of the Day of Atonement, 1913.

On the Day of Atonement, the Jew, though united with his brethren in prayer, stands utterly alone before his God, attired in his shroud as he will be on the day of his death. The Jew is nothing other than man, and God nothing other than the judge of the world. The drama of this day begins on its eve, with the *Kol Nidre* in which the Jew frees himself of unintentional commitments to his fellow man. All guilt against man the Jew must have remitted before commencing this day. Thereafter he is no longer guilty before man; his sin is a sin before God.

The liturgy of the day leads through psalms and hymns to the scriptural readings in which the ancient sacrificial rites of atonement are contrasted with man's obligation "to undo the bands of the yoke, to let the oppressed go free and to deal bread to the hungry" which is "the fast that God has chosen." From here the liturgy leads through the recollection of the ancient Temple service of the Day of Atonement at which the high priest pronounced—this single time in the year—the ineffable name of God (who is near to those who call upon Him), to the reading of the story of Jonah the prophet who tried to flee from God (who is near to those who forsake Him).

The hour of sunset nears when the worshipper once more

expresses his desire to "enter Thy gate," to experience eternity within the confines of time. Then, in utmost solemnity, the congregation cries out the profession: "Hear. O Israel, the Lord our God, the Lord is One!" and finally "The Lord is God: The God of Love, He alone is God!" In this profession, followed by the sounding of the ram's horn, the drama of the Day of Atonement finds its resolution.

Rosenzweig left the services a changed person. What he had thought he could find in the church only—faith that gives one an orientation in the world—he found on that day in the synagogue.[4]

He never mentioned this event to his friends and never presented it in his writings. He guarded it as the secret ground of his new life. The very communicative Rosenzweig, who was eager to discuss all issues and to share all his problems with people, did not wish to expose the most subtle moment of his intellectual life to analyses and "interpretations." His alert mother realized immediately the connection between her son's attendance at the Day of Atonement service and his new attitude, and later confided this conclusion of hers to the present writer. But the mother's contention could only be convincing if confirmed by some internal evidence.

Rosenzweig looked upon the event which he had lived through as incomplete, as a *partial* experience. Once he remarked: "The reasoning process comes afterwards. Afterwards, however, it must come." And he added: "The attempts of our 'irrationalists' to establish separate accounts for faith and knowledge enrage me wherever I meet them."[5] And in commenting on a poem by Judah ha-Levi he said: "To have found God is not an end but in itself a begin-

---

[4] A parallel experience is reported by the great Protestant interpreter of faith, Rudolf Otto, author of *The Idea of the Holy* who conceived his notion of *tremendum* as a central factor in religion after participating in a Day of Atonement service in a simple North African synagogue.
[5] *Letters*, p. 620.

ning."[6] If Rosenzweig had been a mystic—he was not!—he would have found it possible to comprehend the event immediately; the thinker needed time to clarify his experience to himself. But the fact of the experience is certain. The long letter home in which he discusses Christianity and Judaism and which concludes almost parenthetically with the remark that he seems to have found the way back, is written only twelve days after that Day of Atonement. A few days later follows a letter to Rudolf Ehrenberg announcing that he has "reversed his decision" to become a Christian. "It no longer seems necessary to me and . . . *no longer possible.*"[7] "No longer necessary" might still imply an intellectual decision; "no longer possible" hints at a radical personal experience. In another letter to Rudolf Ehrenberg he agrees on what the church means to the world, namely, that no one can reach the Father save through Jesus; but "the situation is quite different for one who does not have to *reach* the Father because *he is already with him.*"[8] This conviction betrays a certainty that does not come to a man through thinking; it points to a profound, instantaneous event.

Only in later years, when Rosenzweig has completed his new system of thought, integrating into it his concept of Judaism, does he emphasize the paramount importance for the understanding of Judaism that must be given to the Jewish liturgy in general and the liturgy of the Day of Atonement in particular. His personal involvement is still hidden from sight, but it becomes increasingly clear to the student of this life story.

In a lecture at the Freies Jüdisches Lehrhaus in Frankfort on the Main he said: "Anyone who has ever celebrated Yom Kippur knows that it is something more than a mere

[6] *Judah ha-Levi,* p. 204.
[7] *Letters,* p. 71.
[8] *Ibid.,* p. 73.

personal exaltation (although this may enter into it) or the symbolic recognition of a reality such as the Jewish people (although this also may be an element)—it is a testimony to the reality of God which cannot be controverted."[9]

In his central work, *Der Stern der Erlösung* ("The Star of Redemption"), Rosenzweig describes the Jew who on the Day of Atonement "confronts the eyes of his judge in utter loneliness as if he were dead in the midst of life . . . Everything lies behind him." Then, "God lifts up his countenance to this united and lonely pleading of men," and grants man a part in eternal life. Man's soul is alone—with God. "Everything earthly lies so far behind the transport of eternity . . . that it is difficult to imagine that a way can lead back from here into the circuit of the year."[10]

In his *Judah ha-Levi* Rosenzweig takes up this theme again. He speaks of the tension between God and man which seems irreconcilable on this day of atonement and reconciliation, until in the last profession of the day "man himself, in the sight of God, gives the answer which grants him the fulfilment of his prayer of return . . . In this moment, he is as close to God . . . as it is ever accorded man to be."[11]

Had it not been an experience of his own life, all this could not have been written. This is the voice of a man who broke with his personal history, and—in an act of conversion—had to become a Jew.

5

We have to ask: What actually made—in Rosenzweig's situation—for the priority of Judaism over Christianity?

[9] *Almanach des Schocken Verlags auf das Jahr 5699*, 1938, p. 60.
[10] *Star of Redemption*, III, 80-87.
[11] *Judah ha-Levi*, p. 182.

We are informed that already in 1910, three years before the crucial year 1913, Rosenzweig rebelled against an over-emphasis on history as the sphere in which God reveals himself. The following years led him—slowly—to an acceptance of faith as a possible orientation in the world. But the form of faith which suggested itself—Protestantism—was intimately tied up with that which evoked Rosenzweig's skepticism: history. Rosenzweig realized that the function of the church —to go out and conquer the unredeemed world of the heathens—involves the Christian in the fate of nations and the unfolding of the world-historic drama. The Christian is always on his way from the first to the second advent, through history and its earthly forms, state and church.[12] Only in his course through world history, only by his active participation in its works, does the Christian "gain the experience of the immediacy of the individual to God."[13] This being-forever-on-the-way marks the Christian with the stamp of incompleteness and keeps him in constant danger of compromising with the world and of turning into a pagan—which is what he was before his inner transmutation made him a Christian.

Rosenzweig's first decisive Jewish experience showed him in practice what later became his "theoretical" conviction: that it is the Jewish faith that is free of "the curse of historicity"—a term he first uses in 1914.[14] The law of Israel is not power and expansion, but the anticipation of eternity within life. The rhythm of the sacred (liturgic) year, its sequence of Sabbaths and holy days, the ideas they represent, the realities they create, mirror the eternity of which the Jew partakes. Freed from historic obligation and destiny, living in the vision of eternity, the Jew "must forever

[12] *Star of Redemption*, III, 104.
[13] *Ibid.*, 91.
[14] *Collected Writings*, p. 289.

remain a strange thing and an annoyance to the State and to world history."[15] The eternal people denies itself growth and foregoes decline, both of which are the marks of history. It suffers rejection by the nations and seeming defeat and destruction. Yet the categories of history do not impinge upon the Jew's inner life. He has already reached the goal toward which the nations are still moving. It goes without saying that Rosenzweig does not refer to biblical Israel with its national history and historiography and not to the Second Commonwealth with its political involvements but to "Judaism" after the destruction of the second temple.

As a metahistoric religion, Judaism cannot be known by its external fate and by its external expressions. It can be understood from within only. "For now," Rosenzweig writes to Eugen Rosenstock, "I would have to show you Judaism from within, that is, in a hymn."[16]

In the concrete historical world in which Rosenzweig started to think philosophically and theologically "there seemed to be no room for Judaism."[17] But then, again, in the world, subjected to historical laws, conditioned by historical forces, there was no room for an unmediated, free relation between man and God. In this dilemma, Rosenzweig discovered metahistoric Judaism.

6

The *Star of Redemption,* written by *Unteroffizier* Franz Rosenzweig at the Macedonian front, in hospitals, and, after the collapse of the front line, on the march of the retreating army, is the most curious of "war books." A militant book it is, especially in its first parts, and confident of victory in

[15] *Star,* III, 95.
[16] *Letters,* p. 688.
[17] *Ibid.,* p. 72.

its final passages. The enemy it attacks is the philosophy of German idealism, the home it defends is the individual, the suffering, erring, loving, doubting, despairing, and hoping human being whom the philosophy of the classical systems has so badly neglected, letting him vanish in the "whole." The proud sweep of the speculative philosophical systems which constructed all reality out of "concepts" independent of experience and empirical knowledge, which identified reality with conceptual, theoretical truth, ignored the deepest anxiety of man: his fear of death, the nearness of death, the perilous nature of his existence; "Only" the individual dies, nothing can ever die in the "whole," says the philosopher; but the "individual *quand même*" does not accept this verdict and stubbornly resists his annihilation within the system. The singleness of the living person, his consciousness, his death, the paradox of his existence within the world, disturb the rhyme and the rhythm of the total view of idealistic philosophy. True, man strives for knowledge, but he also longs for love to redeem him from solitude and death.

The "new thinking," in which Rosenzweig joins in the anti-Hegelian revolt, and which is the thinking of the individual *quand même*, considers the carefully and ingeniously constructed "Whole" and "Absolute" as an arbitrary, impersonal abstraction of the "pure Ego." The new thinking as presented in the *Star of Redemption* goes back to the original three elements of reality, the parts of the "Whole": Man-World-God. Our thinking (dialectical or otherwise) is unable to deduce the one element from the other, to transform the one into the other. In a state of separation these elements appear in heathen imagery. There we find the tragic hero, dumb, alien to men and to God; the plastic cosmos—without a beginning and without an end, unrelated to man and God; the gods of myth in their hiddenness, far removed from the doings of men. This pagan world is not a false world, but a true one—in a veiled, unrevealed state. The paths that link the elements Man-World-God, leading them to a state of reality, Rosenzweig calls by names borrowed from theology: Creation-Revelation-Redemption.

Creation is the process which establishes the relation between God and World. Here God, hitherto hidden in the mythical beyond, appears and gives the world reality. The final word of Creation is transitoriness, finiteness, and that which endows the living creature with the quality of "past," namely death. However, Creation, the first act of God, necessitates continuation and renewal. This process Rosenzweig calls Revelation.

In Revelation, God in his love turns to man, calls him by his name. The awareness of God's love awakens in man the consciousness of an "I." Only as a loved one does the soul of man assume reality. In this love, man overcomes his original dumbness and becomes an individual able to speak and give answer to God's first command: to love. Man loves because God loves him. This love is only of the "present," and the command to love—the highest of all commands—is only of the present. This "command" can never turn into a "statute," cold, scrupulous, designated for the future. Love, ever present, is the basis of ever-present revelation. There is no love that is only "human" or sensual; here human and divine fuse in one; the passing moment mirrors an eternal ground.

Man, awakened to the awareness of himself, receives in Revelation his name and the knowledge of the name of the loving and present God. A name is not an empty sound as in the heathen world, but a living word which ends dumbness and establishes orientation: beginning and end, origin and aim. Now, a concept of world history becomes possible.

Man translates his love for God into love for his "neighbor." In this love man takes part in leading the world toward Redemption. It is in the practice of deeds of love that the fleeting moment is filled with eternity. Redeeming love frees man from the finality of death. Redemption in its fullness, the perfected world, eternity—this a man experiences in his prayer, in the cycle of the days of rest and the rhythm of the holy days which form the sacred year. In living the sacred year, man anticipates eternity in his earthly time. In this experience death is overcome.

Judaism and Christianity are two views of the world under the aspect of Creation-Revelation-Redemption. Both are representations of the real world (and as such equal before God) and spell the end of the heathen view of the world. Judaism, which stays with God, stands in contrast to Christianity, which is sent out to conquer the unredeemed world and is forever marching toward God. The beginning of the way, the advent of Jesus, is the central fact in the life of the Christian who identifies it with the redemption. Revelation is the chief motive in the sacred year of the church. Judaism, in the third part of the Sabbath, in the Days of Awe, and especially in the Day of Atonement, culminates Creation and Revelation by the experience of Redemption.

Rosenzweig's work is the first attempt in Jewish theological thought to understand Judaism and Christianity as equally "true" and valid views of reality. Yet this does not lead to a suggestion of compromise or to a wish for harmonization. The two forms (Rosenzweig avoids the term religion) will exist, will have to exist, to the end of historical time. And forever will the Christian who is eternally on the way through history resent the Jew to whom it is granted to realize eternity in time, in a metahistorical existence.

Is Judaism the "eternal life," the truth? Do "eternal life" (Judaism) and "eternal way" (Christianity) together constitute "the truth"? Rosenzweig's answer gives an insight into the ultimate seriousness of his faith. Man can become aware of the Love of God (Revelation), he can fill the moments of his life with eternity (Redemption), but Truth is beyond man. Only God is Truth, Man (Jew, Christian) is given a part in truth [*Wahrheit*] insofar as he realizes in active life his share in truth [*bewähren*]. The distant vision of truth does not lead into the beyond, but "into life" — which are, not accidentally, the concluding words of the book.

7

Rosenzweig's impatient criticism of philosophical idealism and historicism brings him into the neighborhood of the Kierkegaard revival, and into the discipleship of Schelling in his last period and of Nietzsche. The starting point of Rosenzweig's new approach coincides with existentialism: the human creature in need and aware of its mortality, antedates thinking and the "productive" reason of idealism. The intimate tie between thought and language seen by Rosenzweig is paralleled by a similar insight of Martin Heidegger. These similarities and correspondences, however, are not enough to make Rosenzweig an existentialist philosopher or expressionist writer. What they show us is Rosenzweig as a man of his time.

A different matter is the world view he presents in answer to the quest of the old-new man: his reconstruction of the world out of Creation-Revelation-Redemption. Here, and in the reinterpretation of concepts such as divine love, the miracle, the name, Rosenzweig takes a decisive step in modern Jewish theology. Jewish thinkers have for a period of a hundred and fifty years done their best to devitalize Jewish theology. Blinded by the sharp light of philosophical idealism, they identified Judaism with humanism, with a religion of reason, with man's moral autonomy. Jewish philosophers like Solomon Formstecher and Samuel Hirsch sought to justify Judaism before the throne of philosophy. They presented the Jewish religion as identical with the universal ethical truth of a religion of reason. Such an identification relieved the Jew of the burden of giving a philosophical explanation of Judaism; this work was done by general religious philosophy, and the results were valid also for the Jewish thinker, provided he could prove that the ideas of Judaism were identical with the ideas of the religion of reason.[18] Jewish philosophy then, engaged in establishing this identity, lost interest in the actual theological problems that had absorbed Jewish thinkers before the Emancipation.

The transition from this to a new period is marked by the works of Leo Baeck, Hermann Cohen and Martin Buber, older contemporaries of Rosenzweig, who, each one in his own way, represent a new orientation in Jewish religious thought. Rosenzweig is distinguished from them by his more radical break with the past and his renascence of theological concepts that were last alive in the long forgotten sphere of independent, dialectical Kabbalah. (This parallel, first recognized by Gershom G. Scholem, is doubly significant, since Rosenzweig never was a mystic.) As distinct from the nineteenth-century Jewish thinker who made man the measure of all things in the universe, Rosenzweig restores the position of classical theology: Man before God as the measure of life.

8

The *Star of Redemption* is an inspired book. Yet its inspiration did not prevent it from remaining a book of theories, speculations, doctrines. In a letter addressed to the present writer, a few months before his death, Rosenzweig

---

[18] Julius Guttmann, *Die Philosophie des Judentums*, 1933, p. 318.

calls his book "a theory that grew out of an ardent longing." The longing was to reach the state of a man who stands before God, and who lives in this faith. It was this state that Rosenzweig experienced at the Day of Atonement 1913, and whose reality was further revealed to him in the Jewish section of Warsaw, where his war duties had brought him on a visit shortly before he wrote the *Star of Redemption*.

The vision of the Jew who accepts the world and the fulness thereof as divinely ordered and willed; who even if shaken by the problems of reason and faith, reason and revelation, always feels the ground under his feet; who in misfortune may ask why?—yet trusts that an answer is provided; who in the study of the law, in his daily prayer, is able to overcome innumerable obstacles—this vision of faith captivated the thinker Rosenzweig. He felt that such a Jew would *anticipate* the theoretical insights of the thinker by the simple fact of living as a Jew, without employing the complicated machinery of his intellect.

In his *Star of Redemption*, which we have called a war book, Rosenzweig fought not only against abstract philosophy and for the individual *quand même*, but also against the abstract philosopher *in himself* and in behalf of the lonely individual in doubt, consumed by skepticism and intellectual distrust—whom he also found within himself— and in search of the certainty of faith. Nietzsche, who as one of the first "new thinkers" had a decisive impact on Rosenzweig's own "new thinking," is, after all, also one of the fathers of European nihilism. We do well not to deny the challenge of this aspect of Nietzsche in considering Rosenzweig's journey to faith. It was this nihilist undercurrent in Rosenzweig's thinking which in various disguises threatened to blow up the claims of the spirit. The secret hold of this enemy on the searching man—who in the initial stage of the battle had lost the potential ally of reason—

accounts for the fierceness of the struggle. Modern man's condition (presented with ultimate precision by Franz Kafka) is to stand in a world grown silent, waiting for the message that never reaches him—and it is also Rosenzweig's intellectual position. This is the "death," the initial motive in the *Star of Redemption*. From this battle against his own skepticism and his own tendency toward abstraction in its demonic sense, Rosenzweig emerged victorious. In the process of writing the *Star of Redemption*, Rosenzweig emerged a free man.

Freedom implied a complete autonomy of choice and decision; a rejection of dogma, formula, and prearranged results; an abandonment of all that would prevent a mind from being open to the unpredictable; a freedom from fear of life and fear of death ("fearlessness in the face of the world is a sign of the spirit's presence and aliveness").[19]

As a free man, Rosenzweig freed himself from the bondage of his own book. Freedom of theory, dogma, and abstraction, could not mean *writing* about that freedom; a vision of faith could not mean describing this vision in a book. Only actual day-to-day life could furnish the proof for the validity of a book, or else demonstrate that the victory was only imaginary and the vision but an empty dream. Only life offered a chance for theories not to turn into phrases, for symbols not to be dissolved into play, for a declaration of faith not to sink back into the abyss of nihilism.

With an admirable ease Rosenzweig minimized the importance of his book. Already in 1919, the year of the book's completion, Rosenzweig called it an "episode" in his life.[20] Somewhat later he called the *Star* an armor which

19 *Collected Writings*, p. 502.
20 *Letters*, p. 368.

protected him until he learned to get along without it.[21]
To his teacher, Professor Friedrich Meinecke, he wrote in
1920 that he did "not attach any undue importance" to his
work. In reviewing the "dangerous book," as he called it,
he wrote: "Everyone should philosophize at some time in
his life, and look around from his own vantage point. But
such a survey is not an end in itself. The book is no goal,
not even a provisional one. Rather than sustaining itself,
or being sustained by others of its kind, it must itself be
"verified." This verification takes place in the course of
everyday life."[22]

9

"Life" comes to mean to Rosenzweig Jewish life, in a
very broad and profound sense. That he enters Jewish life
as a free, and thus as a modern, man, makes his biography
a matter of significance for contemporary Jews. That Jewish
life in this day and age became the testing ground for a
modern man's problems that were not specifically "Jewish,"
gives Rosenzweig's life a scope beyond the particular
interests of the Jew.

The period of "verification" lasted ten years, through
eight of which Rosenzweig suffered his paralysis. (The
nature of his illness forced him to go back to writing,
when he had intended to use the living word.) In these
years Rosenzweig was the driving force of a Jewish renascence which, inaugurated by the treatises *Zeit ist's* ("It Is
Time") and *Bildung und kein Ende* ("On Education"),
found its main expression in the Freies Jüdisches Lehrhaus
in Frankfort and similar institutions throughout Germany.
The activities of the Lehrhaus, many-sided and variegated

---

[21] *Ibid.*, p. 421.
[22] *Collected Writings*, pp. 396 f.

as they were—some indeed designed to attract a wide audience—centered around the small study groups which Rosenzweig considered the heart of the school. Here Rosenzweig advocated a reorientation in Judaism to result from reestablished contact with the classical sources, and from a renewed practice of Judaism. The basic attitude is freedom. No recipe can be given, no rules can be set. But the sincere attempt cannot fail in restoring the sacramental quality of Jewish learning. Learning, i.e., turning documents of the past into life-words of the present, led to observance of the Jewish law not as ritual and ceremony but as a manifestation of religious truths. In advocating such a renascence of Jewish traditionalist practice especially in *Die Bauleute* ("The Builders"), an epistle addressed to Martin Buber, Rosenzweig rejected the theory of Western Orthodoxy which overstressed the legal aspects of the law.

Rosenzweig's Judaism, receiving its orientation from classical Jewish texts, encompassed the whole width and profundity of Israel's culture as it had been before the Emancipation; before, in an attempt at Europeanization, it had accepted historical and sociological norms as the measure of spiritual values, and had thus limited the scope of Judaism as well as narrowed down its relevance. Rosenzweig freed Judaism from historically conditioned limitations. He saw again in Judaism one of the supra-human powers and a supra-Western force. He well knew that in order to be of help in the crisis of Western culture, Judaism had to become "secularized," i.e., brought into living contact with the "worldly" life of man. "The ability to secularize itself again and again proves its eternity."[23] (Similarly, Rosenzweig realized that within the Western world social-

[23] *Letters*, p. 476.

ism, even in its atheist form, contributes more to the establishment of the kingdom of God than religious institutions and their adherents.)[24] Unacceptable, however, is secularization as a modernist dogma. Though a force active in time, Judaism must know how to return to its meta-historical source. There, Law resists a pseudo-legal interpretation as given by Orthodoxy; monotheism resists a pseudo-logical, and social justice a pseudo-ethical interpretation, as advanced by religious liberalism.[25]

Rosenzweig criticized, from this standpoint, the theory of Zionism prevailing in his time (and chiefly represented by Jacob Klatzkin) according to which only the soil of Palestine and only the Hebrew language could guarantee the goal: "normalization" of Judaism. Against this uncritical acceptance of ideas of Emancipation, Rosenzweig maintained that mere historical existence has its diabolical limitations; that a normal existence of the Jewish people should be but a precondition for higher aims; that "today" is not only a bridge to "tomorrow," but a board for jumping off to eternity.[26] The liberal critics of Zionism who stressed the "essence of Judaism" and the idea of eternity, were told by Rosenzweig that eternity as understood by Judaism lies not in the metaphysical clouds of timelessness but in its realization in our days. ("There is no 'essence of Judaism,' there is only: 'Hear, O Israel!' ")[27]

In this spirit Rosenzweig translated Judah ha-Levi's poetry and finally undertook, with Martin Buber, to translate the Bible for the modern German reader, to elucidate certain phases of the inner history of the Bible, and to confront the Western Jew with the reality of the Bible.

---

[24] *Ibid.*, p. 580.
[25] *Collected Writings*, pp. 111 ff.
[26] *Letters*, p. 158.
[27] *Almanach des Schocken Verlags auf des Jahr 5699*, p. 54.

These writings were a part of the plan to reveal the scope of the Hebrew sources. It is here where he most successfully showed how much of ageless Israel can be activated and relived by a modern, free, Jew.

It is in the way Rosenzweig applied himself to these activities and to the sphere of classical and traditional Judaism that he "verified" his theory of faith, translating doctrine "into life," and finally conquering the opposition from within.

The greatest test were the eight years of paralysis. Here "life" meant enduring, with an upright spirit, pain, physical privation, and gradual decline of the strength to live; it meant filling every day with spirit; with help and counsel to family, friends, and the community at large; and with a healthy sense of humor. All this in preparation for the great day of death which was to be accepted in faith and in freedom.

Here is a note of the poet Karl Wolfskehl written after a visit in Rosenzweig's home:

"Whoever stepped over the threshold of Franz Rosenzweig's room entered a magic circle and fell under a spell, gentle yet potent—in fact, became himself a charmed being. The solidity and the familiar forms of every-day life melted away and the incredible became the norm. Behind the desk, in the armchair sat, not as one had imagined on climbing the stairs, a mortally sick, utterly invalid man, almost totally deprived of physical force, upon whom salutations were lost and solace shattered; behind the desk, in the chair, Franz Rosenzweig was throned. The moment our eyes met his, community was established. Everything corporeal, objects as well as voices and their reverberations, became subject to a new order, were incorporated without strain, conscious effort, or need for readjustment, into that wholly genuine, primordially true kind of existence irradiated by beauty. It simply couldn't have been otherwise, for what reigned here was not pressure and duress, but utter freedom. . . .

"It was not only that all petty human feelings, anxieties and embarassments were wiped out. It was not only that all the paltry, complacent pity of well-being was purged away. What happend here was much more: in the presence of this man, *well* in the fullest sense, one's own welfare was assured, wholly and in accord with the spirit. Near Franz Rosenzweig one came to oneself, was relieved of one's burdens, heaviness, constriction. Whoever came to him, he drew into a dialogue, his very *listening* was eloquent in itself, replied, summoned, confirmed and guided, even if it were not for the unforgettably deep and warm look of the eyes. . . ."[28]

The freedom achieved in Rosenzweig's life is not identical with existence, as in Sartre's existentialism, where, curiously enough, it refers back to Hegel's *Phänomenologie des Geistes*. It is rather the status granted to man who, in crisis reached the end of the road, and "out of the depths" beheld the presence of God. It is the freedom of Abraham *after* the "Binding of Isaac," his final trial. It is the freedom of man before God. Here, theories, formulas, speculations, doctrines, dogmas and all "isms" are silenced. Now, issues and objects no longer matter.

Rosenzweig, perhaps, never achieved in actuality his vision of the naive simplicity of a pious Jew. He remained a modern man. But his freedom became the freedom of man before God. This consciousness achieved ever purer forms, ever subtler points. In the last sentence which he started to write shortly before his death: "And now it comes, the point of all points, which the Lord has truly

[28] *Franz Rosenzweig: Eine Gedenkschrift,* 1930, pp. 35 f.

revealed to me in my sleep. . ." he might have wished to express something final. The sentence remained unfinished.

The first part of the book, the life story of Franz Rosenzweig, is composed of letters (some presented here for the first time), diaries (published here for the first time), reports and diaries of his physicians, and the notes of some of his friends. The second part, the thought of Franz Rosenzweig, offers a cross section of his major works, as well as the shorter essays and epistles, some in a condensed form. This cross section introduces the reader to the major themes of Rosenzweigs' philosophy and to the ideas of the Jewish Renaissance in Western Europe that he represented. The book is not intended as an analysis and interpretation of Rosenzweig's work.

It is not expected that this volume shall induce the American reader to accept Rosenzweig's views. What may engage the reader is the genuineness of the search for faith without loss of common sense and a sense of humor; the Western European's thrill at discovering the central issues of classical Judaism; and above all, the heroism of his life; there is drama in it, and greatness.

The passages of the biographical part are arranged in a manner to document the life and intellectual journey of Franz Rosenzweig. The short connecting texts (printed in smaller type) are meant to provide information not contained in the quoted material, and supply introductory notes whenever necessary. This biographical part starts with the story of the eighteen-year-old student; from that time on quotable material was available. For the first period of Rosenzweig's life the following notes may suffice.

Franz Rosenzweig was born in Cassel on December 25, 1886; he was an only child. His father, Georg Rosenzweig, was a respected and successful manufacturer of dyestuffs, and an energetic community leader. Adele Rosenzweig, Franz's mother, was a woman of charm and *esprit,* with an intuitive understanding of everything noble in life and in letters. She had a lively enthusiasm for art, for music, and poetry.

The Rosenzweig home was a gathering place for prominent city officials, representatives of the government, and various civic groups; and the family's social and intellectual life was involved with communal and state affairs, and with the literary and artistic events of the day.

Self-respect demanded affiliation with the Jewish community, and any suggestion that the members of the family embrace the state religion would have been rejected. The rudiments of religious tradition—Bar Mitzvah, High Holidays—were still observed, superficially. Franz himself did not learn of the existence of the Sabbath eve until after he was in college. The Rosenzweigs' was a formal Judaism, lacking in devotion and depth.

Franz's early life was importantly influenced by an older member of the family who lived with the Rosenzweigs: his granduncle, Adam Rosenzweig (1826-1908, a brother of Louis Rosenzweig) who was a xylographer by trade. It was through him that the young Franz gained an insight and, even, some access into a "Jewish world." Franz owed his granduncle more than this; it was through him (rather than through home and school) that Franz received his earliest, most formative impressions of the German world—that is to say, the German world of the middle nineteenth century; Moritz von Schwind, Peter Cornelius, Anselm Feuerbach, and Goethe, Dürer, Rembrandt. To be sure, these "German" impressions were later overgrown by others, more powerful and immediate; while it fared quite otherwise with the boy's initial meeting with Jewishness. First, there was the realization of Adam Rosenzweig's passionate heart—the earliest experience of true pathos in Franz's life. Then, there were established a number of concrete Jewish values and meanings; not many, yet sufficiently strong to become a source of strength in later years. "The thin thread of tradition has become the thread around which everything can crystallize."

In 1893 Franz entered grammar school. Joseph Prager, Franz's schoolmate, and later his friend, relates:

"When, at the age of six, he was setting off to school for the first time, full of the scholar's new dignity and proud of his big satchel, his uncle seized him in both arms, shook him violently by that same satchel, and said emphatically: 'My boy, you are going among people for the first time today; remember as long as you live that you are a Jew.'"

In 1896 Franz entered the Friedrichs-Gymnasium. Outside of school, he took violin lessons, and in later years he recalled with disgust the trash of operatic potpourris, etc. he was made to play. This went on until he literally forced his teacher to stop making him play Bériot, Wieniawski, and their like. Meanwhile, he was paying frequent visits to the Cassel Art Gallery; there among other great and treasured works of art, Franz discovered Rembrandt's "Blessing of Jacob," and it became for him the most familiar of all great paintings. Always, later in life, whenever he heard talk of painting, the magnificent "Blessing of Jacob" would be conjured up for him.

Franz read the Bible in Zunz's German translation. It was the family Bible, and Zunz was the Rosenzweigs' "family saint." Much later, he rememberd that he used to read that Bible pantheistically, for, as he said, he "read it without the help of tradition, hence without revelation." Then once, when he was about eleven years old, he came home from school bearing a report with the highest marks. His father offered to reward him with the granting of a wish. "I want a teacher with whom I can really learn Hebrew," was Franz's request.

In 1904 the Rosenzweigs left their original Cassel residence, which also housed the business offices (Untere Königstrasse), and moved to more spacious quarters (Wilhelmshöher Allee). Franz's room was furnished in "Jugendstil": sofa and chairs of pale violet. Here Franz brought together his friends, Hans and Rudolf Ehrenberg, Gertrud Frank (later Oppenheim), and Joseph Prager, for long and fiery discussions. Many years afterward, Franz visited this old childhood home; walked up the stairs, and had the sensation of being his own ghost.

FRANZ ROSENZWEIG

First Part

The Life

Told mainly in Franz Rosenzweig's
own words, in letters and diaries
and in notes and reports of friends

I

A STUDENT OF MEDICINE, HISTORY, PHILOSOPHY

1904-1912

A youth of many talents discovers the adventure of knowledge and of art, the excitement of living and thinking, and of friendship.

Franz Rosenzweig was eighteen, and about to finish his course at the high school; for a time he was undecided as to what field to enter at the university. He vacillated between science, philology, history, and medicine; in the end he chose medicine.

Cassel, December 1904, to Gertrud Frank:
At last I feel really secure, at ease, almost free of the leap-into-the-unknown feeling. Recently, when I expressed concern about doctors having to be so constantly occupied with the sick, X. reassured me with a beautiful maxim which I cannot remember at the moment. So now it is to be medicine, not pure science as I had thought. . . . I am making good progress with the violin. Not, as I once hoped, in a direction contrary to my natural one, but in my own.

Cassel, April 3, 1905, to Gertrud Frank:
I have been taking drawing lessons for a week. Every day I spend either a whole morning or a whole afternoon

1

at it. It is impossible to describe how marvelous this life of constant receptivity is, since I finished my exams. Eyes, ears and mind. Now school is over, I begin to see how much room in my brain this damned institution has occupied in spite of my holding it in low esteem. I wish now I could share something of myself with you. Too bad your visit didn't work out.

I noticed the other day that my onetime Father in Heaven has dwindled to a weather-maker. It amused me, since it represents a backward evolution. Ordinarily it is the weather gods (Wodan, Zeus) who gradually evolve into ethical *melechs hoaulom*,[1] but with me it happened the other way round.—Good night!

His first semester (summer 1905), F. R. studied at the University of Göttingen, the second and third (autumn 1905 to autumn 1906), in Munich. For his mother's birthday, September 1905, he wrote a letter in which he took leave of his childhood home: "It was like starting on a long journey with no certain destination." A Jewish fraternity tried to pledge F. R. October 22, 1905, to his parents:

Rather dismally the following: last night I found rather pleasant so far as I care for this kind of thing at all. The people as individuals were nice-looking, cheerful and well-mannered. Very few typically Jewish-looking young men, some of the handsome racial type, about half without marked traits. The prevailing tone exactly the same as among Christian students, which is meant neither as praise nor censure. Even the beer-drinking code showed no trace of Jewish *esprit*. It was just the opposite.

After this test, racial anti-Semitism seems to me more

---

[1] Kings of the universe ("King of the Universe": Jewish appellation for God).

senseless even than before. These people are, at least at their present age, as completely "German students" as can be imagined.

As for the particular case, Franz Rosenzweig: I've observed in the past with some surprise that other people recognize one sooner than one does oneself; and I've come to believe that I really am blasé, as several of my aunts have been telling me for some time.

I suppose I really am a doddering old man of eighteen, blasé to what gives the "student" pleasure. It seems so, and no doubt it's a bad sign. Yet while I find it bad, I am afraid of drastic remedies; I don't want to slough off my old sink—it's so very comfortable.

Munich, November 12, 1905, to his parents:
I wish I were a symphony by Beethoven, or something else that has been completely written. What hurts is the process of being written. Given my choice I would want to be tonight's, the B flat Major.

Munich, November 25, 1905, to his parents:
As to the dreadful human body, it is actually one of the most attractive, and working on it is pleasanter than you might imagine. At least it gives me much the same feeling as though I were drawing. And in any case dissecting it is a less harmful, more useful activity than dissecting God, spirit, and Goethe, is it not?

In December 1905, prompted by Hans Ehrenberg, F. R. started a diary in which he jotted down his thoughts and observations (the "black book," so called because of its black cover). Only a few entries concern events. Diary, December 14, 1905, about 2 A.M.:
The dread of taking the first step! I only write this to get started.

In order to produce, one must have a certain amount of shamelessness.

January 11, 1906:

"If you take one hundred million years to represent the history of organic evolution of our globe, and then project this time onto twenty-four hours, the entire historical epoch represents only *five seconds*." The other day in the train I wrote the following gloss on this Haeckelian[2] abomination: "Only five seconds! If they were five seconds of love, understanding, and truth, what would the rest of the day be like?"

January 21, 1906, 11 P.M.:

"Why do you want to become a doctor?"

Yesterday for the first time I was *struck* by this question, probably because this semester too I've spent so little time on medicine. —One thing is certain, what I had hoped from it, concentration, absorption, has not come. I fritter myself away, unfortunately most of the time in emptiness rather than overactivity. I don't in the least question my choice of *studies* (I avoid the word *occupation*, since I have resolved not to think beyond my twenty-fifth year), but it remains to be seen whether this is a valid instinct or only the result of my lack of industry until now. *Fiat experimentum! Fiat*, but tomorow rather than the day after tomorrow.

January 28, 1906:

What do I mean by a "real" friendship? A friendship that understands not only what it knows and can assess empirically (to the extent of one's maturity and experience of life)—this I can offer Hans [Ehrenberg]—but also what it does not know and cannot understand empirically: the kind of friendship that after a year's absence finds the

---

[2] Ernst Haeckel (1834-1919), a Darwinian evolutionist.

friend "unchanged," because one has shared unconsciously in all his mutations, so that he seems at any moment close and familiar.

Mephistopheles—a Faust ten years older.

I can't help thinking that our Emperor will come to a bad end.

February 1, 1906:
Listened to a lecture on the form of American business life. Our social institutions (compulsory workers' insurance, organization of white-collar workers, the fight over pensions, etc.) are all signs of weakness, of the desire for a safe berth, however subordinate, in our bureaucracy. In America people are independent, jobs can be given up, insurance is not legally tied to the job but is undertaken by the individual or the union; the goal is not a safe berth but always a better and eventually a high position. Here the attitude is petty bourgeois, there it is generous and resolute. Here society or the state stands as the protector of individuals, there it only regulates the commerce between individuals, who personally don't wish to be protected at all but want to grow continually stronger.

February 5, 1906, on reading Nietzsche's *Zarathustra:*
You can't *build* anything on Nietzsche, as you might on Goethe or nature.
Who can possibly be a disciple of Nietzsche, base anything on him? He is neither a foundation, nor all-embracing as nature. He is a scaler of heights and therefore lonely. Who dares follow him? Who has enough conceit for that?

Munich, February 6, 1906, to his parents, after a dancing party:
. . . All this goes to show that I had a very good time.

5

A word or two about my various "experiences." I danced the last *Française* with a very pretty painter who had a soft, soothing mezzo-soprano voice. I didn't make any conversation at all, except once to praise her garland of violets. But when the dance was over I opened up and gave her a glimpse of a mind dissatisfied with God and the world. She took me quite seriously and I was highly amused by my parody of myself. In this way the rest of the evening passed very cheerfully. Finally I became quite blunt and made her a solemn declaration of love, "having at last found someone . . ." etc. Here she grew rather alarmed and moved away, saying: "Listen . . . you are much too young for . . . this sort of thing." Whereupon I asked, "For what sort of thing?" She made no reply to this and changed the subject to Storm and Stress, etc. I seized the opportunity, and with somber Storm and Stress gestures and exclamations of amorous despair, I escaped to the landing where I ran into Hans [Ehrenberg] and doubled up with laughter in his arms.

Diary, February 6, 1906:

The need for a human being, which I parodied the other day, is really very strong in me. For what kind of human being? One who admires me critically—that's a more honest way of putting it than one who *understands* me.—*Fi donc!* What a hideous spectacle weakness makes of one! When will there be a change? Not until such a person appears. Only unsatisfied desire appears disgusting, petty; satisfied desire makes one tranquil, simple, rich.

February 9, 1906:

The slogan of 1900 is "Race," in 1800 it was "Humanity." Progress? At least in 1800 the scope was wider, the goal greater.

The Bible is a parable of man's advance to the family,

to the tribe, to a nation with a national ideal, to a nation with a universal ideal (the Prophets). Is the last and most ambitious step—toward the universal ideal—now to be rejected, made impossible? Is the wheel to be turned back one revolution?

February 10, 1906:

When I leave here by Easter I shall barely have tasted the cup Munich. I would need the summer semester.

How I have thanked my Maker whenever I've seen signs of productivity in myself! And how often what I've taken for a springboard has turned out to be the height of the arc! At least for the time being!

Only no pathos!

February 12, 1906:

Tonight at Hans's [Ehrenberg] a gleam of light. We talked of schoolmates, Achilles, differentiation, Homer, matters Greek; Hans suggested that I read Eduard Meyer.[3] At the end of the first half hour an idea struck me: after the preliminary medical exam [*Physikum*]—history. Everything points that way: the direction of my thought and preoccupations; my literary ability; my early idea of a history of German culture after 1870; my habit of grasping things immediately in historical terms; my perception of the individual event as a symbol of the universal; my delight in the individual, characteristic, anecdotal trait; my skepticism, which would not render me unproductive in this field;— other people's judgment of me.

February 19, 1906:

Not to think about thinking! Not to doubt one's doubt! Nietzsche's method: distrust and skepticism. Goethe's method: wonder and scrutiny.

[3] Eduard Meyer (1855-1930), German historian of antiquity and early Christianity.

February 24, 1906, night:

To wean a baby from its bottle you give it something to suck. Some people suck radical theories as a substitute for radical action.

March 15, 1906:

The chief advantage of this kind of note-taking is that it disposes of certain things and makes room for new ideas.— It is a mistake to note down problems: better the rashest hypothesis than a question with a question mark—such notations act as barriers to further thought.

March 27, 1906:

In the magazine *Gegenwart* Ellen Key attacks the position of the modern liberal theologians of compromise, who would see in Jesus the absolute human ideal. She cites good examples to controvert this position. The cliff of compromise upon which modern Protestant theology seeks to save itself is as brittle as the other cliff upon which [Adolf von] Harnack stands: "The spirit of Christianity"— Christian ethics. As though pure ethics could ever produce or nourish a religion.

1) Metaphysical notions (soon developed into dogmas)
2_a) Eu- or
2_b) Cacodaemonist moods
3) A disposition toward myth-making
4) Nationalism.
These four produce (and maintain by constantly feeding the child) religions; usually one component is paramount, but the others also contribute. In the course of time the center of gravity of a religion may shift from one of these pillars to another, but it can never base itself upon ethics. Ethics has its origin outside of religion, in the intercourse

8

between men, and is only brought into the domain of religion in order to support it.

And what is my own Judaism based upon?

1. "It is the religion of my forefathers"—number four of the above causes.

2. "I enjoy observing certain customs without having any real reason for doing so." This would come under the first heading, since the ceremonial law is in a sense our dogma.

3. "I believe in Plato." No. 2_a.

4. "I like to think in terms of biblical images"—No. 3. Of these pillars, 1 is the central and strongest; 2 is a circle of slenderer columns that support the periphery of the temple roof; 3 and 4 are pilasters, strong enough in themselves, but in this particular edifice serving only as ornaments.

In the spring of 1906 F. R. spent the vacation between semesters at home in Cassel. March 17, 1906, to Hans Ehrenberg:

Read much, slept even more. . . . I hope to be able to begin my vacation schedule. Tomorrow afternoon I start drawing again from model, on Wednesday a violin lesson; Hebrew I already started several days ago, and right now I again know what I used to know.

Yesterday afternoon it was suddenly spring. I was in Wolfsanger. The walk there and back was delightful. I am happy as a lark, for such a spring must be enjoyed in the old haunts.

Diary, April 1, 1906:

Why does one philosophize? For the same reason that one makes music or literature or art. Here too, in the last analysis, all that matters is the discovery of one's own personality.

9

Today I visited Aunt Julie [Ehrenberg].
What a pity that beauty cannot delight in itself!

Munich, April 24, 1906:
I spent a week in Berlin. Saw [Anselm] Feuerbach's paintings! I have a pretty good idea of the town. The streetwoman on the Friedrichstrasse epitomizes the meretriciousness of the whole city. The architectural tastelessness almost amounts to style. The Pergamene groups might be by [Karl] Begas and vice versa. The impression is one of over-richness, decline, decadence. Indeed, if such a decadent culture is to manifest itself it must do so in buildings like the Dome and monuments like those of William I and Bismarck. The older monuments express a simple, strong, energetic culture, partly naively trying to realize itself, partly calm and secure in itself.

April 29, 1906:
Any relationship between two people that lacks discretion strikes me as immoral. It shows a lack of mutual respect and, in a certain sense, of self-respect. What should by rights be freely given is demanded in a tactless way.—Most family relationships are of this nature, especially, alas, those between parents and children. It is the same, almost invariably, in married life. This is the cause of the well-known stagnation and "philistinism" of the relationship. Friendship too can degenerate this way. When it does it is ripe for separation. And since there are no external bonds the separation will commonly take place. What operates here is an intellectual modesty, which being more sublime than the physical, must be treated with greater tact.
Read a good deal of Heine.

May 25, 1906:
Hans [Ehrenberg] has brought home to me that I have

gone too far in my concern with heredity. The force of heredity may be reduced to *almost* zero through adaptation. Besides I had forgotten that the individual, as such, is always unique, as the gases H and O combine to form the liquid H_2O, which considered in itself is something new and part from H and O.—Thought of in this way the baptism of Jews loses some of its stigma of desertion. But one must adopt this point of view; one must have the courage to commit oneself to the *individual* which is not conditioned historically; and one has that courage as soon as one no longer feels oneself so conditioned. Whoever has managed to do this need not fear the odium of this despised road.

I am not one of them!

> May 29, 1906:
"What is finally left from the semesters in natural science?"
"Big eyes."

> In June, 1906, F. R. made a trip to Venice. June 5, to his parents, on the impression of Giorgione's *Famiglia:*
You sit there for a few minutes on a rococo chair, and then the miracle happens: Everything I've told you about disappears and you look without knowing what it is you are seeing; you simply turn into eyes. Without passion or emotion, without thought, empty of awareness, including self-awareness: pure vision. This is absolute art in the sense that one speaks of absolute music, the kind of music that represents nothing whatever (not even the kind of unspecified program which most non-program music represents), the music that is nothing but music and can only be *heard*.—It is something so mysterious that one might found a religion on it.

> Diary, August 23, 1906:
Have read the Song of Songs in the Septuagint.

August 27, 1906:

Even chemistry is fun now. I manage to breathe my living breath into the abstract chemical clods; I believe I might even have grown to like mathematics!

September 1, 1906:

I don't think that the daemon is congenital with us; rather it comes to visit us one day and stays for good. The child has only *divinations* of what is to come. Happiness is living on good terms with one's daemon. Unhappiness is being stronger or weaker than one's daemon.

September 2, 1906:

What I call daemon is destiny become man, character incarnate.

September 6, 1906:

I have worshipped God in a variety of forms: childish, Hebrew, biblical, Homeric, natural, pantheistic, Platonic, Christian, and—atheistic.

The business of man in this world is to be man—*"lachay roi"* [*see* Gen. 16:14], to live, to look. Speculation serves him only as a protection, a defense against the crowd of visions. He files away what he has seen and experienced in order to make room for the new. The labels on the pigeonholes are not ends in themselves but merely a means of keeping things in order. The things themselves are what matters.

During his fourth and fifth semesters F. R. continued his medical studies in Freiburg (autumn 1906 to autumn 1907). His philosophical bent led him into Professor Jonas Cohn's class, where he made his first contact with academic philosophy. Freiburg, November 4, 1906, to his parents:
About six o'clock I went to see Cohn at the philosophy

seminar. "My name is Rosenzweig." "Yes, Herr Rosenzweig
—what is your field? "Medicine." "I see. Do you know
anything about philosophy?" Here I lied brazenly. "Yes,
I've studied it on my own." "I see. Have you had any
lectures?" "No." "And you are taking none now?" "I have
no time." "In that case, Herr Rosenzweig, I don't want to
tie you down. If you find it doesn't work, you can drop
out." I bowed. Then the wheels began to turn. He gave
an introduction and assigned research projects (we are
doing Kant's *Critique of Pure Reason*). My turn isn't until
after Christmas, and I'm to talk about—paralogisms!! Do
you know what the word means? Neither do I. A man
got up and read a paper on the Preface to the *Critique of
Pure Reason*. I felt like a savage who has been carried off
to Europe: I didn't understand a single word. During the
discussion that followed Cohn made a point of calling
on me frequently, because I was the black "medical" sheep
or the most naive member of the class or heaven knows
what. "Can you follow, Herr Rosenzweig?" "No." He's very
charming, by the way. It occurs to me that he looks like
Moses Mendelssohn.—I'm becoming quite philo-Semitic.

The philosophy seminar made me late for the concert.
I, Franz Rosenzweig, thus missed the first movement and
half of Beethoven's Op. 127!

Diary, September 29, 1906:
The aged Goethe reworks the problems of the young
one: *Faust,* the Prometheus myth, the Orient (*Divan,* the
plan for *Mahomet*), the maze of *feeling (Elective Affinities)*
—not the maze of action (as in *Wilhelm Meister*). The
Romantic Movement is to him a neo-romanticism; his Storm
and Stress period had been the period of true overmastering
romanticism; with the old Goethe it is a classical, i.e.,
mastered romanticism.

October 8, 1906:

Better write than read,
Better write poetry than write,
Better live than write poetry!

November 17, 1906:

Words are tombstones.

Words are bridges over chasms. One usually walks across without looking down. If one looks down he is liable to feel giddy.

Words are also boards laid over a shaft, concealing it.

To be a philosopher is to open tombs, look into abysses, climb down shafts.

November 29, 1906:

Even Plato's "supreme ideas" (as well as all godheads and divinities)—anthropomorphism?

Here we come to a parting of the ways. One might say: "Only man acts upon man" or "Only the divine (in incarnation, of course) acts upon man," that is to say upon the divine in him. Which is as much as to say that only the human acts upon the human, only the divine upon the divine, so that in the end it becomes a matter of taste which way you put it.

December 9, 1906:

The older one gets the more difficult one finds it to make friends, because one's own store is so great that while there may be individual items in common, these items seem too small a fraction of the whole to form the basis of a common fortune. For the same reason, as one gets older it becomes easier to make acquaintances and cultivate them, since out of a large store it is easier to find suitable articles of exchange.

In August 1907, F. R. passed his preliminary medical examination [*Physikum*], although he had already decided not to continue the study of medicine. He went to the trouble of preparing himself for the examinations only to convince his practical-minded father that he could finish the job he had undertaken. To no avail. His father looked on his shift to the study of modern history and philosophy (Berlin, winter 1907 to summer 1908) as desertion. F. R. repented of his considerateness. "It's simply that father has no memory. It was foolish of me not to think of this." He felt that he would not make a good philosopher ("It's really a horribly abstract business and one must pursue it even more devotedly than medicine"), but he was almost certain that he could become a good historian of civilizations.

Jewish problems did not concern him too deeply. They aroused his theoretical interest but left him personally untouched. Joseph Prager relates:

In 1907 we had three months' vacation together for the pursuit of natural sciences and mathematics. F. R. made the following condition for this joint enterprise: there was to be no mention of Jewish problems. "I don't want to hear about it! I'm not going to be a Zionist."

Diary, December 15, 1907:
"What do you think about death?"
"It is a bad sign to think about it."
Nevertheless it seems strange that I should have no relation with it whatever.

Physiologically speaking, man (i.e. man as phenomenon) is dead all his life. As for man an noumenon, such a thing as "death" (cessation in time) does not exist, since noumena are timeless. Man as phenomenon, body *and* soul, i.e., the physiologist's body and the psychologist's soul, does not die since he has been dead from the start; man as noumenon (the personality) does not die since he has never lived (in time).

February 27, 1908:
Uncle Adam [Rosenzweig] died.

April 4, 1908:

The Middle Ages are the East's revenge on antiquity for Alexander's conquests.

May, 1908:

According to eighteenth-century individualism the individual creates society; according to nineteenth-century individualism, society creates the individual.—The eighteenth century is a private century, the nineteenth century a societal one.

History is psychological "materialism;" stated more generally, materialism of events, while true materialism is ontological. Where the latter says that everything exists in space alone, the former says that everything exists in time alone. Values should be rescued from history as well as from science; both space and time are coffins.

Socrates is the most obscure of the great figures of history. Christ is not obscure at all, because we substitute for him the Christ-image that has been elaborated through the centuries—he lives only in this. But there is no such thing as a "Socrates-image through the centuries." He is not embedded in Plato as Christ is in Christianity; he seems rather the occasion than the germ of Platonism.

May 24, 1908:

The following has a place here: Continuous development from autumn 1900 to autumn 1906; from then to autumn 1907 the negation of this development: until then, I had developed "within Goethe"; then I ventured further, moving along his boundaries. Finally, starting with autumn 1907, the attempt to renew the contact: the thesis, Goethe, and the antithesis, Kant, have been followed by a synthesis for which as yet I have no name, unless it be, as I hope, my own.

In August 1908 he invited Hermann Badt, an ardent Zionist of his acquaintance, to visit him in Hain (Riesengebirge). By way of an attraction he mentions the presence of a "very dear cousin" of his, "whom I would like to have meet an actively enthusiastic Jew, for my kind of passive enthusiasm is after all an unimpressive thing; by its very nature it is unable to move anything on the outside, though it may be enthroned on the inside.—Do come then. We will have fun!"—A note by Hermann Badt:

I came early in the morning and found Franz still in bed. I was permitted to witness the levée and teased him about the length of time it took him and the almost ritualistic ceremonial with which he surrounded it. He reacted to this by giving a long lecture that was half-serious, half in fun. Indeed, he said, the moment of daily reawakening from nightly death was for him the greatest and holiest moment of the day. It was impossible ever to dwell too fondly on this daily renewal, one must taste it consciously in every detail. On that occasion, if I remember rightly, he first spoke those words which he was to repeat later under different circumstances, and which gave me much food for thought. He said that he alone is truly blessed who is able not only to experience consciously this daily reawakening, but also in the moment of death to remain conscious and make the step from this world to the next with his senses still intact.

In the autumn of 1908 F. R. returned to Freiburg (where he stayed until autumn 1910) to study history, mostly under Professor Friedrich Meinecke, the author of *Cosmopolitanism and the National State*. F. R. on Meinecke: "He treats history as though it were a Platonic dialogue, not murder and manslaughter."

In September 1908 F. R. made his first acquaintance with the writings of Hegel. His main teacher of philosophy was Professor Heinrich Rickert. Freiburg, February 20, 1909, to his parents:

Today my paper for Rickert was due; I was greatly excited, and Rickert was somewhat apprehensive over the difficulty of the subject. I laid on Rickert's desk an outline covering two foolscap sheets. "Why?" "To make it easier for you to follow." In the beginning he ignored it rather haughtily, then he picked it up and elaborated on it during the pauses, and finally he held it in his hand throughout the remainder of the talk, and when it was over recommended it to the entire class as an innovation worthy to be followed!

July 19, 1909, to Hermann Badt:

What is your opinion of the Kol Nidre prayer? Why is it the preamble to Yom Kippur? (Also why is it spoken then and not, for instance, on Rosh ha-Shanah?)[4] What is your own view and what do you know of other opinions past and present? (And where can I find material on the subject?)

Hans Ehrenberg accepted baptism and became a Protestant. The Rosenzweig family, itself indifferent in matters of religious faith, nevertheless opposed this break with the ancestral confessional affiliation. Rosenzweig's parents felt that Ehrenberg should have discussed his intention with a Jewish theologian. Freiburg, November 2, 1909, to his parents:

Hans is still in Berlin. I really see nothing shameful in the whole matter. It's an excellent thing, after all, to be able to make contact with religion, even somewhat late—if only for the sake of one's children—when one has been robbed of it by early neglect. Of course it would have been best if Uncle and Aunt had had their children baptized or circumcised at birth, but it's better to repair the omission

---

[4] F. R. used the Ashkenazic pronunciation of Hebrew. As a rule, this volume offers the Sephardic transcription.

belatedly than not at all. Because I am hungry, must I on principle go on being hungry? On principle? Does principle satisfy a hunger? Can being non-religious on principle satisfy a religious need? Or can the empty notation in the registrar's office, "Religion Jewish," satisfy a religious need? If I am given the choice of an empty purse or a handful of money, must I choose the purse? Again on principle?

Freiburg, November 6, 1909, to his parents:

About Hans we simply don't see eye to eye. What you say about the three visits to a Jewish theologian won't hold water. Not even three hundred visits would have changed matters. We are Christian in everything. We live in a Christian state, attend Christian schools, read Christian books, in short, our whole "culture" rests entirely on a Christian foundation; consequently a man who has nothing holding him back needs only a very slight push—the "three visits"—to make him accept Christianity. In Germany today the Jewish religion cannot be "accepted," it has to be grafted on by circumcision, dietary observances, and Bar Mitzvah. Christianity has a tremendous advantage over Judaism: it would have been entirely out of the question for Hans to become a Jew; a Christian, however, he can become. To let you know how serious I am about this, I myself counseled Hans strongly in this direction, and would do it again.

This discussion leads F. R. for the first time to consider the question of Jewish religious instruction in the public schools, which was optional in Germany.

Freiburg, December 5, 1909, to his parents:

However, it doesn't rest with the children but with the parents, and religious instruction is of no avail, at least to us, without a religion that is seen, heard, tasted, and visibly exercised upon the body. With the Christians it's different. I grant that obligatory instruction would be a great step forward, and perhaps this should be made the hub of our religio-political demands; compared with this, the legal status of our communities, etc., is unimportant— for what is the use of the most perfect organization of Jews if there are no Jews left to be "organized"?

January 1910, F. R. participated in a convention of young historians and philosophers held in Baden-Baden. The convention examined contemporary philosophy and tried to overcome the then prevailing emphasis on subjective thinking, in order to reach a common objective ground. Hans and Rudolf Ehrenberg took part in the convention. Here, too, F. R. met Eugen Rosenstock; a lifelong friendship ensued. The attempt to found a permanent cultural organization failed.

During the winter of 1910 F. R. continued his studies. He explored the manuscripts of Hegel's posthumous works, especially his early writings, and began an extensive research in Hegel's political doctrine. Berlin, November 11, 1910, to Hans Ehrenberg:

You can imagine that my days are filled to the brim. I seem to have turned into a day laborer: I start theoretically at ten (actually a little later)—I hope in the future to make my theoretical start at nine. I work straight through in the manuscript room until three when it closes. I remain in the reading room until seven, spending quite a lot of time in the catalogue room; by that time I feel tired and stupid, go to the theater indiscriminately, with the single reservation: no music. Here you have the frame; the picture within, you will scarcely recognize. I've joined the philologists. I make excerpts, collate, I experience commas, make tracings, graphologize, and like Goethe's Wagner am infatuated with the noble parchment. Especially in the beginning it was very exciting and solemn, and from time to time I recapture the experience. This feeling of being an eyewitness, a direct observer of Hegel's various attempts to formulate his ideas, is sublime. Besides I have the pleasant sensation of being at the ultimate source and not, as when one depends on books, of forging ahead with the uncomfortable feeling always that one look at the manuscript might bring my house of cards tumbling down. It's a slow process all right but each day I make some progress, and rarely before have I had such a philistine feeling of useful and well-ordered activity. There are no entirely new writings, but there is much that contributes to the understanding of the ones we know: excerpts, sketches, variants.

> As a result of this winter's work, F. R. came to feel "that I have now developed a tendency toward extensive historical universality; my former tendency was exclusively toward the intensive." In the spring of 1911 F. R. interrupted his Hegel research and in two weeks of "concentrated inspiration" conceived a plan for a "history of the tragic individuality in Germany since Lessing."[5] The projected book, an outline of which was found among F. R.'s posthumous writings, was to have been entitled "The Hero." F. R. forced himself to continue the work on Hegel and the State, postponing "The Hero" until he should have completed the former work. Berlin, September 28, 1911, to Gertrud Oppenheim:

Yet I am looking forward to it, for the child will doubtless bring me many surprises. This joy now lies chained in the background of my existence and barks every once in a while. But in the foreground the philological chickens scratch about and among them a proud psychological rooster crows loudly from time to time: this is going to be my dissertation.

[5] Gotthold Ephraim Lessing (1729-1781), critic and dramatist.

One section of the still unfinished Hegel work became F. R.'s doctor's thesis in the summer of 1912, by which time he had concluded his formal studies at the university. "The Hero" was never written. Berlin, November 6, 1911, to Amschel Alsberg, his maternal grandfather, on the latter's seventy-fifth birthday:

I know that like all old people you would, if you were asked, speak more ill than good of old age; and though I know this, I still wish to attain old age, simply to experience this too, this entirely new relationship to things, so consummate, so detached, so "all this really doesn't concern me." Consequently, though I wish I could, I can never really muster the requisite sympathy when I hear old people complain.

In 1912 the Rosenzweigs had a new home built for them in one of the most beautiful sections of Cassel (Terrasse 1). In October 1912, F. R. entered obligatory military training in Darmstadt. At that time the outbreak of a world war was expected because of the tension between Russia and Austria caused by the first Balkan war. Darmstadt, end of November 1912, to Hans Ehrenberg:

This war will not come to a decisive end, but it implies two, possibly three wars; we are on the threshold not of a single war but of a whole epoch of wars, and in the European perspective we are already involved in it. In such times of transition the individual can have only ambivalent feelings. History hasn't yet forced upon him an unambiguous ideal.

What little I have seen so far of our army doesn't make me particularly confident.

In December 1912 F. R. suffered an injury and was dismissed from the service.

II

BETWEEN CHURCH AND SYNAGOGUE

1913-1914

Years of reorientation: A member of the academic bourgeoisie and a believer in the scientific method becomes a religious thinker. A Western European to whom Christianity suggests itself as a natural form of faith, becomes a Jew in the classical sense.

During the first part of 1913 F. R. attended courses in jurisprudence at the University of Leipzig and continued to work on the Hegel book. Joseph Prager relates:

One day, after five years, we ran into each other in the foyer of the University of Leipzig. "How are you?" "Very well, thanks. I'm reading Isaiah with might and main! Believe me, it's magnificent!" He left me standing there.

F. R. had chosen Leipzig because it was there that his friend Eugen Rosenstock, whom he had met in 1910 in Baden-Baden, was a lecturer in medieval constitutional law. The two friends met daily for their noon meal. Frequent conversations between the two concerned contemporary academic philosophy, and its failure to satisfy the spiritual needs of the individual. Rosenstock, of Jewish origin, had found the solution in Christianity; Rosenzweig was living through an intellectual dilemma. The most decisive of these talks took place on the night of July 7, 1913.

During our conversation that night in Leipzig, when Rosenstock forced me step by step from my relativistic position into a non-relativistic one, I was at a disadvantage from the start, since I myself had to admit that his attack was justified.

> That night Rosenzweig realized that he had only one course: acceptance of the Christian faith. October 31, 1913, to Rudolf Ehrenberg:

You know very well what made me not only stand up to him but also submit to him: that I Christianized my view of Judaism, that I shared your faith, or at least thought I did. Consequently I was immediately disarmed by Rosenstock's simple confession of faith, which was only the start of his argument. The fact that a man like Rosenstock was a conscious Christian (in your case these things were still in the liquid state of a problem) at once bowled over my entire conception of Christianity and of religion generally, including my own. I thought I had Christianized my view of Judaism, but in actual fact I had done the opposite: I had "Judaized" my view of Christianity. I had considered the year 313[1] as the beginning of a falling away from true Christianity, since it opened a path for the Christians in the opposite direction to that opened in the year 70[2] for the Jews. I had begrudged the church its scepter, realizing that the synagogue bears a broken staff.[3] You saw how, on this assumption,[4] I began to reconstruct my world. In this world (and anything outside the world unrelated to what is inside I did not then or do I now recognize)—in this world there seemed to me to be no room for Judaism. In drawing my conclusions from this, I made a personal reservation whose

[1] Edict of Milan which recognized Christianity as a legal religion.
[2] The destruction of the Second Temple.
[3] Reference to the representation of church and synagogue in the cathedrals of Freiburg, Bamberg and Strasbourg.
[4] The assumption that the year 313 meant progress and not distortion as understood by liberal historians.

importance to me you know well enough; I declared that I could turn Christian only *qua* Jew—not through the intermediate stage of paganism. I considered this reservation purely personal, and you approved of it, remembering early Christianity. In this you were correct: the mission to the Hebrews actually rests on this basis, which I had thought purely personal, and urges that the Jew remain faithful to the Law even during the period of preparation and up to the moment of baptism.

From Leipzig F. R. went home to Cassel, and he attended the New Year's service at the Cassel synagogue (October 2 and 3). A day or two later, after a night spent in discussion with a friend, he came down from his study into the living room to his mother: "I want to talk to you." His mother, guessing what was on his mind, said excitedly: "You want to be baptized!" Franz pointed to the New Testament in his hand: "Mother, here is everything, here is the truth. There is only one way, Jesus." His mother asked him: "Were you not in the synagogue on the New Year's Day?" Franz answered: "Yes, and I will go to the synagogue on the Day of Atonement, too. I am still a Jew." His mother said: "When I come in I will ask them to turn you away. In our synagogue there is no room for an apostate."

F. R. left Cassel and went to Berlin. There he attended the Atonement Day service (October 11) at a small orthodox synagogue. The experience of this day was the origin of his radical return to Judaism.[5]

About that time his mother received a letter from a Protestant minister, ParsonJ., who was an acquaintance of the family. In the letter he discussed the question of Judaism and Christianity. Apparently the minister did not advocate outright baptism, although he maintained that the princi-

[5] *See* p. xvi-xx.

ples of the Jewish religion can only be realized within the church. Adele Rosenzweig mailed this letter to Franz with the remark: "People like us approve, of course, of an idealist who preaches humanity and has so much optimism."

Berlin, October 23, 1913, to his mother:

I'm surprised that J.'s letter should appeal to "people like you." Although he puts his arguments very cleverly (too cleverly for my taste, who am repelled by the sanctimonious guiding and manipulating of souls instead of a frank and open staking of the individual personality for good or ill), you should not have attended only to certain passages that struck you but to the whole meaning, which is—as one might expect from a man who is dishonest only for tactical reasons, but honest in his convictions—Christian in a very narrow sense. He is generous only tactically; he rejects the mission in its present form because it contravenes his tactics, but he wholeheartedly approves its ends.

Can you really discover "humanity" in his attributing "mere elements of truth to the Asiatic religions? In his suggesting that Christian missionaries should act as leaven to the insipid dough of Buddhism, etc.? (Imagine Herr Licentiat Fridolin Müller acting as leaven to such men as Buddha and Confucius!) Christianity has all along, even in the early centuries and the Middle Ages, acknowledged "elements" of truth in paganism and even ferreted them out with passion! But only "elements": it considered itself alone to be in possession of the whole truth, and this applies to Tertullian and Augustine as much as to Parson J.—And what is J.'s attitude toward Judaism? Don't be surprised if I answer at once: the official attitude of the Christian church, none other.—He says Judaism is "not dead"; as if speaking from the Jewish point of view, which he—a polite man—adopts in addressing a Jewess; it is still in existence—a historical phenomenon that "deeply interests" him. (Many thanks, Reverend, on behalf of Jewry, for your extreme "interest." It's also interesting, even extremely interesting, that there are still cannibals on the Bermuda Islands or elsewhere, *extremely* interesting—is that all? Then I decline your interest with thanks.)

The Jews simply refuse to see that their development leads through Jesus, in whom alone Jewish religion could "consummate (!) itself." Judaism has not taken this step; on the countrary it rejects with all possible force the notion that he has already arrived through whom their historic mission is to be fulfilled; it is still waiting for him and will continue to wait so long as there is Judaism. The development of Judaism has by-passed him whom the heathens call "Lord" and by whom "they reach the Father"; it does not pass through him.

Here an abyss opens between J. and his church, on the one hand, and every Jew on the other—an abyss that will never be filled up. That "connection of the innermost heart with God" which the heathen can only reach through Jesus is something the Jew already possesses, provided that his Judaism is not witheld from him by force; he possesses it by nature, through having been born one of the Chosen People. . . .

A Christian need only be a Christian to be at the same time a missionary—by this I don't mean the Christianity of the registrar's office. Just as a Jew only needs to be a Jew to arouse a Christian's Christianity if he has forgotten it—here again I am not speaking of the Judaism of the registrar's office.

> The letter—the first expression of F. R.'s affirmation of Judaism—ends with a reference to his own situation:

You have gathered from this letter that I seem to have

found the way back about which I had tortured myself in vain and pondered for almost three months.

Berlin, October 31, 1913, to Rudolf Ehrenberg:
I must tell you something that will grieve you and may at first appear incomprehensible to you: after prolonged, and I believe thorough, self-examination, I have reversed my decision. It no longer seems necessary to me, and therefore, being what I am, no longer possible. I will remain a Jew.[6]

The liturgy and ritual of the Day of Atonement—in fact the liturgical year as a whole—became for F. R. the key to the body of Jewish doctrine, which from then on he made the object of devoted study. November 1, 1913, to Rudolf Ehrenberg:
You will see that I no longer borrow my concepts from Christianity (linguistically and terminologically I still do, but no movement can be autonomous in these matters). In the most important points, especially regarding the doctrine of sin, where I had most strongly disagreed before, I am now in complete agreement with Jewish doctrine—complete as it is involuntary, simply the result of what I have been telling you here. That Jewish doctrine of which I could not see any sign in the Jewish cult and in Jewish life before, but which I now recognize. As I have said, I am now engaged in making clear to myself the entire system of Jewish doctrine. I am no longer the heretic of your eighteenth sermon,[7] who has faith but not charity; I now pronounce different names and profess different tenets. And yet I know that I have vanished only "before the will of

[6] For the continuation of this letter, *see* pp. 341-344.
[7] Rudolf Ehrenberg, *Ebr. 10:25—Ein Schicksal in Predigten,* Würzburg 1920.

your *Lord*"; but I am not forgotten by *God*—that God whom one day your *Lord* too will serve.

The following year (fall 1913 to 1914) F. R. remained in Berlin studying the sources of Judaism. He became a student of Professor Hermann Cohen, the founder of the neo-Kantianism of the Marburg school, who had left the University of Marburg in 1912 to teach Jewish religious philosophy at the Lehranstalt (later Hochschule) für die Wissenschaft des Judentums[8] in Berlin.

F. R. on Cohen's lectures in the Lehranstalt:

I had the surprise of my life. I am used to professors of philosophy who are subtle, acute, lofty, profound, and whatever other attributes are used to praise a thinker—instead, I found something I hadn't expected, a philosopher. In place of the tightrope walkers who execute their leaps on the taut wire of thought more or less boldly, more or less adroitly, more or less nimbly, I saw a man. Here was no trace of that desperate lack of content or indifference to content from which almost all contemporary philosophizing seems to suffer—an indifference that always makes one wonder why on earth this particular man should be philosophizing and not doing something else. With Cohen, you feel perfectly convinced that this man must philosophize, that he has within him the treasure which the powerful word forces to the surface. The thing that, disenchanted with the present, I had long searched for only in the writings of the great dead—the strict scholarly spirit hovering over the deep of an inchoate, chaotically teeming reality— I now saw face to face in the living flesh.

This and the following is from a notebook in which F. R. tried to transcribe the most significant of Cohen's dicta, as

[8] Liberal Jewish theological seminary.

it was impossible to take systematic notes—writing, one might have missed the best of what was being said. "Sometimes," F. R. notes, "an entire train of thought was concluded with a gesture, and this gesture was more conclusive than any possible conclusion":

About the Sabbath: "All of it is miracle!" About the love of one's neighbor: "This is beyond the sphere of development; here all patience with evolution must come to an end. This must not have anything to do with development—*a priori* is what the philosophers call it." About the voluntary acceptance of suffering on the part of the devout: "Can we imagine it? Isaiah replies: Behold Israel!" And again, about the Suffering Servant in the book of Isaiah: ". . . that is, of course, as we venture to approach such matters from the human standpoint, from the standpoint of human history" On the origin of the idea of prophecy: "How? When? We shall never be able to understand it, we shall never wish to be able to understand it." Concerning the unity of God, this "most abstract" concept "for which we would suffer death any day": "As far as I am concerned, God can be whatever he will, but he must be One."—"Here is the point on which we cannot come to an understanding with Christians—I cannot help but say it."—"Balaam's words about the 'people that shall dwell alone' [Num. 23:9]—modern man, the cultured mind, simply does not understand it. All of nature, the model for art, is opened up in the second commandment —and then sealed." And again: "But this they will not forgive us down to the present day," and—after a pause full of emotion—"It is something that cannot possibly be understood—"Monotheism is a psychological mystery. Whoever does not accept it as such, must fail to comprehend it in all its profundity."

In April 1914, F. R. attempted for the first time to formulate his ideas on Jewish religious thinking. Martin Buber, whom he visited in Berlin, invited him to contribute an article to the projected second volume of the book *Vom Judentum*. F. R. then wrote the essay "Atheistic Theology," wherein he criticized certain trends in modern theology that ignore the concept of revelation: "The offensive idea of revelation, the sudden pouring of higher meanings into an unworthy vessel, has been silenced." F. R. characterized his essay as "a programmatic affirmation of the idea of revelation." The restoring of revelation to its proper place within theology, which Rosenzweig demanded in this essay, later became his own appointed task. (The projected volume never appeared.)

In examining some Hegel manuscripts, F. R. came across a folio page in Hegel's handwriting marked "Essay on Ethics." Recognizing this sketch as the oldest program for a system of German idealism, F. R. was able to prove that its author could not have been Hegel but must have been Schelling, and that the folio page was a copy made by Hegel in 1796. He elaborated this thesis in a paper entitled "A Prolegomenon to German Idealistic Philosophy," which was published by the Heidelberg Academy of Sciences in 1917.

Toward the end of the summer F. R. began the study of Arabic, and he kept at it throughout the war.

Diary, July 23, 1914:

Jews and Christians both deny that the ethical and religious principle of "Love God and thy neighbor" is their common possession. Each tries to impute paganism to the other: the Christians by disallowing our love of neighbor, we by disallowing their love of God. Both are right and both wrong. Here the insincerity of liberal theology becomes apparent.

III

THE JEWISH THINKER IN THE TRENCHES

1914-1919

*The soldier in the trenches plans the renascence of
Jewish learning. The contact with Polish Jewry and its
vigorous, natural religiousness opens new vistas. The intellectual journey so far finds expression in the Star of Redemption.*

After the outbreak of the First World War, September
1914, F. R. entered the Red Cross service in Berlin. On
September 19 he was sent to Belgium as a male nurse.
Early in 1915 he enlisted in the regular army. Berlin, April
14, 1915, to his parents:

Turkey is out. The unit has canceled its list for Turkey
and asked me to join a hospital detachment for eastern
Europe. I then resigned from the Red Cross and shall before
long be attached to the Landsturm. There is a ninety-five per
cent chance that I'll be an infantry man, and reach the front
after eight weeks of training. You know, dear parents, that
I haven't taken this step for my own pleasure, and that I've
been putting it off for a long time. Besides, you remember
that I told you here last month that now the Landsturm is
being called up, I consider it my duty not to dodge danger
by remaining a nurse. Since my turn has now come, and it's
no longer a matter of volunteering as it would have been in
August, I no longer see anything to withold me from my

duty. No decent alternative presents itself. Naturally I don't feel enthusiastic about it; I am a coward by nature and shall be much too nervous to make a good soldier. But it had to be.

I realize, of course, that this is a heavy blow to you; pessimists of the imagination (I myself, unfortunately, am one) always expect the worst in such cases, and are not light-hearted enough to dismiss such thoughts.

> He received his army training in Cassel, in the field artillery. In July 1915 he managed to work on Hegel and the State.

> When Hermann Cohen's essay "Deutschtum und Judentum" ("Germanism and Judaism") appeared, F. R. set to work on a critical review ("Judaism and Germanism"). One passage reads:

A nation always concentrates its strength in those spots where it senses danger; in the next few decades it will be the *galut* [exile, dispersion] (no matter what its outward destiny) that must prove the inner strength of Judaism. This strength is what it always was and must be: an assimilative holding of one's own. Neither invidious recriminations nor wounded vanity must ever bring us to deny this psychological mainspring, which propels us through the centuries. It is our lot to remain strangers, alien to all spiritual possessions of the nations, of which they allow us to partake; alien at heart even to that share which we ourselves try to contribute in recompense. Whatever we receive we must not receive as Jews, whatever we perform we must not perform as Jews; and yet, in order to guarantee our own integrity, we must put our Jewishness in some kind of relation both to what we give and what we receive. And while in all else we are subject to the judgment of the nations, and permit them to tell us whether or not they find our contributions acceptable, in this we are outside their jurisdiction: we are the sole judges of any efforts to grasp the world in Jewish terms.

On January 1, 1916, F. R. was sent to the Ballistics School at La Fère in France. On February 19 he joined an anti-aircraft unit; March 12, this unit was transferred to the Balkans, where F. R. remained almost to the end of the war. Early in March, 1916, to Rudolf Ehrenberg:

As soon as the war is over I shall look (I feel increasingly sure of this) for some kind of public forum: my udders are full to bursting, and I know on the other hand (or at least want to know it this way and no other) that my real book will only appear posthumously; I don't want to have to defend it, nor do I want to have to witness its "effects." Until then, I'll nourish my reputation on by-products of this "real product" ("Studies in the History of Islam," "The Aesthetics of the Church Fathers," "Plato and History," "The Hero," and the like; it will be largely a matter of accident which of these will get written down). Yet these scholarly productions won't help me directly; I must risk myself, not posthumously but while I live; I'll either teach in Berlin at the Lehranstalt[1] or, should the faculty in Jewish theology at Frankfort[2] materialize—which seems likely—I'll teach there. The need for compromise and for comprehensive formulation implicit in both plans is exactly what I am looking for. My work requires that the author be poised on a needle point. The "needle point" is to me what "chaos" is to you—namely, danger, "fear and trembling."

The strangest thing about war is that one gets buffeted about among people. This is the one lesson I have learned:

[1] See p. 29, note 8.
[2] At the University of Frankfort. See the letter of January 12, 1923 to Martin Buber.

before the war we made things too easy for ourselves, or rather, things were too easy for us; associating, as we did, exclusively with people of our own kind, we came to underestimate the difficulties. The road to mutual esteem (meaning mutual tolerance, and that's all) is covered much more rapidly between two scholars, no matter how hostile their views, than between myself and a Rhenish merchant who calls himself an idealist. And even this difficulty is dwarfed by the difficulty of associating with men of the lower middle class or the proletariat, who object—and one suddenly recognizes, rightly so—to one's considering oneself something more than a member of a different class. But I don't believe that one should base a program for future action on this insight. It is unwise to court a second danger while one is still in the middle of the first; the war should teach us simply that beyond the first circle there are many concentric circles. Only he who has traversed the nearer circles without friction has a right to settle in the outermost one (mendicant monk, hermit). One should not become a saint (a man of the outermost circle) from choice, but from destiny. But how far my own task is from that of the saint (the man in whom everybody must believe because no one any longer has anything in common with him) has never been so clear to me as it is now.

Near Belgrade, March 17, 1916, to his parents:
Approaching Belgrade. Trip still going well. There's no longer any doubt that we are bound for the Balkans. All we have seen en route was what we could see from the train. Hungary is colossally monotonous, the most beautiful sight being the white buffaloes yoked to plows in sixes and eights. —It was surely a stroke of luck being attached to this unit— of course, only geographically speaking.—Please get me Augustine's *De Civitate Dei*, the Teubner edition, unbound,

only the first volume (there are two). Wait until you have my exact address (I'll wire it if possible) before sending.

In the Balkans, March 19, 1916, to his parents:

I can't imagine that we will stay here long. Everything seems to move on. So long as we are here you may feel perfectly at ease. The front is about a hundred kilometers from here, and no enemy aircraft has been seen over Veles since January. It's a perfect summer resort, disfigured by a few superiors, but they are no more bothersome than the waiters in Switzerland. Flowering trees, snowy peaks, cattle, Arnauts, Turks, Bulgarian soldiers.

The last package that reached me at Karlsruhe contained no book except Buber's.[3] You can send the rest of the New Testament and the Augustine. I have sent back the first two sections of Wagner's autobiography—one of the most instructive of books; I wonder whether they'll arrive all right. Not many things get lost.

In the Balkans, April 30, 1916, to his parents:

The weather stays warm. No sign of aircraft. It seems that we'll stay here, at least for some time. You'll be amused to hear that I've taken up the violin again, in the evenings, of course. I actually make tremendous progress; if I tried hard I could master it again in a relatively short time. You might send me a few of Bach's solo sonatas, that is a few pages from the G Minor Prelude (maestoso) and Fugue, also the Prelude in E Major, the Gavotte and the Minuets, the Bourrée, and the Chaconne—in other words all my old favorites.

In the Balkans, April 30, 1916, to his parents:

Have I ever told you that I lecture every Sunday afternoon on the history of the World War—today was the sev-

---

[3] Martin Buber, *Vom Geist des Judentums*, Berlin 1916.

enth time? The first five lectures dealt with the political antecedents; last time I began on the history of the war itself. Today I discussed Hindenburg's two victories of the fall of 1914. Naturally, it's all on a popular level, but quite outspoken in content. I don't suppose it will do much good, even though I am trying to present it as well as I possibly can.—Please send me a G string (a good one).

> Toward the end of May 1916, after F. R.'s unit was moved to the battle front, an exchange of letters began began between F. R. and Eugen Rosenstock, also a soldier and stationed at the Western front.[4] The correspondence lasted until the end of the year, and continued the discussion that took place in Leipzig in July 1913. But whereas in 1913 the Christian philosopher had confronted a man who was going through an inner crisis, a seeker and a doubter, in 1916 the issues were more clearly defined: the Christian confronted the Jew.

> In the Balkans, June 7, 1916, to his parents:

There's no such thing as the problem of East European Jews; there's only the Jewish problem—and strictly speaking even that doesn't exist. Bear in mind that the whole German fear of the East European Jew does not refer to him as such, but to him as a potential Western Jew, i.e., one like you.

> July 9, 1916, F. R. wrote to his parents on the subject of the autobiography of Solomon Maimon, the eighteenth-century Jewish student who escaped from his East European town to become a philosopher in Berlin:

It's nonsense to brand the state of the Jews at the time as barbaric, degenerate, etc. It's really an integrated culture; it's only the individual (Maimon, for instance) who becomes

---

[4] *See* pp. 344-348.

a barbarian by relinquishing it. If one looks at it from the outside, without a knowledge of the language and customs, it may appear barbarous; but so does present-day German culture in the eyes of Western Europeans, though actually it's only a matter of being different. Jewish culture has been "decadent" not for a few centuries only, but ever since its inception (538 B.C.E.).[5] What seems decadence to the *goy*— who was then a pagan and is now a Christian—is of the very essence of Judaism. These are not my own private opinions but those of the Christian scholarly world (the Jewish scholars are an interested party and judge differently).

In the Balkans, August 17, 1916, to his parents:
War is no more immoral, i.e., irreligious, than peace. It is the *men* who are good or evil. What makes pacifism such an abject doctrine is the assumption that good and evil depend on outward circumstance and not on men's inner condition. The religious doctrine of peace, insofar as it is not simply an allegory of the condition of the individual soul, is an idea of a concluding era: peace appears at the moment when world history has run its course. Consequently religion does not regard this ultimate peace as man's work but as a direct act of God to be prepared by a final and incredibly terrible series of wars. These wars are not to teach men the horror of war (men have known this all along, i.e., as long as there have been wars, i.e., history, i.e., human beings—animals do not wage war any more than they pray, laugh, write poetry) but to bring about the last definitive separation of men (as individuals) into good and evil ones; they are the last and strongest "temptation" to confront mankind.

In the Balkans, September 1, 1916, to his parents:
Life, insofar as it is good or evil, is not enacted upon this

---

[5] The return from the Babylonian exile; the beginning of the period of the Second Temple.

earth, even today. (Hence the immeasurableness of actions considered morally.) The categories of "good and evil" posit a world radically different from the terrestrial. This and nothing else is what is meant by the religious belief in immortality (which only in its Islamic Bowdlerization can be conceived as being contrary to Kant's concept of morality).

In the Balkans, September 3, 1916, to Rudolf Ehrenberg: I received your letter just as I was assigned to an observation post on Dub mountain. I am still there, as I declined to be relieved. I live more primitively here, but on the other hand am removed from the whole enervating mechanism of commanding and obeying. Things are easily arranged between a sergeant-major, another noncommissioned officer, and two telephone operators.—On the mountain we have a concrete shelter, so that we are quite safe, though not while actually on duty.

My subjective interest in the war is of course entirely exhausted by now. As far as I'm concerned it may come to an end any minute. . . . As for my parents, though, I'm still in Walandowo; in fact, unless you have spilled the beans, you are the only person who knows that I'm at the front.

In September 1916, F. R. began to collect information on the status of Jewish religious instruction in Germany, and to formulate plans for the reconstruction of Jewish education on a broad scale. His suggestions were later outlined in the treatise *It Is Time*. In the Balkans, September-October 1916, to his parents:
Who pays for Jewish education in the high schools in Cassel (or elsewhere, if Father knows)? I suppose it's the community. And how much does one student's instruction cost? Also, what percentage of Jewish students in Cassel participate, since it is optional? Do they still put three

grades together in the same class? In case S. happens to know of any recent important pamphlets on the subject (also on the question whether Hebrew should be taught or entirely eliminated), also on the question of procuring teachers (to what extent college graduates are being used) I should like to see any such material.

I would like to understand clearly for once exactly what the anti-Zionist majority is doing to promote their notion of Judaism ("confession only").

At the same time I suspect that the problem here can only be solved in conjunction with a greater one, the most urgent the anti-Zionist German Jews have to solve, now that the war is drawing to an end: I mean the establishment of a Jewish theological faculty at the University of Frankfort on the Main. The state can grant this reward for good conduct in its own right, and will do so if the necessary fund of two million marks is laid on the table; in this way at least one institution would be firmly established.

Once the state has created this nucleus, an autonomous academy should be added to it, partly by consolidating present facilities, in such a way that the professors would *ipso facto* constitute its permanent staff, with the right of further co-optation.

But unless we act at once, the matter will be taken up by the Christian theologians, who will introduce lectureships in rabbinics into their Protestant faculties. Such an action would fit in with the prevailing ideas of higher learning. Then you would be out of the picture. For if hitherto your "confession only" doctrine has met with no favor in the eyes of your Christian fellow citizens, the reason lay in the fact that the educated Protestant found in the controversies of his theological faculties ("pure" research, entirely divorced from parish duties) the strongest guarantee of modernity, of Christianity's effectual survival. . . . And since they saw nothing of the sort among us, but only synagogues, rabbis, and charitable organizations, they refused to acknowledge the existence among us of something that existed among themselves.

A program I should regard as adequate would comprise nine years (nine stages) of two weekly hours of mandatory religious instruction centered around the study of Hebrew (no German Psalms, biblical sentences, Jewish history—let alone ethics—but everything drawn from the sources), with no outside work, everything done in class—to reassure the state official, who might fear too heavy a load—provided that, by shifting one of the hours of perhaps the entire Christian religious instruction, obligatory attendance at the synagogue can be obtained for Jewish students. . . . In this way they would learn more Hebrew than they possibly could through outside assignments.

Today elementary instruction has passed out of the hands of the Slaughterers[6] and into the hands of certified teachers, but now we need an academic faculty to achieve the next step, that is, college-trained Jewish teachers of religion. The time has come to begin working down from the top: we need the faculty for training teachers.

In the Balkans, September 30, 1916, to his parents:
Perhaps I will write one day to [Hermann] Cohen on this subject: he should know exactly what mud the cart got stuck in, or whether it is simply standing forgotten in a corner.

October 1916, to Rudolf Ehrenberg:
I have been on Dub mountain now for almost exactly three months as an anti-aircraft observer, and I hardly ever get down; I still feel no desire to be relieved. (So far as Cassel and the rest of the world are concerned I am still

---

[6] Ritual Slaughterer (who used to give religious instruction to Jewish children).

at Walandowo, protecting the Army High Command which has long since been moved.) Nothing much has happened since the end of August; the platoon is still the same; its former position was among the rest of the artillery, and now it is once more in rather dangerous proximity to an Austrian 30.5 mortar. But up here I lead a hermit's existence. It's getting to be mighty cold, which diminishes one's enjoyment of the scenery but gives one more free time. I've been reading a lot in Tertullian and studying Aramaic assiduously; Tertullian teaches you a lot about the gnosis, which is in every respect tremendously interesting.

I've also developed a great taste for writing and write endless letters; my letters home are full of witticisms and consequently I have become very popular with the family: my mother reads excerpts aloud, a success I had never dreamed of. I carry on a correspondence with Rosenstock too, which I find rather difficult since we are still paving the way; I am still paying for not having talked to him or having been able to talk to him since that night in 1913; I am forced to continue the conversation with his phantom of that evening. . . .

> F. R. was stimulated by an article of Victor Ehrenberg's to develop, in his Dub mountain solitude (October 1916), an extensive program of German education, "People's School and State School." He proposed a school that would restore the cultural unity of the nation, which had been destroyed by denominational and social differences and an overemphasis on specialization. The plan was intended as a "Central European educational program for Germany."

In the Balkans, October 1916, to Hans Ehrenberg:
The war itself in no way represents an epoch to me: I experienced so much in 1913 that 1914 would have had to be a cataclysm in order to impress me . . . I have been compelled to adopt a system of ignoration, which I still observe

consistently. Even those few features of the war that have been of positive benefit to me (the fact that it enabled me, as you observed, to get rid of small, persistent inhibitions, repressions, subtleties, in short, to take myself less seriously)—even this was only seizing an opportunity, and entirely in line with my organic development. Consequently I haven't experienced the war and know nothing about it (and it is perhaps this very fact that has given me from the start an ability to foresee its course accurately, which I myself sometimes find surprising). I neither expect nor hope anything from it, but carry my life through it, as Cervantes did his poem (not even in the left but in the right hand; with the left I master as much of the war as I can). Whether this vacation from life's responsibility, which I have feared and still do, will or will not benefit me, I do not know; in a sense I enjoy it, as I will not have another such chance. To enjoy it *entirely* would be equivalent to experiencing the war, which I am prevented from doing by my future life, whose servant I am even now, in every leisure moment. In any event, I manage to spin out some thread or other that I had begun to spin earlier, and which at that previous time I thought to have done with for good (I'm speaking of the soul; in intellectual matters, I'm certain I shall never leave anything hanging, but that sometime or other I shall take up every thread, even if my literary projects cease to exist in their old form). During military service, any long, sustained composition takes too great a toll of nervous energy.

If it weren't for that, I would sit down and dash off a theory of the state, say about three hundred printed pages; it's all so simple and so interesting. Later on I probably shan't be frivolous enough to write without research.

October 20, 1916, to his parents:
What is it that becomes "unchained" if you go insane?

(A very good question!) Answer: man at his most profound. But only in the *act* of becoming insane, afterwards one vegetates like a plant; yet as the building collapses the flames soar for the last time, illuminating it with a clearer light, detaching it more sharply from the surrounding world than the sun ever could. Afterwards, all that remains is a ruin, with a buttress standing here and there to remind the beholder of the building as it was, and perhaps quite "touching," too, overgrown as it is with flowers and buried in the earth—but the tremendously exaggerated image of the total structure is seen only in the moment of collapse. It was a superstition of antiquity, to call insanity "divine," but the road *to* insanity is divine. Thus, genius is man on the way to (his) insanity, regardless of whether, later, it can be medically attested to (the ruins for the doctor's inspection) or not, as in the case of Goethe. (There is much in the writings of the old Goethe that, had he become insane, and even without this—as in the case of Beethoven and Rembrandt— might be diagnosed as forewarnings of insanity.) Consequently, no one should *fear* insanity; it is man's destiny, and one ought only to fear the being unworthy of this destiny, that is, lest the building prove, as it is seen going up in flames, to be of insignificant, commonplace proportions. The fear of insanity need not be greater than, or different from, the fear that ought to dominate life as a whole: the "fear of the Lord."

In the Balkans, November 24, 1916, to his parents:
Unfortunately I am a poor soldier, since I am so unpractical and awkward (the former only with regard to the latter, for I could be useful at a desk job); nevertheless, I get some fun out of it. My solitary tour of duty as an aircraft observer has made a romantic childhood dream come true: to be "alone" on a high mountain with a magnificent view.

In the Balkans, January 6, 1917, to his parents:

I've always regarded funeral oratory as a nuisance; myself, I would prefer simply the traditional rites, and if possible, not a single German word included. However, I am against the "dignified ritual grab" of the Hevre,[7] as I am against everything "dignified" in our worship. Prose is our poetry. All these artificial solemnities without traditional roots are false, like the rabbi's gown, and, in a certain sense, his entire contemporary position. One should preserve forms with genuine meaning, and we have enough of those.

In the Balkans, January 9, 1917, to Gertrud Oppenheim:

I still can't get over W.'s death; I shrink from the idea. While he was alive it never occurred to me that his absence would leave such a gap, one more irremediable than any made by the loss of much closer friends. But the very fact that my relationship with him was so entirely unintellectual, that I loved him as one loves a beautiful object or animal makes him now so *entirely* dead, simply gone, without a trace of immortality; there's nothing left to me of him, and I dread the return to Berlin with him not there.

In the meantime I have turned thirty, and if it weren't for the war I should have to be ashamed of myself.

By way of compensation, I have become such a family hero as I've not been since I ceased, to everyone's disappointment, to be a child prodigy; this brings home to me how standoffish and obnoxious my attitude must have been even as late as 1915, in Cassel.

January 11, 1917, to Gertrud Oppenheim:

There are sheerly arbitrary moments when I feel Goethe the man almost within physical reach, and such moments open my eyes upon a view of my own life that makes me

---

[7] *Hevra Kadisha:* holy (burial) society.

literally *dizzy*. That valley through which I once expected to travel the whole course of my life on toward the heights now suddenly lies far below me, and I am running along a rocky and unknown mountain path. The valley too would lead eventually to an eminence of some kind, but it is the suddenness of the sweep upward that fills me with horror. Without sleep, real physical sleep, life would become altogether intolerable: I must constantly shake myself free from the daily somnolence called happiness. Unless it spring upon me with the irresistibility of a *force majeure*—I dare not *search* for it.

January 12, 1917, to his parents:

Just received your letter of the 4th, honey cakes, fish, and parcels of books. I read the Kafka[8] at once. The old man is insane of course (what else?), but he is a mere prop; the real drama is enacted by the son, and the fable is that of a man who loses what little reason he has by delivering himself up wholly to the flow of events and (which is the main thing) in so doing, makes the assumption that *because* things happen they must be meaningful (hence the term Expressionism, on which this piece throws quite a little light; the Impressionist also has dedication, but only the Expressionist holds the belief that all the separate phenomena hailing down upon our nerves, when taken together, not only mean *something* but mean what they themselves purport to mean—the judgment! Therefore the Expressionist is the caricature of the religious man, as the Impressionist is the man of science.)

In January 1917, F. R. wrote a long geopolitical essay entitled "Oekumene." January 20, 1917, to his parents:

Heaven be thanked, the child "Oekumene" has been brought to birth. Now it must be washed and swaddled.

[8] Franz Kafka, *The Judgment*.

Mother and child are doing nicely—but I exclaimed as I did after "People's School and State School," and as some member of the family, I forget who, did after her first child: "Never again!" It's an intolerable situation. Now I'm curious to see how I'll like the child when I begin soaping it tomorrow.

January 23, 1917, to his parents:

Truth is a sea into which only he may dive whose heart has a specific gravity greater than "truth," that is, a heart full of irreducible reality. If a person consists entirely of brain, that is, of a substance with the same specific gravity as the water of truth, he will always remain on the surface no matter how he kicks and thrashes.

January 27, 1917, to Rudolf Ehrenberg:

I have been wondering whether, to make better use of my time, I shouldn't have done with Macedonia and try to get somewhere on the Russian front or into Turkey. I ought to try to make the most of this opportunity that has been forced upon me to pollon anthropon nóon gnonai,[9] otherwise I would have to live for some time among East European Jews after the war is over.

February 5, 1917, to Gertrud Oppenheim:

Every act should be performed as though all eternity depended on it.

All our seeming contradictions arise from the equation between the *today* that is merely a bridge to tomorrow, and the *today* that is a springboard to eternity. No day has written on its forehead which of the two *todays* it is. One can never tell.

I have glided into autobiography since I have come to notice in myself so many certainties and conclusions of some phases of development (and new beginnings). This leads

---

[9] "Know the customs of many men."

one into retrospection. It is a time for writing one's autobiography for oneself and one's closest friends. For the public it should be done only after fifty, since for the public one's life does not exist until enough of it has been lived before their eyes.

February 17, 1917, to his parents:
War is a "divine *judgment*" but not a simple tribunal; it is crisis, division, goats and sheep. Within each nation a judgment upon internal politics, between nations upon the nations themselves. The touching thing about the "just" is that they place themselves fundamentally under the same law as their opponents.

The Army High Command asked F. R. to give a series of lectures to officers. March 5, 1917, to his parents:
In spite of rather trying conditions, my "inaugural lecture" went very well (and it really wasn't bad—criticism follows presently). Though I didn't have to report until seven-thirty, I left in the morning, paddling through snow and slush and mulling over my lecture. . . .
Major von E.: "Ah, so you're the professor." "Not yet, Major." "What *did* you do in civilian life?" "Nothing, Major." (Baffled): "What was your intended profession?" "Professor, Major." "So then, what are you going to talk to us about?" "I have received orders to talk about Mohammed and Islam." "I hope you won't make it too long!" "I have received orders to talk for three-quarters of an hour." "That's mighty long! Do you think you can stand it?" "*I* can." (Laughing): "You mean that perhaps we . . . well, so long until tonight."—Then I went to Captain von E. who himself showed me to the guest room, with a bed in it (the first in a year!) . . .
It has been one of the most important days of my life, one of those days that show how right the New Testament is: strive after the Kingdom of Heaven and the rest shall

be added unto you. All I ever wanted was to *understand,* and now I find I am able to speak as well.

In March 1917, F. R. wrote *It Is Time* [Ps. 119:126], the treatise in which he outlined his ideas on Jewish education and the training of teachers, and presented his plan for the establishment of an Academy for the Science of Judaism. The purpose of the plan was to develop a new type of Jewish academician. As members of the Academy, Jewish scholars would collaborate on certain scholarly projects, and spend a part of their time giving Jewish instruction in the local high schools. Elaborating on the letter to his parents of September 1916, F. R. developed a detailed program of Jewish studies. The essay was dedicated to Hermann Cohen.[10]

March 23, 1917, to Hermann Cohen:
The essay I am sending you as my first—and all the more comprehensive for that—sign of affection, has changed in the process of writing from a letter to something more weighty. Consequently I feel obliged to add a regular letter to it, especially since that original letter, despite the date of final composition, was conceived over half a year ago, on Dub mountain, "between Wardar and Lake Doiran," as the daily communiqués say. I was stationed there at the time as an aircraft observer, was shone on by the sun and occasionally shot at from Sarrail, and had plenty of time to think during both. At present we are stationed in a different sector of the Macedonian front; I keep well and unharmed, and despite the inevitable discomfort, which one becomes used to in the end, I am enjoying it here quite a bit. I've also had a chance to do some work, particularly reading, though as you see from the enclosed I've done some writing too.

[10] *See* p. 251.

I hope that the essay I am sending will give you pleasure. On the whole, I mean. As to details, you will approve some and not others; after all, in writing it I concentrated more on the subject matter than on the addressee. But no matter —now that it is finished I feel as strongly as I did when I started that the whole thing belongs to you. For this reason, I ask you to decide whether or not it should be published, and in what way. Of course I am chiefly concerned not just to "be read," but to be effective.

March 25, 1917, to his parents:

If we were still cooking kosher I could have spared myself the effort of writing It Is Time, but now that the way to the heart is no longer through the stomach, it must be through the spirit.

March 29, 1917, to Rudolf Ehrenberg:

I have never had any "forebodings" about my personal destiny, yet I have reason to believe that Goethe is right when he says that "our wishes shadow forth our faculties." Thus I feel a kind of somnambulistic certainty about my future actions though not about my future sufferings: with regard to the latter I have confidence rather than forebodings, a confidence which I rationalize into an alternative: either I am to be killed, in which case He does it without me and I am spared work and worry—or I am to survive, which means that He needs me and that I must assume my duties. If I thought that *you* would be killed, I should certainly remain at my post, and the adversity of life would remain the same; but the air I would breathe would be a more rarefied air, too rarefied for comfort. This thought is like another: that I might not find a wife and might remain unmarried (which is not quite so impossible as you perhaps think, and as I myself thought at one time); it is not impossible, but I don't think about it and have a feeling that by not thinking about it I prevent its coming true.

> Easter 1917, F. R. spent his furlough in near-by Üsküb (Yugoslavia). Here he had his first contact with Sephardic Jews. To his parents, April 6, 1917:

I have also seen many Sephardim and paid a visit to the president of the community, a merchant whose manner is very dignified but even more markedly astute; his wife looks not at all Jewish, his daughters very much so. The older one, Oro (Goldchen!), went to a German school in Saloniki, the younger one, Fortune (Glueckel!), fourteen years old, doesn't know German yet. All of them know French, but among themselves they speak Spanish, which the men write in Hebrew characters and the women in Bulgarian characters; it's rather easy to understand them if one knows Italian, probably because it is *old* Castilian. Their Jewish knowledge is nil, but the Jewish way of life is entirely natural to them. They consort only with one another, and rightly consider themselves an elite, but as regards hospitality, etc., they are a living proof of the saying that too much comfort demoralizes. This is the general verdict, which I have also found to be true. The *hazzan* [cantor] calls himself *hakham* [the wise] instead of rabbi; I have yet to attend a service. The name of the president's family is Navarro! Imagine, by the way, a thoroughly drab lodging-house interior; they receive guests in one of their bedrooms! All the names are magnificent, e.g., Isaac Calderon. . . .

Whoever says that the Sephardim are of a different race from us is a liar. But their destiny has been different.

> F. R. admired their perfectly natural, unapologetic Judaism. Speaking of a conversation with a ten-year-old boy, he says, "It was as though the very race were interrogating

me." Of his experience, F. R. says: "Those were marvelous days, which I should hate to delete from my life."

April 10, 1917, to his parents, on a comparison of "People's School and State School" with It Is Time:

The blond brother ["People's School and State School"] is by Franz Hesse,[11] whom I don't know; if anybody spits at him I shan't defend him. My "power" may do some good over there, my "energy" keeps to its own domain. I am every bit as pessimistic as you are: it has never benefited anyone *as a Jew* to trouble himself over the Jews as Jews, ever since Moses. To each of them the same offer has been made that was made to Moses, namely that *his* name should become great but that the nation should perish. Moses answered, Let my name perish, but the nation shall live.

April 12, 1917, to his parents:

You still expect too much of the Jews. They would only "admire me" if I had a German-indorsed fame. When a man is a great bacteriologist his views on Jewish matters are listened to more reverently than when he has devoted himself expressly to such matters. I have cast off all illusions, at least so far as my own lifetime is concerned. "Mission?" No, because in that case I would have to *believe* in myself, but I definitely feel that having once chosen I no longer have a choice.

April 21, 1917, to his parents, concerning Hermann Cohen:

You really should have asked him to stop over on his way back, but I'm afraid you will not have done this. Perhaps there is still time. It would be worth your while: Terrasse 1[12]

---

[11] The pseudonym chosen for a possible publication of this general school program.
[12] Home of F. R.'s parents.

won't have harbored so distinguished a man. He is easier
to converse with than you seem to think, and the only way
to get to know him is "face to face."

May 1, 1917, to Gertrud Oppenheim:
Do you want to know my exact position? Ever since the
emancipation Jewry has been split into two main bodies:
the assimilationists and the Zionists. Both are paths, direc-
tions, and as such unassailable. But both are in danger of
changing from paths through the universe to streets leading to a certain house. That is to say, both are in danger
of attaining an attainable goal. The assimilationists by becoming, instead of brokers, lecturers, journalists, bohemians,
and usurers—that is, the Jewish brains that again and again
arouse the nations' hatred—petty civil servants (as is now
being urged), artisans (which was urged as early as 1800,
e.g., the Humanität[13] in Cassel, the Gans-Heine ethical Kul-
turverein of 1820[14] in Berlin) or, God forbid, German peas-
ants. The Zionists will attain that goal by managing to
found their Serbia or Bulgaria or Montenegro in Palestine.
I don't think that the first danger is serious, for in this
Europe replete with history the past cannot be simply dismissed; we have to swim with the current. But the second
danger holds a serious threat, for Asia is today relatively
unpopulated. It is for this reason that Hermann Cohen, with
absolutely trustworthy instinct, hates the Zionists. He once
said to me something he has never put on paper (nor ever
will, for think how the Verein,[15] and the Central-Verein[16] and

[13] "Moralische Anstalt" Humanität.
[14] Verein für Kultur and Wissenschaft des Judentums in Berlin, founded by
Eduard Gans and Leopold Zunz in 1819. Heinrich Heine was a member of
this group. In 1824 the Verein was dissolved; E. Gans accepted baptism.
[15] Verein zur Abwehr des Antisemitismus, founded in 1890.
[16] Central-Verein deutscher Staatsbürger jüdischen Glaubens, founded 1893;
organization of German citizens of Jewish persuasion.

the Verband[17] would react!): "These bums want to be *happy!*"—There's the *rub!* Verein, Central-Verein, and Verband have precisely the same wish, yet Cohen senses that it will never be fulfilled; in the case of the Zionists he feels that they *will* be happy, eventually.

. . . The Zionists will be lost once they lose touch with the Diaspora. Their contact with the Diaspora is the only thing that makes them hold fast to their *goal,* which means, however, that they must be homeless in time and remain wanderers, even there. Ahad Haam's[18] conception of Zionism is thus quite (unconsciously) correct; only by realizing its connection with Berlin, Lodz, or, someday if you like, New York, Valparaiso, and Tobolsk, will Palestine remain Jewish and also make life in the Diaspora really possible. This explains my position. Not so much my position while I live as my posthumous one, for only posthumously shall I wholly speak out. Because I don't concern myself with the means, I will clarify the unity of their goal for the Jews of the coming era. I cannot tell what this book will look like or when I'll be able to write it, but I am subjecting my entire life to this posthumousness. There will be nothing in the book but the idea that the Jewish *must* and the Jewish *will* are one (the "blood" and the "mind," "race" and "religion," capitalism and the Torah, the journalist and the talmudist, Buber and Cohen, Klatzkin[19] and Ahad Haam, and any other antitheses one might produce)—incomprehensibly one, for everything we call history happens by a volition thrusting past a compulsion and in the process becoming another compulsion, after which the whole process begins again;

[17] Verband der deutschen Juden, founded in 1904, an organization representing Jewish interests in dealing with German state authorities.
[18] Ahad Haam (1856-1927) advocated "cultural Zionism."
[19] Jacob Klatzkin (1882-1948) advocated formal Jewish nationalism based on the land of Israel and the Hebrew language, without further traditional Jewish content. *See* p. 263.

here a fragment of the ahistorical is thrown in the middle of history. By whom? Do you *ask*??—As to the question "For what purpose?"—I will try to answer it in all humility as a questioning and speaking person, so that the book may not only describe but also explain.

> F. R. wrote a series of articles dealing with political, strategical, and historical questions, which he published under the pseudonym Adam Bund in the *Vossische Zeitung* and the *Archiv für exacte Wirtschaftsforschung*. In collaboration with his uncle, Professor Richard Ehrenberg, he also wrote a series of articles for the *Thuenen Archiv*. May 1, 1917, to his parents:

The vicissitudes of these trifles on their way to publication interest me tremendously; I learn a great deal about myself, and I will benefit from it all in the future. I have always deplored the idea of losing my literary virginity with the fat Hegel book rather than with a few odd and casual debauches. I don't want to elaborate on the comparison (even though it holds down to the slightest detail), since it points the moral that "these make the best husbands."

May 2, 1917, to his parents:

I just learned over the telephone that because of the plane the other day I have received the Bulgarian medal for bravery, a very pretty, light blue ribbon (besides myself, the cook and—the orderly). Because of its exotic character it pleases me even more than the E.K.,[20] though it is worth less.

May 8, 1917, to Hans Ehrenberg:

A few days ago we got another lieutenant, with whom I hope to get along better . . . but, between you and me, every man counts here. We had a bad day on the 5th, losing

[20] Eisernes Kreuz; a German medal.

five of our seventeen gunners (two men are dead: our best head gunner, who shot down our third plane only a few days ago, and our second-best computer; besides there are three men wounded, two seriously and one slightly). It was a terrible day; we had to carry them across exposed terrain. At night we moved to a new position; since then nothing has happened; we are now lying between two targets and consequently get only a few splinters. At the moment it's pouring rain, but nobody seems to care any longer.

May 28, 1917, to Rudolf Ehrenberg:
I'm reading a great deal in the Psalms. I have a hunch that someday I may write about them, possibly from two angles: on the one hand the Septuagint, the Vulgate, Luther and his influence on language and literature; on the other Jewish textual interpretation, possibly as a study of individual psalms.—I too am now anxious for a furlough (bath, carpet, sofa, chair, Beethoven variations, old manuscripts, which again interest me). How autobiographical a man becomes in this solitude!

Of course there are no plays or concerts in June. The separation of mankind into two sexes is also a kind of sensation: for seven weeks now I haven't seen a woman, and before that it was three months; and complete houses; and no noise of shooting, in short, what the profound philosopher [Georg] Simmel tellingly calls security.

In June-July 1917, F. R. spent an eighteen-day furlough in Cassel with his parents. He had a meeting with Hermann Cohen. July 9, 1917, to Rudolf Ehrenberg:
Cohen was grand. He is the most alive person, even though *and* because he's a Jew. Aunt Julie[21] asked me how old he was. Seventy-five. Oh, she said laughing, a child!—

---

[21] Julie Ehrenberg was then ninety years old.

But it's really true. A child still wholly rooted at home. His spirituality is more that of a plant than an animal (*non sponte se movet*).—Altogether it was delightful. Eighteen days in mufti, risotto, peas, wine, real coffee, the cake you know, three times (we were thinking of you constantly), human beings!

On returning to the front, July 23, 1917, to his parents:
What concern of mine is this war waged for Brieg or for Belgium? I don't know this Germany. I was born in it but I'm not responsible for that. It may be that Michaelis[22] is better than the clown Bülow.[23] Evidently his looks are rather comical. But it makes no difference.

War-weary? In another twenty-seven years perhaps the whole world, or at least the iron-ore district of Brieg, will have been conquered. Let's hope for the best. To the gallows with all Social Democrats! Ditto all non-Germans outside Germany! Ditto, or more in style, burn everything non-German inside! Until only Count Reventlow[24] is left to save the world. Feel like vomiting.

August 21, 1917, to Gertrud Oppenheim:
One thing is certain, I have no real feeling about my first name. I can only guess why this is. It seems to me that it may be because my parents gave it to me without any particular feeling, simply because they "liked it" (and why did they like it? because at that time it was "different"; only later were there other Franzes in the Jewish community of Cassel). It's as though my parents had seen it in a shop window, walked inside, and bought it. It has nothing traditional about it, no memory, no history, not even an

[22] Georg Michaelis, German Chancellor, July to November 1917.
[23] Bernard von Bülow (1849-1929), German diplomat.
[24] Ernst zu Reventlow (1869-1943), pan-Germanist.

anecdote, scarcely a whim—it was simply a passing fancy. A family name, a saint's name, a hero's name, a poetic name, a symbolic name, all these are good: they have grown naturally, not been bought ready-made.

One should be named after somebody or something. Else a name is really only empty breath.

> Hermann Cohen and his wife visited F. R.'s parents in Cassel. In looking through F. R.'s library, Cohen remarked that there was no complete edition of Kant on the shelves, and he added: "And he has nothing of mine." His wife comforted him: "He will have your writings with him."

September 20, 1917, to his parents:
Evidently you have got to know Cohen very thoroughly. What you write about Cohen's isolation has never been so apparent to me, but you are undoubtedly right. His "vanity" is of course well known. But there is something that is less well known and yet very important: I can assure you on the strength of my personal acquaintance with him, his vanity is justified. Of the professors of philosophy I have known, the following have made a personal impression on me [F. R. mentions thirteen names]. Yet none of them in the least gave me the feeling: he is a philosopher. They were decent people, keen minds, contortionists, self-devourers, or to put it more bluntly, nail-chewers, subtle spirits—but not philosophers. Then I met him, rather prejudiced by several things of his I had read, and immediately knew I had found one. For the first time the word "philosopher" came to my tongue. There was the personal fund, heart, love, hate, in short a man who was worthy material for philosophy. I cannot tell whether racial kinship had anything to do with this instantaneous impression, that is, an instinctive understanding for the kind of transitions, the way of spinning out an idea to a certain point and then descending with a

swoop, the *crescendi, decrescendi, sforzati,* in short, for all that can be felt by instinct only.

In any event, he was the genius, the others artisans, often very competent. It might have been very nice if I had "gone to school" at Marburg instead of Freiburg; it *might* have, for perhaps it was a good thing that I took my first steps not under this overwhelming impression but under slighter ones.

His Germanism and Judaism. The "and" becomes a problem only when the two terms are taken in their strict sense. Fundamentally, though, he feels the same way as you. When you want to feel yourselves Germans you, too, look toward the small group of Germans who approve of you, such as (1) those "Germans" who are in the same position as yourselves, namely, the other Jews; (2) a handful of déclassés and bohemians; (3) a few dogmatic liberals and sympathizers; (4) the Jew-lovers; (5) your dependents. In Cohen's case all this becomes heightened because it is purely intellectual. He allows nothing as German, save his own philosophy and whatever he can muster in support of it. Under the circumstances it is easy for him to "consider himself a better German than the 'real ones.'" Of course he is a better Cohenite! The tremendous *hutzpe* [impertinence] of this statement pronounces its own sentence. I have got at the root of the whole problem in a short critique which I have all along asked you to copy out for me.[25] To be a German means to be *fully* responsible for one's nation, to harmonize not only with Goethe, Schiller, and Kant, but also with the others, and especially the trashy and mediocre ones, the assessor, the fraternity student, the petty clerk, the pig-headed peasant, the stiff school teacher; the true German must either take all these to his heart or else suffer

[25] *See* p. 33.

from them; he can calmly ignore the average Frenchman; just as we blush for the average Jew when he "disgraces us." This need not be a secret racial instinct; it is quite enough for a people to be sufficiently hard-pressed from without, as we are by the eternal *rishes* [anti-Semitism] to coalesce into a nation; it is enough to "experience a common plight" (Richard Wagner), or in our case a common pride (Paul Ehrlich, Rathenau, Disraeli, Gambetta, Spinoza) and a common embarrassment (the shirker, the profiteer). Cohen confounds what he as a *European* finds in Germanism with what the German finds in it. Sure enough, German philosophy and music are European phenomena, but so are French painting, English politics, the Russian novel, and the Russian religious spirit. Compared with the Russian kind of piety the German seems as contemptible as Western European philosophy does compared with German philosophy. The Europeanism of the educated man is combined in the case of the German with a kind of folk quality which he has too, and which alienates him from the educated man of another nation as it allies him with the unlettered people of his own. Cohen, however, has only Europeanism; there is no genuine Germanism for it to combine with, and Judaism, of which he has plenty, is notoriously incapable of crossbreeding. So in the man everything remains merely juxtaposed, while in his writing we find the mad acrobatics of "Deutschtum und Judentum" ("Germanism and Judaism"), in which Cohen, after speculating upon the Christian element in the German, proceeds to pronounce this element Jewish. A tasty dish! Yet all this is really no more than the same caricature which you represent on the social level, transposed to the intellectual level. Cohen's intellectual Germanism is every bit as precarious as your social Germanism, and neither fiction can be maintained without constant antics. The magnificent thing about

Cohen is that he exhibits highly magnified that which in others is only faintly visible.

I detest sets and love the single book. Apart from Schopenhauer, I have all my authors in separate editions, also most of the poets except those I was given for Bar Mitzvah. To this day I own no complete Shakespeare! As for Kant, I think the number of *Critiques of Pure Reason* alone should have impressed Cohen; I believe there are six in a row. Incidentally, I got so worried last night that I started examining myself on the subject of Kant before going to sleep; I passed with flying colors, gave myself a regular lecture on "schematism"—a chapter considered particularly obscure, which I hadn't read in eight years—was quite satisfied with myself, but of course didn't fall asleep until late. Such are the consequences. . . . "He will have your writings with him" is really marvelous!

During the High Holidays of 1917, F. R. attended the Sephardic synagogue in Üsküb (Yugoslavia). September 29, 1917, to his parents:

The nave has great architectural beauty. The *mahzor* [Festival Prayer Book], except in its main sections, contains only texts we do not know. They sing the Kol Nidre to a strange tune! Only the *hakham* [rabbi] was dressed in white.[26] During the *alenu* prayer they don't prostrate themselves (so I was told).

During these months F. R. had some favorable response to It Is Time, expecially from his friend Joseph Prager. F. R. said: "Here for the first time was the kind of response I had hoped for—the reader gave a start and said: Something of the sort *must* be done!" September 30, 1917, to Joseph Prager:

[26] In a white "kittel" as is customary in Ashkenazic Judaism.

The "teaching program" should be discussed as little as possible (except with the teacher). It may be added to or subtracted from almost at will. But one thing must be preserved, namely, the central position of Hebrew.

September 30, 1917, to Hans Hess:

You are certainly right to reduce my political pusillanimity *ad absurdum* by means of my own words, nor are you the only person to do this. It wasn't until the overthrow of Bethmann[27] that I realized how much my politics savored of hero worship, a kind of hero worship that I could not theoretically defend in so radical a form. I suppose it is my lack of a direct (autochthonous) relationship to the German people that has made me cling to the idea of a personal mediator. Just as Germany means only Schiller and Goethe to me and not, as to you, and rightly so, also Müller and Schulze. So you had better add a large grain of salt to my current political expectorations.

October 1, 1917, to his parents:

[Professor Friedrich] Meinecke's fundamental error is that in spite of everything, he still thinks in terms of *states* and not federations. He says: Federations make it impossible for wars to be politically creative, and by this he means a creative influence upon the individual *state*. But states are no longer the agents of history; their role has been usurped by federations, and upon these war—at least this war—has a highly creative influence.—There is a politically sound kernel to the pacifist idea, namely, the overcoming of nationalism through a federation of states.

October 1, 1917, to Rudolf Ehrenberg:

The true goal of the mind is translating; only when a

[27] Theobald von Bethmann-Hollweg, Chancellor of the German Empire; forced out of office in 1917 by Hindenburg and Ludendorff.

thing has been translated does it become truly vocal, no longer to be done away with. Only in the Septuagint has revelation come to be at home in the world, and so long as Homer did not speak Latin he was not a fact. The same holds good for translating from man to man.

October 19, 1917, to Margrit Rosenstock:

The kind of anti-Semitism that also includes baptized Jews seems to me the really objectionable one, simply because I begrudge them the triumph of this disgrace.

In October 1917, F. R. worked on a clarification of the concept of revelation; this became the central idea of his theological system. In November he formulated his "philosophical Archimedean fulcrum" in a lengthy letter to Rudolf Ehrenberg. Later, F. R. called this letter the "germ cell" of his *magnum opus*, the *Star of Redemption*.

October 24, 1917, to Gertrud Oppenheim:

Do you know that I no longer consider the Russians (that is Dostoevsky, Tolstoy, though not Turgeniev) as alien? I take them too seriously for that. To me they are on the same plane as the Greeks and the Germans.

December 18, 1917, to his parents:

We [Jews] will never become decadent because—we have been from the start. With other nations the birth of self-consciousness is the beginning of the end; with us it was the *beginning*. We didn't develop into a nation but were constituted so (no matter whether by Moses or by Ezra,[28] no matter, that is, whether one follows the Bible or today's radical historical research). The intention, the constitution, came first, the nation followed. Consequently, with us spir-

---

[28] Ezra: Scribe and religious leader in Jerusalem at the beginning of the era of the Second Temple (5th cent. B.C.E.).

ituality is tantamount to national health. If Zionism were to gather all the Jews into Palestine there would be no Jews left after two hundred years. But since it only desires to create a Jewish *center* (this it knows) and this center (this it doesn't know) will be governed by considerations of the "periphery," and not, as it hopes, the other way around, all Zionism amounts to is one more root gripping the earth, in addition to all others.

December 26, 1917, to Hans Ehrenberg:

Jewish piety and Jewish wit dwell in the same organ, namely, the Jewish heart; there is no road thither from alien minds and hearts.

December 28, 1917, to Richard Ehrenberg, on the subject matter of It Is Time:

I have deliberately made the study of Jewish sources the center, and shoved history toward the margins. You may believe me when I say that I don't underestimate history, but if you use it as your main weapon it's a double-edged sword; a man whose sole relation to Judaism is through history will be more apt to become confused in his Judaism than confirmed. It's quite different in the case of a man who has a bit of Judaism in him already: he may use it as a weapon, but a defensive weapon, as a shield, not a sword. The following may serve as "swords": Jewish race consciousness (as the Zionists know better than I, though I am far from denying it); Jewish life (wherever that exists I can add nothing); and—what else remains that doesn't function? For that is what we must assume almost throughout in the case of *our* "material"—what else can, be used as a sword? What *tertium datur* is still left? I can only think of one, Jewish *spirit*. The school cannot do much, but if it can do anything at all it can transmit spirit. Our present situation is about as fortunate as that of the general schools in transmitting German spirit: all the school needs to do is to stimulate, introduce, arouse respect; all the rest, all that really counts, is provided through the magnificent object lesson, e.g., the court theater, subscription concerts, chamber music. Our own object lesson is given in the synagogue. The more single-mindedly our teaching envisages this object, that is, the synagogue, the less likely will there be any conflict with the home. To a certain extent, the home will simply be ignored. This is not ideal, and it actually flouts the *Jewish* ideal, but "In a time when it is necessary to work for the Lord the Torah may be made void," as a famous saying from the Talmud interprets the words of the psalm [119:126], and it was this interpretation I had in mind when I made these words the title and conclusion of my pamphlet.

During a furlough at the end of January and into February 1918, F. R. was twice in Berlin, where he visited Hermann Cohen. On his second visit he was accompanied by his father. The three men discussed the foundation of the Academy for the Science of Judaism according to F. R.'s plan in *It Is Time*. In Cohen's bathroom F. R. happened by chance upon a discarded carbon manuscript copy (on very thin paper) of Cohen's *Religion der Vernunft aus den Quellen des Judentums* ("Religion of Reason from Jewish Sources"), which he appropriated. On his return to the battle front in Macedonia, March 9, 1918, to Hermann Cohen:

All I can do is thank you. These pages have helped me through dark days.

F. R. was taken up with It Is Time and with the way it was being received. March 7, 1918, to Hedwig Cohn-Vohssen:

"I have always found that it is a good thing to know something," as Goethe once said in a rather Mephistophelian mood, to his disciple Eckermann; I have always thought that a more widespread Jewish scholarship would benefit everyone. I am personally quite indifferent to parties; I wish that both the Zionists and the members of the Central Verein would become a little more—Jewish. To this end I wrote my pamphlet. It was meant to shake them up a bit.

Once there is a Jewish theology within the German *universitas literarum* (and of course also within any other) the Rathenaus will no longer be able to overlook it. Walter Rathenau[29] hasn't really overcome Judaism so far as what concerns religion, he just thinks he has. Individual scholars alone cannot make it impossible, or at least extremely difficult, for him to imagine this; it can only be done through the visible existence of a corporate "ism." At present the Rathenaus are as naive as children; *then* they will at least know what they are doing. And keep doing it anyway, fifty per cent of the time. But the other fifty per cent they won't do it, and on this I place my hopes.—There is doubtless an element of contraband in this: I should like to smuggle Judaism into universal education—the kind of education the Rathenaus want so much. The German Jew would have to be ashamed of knowing as little as most of them do now. The first signs of shame can already be seen, at least in some of the younger people. Martin Buber's monthly, *Der Jude* seems to be a powerful agent in this direction. He is also a smuggler. The phony address reads: To the Intellectuals. But inside one hears the voice of Rabbi Martin Salomonides.[30]

On March 19, 1918, Georg Rosenzweig, F. R.'s father,

---

[29] Walter Rathenau (1867-1922), leading German-Jewish industrialist; foreign minister in post-war Germany; assasinated by reactionaries.
[30] Rabbi Martin, grandson of Solomon [Buber]; Solomon Buber, a noted Jewish scholar.

died. Shortly after the funeral, F. R. got a few days furlough to visit his mother. April 5, 1918, to his mother:

My mind is still full of the days in Cassel. I know very well how little I can be to you, notwithstanding the consensus of opinions expressed in all the letters on this subject. There is something in you to which I lack the key. I clearly sensed this alien area when you talked so matter-of-factly about your life coming to an end if anything should happen to me. It isn't simply the difference in age that makes me think it impossible that any contingency, any loss, whether present or future, could alienate me from life. It is true that every loss makes us more familiar with our own death, but none can bring me closer to it, none has the power to turn me out of the house of life. In spite of all losses I still retain Myself, with the unfathomable and continually surprising store of tasks that each new day brings. And each loss, by making me more familiar with death, makes me more ready for life. The less I fear death, indeed the more I love it, the more freely I can live. That is to say, the more I cease to expect happiness on this earth. Happiness and life are two different things, and it's no wonder that men finally came to ascribe bliss to the dead alone. In any event, it is not the portion of the living.

I am speaking to you as one who has not yet reached that point, as one who has not untaught himself expectancy, and I am speaking to *you*, who likewise must not unteach yourself: Father is dead, but your grandchildren are not yet born. We are both still too young to need this kind of wisdom. But if it should happen one day (which is not at all likely), and if you should then feel the despair of having nothing more to lose, remember what I have just told you: that it is only then that the perfect life commences, the perfect freedom to do and suffer anything. Be close to me then; I know that until then you cannot be, that until then you must blindly cling to anything you possess, and that we meet only at those points where I too cling, though not blindly. But should that which I hope will never happen, happen, then be such that I may wholly understand you. Not for the sake of my literary remains and trifles of that kind—you may bother about them or not, as you please— but in order to be then close, understandable, and beloved. Today you needn't take all this very seriously; it is not for today, it is for *then*.

For today, just a hearty kiss, from your Franz.

> On April 4, 1918, Hermann Cohen died in Berlin. April 7, 1918, to his mother:

We still occupy the same position. I had hoped never to see the place again. Yet I am glad in a way, for there has been no gunfire in this region for many months; evidently the enemy doesn't suspect anything. As telephone operator I am very safe, because I have a very strong shelter.

My thoughts continually go over the days of January and February, particularly those I spent in Berlin, which now mark a double terminus in my life. How strange that I should have met Hermann Cohen so late, in 1913! It must have been a great thing in his life too, at least ever since It Is Time. I told him as much, as early as the spring of 1914, before he went to Russia. I walked home with him from the Lehranstalt, and he complained of not having had the response he had hoped for when he moved to Berlin. I became excited and told him that it was perhaps more important to have influenced me than the whole of Berlin W.[31]

I only made him really angry once, at the beginning of the war, after hearing his lecture "On the Peculiar Characteristics of the German Mind"; I was deeply disturbed, I thought he had fallen a victim to chauvinism. I asked him

[31] Berlin-West: well-to-do residential section.

for an interview, and then I behaved very crudely, starting with an accusation that he had betrayed the messianic idea. He gave me a terrific dressing-down, defended himself— partly well, partly ill—and everything was all right again. I should like to reread what I wrote you about him in the fall when he was visiting you. Now it is over. And yet I think this past year was a great blessing. Good night, mother.

April 10, 1918, to Hans Ehrenberg:
Thank you for your letter; there was in it something of our old friendship, of that which cannot age—fortunately there are things that cannot be discarded and do not need to be.

My mother is surprised to learn from the recent letters that my lack of rapport with Father was taken so seriously by my friends and acquaintances. I am not. It always troubled me, and when our relations improved during the war (partly *because* of the war, through the simple, *undemanding* concern with survival) I was very happy indeed. They would have gone on improving. Outward success, which would have come with time, would have satisfied Father's need (a need, after all, very easily satisfied) to be "proud" of me. Perhaps he *was* toward the last; people have told me as much.

Nevertheless, I can't reproach myself for what happened earlier: our natures were too different. It wasn't merely a question of "social" vs. "unsocial" (if it had been, I would have been obviously in the wrong), but it had to do with Father's lack of direction in his activities. To put it more sharply: the lack of idea in his activities. This made him a remarkable *man,* but estranged me from his actions. I have always admired him (you will remember how once as a freshman I worked in the office for three weeks; I pre-

tended that I did it in order to learn how a business operates; actually I did it simply in order to see him at work),
but could never become interested in what he was doing.
The fact is that in his hands everything turned into a "piece
of business," never into a subject. Once one has been bitten
by the mad dog of the *idea,* one is no longer interested in
anything but subjects. It wasn't the theoretical man defending himself against the practical man—I needn't tell *you*
that this is a false dichotomy; especially toward the last,
Father came to know my practical side—a practical side so
strong that anyone knowing it might never suppose that I
had also a not inconsiderable theoretical talent, but might
think my true vocation lay in the realm of organizing and
propagandizing. (This has actually happened recently.)
Rather, it was the man possessed of ideas defending himself
against the father who grappled indiscriminately with whatever came to hand. I shall always be grateful that toward
the very end my own obsession and his grappling converged
in one of my "subjects,"[32] which he converted into one of
his "pieces of business."

I have tried to perpetuate his memory as I have described
him to you, in the foundation[33] which mother has erected
according to my instructions . . . perpetuate it at least as
long as the town [Cassel] survives.

April 14, 1918, to Rudolf Ehrenberg:
Hermann Cohen too is dead.—I visited him at the end of
January and again in the middle of February; Father was
with me the second time, and helped me with the Academy
project. I was very grateful to him at the time, because I
realized how little he liked, not the project itself, but my

[32] Academy for the Science of Judaism.
[33] A foundation established by the Rosenzweig family in memory of Georg
Rosenzweig. The inflation of 1921 wiped out the funds.

share in it. I felt it very strongly because it was something entirely new in my relationship with him, something I had always wished for but which had never before happened; but unfortunately I didn't let him see how I felt. Once when Cohen had left the room I felt an urge, perhaps for the first time in my life, to fall on his neck. But I didn't do it; shame prevented me.—Shouldn't this be set aside for him? After all, evil thoughts too remain efficacious until they shatter upon God's throne. Then why shouldn't the good ones?

Everything else is as you would imagine it to be: Mother alone in the house, I in the war, no daughter-in-law, no grandchildren. A deadlock that will be broken in time, if nothing dire happens.—Your father has no doubt written you about Mother's great and beautiful composure, but this lasted only during the first few days, so long as Father was actually, in a sense, still there—first the corpse, and then the civic personality. While she still had the feeling of being able to do him a last service, she did it magnificently. She, who always refused to "assume a role" when he asked her, seems to have done it this time quite purely and grandly. But this is something that cannot be maintained for long, and even while I was still there she went to pieces. Her strength sprang from a wholly terrestrial source, and was bound to dry up. I would be so happy to show her the other one, but you know yourself how difficult it is, especially with close kin (who really believe nothing one says); I have joined battle with her, but I don't hope for success. The chances are that from Father's remnants and from myself she will construct an emergency existence for herself. Should I be killed, this too would no longer be possible. Since she knows this, and has told me so, I have insisted on this point by letter (I can't bring myself to do so orally). But, as I have said, I have little hope.

In your letters to Cassel you have harped on the danger
of my letting myself be too much absorbed by the practical
repercussions of It Is Time. But up to a certain point these
are exactly what does concern me. I *mustn't* become a mere
writer even if I should like to. When I wrote It Is Time I
thought it might open the way for me to teach some day
in a metropolis. Now it looks as though it might lead to my
organizing and proselytizing in connection with the Academy. No matter, so long as it isn't mere literature. This
Berlin affair moves forward, in spite of Cohen's death and
Father's. Of course, I'm not sure I'll recognize the child by
the time I get back. Cohen himself didn't understand fully
what I wanted until my last visit. But I can't change anything.

April 25, 1918, to his mother:

I feel great compassion for you, but not all songs can be
sung to the end; things may yet turn out quite pleasantly
for you. Of course it will involve a degree of resignation on
your part when I marry some day, but as you said yourself,
this would have been the same had Father remained alive;
and after all, in this too we meet each other halfway; I have
some talent, though not too much, for being a good son.
Don't try to weigh yourself down with tasks now. No one
need live a moment longer than he enjoys living simply for
the sake of tasks—they will be taken care of, if not by oneself by the next person.

The thing is simply to live in the conviction that one cannot tell what good may come of it. Also, not to close the
door on oneself, at least not out of principle, for this principle is of as little value as any other. Who has the right to
ask you to force yourself and "to be strong"? It was a good
thing for everyone that you were strong during the first few
days, but why should you want to harden yourself deliberately and become callous now? It's our own business

whether we are happy or sad; we are human beings, not Japanese. Don't be afraid of your own heart. At least before ourselves we shouldn't dissemble. Please let's not!

April 28, 1918, to his mother:
Do you too feel that with each day Father's death becomes, not more accustomed, but more incomprehensible? That, in a sense, it comes as a cumulative wrong that he has been dead one day more. He possessed nothing beyond this life; his delight in living was so unmixed and so free, I am certain he never felt fed up for a single moment. It makes one wonder what business he has being dead; I can imagine him only as living. And now this is denied, and one is confronted by this finality, this disallowance.

May 2, 1918, to Erna Jaeckh:
I know only in general what destiny is. And thus I know that there is but one way to keep one's soul alive in the face of misfortune: namely, to say *yes* to one's fate, to swallow it down (not necessarily skin and all, but in all its somehow digestible portions). A soul that thinks it can say *no* to its destiny will find out that it isn't free but simply naked. But to be naked, without destiny, is permitted only to the "sleeping babe"; after that life marches on pitilessly, and if the soul wishes to preserve its identity, it can never take a step back—its one choice is to keep in step.

In May 1918, F. R. was sent by the army to an officers' training center in Rembertow near Warsaw, in that part of Poland occupied by German troops. Here he came in personal contact with the native Polish Jews, an experience of the utmost importance in F. R.'s life. Rembertow, May 23, 1918, to his mother:
Rembertow is a beautiful park; I haven't seen a village yet, just the barracks in which only Jews are housed; they

all seem to depend on the gunnery school for their livelihood. So far I have seen only the younger generation. There
were also a few Polish children among them. The Jewish
boys are magnificent, and I felt something I rarely feel,
pride in my race, in so much freshness and vivacity. Driving through the town, too, I was impressed by the masses
of Jews. Their costume is really very attractive, and so is
their language (*vun vannen kummen zey?*). I noticed that
what, among us, is characteristic only of the upper stratum
is here typical; I mean the extreme alertness, the ability to
place each trivial detail in an interesting context. If you
tease a toddler by telling him he's crafty, he answers you
with a whole diatribe on craftiness that might have come
out of Shakespeare. I can well understand why the average
German Jew no longer feels any kinship with these East
European Jews: actually, he has very little such kinship
left; he has become philistine, bourgeois; but I, and people
like me should still feel the kinship strongly.

Don't forget to send me Cohen's *Logic* by the pound
(return covers!) or preferably by the half-pound, otherwise
it's too slow. Our officers seem to be nice. There are tub
baths.

May 27, 1918, to his mother:
The nation [i.e., the Jews] is "stiff-necked," but really "a
unique nation on earth";[34] true, we in Germany are degenerate parvenus.

May 28, 1918, to his mother:
I visited Warsaw Saturday evening shortly before seven,
Sunday from 3:00 P.M. on. It's a very beautiful town, though
I've seen very little of it yet; I spent most of my time in the
Jewish quarter. It consists of rectangular streets with tene-

[34] Biblical and liturgical phrase.

ment houses, usually built around several square courtyards so that most of the apartments have rear views. I haven't been inside one yet, but you can imagine from the type of construction what they must be like. The strange thing to me is that the people living in them are not regular proletarians but—Jews. I did not get an impression of abject poverty, such as I expected from descriptions, nor of filth; least of all on Saturday, when I saw many "extra uniforms." I can't help finding the costume very beautiful.

On Saturday I chanced into a hasidic *steebel* [prayer room]: on Sunday I went into several bookstores and two *heders* [Hebrew elementary schools]. There were two classes in one of them, one for the older children and one for the younger. The contrast with the Mohammedan school in Üsküb was very pronounced. First because there were only boys there. Also, among the hasidim the purely masculine character was striking; all the more so because the meal came between *minhah* [afternoon prayer] and *maariv* [evening prayer], at dusk, the so-called *sholeshsudes*, "the third meal." The "first" comes Friday evening, and Sabbath lunch is the "second." It was only a token meal, whether because of the war or by custom I don't know; the singing was the main thing; I have never heard anything like it. These people don't need an organ, with their surging enthusiasm, the voices of children and old men blended. You'll find one of the songs in one of the last issues of *Ost und West;* I'm sure there has been some reference to it in *Der Jude.*

Nor have I ever heard such praying. I don't believe in all that talk about "decadence"; those who now find all this decadent would have seen nothing but decadence even a hundred and fifty years ago. An adjoining room, smaller, contains the library.

The important thing about the *heder* is that the children

do not learn by rote without undestanding the meaning, as in Üsküb, where the Koran is committed to memory without any idea of its content. I was also struck by the comprehensiveness of the instruction within such a limited sphere. Unfortunately, thus far I can scarcely understand the Yiddish language; reading I find easy, and I try to speak it, but as yet with little success. There were two teachers and one *belfer* [assistant] . . . I have also been to the *tatshe shil* ["German" synagogue], a large, magnificent synagogue of the assimilated Jews, with, over the portal, a Polish inscription to the Creator by Alexander II who donated the site. Very gorgeous, very assimilated, coiffured, and *so* cold!

Ludwig Haas, a Jewish assimilationist, and a member of the German Reichstag, was appointed by the German authorities to represent Polish Jewry to the German administration. In Warsaw F. R. also met his old friend Hermann Badt. June 3, 1918, to his mother:

Oddly enough it was with Badt that I first visited the Gentile part of Warsaw. Of all people!—Haas is personally delightful; he has the most beautiful gray eyes I ever saw, like two polished metal mirrors. And yet, and yet . . . He outlined his views on Jews, Judaism, religious education, etc. in a thirty-minute parliamentary speech (quite excellent in its way)—we couldn't get a word in edgewise. He is very intelligent for a politician, very honest as a person, but as a leader and representative of the Jews he has dreadfully little Jewishness. The idea of this man's being allowed to play the part of destiny for the Polish Jews is a ghastly one. Later, when I was finally allowed to speak, I grew polemical, but still not enough. His Judaism consists in a sense of pride in belonging to this time-honored, and nowadays quite well-situated, "sociological stratum." He regards himself as "an aristocrat." Really the same point of view as yours and

Father's. Yet it became especially clear to me in Haas's case that what is really good in the Western Jews does not pertain at all to aristocracy but to the *homines novi*. The little East European Jew is more of an "aristocrat" than such a Haas. Afterwards, to point this up, I told Badt about an incident that was witnessed, I believe, by Moltke[35] in the fifties in London. Empress Eugénie was paying a visit to Queen Victoria. A theatrical performance was being given in their honor; they entered the King's box, approached the railing, thanked the audience, and sat down—Victoria without looking round, Eugénie after she had made sure by a glance that there was a chair. Eugénie was probably more of a person than the tedious queen, but only Victoria was a descendant of kings. The East European Jew has his chair behind him and sits down on it without looking around; even the most intellectual of them are more naive than the least intellectual Western Jews, whose life-element is tennis, etc. The Western Jew always looks round before he dares to sit down.

German city children are essentially proletarians without tradition, without substance, and hence without imagination. Here the five-year-olds already live in a context of three thousand years.

June 4, 1918, to his mother:
I remember, not only from S.M.E.'s [Samuel Meir Ehrenberg's] autobiography, but also from many other sources, reading of the worthlessness of the *heder*. So I was particularly struck by its positive virtues. In its actual effect it corresponds much more to the ideal of an educational institution than any Western European school. The latter turns out fragmented human beings, disoriented and incapable of

[35] Count Helmuth von Moltke (1800-1891), chief of the Prussian General Staff.

orientation; through the *heder* a nation constantly rejuvenates itself. Of course this has to do not only with the *heder* and Gymnasium, respectively, but with the whole context of which these are a part; there is after all only one true people, and it is really no people. The other peoples, which are indisputably peoples, are all just setting out on the road toward peoplehood. That is why outbreaks of war and the like are so important to them, since only during those brief periods do they really experience what it is like to be a people.—It is understandable that S. M. Ehrenberg should have disliked the *heder*: for men who were out to have their grandchildren baptized, I daresay it was not the right kind of school.

June 10, 1918, to his mother:

I don't seem to be able to get around to writing to Hans [Ehrenberg]; I've put all his letters in order, but I won't be able to make it today either. But it isn't because of Poland and other countries of his ancestors that I don't write to him; the Poland that fails to connect us would be between us also in Heidelberg. The real Poland, as I judge from your letter, lies more between myself and my *Jewish* relatives. Only Jews get nervous when they see Jews. Christians turn spiteful but not nervous. Our craven chiming in with the chorus of obloquy against the Polish Jews is the most shameful of the many shameful things that make up Jewish life in Germany. At least, like the rest of our mean acts, it has done us no good; the great goal hasn't been attained.

June 26, 1918, to his mother:

Whether I "need" you? I shrink from the idea of "needing" people. I don't want to "need" anybody, and I don't think there is anyone from whom I could not bear to be separated by death. This holds especially for those from whom I could not bear to be separated by life. This is the difference between you and me, and in this sense I should have to answer your question, Do I need you? in the negative. I do not need you, nor do I wish to need you. But I love you very much. And I feel a great pity for you, because what you want is not to be loved but to be needed. For whose sake must you continue to live? After Father, who even now needs you in your sense, since he goes on living as long as you live, in people's memories and especially in the kind of life he loved—after Father's living memory, I should say: simply for your own sake, for the sake of a future unknown to you or anyone else, unknown and unimaginable today, and yet forthcoming. Such a simple, unreasoned "for your own sake" will one day become a meaningful "for others' sake." Therefore I ask you quite simply: first get well physically, learn to sleep once more, don't puzzle over for whom or what you must get well, but first get well. And please don't shrink from lamenting to me; it can never become "tiresome" to me. "Tiresome" is another word that is not in my vocabulary. In any event, unhappy people, and really happy ones, can never be tiresome. The reason why most people are tiresome, just the same, is that they are capable of neither happiness nor unhappiness, but only of "good luck" or "bad luck." Your complaints can never upset me; on the contrary, they only make me love you the more and wish (in vain, as I well know) to help you. But what does upset me (I may as well tell you since you know it yourself) are not your complaints about yourself but your worries about me, through which you touch upon my life. For instance, your evident passive resistance to my Sunday letters from Warsaw has somewhat offended me. I have not been able to write about these matters since.

Franz's mother took note of his enthusiasm for Polish Jews with apprehension. In her letters she spoke of his "fanaticism for the Jews." She was afraid this experience might influence his postwar professional aims, and that he might, unlike other talented Jewish academicians, decide against becoming a *Privatdozent,* or junior lecturer, at a university. July 3, 1918, to his mother:

What do you fear on my account from "the Jews"? I think you would really be at a loss to say what damage my "fanatical, enthusiastic," etc. disposition has done me. I think I have always managed my life very well. I think few sons have given as little cause for concern as I.—And yet few have been more surrounded by concern than I. The only abnormal thing in my life has been that I did not become a *Privatdozent* and I refrained precisely in order to avoid external complications.[36] If X. finds the Zionist viewpoint impossible in the civil service, how much more would he find mine. A Zionist would be as possible in the civil service as a Prussian Pole, but I would find myself between two stools, and it is in order to avoid this that I shun a job in a state institution.

At the end of the officers' training course in Rembertow, F. R. was given a furlough (beginning of July). On July 11 he contracted influenza and pneumonia. He was confined in the military hospital in Leipzig until August 1. Soon after this he returned to the Balkan battle front, where he remained until the front collapsed.

August 18, 1918, to Mawrik Kahn, a young fellow soldier who had been his neighbor in the Leipzig hospital:

Personally or factually? "Or"?—When I was born (and even more so, prior to that) I was highly factual; when I die (and even more so thereafter) I hope to be highly per-

---

[36] German university lecturers were state officials since the universities were state institutions.

sonal. So, probably, I find myself between the two extremes today. For these *are* extremes. The world was created as a fact, and it must be redeemed into personality, personality down to the last barber's apprentice, the last waiter, prostitute and fraternity student (*see* Joel 3:1-2).[37] Therefore each step, each action—consciously for the knowing, naively for the naive—is a step toward the personalization of the factual, the humanization of "things." Also a road for each individual from his birth (which is very little "his") to his (truly his) death. And because this is so, no other road is valid, no side road, nor the tempting path that by-passes things; the road to our personality must lead through the entire *factuality*, through the whole object-world that has been given us with our birth, our body, our time, and our world.

On August 22, 1918, F. R., struck by a sudden inspiration, began writing his Star of Redemption. August 27, 1918, to Gertrud Oppenheim:

. . . I am deeply involved in developing my letter [of November 1917] to Rudi [Rudolf Ehrenberg] into a book. It's going to be quite fantastic, entirely unpublishable, equally scandalous to "Christians, Jews, and heathens"—but I'll learn what I need to learn in the process, and that's enough. For the present . . . the introduction. I'll probably write to you again tomorrow. I just noticed that I am sending you this insolent announcement of my system on Hegel's birthday. It's a pity about him! Only Nietzsche (and Kant) pass muster!

September 4, 1918, to Rudolf Ehrenberg:

It's quiet here, probably the quiet before the storm, since the enemy is planning an offensive. We have counted sixty

[37] "And it shall come to pass afterward, that I will pour out my spirit upon all flesh . . . And also upon the servants and upon the handmaids . . ."

tanks here and eighty in the Wardar sector. Now we are preparing to defend ourselves at close range; let's hope it won't happen. I could use a quiet winter, for after a few days of irresolution I started writing a book. Not my "real one" (this I won't do until I can, may, must, that is certainly not during this nomadic war existence) but at least the prolegomena for it; my system, as I may well say. It suddenly became clear to me a fortnight ago, and ever since I have been sitting in a shower of ideas. It concerns you particularly for it is really nothing but the development of my letter to you of last November.

It contains really everything that is in me, consequently all the influences I have undergone. I am sending you the outline (reserving the right to make changes, for there is little point sending you separate sections; it will be easier for you to read the whole than parts; provided I have some quiet I hope to finish it in the course of the winter).

August 31, 1918, for his mother's birthday:
Now that you are as unhappy as you were once happy I feel the need to *wish* you happiness (a need which, without knowing why, I had never felt in the past). To wish you happiness, the kind of happiness that may yet come to you. It is not the opposite of unhappiness, as was your former happiness; it should not blot out unhappiness, indeed it shouldn't diminish its weight by a single ounce; it should simply walk side by side with your unhappiness and offer its hand, and by degrees it should come more and more often until your unhappiness will feel that it can no longer live without this quiet companionship. This happiness will come, believe me; there is room for it; and it comes always and only when there is room for it. It comes when it is "needed." Everything else on which you now place your hopes—such as any happiness that might come to you

through me—is small by comparison; these are trifling weights in the scale from which the heavy weight of your former happiness has fallen; they don't turn the scales by a single jot, but the happiness I mean, placed in the same scale with the weight of unhappiness, will make the scale slowly rise.

Dear Mother, thirteen years ago I had the feeling that I had set out on a long journey, the end of which was uncertain. I can't say that I have "returned home"—and wouldn't it be sad if I were forced to say it? Rather, I have made my home outside. There's no longer any uncertainty about this, nor is there any danger that I'll disappear from your sight in the mist and you won't be able to find me. I'm settled in such a way that I'll always be within reach if you need me; distance matters little, so long as we know where we can find each other. It's no longer necessary for me to urge you, as I did once, to have "faith" in a future that is equally dark for you and for me. There is none of that darkness left, through which, indeed, "faith" would need to guide us, but rather a clear daylight shines on our relationship, illuminating my *here* and your *there* indifferently. The day is indifferent, but only a little love is needed to bring together our *here* and *there*. Faith was so much more difficult; it is so much easier to love. If you ever should find it difficult, remember how much harder it was when only faith and hope could lead you to me. It is much easier for me too, now that I can see you from where I sit (for this is really so) after the long years of wandering when I had to turn around to see you.

Presently F. R. decided to send the finished parts of the manuscript of the Star of Redemption to his mother, who had them copied. The "ms." consisted of army postcards and letters, which F. R. mailed one by one.—The Balkan troops were forced to retreat. F. R. came down with an attack of malaria. On September 25, he was brought to the army hospital in Belgrade. To Gertrud Oppenheim, on that day:

The mail service is confused, and so are many other things. So far I've had a very strange and comfortable retreat as an invalid. But all the same it was an interruption, and as such unpleasant. I'm afraid that I won't find much peace for some time now. I had been writing very smoothly, and had nearly reached the end of part one; I can't remember whether I sent you the outline. Since the interruption I have had too much time to think but none for writing, and "such men are dangerous," also in this case since only writing gives one the inner peace and security one needs; mere thinking of necessity leads one to doubt whether it will really *work*, etc.

To his mother, October 11, 1918:

Our platoon still hasn't arrived; the hospital is full, and the nurses are partly overworked, partly lazy; consequently they no longer take our temperatures. . . . Perhaps I'll have a bath today. I've also been working hard, and by tonight I may send you another ms. in letter form; still another, that comes between the last one and this one, is nearly half copied out, and I'll send it to you either today or tomorrow.

From October 29 to November 30, 1918, F. R. was stationed with his unit in Freiburg. November 13, 1918, to his mother:

My mail sent to the platoon has been lost after all, since German troops will hardly be able to leave Austria without being interned. Today I stayed "home" all day. Tomorrow I'll be on duty again. I don't care too much for living in a furnished room like this. One really works better in a dugout. One is bothered by the house fronts across the street until one gets used to them again. It's better in the evenings when the stores are closed. But the bed is magnificent.

In December 1918, after his release from the service, F. R. returned to Cassel; here, and in Berlin, he continued working on the Star of Redemption. Cassel, January 5, 1919, to Mawrik Kahn:

I have been deep in work, almost without interruption, since the end of August. Whatever has happened, personally and politically, since then, I have experienced as though with a second self. I hope to be finished sometime in February.

On February 16, 1919, F. R. wrote the concluding words of the Star of Redemption.

IV
THE SAGE OF FRANKFURT
1919-1922

Foundation is laid for a home, for a house of study (Lehrhaus), for a life dedicated to Hebrew wisdom and Jewish living.

F. R. was advised that Frankfort on the Main might offer the best opportunities for the advancement of Jewish learning. Joseph Prager gave F. R. a letter of introduction to Dr. Nehemiah A. Nobel, one of the leading rabbis of the city. Frankfort, April 15, 1919, to his mother:

In the afternoon I took Prager's letter over to Nobel. He at once invited me for both days [the two Passover Seder celebrations], and I didn't have the heart to say no. He impresses me as an honest and *almost* remarkable man.

The evening turned out to be very delightful, very good food, incidentally. He gave the Seder very fully for the child's sake, and added things on the spur of the moment. During the meal he became abstracted for a while, tried to make conversation, and then didn't listen to one's answers; he was evidently thinking about something.

This morning I found out what had exercised him to such an extent yesterday. An aperçu he had uttered during the Seder had developed into such a sermon as I have never heard before; he is a preacher of genius. He speaks freely, sovereignly, and with utter simplicity; without a single trace of unction, simple even when he takes fire, the ideas very arresting to me, who am not easily satisfied, rich and yet so concentrated that everything remains quite plain. I've never heard anything like it. An open mind, a Cohenite, with a feeling for the shape of words, German as well as Hebrew. I'm still quite enchanted, and I've told him so. Afterwards I had breakfast with him, and now I'm writing this in the waiting room in order to get this letter off if possible on the 1:15 train.

Please give my regards to Prager, and tell him that I am grateful to him.

F. R.'s thoughts centered around the Star of Redemption and his Academy project. He was studying classical Hebrew literature. June 8, 1919, to Gertrud Oppenheim:

I expect that the real thing for me will somehow come out of the Academy. After all, I would be crazy to kick aside the springboard I've constructed for myself, in order to make the leap *without* a springboard. The other thing is the Star of Redemption. I think I'll publish it after all. I must come out in the open. It's nonsense to stay in hiding, as I've learned during this past fortnight. A fortnight is a short period, and I was simply too impatient, more impatient than I have a *right* to be.

What you write me about the Star makes me very happy. This is just when I need to hear something about it. *It* is what keeps me going now, as a pledge for the future, as well as a hieroglyphic of the past and present. You'll understand.

Berlin, June 24, 1919, to Hans Ehrenberg:

Furthermore, you don't know how I happened to decide to have the Star of Redemption published. . . . I noticed during the first week of my stay here that I'm not sufficiently thrown into relief, that I really *am* nobody. So I said to myself that it's better to be in ill repute than to be nobody. As a nobody I have no connection with anything, while as a person of ill repute (as a "heretic") I am at least "interesting" and talked about as such.

> F. R.'s Christian cousins and friends tried to persuade him to publish the Star of Redemption through a Christian publishing house. Stuttgart, July 6, 1919, to Hans Ehrenberg:

A Jewish book under Christian aegis is no longer a Jewish book and means nothing to Judaism. . . . You will still be able, later on, to translate the Star into Latin and make a "stella ex Juda" out of it; but the only thing left for me to do with it is prepare the Hebrew edition. The rest must happen as it will.

> In the autumn of 1919, F. R. visited Frankfort again, and he made the acquaintance of Dr. Eduard Strauss, a chemist by profession, who was interested in adult education among the liberal Jews. At that time a few intellectuals were planning to establish an Institute of Adult Jewish Education [*Volkshochschule*]. F. R. again visited Rabbi Nobel. A note:

Nobel made a vain attempt to marry me off, I don't know to whom, and when I declined politely but firmly, he asked me if I wouldn't at least come to live in Frankfort. I had myself entertained this idea, and I told Nobel that I would come, but not as a "globe trotter," only if I had a position. Nobel immediately thought of the *Volkshochschule*, which was in the air at that time, and promised to use his influence. Strauss, who was also enthusiastic about the possibility, promised to do what he could.

F. R.'s Academy plan underwent many changes in the months after the war. There was no lack of intelligent Jews and community leaders who were ready to lend their support. However, certain education experts objected to F. R.'s suggestion that school reform be combined with the reorganization of scholarship. Also, the death of Hermann Cohen, and the breakdown of Germany in 1918, made it necessary to curtail the original plan. An institute devoted solely to research was established. F. R. fought desperately, in numerous committee meetings, against the modification of his project, only to realize in the end that it was a lost battle. He found himself undertaking a new task, the reorganization of Jewish adult education.

In December 1919 and January 1920, F. R. gave a series of public lectures in Cassel on Lessing and *Nathan the Wise*. The series concluded with a reading of the first chapter of the third part of the Star of Redemption. Joseph Prager relates:

I'll never forget the evening after his lecture. I disagreed with his interpretation, and late in the evening I went up to his room to talk about it. We immediately got involved in a vehement discussion, which grew livelier by the hour, for we were both concerned with the ultimate bases of our Judaism. When the night was nearly gone we were still arguing. Suddenly he disappeared into the next room and came back with a big manuscript. It was his Star of Redemption, and he began to read me sections from the third book. As he read our quarrel dissolved. I realized how far he had already gone along the road that leads from the spurious to the real Judaism; and he himself realized how much further he had to go.

The next day he came to me to study the Talmud. Anyone who knew Franz Rosenzweig in his vigorous days knows that it wasn't easy to have him for a teacher. Neither was it easy to have him for a pupil, or, as more precisely fits the case, for a fellow student. He found no time unsuitable for study. Early in the morning before I went to work, at noon, in the evening, every minute I could spare from my professional work he claimed. The assignments were never large enough for him, the pace was never rapid enough. He rushed forward with tremendous verve, never stopping until the material was wholly assimilated.

On January 6, 1920, F. R. became engaged to Edith Hahn, whom he had met in 1913-1914 in Berlin. January 16, 1920, to Edith Hahn:

Do you know why you were unable at that time to know "the meaning of love"? Because one only knows it when one both loves and is loved. Everything else can, at a pinch, be done one-sidedly, but two are needed for love, and when we have experienced this we lose our taste for all other one-sided activities and do everything mutually. For everything *can* be done mutually; he who has experienced love discovers it everywhere, its pains as well as its delights.

Believe me, a person who loves will no longer tolerate anything dead around him. And since love teaches him "not to run away," there's nothing left him, whether for good or ill, but to love. (More precisely, for good *and* ill.) "As He loves you, so shall you love"—this passage from the Talmud,[1] which effects the transition in my book from revelation to redemption, from "And thou shalt love the Lord, thy God . . ." (Deut. 6:5) to "Thou shalt love thy neighbor as thyself" (Lev. 19:18), is a great passage, and means nothing else. We never awaken for our own sakes; but love brings to life whatever is dead around us. This is the sole proof of its authenticity. You see, I can no longer write a "book," everything now turns into a letter,

[1] The original letter quotes the passage in Hebrew. The exact quotation reads: "As He is gracious and compassionate, so be you gracious and compassionate" (Shabbat 133 b).

since I need to see the "other." That is how I feel now in writing the piece on education. Since today I am really at it. Every once in a while I have a fit of laziness because it is mere "writing"—I had rather speak—but I go on all the same and make my pen shout.

January 17, 1920, to Edith Hahn:

I'm sure you understand why I neither can nor must take too solemn a view of kosher eating. I look forward with pleasure to it, since we will do it together, in our house! But I can't be solemn about it or find "educational value" in it. (I grant that it *has* some, but it can also ruin one's character. Just see the emotional sclerosis of many orthodox Jews, especially the sclerosis of their Jewish feelings! How they are unable to accept any Jew who does not live by the Shulhan Arukh[2].) No, I can't find it "highly important" (though it *is,* granted, but there are more important things). And believe me, this is also the way I regard the "Sabbath and the holidays" (Isa. 1:14!!!). I also look forward with pleasure to these. But, Edith, what has happened between us, between you and me, means more to us than the Sabbath. . . .

Look, the whole secret of life lies in truthfulness, in not denying what great things have happened to us. I have felt upon my own body His rod as well as His gentle hands —then why should I become excited about "educational arrangements"?

The epistle *On Education*,[3] written in January 1920, laid the theoretical foundation for a new institute of Jewish studies, the Freies Jüdisches Lehrhaus soon to be established at Frankfort. Cassel, January 18, 1920, to Edith Hahn:

---

[2] Code of Jewish law.
[3] Addressed to Eduard Strauss. *See* pp. 214-227.

My fingers are stiff, for I have just finished copying with mother a third of On Education (Eccles. 12:12). . . . When I wrote It Is Time I was playing the pundit, so I had it coming to me that later on my ideas were "pundited" by the pundits. This time I have put my real self in it, without any pose.

March 11, 1920, to Ilse Hahn, the sister of his fiancée Edith:

Thank you very much for your kind words. You know, you needn't feel bad because you lack the power to "tell yourself the whole truth," for once, for your own good. Believe me, *no man* has this power; no man can help himself. Though the world is full of people who try to make themselves believe that they can, they succeed no better than Muenchhausen did when he tried to pull himself out of the mire by the scruff of his neck. Each of us can only seize by the scruff whoever happens to be closest to him in the mire. This is the "neighbor" the Bible speaks of. And the miraculous thing is that, although each of us stands in the mire himself, we can each pull out our neighbor, or at least keep him from drowning. None of us has solid ground under his feet; each of us is only held up by the neighborly hands grasping him by the scruff, with the result that we are each held up by the next man, and often, indeed most of the time (quite naturally, since we are neighbors *mutually*) hold each other up mutually. All this mutual upholding (a physical impossibility) becomes possible only because the great hand from above supports all these holding human hands by their wrists. It is this, and not some nonexistent "solid ground under one's feet" that enables all the human hands to hold and to help. There is no such thing as standing, there is only being held up. "As an eagle . . . hovereth over her young" [Deut. 32:11]. Let Edith tell you where this comes from. And give her a kiss from her—and also your—Franz.

On March 29, 1920, F. R. married Edith Hahn. On their wedding trip, F. R. translated from the Hebrew the "Grace after Meals." During May and June 1920 he conducted courses in Cassel, in preparation for his work in Frankfort. July 4, 1920, to Rudolf Hallo:

Frankfort seems more permanent to you than it does to me. I think it may be two years at the most. I'll probably be through just when I can be of most use. The lectures here in Cassel should have taught me how consuming it is to speak *nothing but* the truth. The chances are that after a year or two I'll simply *need* something more normal, more professional, more routine. But not yet, thank God. Nor do I have any routine yet, thank God—which is wonderful.

On August 1, F. R. became head of the Freies Jüdisches Lehrhaus in Frankfort.[4] The program of the first trimester included a number of lecture courses, study- and discussion groups and a course in the Hebrew language given by F. R.; he considered this course the core of the Lehrhaus program. "In the elementary Hebrew course, you have to fight for every student," he wrote.

At the end of the semester I assembled all my students . . . and made my usual speech about the program that was being handed out at the door. The separate lectures become illustrations for a system of Judaism, and the students would feel ashamed not to attend them all.

Summer 1920, *Hegel and the State* was published. F. R. showed Hegel's original conception of the military state as being rooted in a dim, obscure, rigid, superhuman fate which sets itself against the individual. Later Hegel introduced a notion of the state as a moral structure. For some time these two ideas of the state coexisted without connec-

---

[4] For the opening address, *see* pp. 228-234.

tion in Hegel's thinking. Only in his philosophy of law did Hegel force the two concepts together.

Professor Friedrich Meinecke, realizing the scholarly faculties in F. R., offered him a university lectureship. F. R. decided to reject the academic career so as not to have to serve two masters. In the summer of 1920 F. R. visited Meinecke, but somehow he did not succeed in making himself understood. The deepest motive in the heart of his former Jewish student remained a riddle to the Christian professor. August 30, 1920, to Friedrich Meinecke:

I wish to thank you for the kind things you wrote about my Hegel book. Before long I hope to be able to place the second volume too in your hands.

After our meeting in Berlin I felt that I had failed to convey to you the personal necessity of my recent course of life—and yet I was so anxious to succeed! I stress the adjective "personal," for while I also believe in the objective necessity of the course I have taken, I am quite aware that I may be deluding myself in this, and I am not conceited enough to hold on to it at all costs. The error I made in Berlin arose precisely from the fact that I tried to explain the personal element—decisive in my case—through the objective, while actually the latter was nothing more than the visible confirmation of something I had long since felt to be right. In other words, it is quite possible that I misjudge—in historical and philosophical terms—the significance of the crisis we have just passed through; the world in which I was born and bred is so dear to me that I would almost *wish* to be proved wrong. But what has happened to me, blocking as you say, quite correctly, "the simple and straight path laid out for my talent," is quite independent of any speculative optimism or pessimism (or dependent on it only to the extent personal premonition—if there is such a thing—may be said to depend on the world catastrophe that follows it). It is difficult to talk about these matters. It was a kind of moral cowardice that made me expound myself to you in objective terms. It simply didn't work, and so I have decided to put by embarrassment and speak in a very personal way to you. Please listen kindly to what I have to say.

In 1913 something happened to me for which *collapse* is the only fitting name. I suddenly found myself on a heap of wreckage, or rather I realized that the road I was then pursuing was flanked by unrealities. Yet this was the very road defined for me by my talent, and my talent only! I began to sense how meaningless such a subjection to the rule of one's talent was and what abject servitude of the self it involved. I felt a horror of myself, quite similiar to the horror [Siegfried] Kähler felt in my company when we were both studying in Freiburg: I remember how sinister my insatiable hunger for "forms" [*Gestalten*]—a hunger without goal or meaning, driven on solely by its own momentum—then appeared to him. The study of history would only have served to feed my hunger for forms, my insatiable receptivity; history to me was a purveyor of forms, no more. No wonder I inspired horror in others as well as in myself! Amidst the shreds of my talents I began to search for my self, amidst the manifold for the One. It was then (one can speak of such matters in metaphors only) that I descended into the vaults of my being, to a place whither talents could not follow me; that I approached the ancient treasure chest whose existence I had never wholly forgotten, for I was in the habit of going down at certain times of the year to examine what lay uppermost in the chest: those moments had all along been the supreme moments of my life. But now this cursory inspection no longer satisfied me; my hands dug in and turned over layer after layer, hoping to reach the bottom of the chest. They never did. They dug out whatever they could and I went away with armfuls of stuff—forgetting, in my excitement, that it was the vaults of myself I was thus plundering! Then I climbed back again to the upper stories and spread out before me what treasures I had found: they did not fade in the sheer light of day. These, indeed, were my own treasures, my most personal possessions, things inherited, not borrowed! By owning them and ruling over them I had gained something entirely new, namely the right to live—and even to have talents; for now it was *I* who had the talents, not they who had me.

Now, to leave metaphor aside and apply an awkward dichotomy to a crucial experience: I had turned from a historian (perfectly "eligible" for a university lectureship) into an (utterly "ineligible") philosopher. The one thing I wish to make clear is that scholarship no longer holds the center of my attention, and that my life has fallen under the rule of a "dark drive" which I'm aware that I merely *name* by calling it "my Judaism." The scholarly aspect of this whole process—the conversion of the historian into a philosopher—is only a corollary, though it has furnished me with a welcome corroboration of my own conviction that the "ghost I saw" was not the devil; it seems to me that I am today more firmly rooted in the earth than I was seven years ago. The man who wrote the Star of Redemption to be published shortly by Kauffmann in Frankfort—is of a very different caliber from the author of Hegel and the State. Yet when all is said and done, the new book is only—a *book*. I don't attach any undue importance to it. The small—at times exceedingly small—thing called [by Goethe] "demand of the day" which is made upon me in my position[5] at Frankfort, I mean the nerve-

[5] As head of the Jüdisches Lehrhaus.

96

wracking, picayune, and at the same time very necessary struggles with people and conditions, have now become the real core of my existence—and I love this form of existence despite the inevitable annoyance that goes with it. Cognition [*Erkennen*] no longer appears to me as an end in itself. It has turned into service, a service to human beings (not, I assure you, tendencies). Any kind of tendentious work is not only distasteful but downright impossible to me. Cognition is autonomous; it refuses to have any *answers* foisted on it from the outside. Yet it suffers without protest having certain *questions* prescribed to it from the outside (and it is here that my heresy regarding the unwritten law of the university originates). Not every question seems to me worth asking. Scientific curiosity and omnivorous aesthetic appetite mean equally little to me today, though I was once under the spell of both, particularly the latter. Now I only inquire when I find myself *inquired of.* Inquired of, that is, by *men* rather than by scholars. There is a man in each scholar, a man who inquires and stands in need of answers. I am anxious to answer the scholar *qua* man but not the representative of a certain discipline, that insatiable, ever inquisitive phantom which like a vampire drains him whom it possesses of his humanity. I hate that phantom as I do all phantoms. Its questions are meaningless to me. On the other hand, the questions asked by human beings have become increasingly important to me. This is precisely what I meant by "cognition and knowledge as a service": a readiness to confront such questions, to answer them as best I can out of my limited knowledge and my even slighter ability. You will now be able to understand what keeps me away from the university and forces me to follow the path I have chosen: not an extreme degree of consciousness (lucidity of this kind I can only summon when I am called upon to vindicate myself, as I am now) but precisely that "dark drive" to which you appeal in your letter.

You'll be sure to understand me now, and this is all I can hope for. Nor do I really hope for anything more. My sole purpose was to spread myself out before you so that you may see me as I am. It is for this reason that I have talked of myself only, at the risk of straining your patience. Now a great weight has been lifted from my heart, for when we parted in Berlin I was extremely distressed over my failure of communication. I had cunningly woven a net of conversation—we discussed the "present age"—which I was then unable to unravel in order to acquit myself of the only duty of the disciple toward his master, the younger man toward the older: the duty of reverent confession as soon as one's own path diverges from that of one's master.

Will you believe me when I say that in reading your letter I have been deeply aware of your kindness and concern for me? And may I hope that you will believe this all the more in the light of my answer?

Meinecke did not fully understand F. R.'s decision. He felt this decision to be motivated by the postwar disillusionment which took the breakdown of German ideals to be final. Under the circumstances, Meinecke thought, F. R. had taken recourse to Judaism "in its spiritualized form."

In the middle of December 1920, unable to find a regular apartment because of the housing shortage in the city of Frankfort, Franz and Edith R. moved into the attic of the house at Schumannstrasse 10, situated in the residential section of the city. This attic remained their home throughout F. R.'s lifetime. The study contained bookcases that fairly covered the walls, as well as a work desk, chairs, a small couch, and a cabinet which was later used as an ark for the Torah scroll. At the left of the entrance to the study hung a large painting of a venerable old lady, Julie Ehrenberg, F. R.'s great-aunt and the daughter-in-law of Samuel Meir Ehrenberg. Soon after settling in Frankfort, F. R. became a member of a group that met every morning with Rabbi Nehemiah Nobel to study the Talmud.

Hans Ehrenberg, who had been a convert to Christianity since 1909, was invited to visit the Rosenzweigs. September 15, 1920, to Hans Ehrenberg:

When are you coming? Be sure that you don't come too late. I'll give you a list of the Jewish holidays, which all, unfortunately, come together at this time, so you won't arrive smack in the middle of one if you can avoid it. [Here follow the dates of the holidays.] It's a rather complicated time for a meeting—a fantastic calendar, isn't it?

The Sabbaths (starting on Friday afternoon) are always out. . . . You must imagine the Sabbath as a *family* celebration, like a birthday. On birthdays too, the family stays home, and if there's a visitor in the house he naturally joins in the celebration even if he doesn't belong to the family. It's the same if a visitor is expressly invited. Mere acquaintances won't come in for a meal on that day, or even for an after-meal visit of an hour or so, but they'll leave the family to themselves—though the family is bound to be at home. It's a family celebration, not a day for receiving.

I'm anxious for you to understand this right, and not suspect me of "holding anything back." There's nothing of the sort. Stay with us, as I stayed with you last year, and conform to the rather strict domestic rule of the Sabbath (no telephoning, for instance), and you will be a part of it. But don't drop in unannounced unless it's absolutely necessary, out of consideration for the lady of the house, who must prepare for the Sabbath from Thursday on—and it's a real job—since on the Sabbath itself no work may be done. An emergency breaks the Sabbath, but it also breaks it apart, and the fragments are valueless. My unhappiness the other day when I missed the train in Heidelberg was not for nothing; a violated Sabbath is destroyed, no matter whether I myself am responsible for it, as in Heidelberg, or somebody else.

The problem of how to translate adequately from Hebrew into German had occupied F. R. since 1920. "My true 'literary development' since 1920 has been in the field of translation," he remarked. Old Hebrew hymns and liturgical pieces interested him most. March 10, 1921, to Gerhard Scholem, himself a distinguished translator from the Hebrew:

My sending you my little book "Grace after Meals" was not a mere act of politeness. I had the clearest recollection of an essay of yours that appeared, I believe, in the *Jüdische Rundschau,* in which you expressed so precisely what I was thinking that when Rudi [Hallo] spoke of you recently, I seized my chance, and I am glad I did.

For your letter, both where you approve and disapprove, is so thoroughly to the point that I should scarcely have any reply to make if the question were one only of the worth of my translation. But you quite correctly feel that there is something more essential at issue, a principle which rules out the elimination of those errors that the art of translation by itself might very well eliminate. And I think we must decide just what this principle is and come to an agreement about it.

Only one who is profoundly convinced of the impossibility of translation can really undertake it. Not by any means of the impossibility of translation in general (that isn't the case at all; rather, all life beyond one's own soul is conditioned by the possibility of this miracle, as you so rightly call it), but of the impossibility of the particular translation he is about to embark on. This special impossibility is different in every case. In this case its name is: Luther. And not Luther alone—he is only the point of intersection where the newest and the oldest meet—but more precisely: Notker,[6] Luther, Hölderlin.[7] The German language, in the names of these three men, has become a Christian language. Anyone who translates into the German language must to some extent translate into Christian language. To what extent he does so depends not on him but (especially if he translates well) solely on the material to be translated. The nearer Christianity has compelled the translated world to move toward itself, the more Christian will be the German of the translation. Thus it will be most Christian of all for Christian texts, less so but still strongly Christian for the "Old Testament," much less with biblical passages that have been incorporated into the text of a basic prayer, even less for Bible quotations in hymnal prayers and, in fact, in hymns in general. Any arbitrary or deliberate evasion at all is impossible here. So, for example, I simply had to let the verses at the end [of the Grace], especially since they are spoken in a low voice, be really Lutheran. And that is how all the things you correctly saw and noted came about.

What conclusions must be drawn? May I tell you how the thing originated and how I use it? The original idea was to make it possible for some of my guests—Christian friends and those Jews who don't read Hebrew—to take part somehow. I could not bear the thought of using one of the existing translations which render the prayers into

[6] Notker Labeo (10th-11th cent.), translator of Latin classics into German.
[7] Friedrich Hölderlin (1770-1843), translated Greek plays into German; he discarded rhyme in favor of the verse measures of antiquity; he wished to see the Greek spirit expressed in German literature.

the German of the newspapers or of religious instructors. I should have preferred no participation at all rather than feel that the participation was of such an order. If I happen to have a Jewish guest who can just read Hebrew—even if he cannot understand a sentence and, so to speak, not a word—I conceal the existence of the translation from him. The uncomprehended Hebrew gives him more than the finest translation. There is no getting away from it. Jewish prayer means praying in Hebrew. The only compromise I would admit at all are the translations into Yiddish, one of these I have been using all along for my rendition.

Such is our dilemma. But after all we're deep in it. In a sense we are ourselves guests at our own table, we ourselves, I myself. So long as we speak German (and even if we speak Hebrew, Modern Hebrew, the Hebrew of "1921"!) we cannot avoid this detour that again and again leads us the hard way from what is alien back to our own. All we have is the certainty that ultimately it will lead us there. An "ultimately" that of course can arrive at any moment. Otherwise it would surely be unbearable. . . .

An anniversary volume was planned for the sixtieth birthday of Friedrich Meinecke, and F. R. was invited to contribute a scholarly article. July 12, 1921, to Edith Rosenzweig:

I'm still laboring over the piece for Meinecke. Or, rather, I realized this morning that it won't work. I'm too far removed from these things. I hope I can find something to substitute, as I should like to contribute to the volume. Perhaps I can find a short unpublished ms. In order to carry out my original plan I would need much time and energy. And I have time and energy at present only for those books you are jealous of, the Sefarim.[8] The only

[8] *Sefarim*: the Hebrew word for books, used to denote works of classical Hebrew tradition.

thing that gives me pleasure these days is to have learned a few folios of Gemara [Talmud]. I have now reached page 6a in Megillah [a talmudic tractate]; I'm getting more and more into the spirit of it.

In July 1921, F. R. wrote, upon a publisher's invitation, a small philosophical book: *A Treatise on Healthy and Unhealthy Thinking.*[9] He withdrew the book before publication. August 30, 1921, to Gertrud Oppenheim:

I don't feel particularly bad about this book having been done to order, rather than growing organically. . . . What the whole thing comes down to is that one must learn to be grown-up. Fundamentally this is the only thing that matters to me now. You wrote me about this several years ago; it was too soon for me then; at that time I wouldn't have been able to do the work you asked of me. Today I do practically nothing else; the weeks spent here have, I think, brought me a good deal further. However this is nothing one should talk about—not to talk about things is precisely what one must learn. I'm still a long way from mastery; each day still brings pain.

Nevertheless I must be grateful to fate. It isn't given to many to see their boldest childhood dream realized at thirty-two, something for which I have striven desperately for fifteen years: to have a book, a real timeless work (or what we mortals call timeless), finished, behind me. The rest of my life is now really a kind of magnificent gift— something that Goethe could only say after his eighty-second birthday, when he had finally sealed up the manuscript of *Faust*.

October 5, 1921, to Gertrud Oppenheim, after attending High Holiday services at Rabbi Nobel's synagogue:

Nobel's sermons were incredibly magnificent; it's a pity

[9] *See* pp. 211 ff.

that you've never had a chance to hear him. It's impossible to describe; even his lectures are a far cry from such a "sermon" (which is no sermon at all). What is it then? I have nothing to compare it with. Only the very greatest can be mentioned alongside of it. I, too, might have the ideas, after all, and many men have the rhetoric, but something else is involved here, a final quality, a rapture of the whole man, so that one wouldn't be surprised if he took wing in the end and disappeared. Nothing would be too audacious for him to risk saying at such moments, and there's nothing that would not be true coming from such a mouth. Think of this happening to me, who hate and detest all sermons, think of my going to the service for the sake of the sermon, of its happening at a *conservative* service and through the mouth of a Zionist, mystic, and idealist (each, to me, a worse term of obloquy than the last), and of all of it, Zionism, mysticism, and cursed idealism rising to heaven in a vast flame! He prays the way one thinks of people praying only thousands of years ago when the great prayers originated; he speaks to the people as one thinks only the prophets should have been allowed to speak. It's really the Spirit as "cloudburst."

Another rabbi in town mentioned F. R. in his sermon. October 5, 1921, to his mother:

I understand I was put in a sermon yesterday and my book referred to as "the sublime book of a new thinker who lives in our midst." But it won't be really good until they use me in sermons without quoting me, and best of all, without even knowing that it is me they are using.

During the summer of 1921 F. R. edited an anniversary volume in honor of the fiftieth birthday of Nehemiah Nobel.

In December 1921, F. R. and his wife visited Martin Buber in Heppenheim. To Rudolf Hallo:

We reached Heppenheim in the afternoon. I had no settled intention of asking him to join the Lehrhaus; the thought hadn't occurred to me, since from the start I had given up the practice, from the days of the popular lectures, of enlisting university teachers from Marburg or Heidelberg; and besides I didn't see the necessity of bringing Jews to Frankfort. In the course of conversation, while we were having coffee, I suddenly realized that Buber was no longer the mystical subjectivist that people worship, but that even intellectually he was becoming a solid and reasonable man. I was rather astonished and impressed by the extreme honesty with which he spoke. In referring to his books on hasidism, he remarked that he was surprised only one person had asked for his sources in all these years. He was planning to add a list of sources to his new book.[10] What he said struck home with me. I had been searching all along for the original East European Jewish sources of his tales, with some success. I told him I thought there were quite a few people, including myself, who simply hadn't written to him. He said he would like, sometime, to present the sources to a few persons, whereupon I said I could gather together those few persons, not during the winter but during the summer, and I at once outlined a plan how in the mornings we could take hikes and then stop over at his place in Heppenheim in the afternoons. But I had to know how he would go about it so that I could tell people. When he said he couldn't tell exactly, I suggested that since he and two of his students were there, he might given us a trial lesson. We moved into the other room. He disappeared among his bookshelves, returned with two or three texts, and we started reading. He proved a rather

[10] Martin Buber, *Der grosse Maggid und seine Nachfolge,* Frankfurt am Main 1922; now included in *Tales of the Hasidim,* New York 1947.

awkward teacher; he tried to explain to me very circumstantially, in connection with one text, the importance and reality of the "word." Something that wasn't entirely new to me. At that time he didn't know the Star of Redemption. Only during the trip home did it occur to me that it was cheaper to transport the prophet than twenty of his disciples. I wrote him to this effect. I had already told him about the Lehrhaus, perhaps also shown him one of the programs. He replied that, to his own surprise, though refusing had been second nature to him for many years, he had immediately felt disposed to accept my proposal. After some further exchange the rest of the arrangements were made. . . .

In November or December of 1921 F. R. noticed symptoms of a disturbance of the motor system. For no apparent reason he stumbled and fell several times. A friend, Dr. Victor von Weizsäcker, examined him and informed him of the seriousness of the trouble, which he recognized as the beginning of a paralysis. F. R. remarked: "I do not ask my physicians for advice because I do not want them to lie." The two friends went to the dinner table as if nothing had happened.

On January 22, 1922, Rabbi Nobel died. End of January, to Joseph Prager:

You evidently don't know how I stood with Nobel. More particularly, you are unaware of the negative side of our relationship. I respected only the talmudic Jew, not the humanist, only the poet, not the scholar, only the prophet, not the philosopher. I rejected the qualities I did reject because, in the form in which he had them, they were deeply un-Jewish. At least this is what I always felt. All my veneration and love never blinded me to his toying with Christian and pagan ideas. True, it couldn't do me any harm, since I am armored against this kind of temptation as perhaps no Jew in *galut* [exile] has been before me. But in the effect he had on others I was always aware of the poison mixed with the medicine. I always tried to steer people away from his mostly horrid lectures to his sermons, where at the decisive moments the Jew in him came to the fore. Only there did he believe himself able to manage without loans from the Christian and pagan cultural spheres, and even *there* one was never sure one wouldn't be handed a quotation from "the master" [Goethe]. Also in the *shiur* [talmudic course] he made the most of its weaknesses, i.e., the silly quibbles of philological criticism (the original *mishnah*, first, second, second-and-a-half, etc. strata), while he often seemed to present genuinely Jewish matters almost reluctantly or with the cool, ironic remark, "As they say in the Yeshivas"[11] (what followed was always particularly good).

This is how the matter stands. I can't help you. Had I met him sooner, say ten years ago, he might *possibly* have driven me away from Judaism, more likely he would have completely ruined me.

But things happened otherwise. And I am thankful that I got to know him only three years ago, in the spring, after I had finished forging my armor, the dangerous book. For then I did need him, especially to teach me to lay this armor aside if necessary. Through him I have become more tolerant than I was formerly. Three years ago I was more orthodox, anti-Christian, anti-heretical than I am now. What I have learned from Nobel is that the soul of a *great* Jew can accommodate many things. There is danger only for the little souls.

[11] Talmudic academies.

V

PARALYSIS. FIGHT AGAINST DEATH

1922-1925

A period of suffering commences. Yet affliction is not taken as final doom but as the start of new life. Spirit emerges triumphant.

On February 8, 1922, troubled by his nervous symptoms, F. R. visited his friend Professor Richard Koch. Koch tells:
. . . We had been chatting and were standing together at my front door, when suddenly he broke off the conversation and said, in his abrupt, shy way, that there was something important he wanted to discuss with me as a patient. He added that there was no hurry about it. I knew him well enough to know that a great deal had preceded this question, that what he had to tell was important, and I asked him to come into my office there and then. IIe immediately agreed. It was clear that he had arrived at some momentous decision, and that he was now ready to let events take their course.

In my office he told me, in the frank and charming way which he commanded in serious conversation, that he had lately been noticing strange symptoms in himself. On the advice of a common friend he had already consulted a distinguished specialist, who had diagnosed a disease which, from his medical studies, he knew was no trifling matter. But he would like me to examine him also; perhaps it wasn't so serious after all. He showed no signs of anxiety, as most people would in his situation. Nor did he seem to be curious, but rather exhilarated. Before long I came to understand the nature of his exhilaration.

He told me that in September of the preceding year for the first time his knees had given way during a pleasurable excitement. In November or December he had, on four occasions, felt giddy for no special reason. And during the same period he had twice found himself sitting on the pavement after getting off the street car. On December 28 he had noticed that he was able to go downstairs only very slowly, and this condition had not changed. Quite recently he had been having difficulty pronouncing sibilants. Every excitement affected his legs markedly. He was also unable to swallow normally, and often after eating had to cough up food. When I asked him to describe in greater detail the trouble with his legs, he said he had to lift them more in walking than formerly, and that he was afraid of falling. What he said was that he was "afraid he would come a cropper after the eighth or ninth step." I quote so exactly to show how closely the patient had already observed himself, and because the phrase which this man who weighed words so carefully, used for "falling down" showed a sense of humor that must have been, from what we can imagine of his state of mind, very great indeed. Without bitterness, without a trace of "gallows humor," he transformed a dismal situation tactfully and gracefully into one devoid of pathos. In answer to my questions he told me that there had never been any organic nervous disorders in his family, and he himself had never been seriously ill until the summer 1918. In Warsaw in June 1918[1] he had contracted a slight case of grippe from which he had quickly recovered. But it had left behind a barking cough and a few days later the doctors had diagnosed pneumonia; this had seemed serious for a day or two. He

[1] Actually, July 1918.

said that he himself didn't remember any details since a few days after the grippe he had gone into a coma, which persisted while pneumonia was serious. He had been able to converse while in the coma. On the fourteenth day of his illness he was unable to breathe deeply, and then suddenly he was entirely well. Sometime later he said to me that after the grippe he had slept his way out of a serious illness. A month and a half later he had contracted malaria, but had had only one or at the most two attacks. During the summer of 1919 he had a relapse, with three or four attacks.

After I had examined him I wrote down my findings; in the first line there are two words that must, from the context, be "articular disorder," which, however, are undecipherable in the otherwise clearly written report. The syllables are garbled in a way most unusual for me. This proves to me that I must have been in a state of extraordinary excitement and confusion. Immediately afterwards the writing becomes normal again, so I must have pulled myself together. The diagnosis shows that even at that time the entire motor nervous system, from the cortex of the cerebrum to the muscles, was disturbed, more on the left side than on the right, that both legs were slightly paralyzed, again the left more than the right, but that the arm muscles were normal. The medulla oblongata was already affected, and thus the patient seemed to be doomed. There seemed no likelihood of the case being a lingering one.

The patient took my findings very calmly, and even showed signs once more of the previously mentioned exhilaration. His whole interest seemed centered on the diagnosis.

The diagnosis: Amyotrophic lateral sclerosis with progressive paralysis of the bulba. The end was expected within a year.

On the advice of the doctor, F. R. stayed in bed most of the time from the middle of February to March 20. His Lehrhaus lectures were transferred to large rooms which his landlord offered for the purpose in his own home. Seminar groups met in F. R.'s study. March 14, 1922, to Gertrud Oppenheim:

I do not take my illness lightly. The trouble is central. In addition to the paresis of the legs there is a slight aphasia and trouble in swallowing (but this strictly between you and me! It would be very embarrassing if other people noticed it, until it can no longer be hidden, and perhaps it will pass after all).

How slight it is you may judge from the fact that I can dissemble it by putting increased effort into the mere act of speaking. But you can imagine how unpleasant that is for me. Staying in bed hasn't helped me in the least; my trouble in walking is more pronounced than ever. The thing is simply taking its course, and while one might try any number of things, all one can really do is wait and see. Koch is a wonderful doctor, and I consider myself lucky to have him. Nor do I intend to let the family's nervousness about "consultations" change my feeling in this matter. If I must be ill, I want to enjoy it in peace, and not be distracted by "other gods"—all the more since he himself discusses it with any number of people and is not at all stubborn or opinionated.

Enjoy it? Yes, in a sense, for I am now reading a regular tutti-frutti, such as I have scarcely been able to do since my Leipzig illness of 1918 (which they say is connected with this one).

Now something pleasant: we are at last to have a child. It's in its twelfth week. We noticed it one week after Nobel's death. It helps to make up for everything. All in all the future begins to press uncannily close on me now, as though it no longer had time to wait until I reach it.

Just now I had to negotiate a few steps of the stairs and noticed how much worse my legs have become in the past five weeks.

March 27, 1922, to Gertrud Oppenheim:

I'm afraid grandmotherly optimism is unjustified. But there is nothing to be done, medically, except wait. I don't feel yet that the disease has been halted. The only thing that really upsets me is the aphasia, even though hardly anyone notices it unless I draw attention to it; not even doctors, only very observant people.

Anyway, so long as energy suffices to hide it somewhat, I want to go on giving lectures, even though I no longer take much pleasure in them: the best thing about them, the effortless flow of words, is not possible when one has to concentrate continually on the forming of those wretched consonants. You know how important speaking has become to me since, through the writing of the Star of Redemption, I cut myself off from further literary work; speaking was the only productiveness still open to me. I'm very doubtful that such an impediment can be overcome successfully.

March 27, 1922, to Rudolf Hallo:

I want to tell you something about Nobel, about my relations with him and what I have lost in him. You must have seen that in planning my life I took the long view. I needed seclusion, the novice's subordination. Nobel gave me both, because of the very fact that, as I told you the other day, he did not see me. It was a wonderful support for the kind of life I was then leading. I didn't need to rush anything. Now I must rely on myself to such an extent that, even before my illness, I had given up hope

of ever reaching my goal of being able to teach the Law.
My career will end before I achieve that goal, as simply
one among many goals, and I shan't be able to speak my
piece out loud (which after all would be asking a great
deal).

Diary, March 29, 1922:
After 1800 we ceased to pray for the "return" because we
ceased to *pray*. Had we continued to pray we would have
prayed for the return. Liberalism wrongly assumed that we
had ceased to pray because we would no longer pray for
the return.

April 12, 1922:
The day Zionism produces the Messiah my Star of Redemption will be superfluous. But so will all other books.

Speaking to Richard Koch:
Zionism is perhaps after all one of the nation's roads into
the future. This road, too, should be kept open.

April 10, 1922, to Gertrud Oppenheim:
My condition is unchanged. Walking is sometimes a little
better, but often worse. The speech is at times desperately
bad. As yet little trouble with arms and hands, more in
swallowing. Koch is relatively optimistic. But this is partly
the result of the amazing inadequacy of our diagnostical
methods. A speech defect is determined by means of "tests,"
in which, of course, I come out very well; for one stumbles,
of course, not when one is asked to pronounce a word but
when one happens *not* to be concentrating. But all medical
methods are concentration methods.

I always write to you more gloomily than I actually
feel. You mustn't imagine that things are too bad. In a
sense these two months have been quite pleasant. For

113

one thing, after a long spell, I got back to reading books, something I had really needed. And once I reach the point of resignation—that is, when I can no longer have any hopes concerning my condition—things will be all right. What is very difficult for me to endure right now is the feeling—at least Koch fosters such a feeling—of there being still some slight hope.

Speaking to Richard Koch:
People think I am unhappy. They feel sorry for me. Nobody has a right to feel that. Nobody knows whether I may not be happy. I am the only one who can know this.

May, 1922, to Hans Ehrenberg:
My days are now very short, partly on account of the many visits. Another reason is that I don't like to write too much since my hand is now beginning to refuse service.— You needn't worry about my losing "the will to live." I cheerfully begin all kinds of business for my own and other people's sake, as usual. I shall also outline the winter program [of the Lehrhaus] and do what I can to further the lectureship business,[2] and in fact take devilish delight in it. The chances are, though, that neither project will be realized, for unless there is considerable improvement, I won't be able to lecture this winter. To speak without being able to convey nuances becomes lying, and consequently my lectures, etc. have become a torment to me.

May 27, 1922, to Gertrud Oppenheim:
It's possible to "go along," just as it is possible to go as far as the railway station, that is, up to the moment that the whistle blows and the train disappears. And one doesn't

[2] This refers to the newly instituted division of religious philosophy at the University of Frankfort. *See* letter of January 12, 1923.

want to be accompanied even to the station by just anyone. And while those who are left behind have only the grief of separation, the traveler in the window has, besides, an obscure anticipation of what waits for him. This interposes a feeling of strangeness between him and those who have come to see him off . . . Gritli [Margrit Rosenstock] has probably told you that the deterioration in speech has progressed rapidly in the past fortnight. It can no longer be dissembled.

It's drawing toward evening, and I must stop. I'm reading the large Graetz[3] with eagerness and enthusiasm; it's a magnificent book, and I never knew it.

> From the beginning of June until the beginning of July the Rosenzweigs spent their vacation in Königstein, in the Taunus mountains, where F. R. was brought by car. During these weeks he was busy preparing the second edition of the *Star of Redemption*. To Gertrud Oppenheim:

Our lodgings in Königstein are really excellent. Handsome rooms, verandah, magnificent view, delicious kosher food, and a simply fabulous confectionery.

I read, carry on business, pull strings, and, all in all, enjoy life, and besides I have something looming in the background for the sake of which I am almost tempted to call this period, in spite of everything, the richest of my life—which has not been lacking in such periods. This might strike the bystander as funny, and even during the war I myself had only weak and rare intimations of it, but now it is simply true: dying is even more beautiful than living.

For the second edition of the Star of Redemption, to

---

[3] Heinrich Graetz, *History of the Jews*, the large edition of 11 volumes, as against the abridged 3-volume edition.

come out next year, I hope, I am preparing a guide which will be printed in the margins alongside the paragraphs. It is a strange and difficult undertaking.

The Rosenzweigs were anticipating the birth of a child by fall, an event which F. R. did not expect to live to see. Diary, June 9, 1922:

The child, if a boy, may be called Franz. But if it is a girl, for heaven's sake not Franziska; in that case we will keep to the Hebrew name already agreed on.

I am asking my wife to remember that I fervently wish to have the Star of Redemption translated into Hebrew. I am also asking her not to spare considerable expense if she finds a translator. The title might be "Kokhav mi-Yaakov,"[4] since "Kokhav ha-Geulah"[5] has the wrong ring to it.

June 18, 1922:

I ought to be writing my "Parerga und Paralipomena." But it bores me to death. And yet it's a shame. For in the Star these things are not phrased so that everyone gets them. Perhaps I ought to write them as aphorisms. So that I should always have to make only the main point.

F. R. returned from Königstein to his attic apartment in Frankfurt, which he was not to leave again. August 29, 1922, to Gertrud Oppenheim, on Buber's lectures at the Lehrhaus:

Buber? Yes, he might have marked an important epoch in my life; the day after Nobel's death I wrote him to this effect. Now it has turned out not to be an epoch, since epochs imply long perspectives; an epoch can only be

---

[4] "A Star Out of Jacob," referring to Numbers 24:17.
[5] Literal translation into Hebrew of Star of Redemption.

such when we feel that it is still the penultimate one. Death no longer marks an epoch. Just think how different was Goethe's feeling for Ulrike von Levetzow than for any earlier love. Or Heine's for the Mouche.—But it's marvelous for me, and a great blessing. He is approaching the peak of his life; this fall the first volume of his projected five-volume system,[6] based on the lectures you know, will come out.

By August 1922 writing had become increasingly difficult, speech even less articulate. At times F. R.'s food went down the wrong way, resulting in severe choking. Doctors considered this a sign of incipient paralysis of the diaphragm. It became necessary to choose a successor for the administration of the Lehrhaus. End of August, to his mother:

At last I am able to tell you what has exercised me since August 5; last night it came to a head. I am very happy: the Lehrhaus, whose dissolution, or more likely and worse, normalization (according to Buber, in a confidential remark to some Zionists, it is the only distinguished cultural institution today among all of Western Jewry) I had considered inevitable, is to be continued: Rudi [Rudolf] Hallo is to "substitute" for me. Thus its main direction (non-specialist, non-rabbinical, non-polemical, non-apologetic, universalist in content and spirit) has been assured. It's not going to be a committee affair but will retain its personal features. Moreover, as long as I'm still here, I can speak and act through this prophet.

Toward the end of 1922 F. R. wrote a letter, extending over forty pages, to Rudolf Hallo, to acquaint him with

---

[6] *Ich und Du* ("I and Thou") based on the lectures in 1922 on "Religion as Actuality."

the origins of the Lehrhaus, its work, its lectures, and its students.

To work with this crêpe de Chine audience is terribly unrewarding and yet necessary, in fact the most necessary of all. For those who are still Jewish, or once again Jewish, the Lehrhaus is only qualifiedly necessary, that is, as introduction and stimulation. There is even a real and typical danger of restricting their Jewish activities and studies to attendance at the Lehrhaus, since their work there readily bears fruit. It is one of the tasks of the director to help those who have really gone through the Lehrhaus to get out of it again and to stand on their own Jewish legs in doing and learning. . . .

In [Eduard] Strauss's Bible class there are several such people who have stayed there too long and can't shake themselves free. Yet these are the very ones whom it is easy to induct; with the others it is an ungrateful task and must be done by crude and showy methods, with famous names, sensational themes, elegant programs, high prices, and rough treatment. In terms of numbers success will always be slight, but those few are sufficient reward. It is the mystery of Judaism that the talisman can only be passed on through inheritance, but that whole generations may be overleaped in the process. Overleaped, that is, so far as conscious possession of the talisman goes, not in the sense of the instinctive, racial transmission of the talisman. This has already been shown by Judah ha-Levi in his *Kuzari,* where Abraham is presented as the scion of Adam, Seth, Noah, and Shem, but the son of Terah.

I was glad that [S. Y.] Agnon could be prevailed on to read some of his own things from a collection of stories, like "The Legend of the Scribe," and discuss them afterwards in Hebrew. . . . It became clear at the lecture that no one could speak Hebrew though everyone pretended to be able to. Consequently, no one spoke, for fear of saying something that couldn't be found in [Moses] Rath's Hebrew text.

I could see clearly that my work, although it had led to the threshold of success, would be objectively fruitless (not in individual cases but as an institution). A local institution such as this is in a different position from a periodical, which can have a historical effect in a very short time precisely because it isn't confined to one locale. An institution like the Lehrhaus, whose immediate effect is confined to one place, needs permanence for the immediate effect to be translated into a broad, normative one. And this goal had barely begun to be reached. So I relegated the Lehrhaus to the limbo of those personal things that are over and done with.

This is how matters stood when, early in August, I received your letter and in the course of replying to it had the sudden inspiration which, against all probability and contrary to my own expectation, has—as I know for certain now, after your being here only a few weeks—saved the Lehrhaus.

> On September 8, 1922, Edith Rosenzweig gave birth to a son who was named Rafael. His circumcision was celebrated at home. Joseph Prager says:
> F. R. took part in the celebration, silent and immobile but with veritable *simhat mitzvah* [joy in fulfilling a commandment], although he could hardly move at all or speak intelligibly. He had asked me to carry out the *mitzvah;* and when the ceremony was over he asked me to stay on a while. Again we talked for many hours, late into the night; he spoke with difficulty, in a voice that only a trained ear could understand, of suffering, death, and living on in the coming generation.

> Diary, September 13, 1922:

I wish my library to be given to my son. Until he's old enough to read, it can be packed in crates, but afterwards, if there is any space for it at all, it should be put on shelves. It is a library that will mean something even to an intelligent businessman, lawyer, or doctor; it is certainly not meant merely for a scholar. It may be borrowed from freely, but only if proper receipts are given. From these books, which were never bought en masse but always as needed, my son will learn a great deal about me that he could learn in no other way.

September 20, 1922, to Martin Buber:
My wife got up for the first time today. The boy is a fine child, a human being in miniature, not quite four and a half pounds, but a "complete child with hair and nails" and with a real face, a face that I like to think foreshadows, for my benefit, many future faces. By the way, he has been named Rafael Nehemiah, after Nobel, his third name being Georg after my late father, whom, during the first hour or perhaps the first day, he not only resembled but looked as much like as one face can possibly look like another.— When are you going to take a look at him—and the parents?

October 6, 1922, to Gertrud Oppenheim:
Rafael is getting handsome now and has begun looking around at the world, though up to now he treats it all under the heading "not-breast" and disapproves of it, or occasionally, because of its evident uselessness, wonders at it. Yet another example of the "fruitfulness of infinite judgment," to quote Cohen.

October 2, 1922, the Day of Atonement. October 6, to Joseph Prager:
On Yom Kippur Ernst Simon gave me great pleasure by assembling a *minyan*[7] for *kol nidre*, *minhah* [afternoon prayer], and *neilah* [concluding service]. It was marvelous.

[7] A quorum of ten men for worship.

We had prepared the blue room with a great display of tablecloths and other cloths and fifteen candles, and partitioned off a women's *shul* at the west window by stretching a curtain across. Erich Fromm, Fritz Goitein, and someone whom you don't know[8] read the prayers—all of them fine fellows of my acquaintance; the older men were Eugen Mayer and [Richard] Tuteur. The Torah also was read; the white and gold cloth was spread over the cleared cabinet near the window. The ceiling light had gone on the blink Friday afternoon and fortunately could not be repaired in time. By another lucky accident Goitein finished with *neilah* a good five minutes too soon, so that there was a long silence before *shemot*.[9] Perhaps they'll do it here quite often from now on.—For *maariv* [evening prayer] all of them went into the living room, while the blue room was being made ready for the breaking of the fast.

Somewhat later to Joseph Prager:

Last Sabbath we had another *minyan* here, and it will be continued from now on as long as I can participate. Again it was splendid. Afterwards we had breakfast with a *derashah* [exposition]—each taking his turn—to the *sidrah* [weekly portion of the Torah]. Here, too, my long cherished wishes have been fulfilled.

This private worship on the Sabbath and festivals was held in F. R.'s study up to a week before his death.

November 30, 1922, to Hans Ehrenberg:

I am bothered by your excess of pity rather than by the technical difficulties of carrying on a conversation. I always feel like calling out, "You are a parson, after all." Parsons

[8] The editor of this volume.
[9] Concluding solemn recitations.

and doctors shouldn't take a sentimental view of death; they are the *companions* of the dying man, not mere bystanders. Sentimentality is proper for the bystanders. The dying themselves are not sentimental. And the bystanders are the less so the less they are mere bystanders. I don't consider myself at all a "poor invalid"; I wouldn't change places with anyone. Not with you—which doesn't mean very much, since nobody readily exchanges his identity—but not either with my own self of a year ago. And there are few periods of my life which I would be sorrier to lose than the past ten months. (I have just noticed that it is exactly that today.)

During 1922 F. R. worked on *Sixty Hymns and Poems of Judah ha-Levi, in German,* a volume of representative selections from creations of the medieval Hebrew poet, faithfully rendered in meter. The book, published in 1924, included an epilogue, written in 1923, on the art of translating, and notes to each poem. F. R. first attempted to translate Judah ha-Levi in 1921. The actual incentive to this work was a volume of translation of Judah ha-Levi by Emil B. Cohn (published in 1921), "which annoyed me so much that verse came out of it." December 23, 1922, to Martin Buber:

The notes [to *Judah ha-Levi*], which I look forward to so much more, I haven't been able to begin yet, as my wife has not had time. The interim, however, has enabled me to add two magnificent poems, and there is no getting away from it: one's time is better spent in translating ten lines than writing the longest disquisition "about." But the public wants the "about," and spurns the most delicious meal (or worse, gulps it down carelessly) if no menu is held in front of its nose.

After the publication of the book, to Margarete Susman: With each new poem the technical problem has been so overwhelming during the actual work that it has entirely robbed me of perspective, and I need others to tell me that something has finally been achieved. In the critical moment this "other" was Buber. Without him the book would never have got itself written. I had translated "Yah shimkha" ["O God, Thy Name!"], after hearing it in 1921 during a memorial service for the synagogue composer Lewandowski, [Hermann] Cohen's father-in-law. I was immediately transported by the text. My wife, who knew it from Berlin where it is used in services, told me the author. I tried my hand at it then but without success. During the first autumn of my illness I succeeded. At first the only text I had at my disposal was the Berlin Prayer Book, where precisely the stanza from which you quote is omitted because it has angels in it, and of course they don't exist! So I translated it and at once had the experience that apparently goes with these translations: the three important women in my life, who happened to be gathered around the new product, unanimously found it terrible and made fun of me. The same thing happened that has been happening ever since: I *almost* believed them, but just for the sake of having an outsider's opinion I sent it to Buber, who saved the poem and the book that grew out of it. Since then I have compiled quite a collection, printed, written, and oral, of repetitions (more or less outspoken) of this first three-voiced "terrible." I've found out that practically everybody still stops short at [Heine's] *Buch der Lieder,* and only those who write themselves, and not even all those, at the late Goethe and Hölderlin—which corresponds to your "after Stefan George"; a ghastly discovery for a man who on principle objects to writing for writers only. Yet I have witnessed a few conversions, my wife through long training, my mother through Buber's reading aloud.

At the end of December 1922 F. R. lost his ability to write entirely, following a gradual decline during the previous months. He maintained the ability to speak, however indistinctly, to his wife and those closest to him until the spring of 1923. Up to that time he dictated to his wife, who wrote down his letters and his other compositions.

January 5, 1923, to Gertrud Oppenheim:

I have a guilty conscience about my long silence, but I must husband my time very carefully. You can scarcely imagine how it is now that I can hardly write myself any more, and only a few specialists can understand me by putting all their effort to it. The redaction for print of the "Friday Evening Service"[10] and the Judah ha-Levi book was a task that makes the composition of the Star of Redemption at the front, during the retreat and in the hospital, a mere trifle by comparison. It costs me more effort to turn a page than cutting the pages of a whole book does a healthy man. Under the circumstances I dare not invite you. We would be able to speak only through the mediation of Edith or possibly Gritli [Margrit Rosenstock]. Edith is terribly overworked, through an accumulation of tasks (the baby, the household, dictating, and especially interpreting) not to mention the frequent interruptions of her nightly sleep on my account.

January 6, 1923, to Joseph Prager:

The Lehrhaus has reached its maximum enrollment to date, with eleven hundred registrants (this time last year there were seven hundred). Hallo is doing very well in this.

January 1923, to Rudolf Hallo:

Do you really believe that you view the Lehrhaus more skeptically than I do? . . . But—and this simply proves that I am older—my skepticism doesn't blind me to what is already there and what may yet come. You must be patient about seeing its influence become manifest; a number of

10 Translated toward the end of 1921.

experiences have taught me not to despair too soon.

You have done an excellent job as director. I honestly believe it, no matter what you say, precisely because of your skepticism and critical attitude. I couldn't think of a better one. Or, more accurately, I can't think of another one. I can easily imagine that you may want, now or after my death, to make sweeping changes. I can tell you right now that I agree to them, unseen, so long as *you* are the one to make them. Yet I would turn in my grave if anyone else were to direct it "strictly in the spirit of Franz Rosenzweig."

The University of Frankfort instituted in its Department of Philosophy a nonsectarian division of theology and religious philosophy. In spring 1922, F. R. was called to represent Judaism. January 12, 1923, to Martin Buber:

I could not talk to you about the matter I now take up in this letter because it requires a rather epic scope. It is of some importance, and you inadvertently gave me quite a number of suggestions in the course of conversation. So listen quietly, and remember that I am aware of the objections and nevertheless consider it necessary to propose the matter to you. I have thought it over for weeks.

I shall begin *ab ovo*. When the University of Frankfort was founded, various persons suggested that a "Jewish Theological Faculty" might be established here. At the time the idea fell through because (the Christian sponsors naturally did not suspect this reason) the Jewish founders of the university sabotaged it, fearing as usual to do anything "too Jewish." The idea was not entirely suppressed, but it did not get going again until intervention came from another quarter: early in '21 the Bishop of Limburg provided funds for a lectureship in "Catholic Ethics." Then the Protestants and the Jews decided likewise to promote such lectureships. Since we have no bishops, the right to propose candidates for the Jewish lectureship devolved upon the Jewish community here. The government asks the Philosophical Faculty—to which the lectureships are loosely affiliated . . . for a report and then makes its appointments. The first candidate the community proposed was [Rabbi N. A.] Nobel, to whom it was a matter of tremendous import because he still believed in the university. At bottom he probably thought he could have accomplished more in a Goethe professorship than as a rabbi, which was of course a very serious error. . . . Nobel died before the official appointment came from Berlin. In March came my nomination as successor; I was already ill at the time, but they did not know how grave my illness was. What I ultimately hoped for from it was the chance, if I was able to lecture for one semester, during the summer, of setting the issue in the right direction and on the right level. At the very least I thought I would be in a position to influence the choice of my successor. You know I am entirely free of silly academicism; when [Professor Friedrich] Meinecke wanted me to accept a university position I wrote to him refusing on principle.[11] And when the Frankfort Jewish community hinted that I should embark on a regular university career in connection with that special lectureship, so as to have a different status with the university and the government, I declined scornfully; I told them if they did not care to have me as I was, I did not care to have the post.

The reason I wanted the post was precisely that this was a new establishment whose character had yet to be fixed and that I considered the university framework to be exceedingly elastic. The title of the lectureship, "Jewish Religious Philosophy and Ethics," did not alarm me in the least; I could just as well lecture against that title.

[11] *See* letter of August 30, 1920.

But this time, too, the Prussians held their fire. The appointment did not come until December. I then accepted, especially since the matter would not come to a head before the summer semester, so that it was essentially a question of "representation." By doing it this way my influence is naturally stronger than if I had formally declined on account of my illness.

I should now like you to consider whether you can take over this task. The whole matter is still in the stage where anything can come of it. The danger, of course, is that some rabbi will take over now and that the "faculty" which will undoubtedly emerge from it (there is already talk of *three* lecturers) will become just one more institution, among numerous others, for the training of rabbis. That is just what I should like to prevent, and it *can* be prevented. Nowhere are traditions created so rapidly as at a university, because there the life span of a generation is two years at most, and consequently the students who come the third year assume that what exists has been "forever in place here." First come, first served; the other lectureships will not be filled without consultation with the holder of the first, and above all they won't be filled in such a manner that the second and third lecturer will appear ludicrous when contrasted with the first. In other words, at issue here is a small latch that can open a wide portal. I am aware that the portal bears the inscription: Theological Faculty; but behind this it is possible there will be that Theological Universality for which we are all working, both for the sake of theology, which must be detheologized, and for the sake of the university, which must be universalized.

How do I think you fit in? It starts in May at the earliest, but probably, considering all delays, not until November. You will be sacrificing your Mondays to the affair; in the forenoon you'll have a two-hour and a one-hour seminar, the first on some "non-Jewish" subject (gnostics, primitives, or whatever interests you at the moment and on which you want to stimulate studies), the second on a Jewish subject, in which you have free choice all the way from the Apocrypha to hasidism; ultimately the two seminars may even run parallel to each other in subject matter. You will save the biblical subjects for the evening from six to eight-thirty, in the Lehrhaus. So you see you will have nothing but seminars. If perhaps you should again feel the urge to lecture, there will always be time for that. If you go to Eretz Israel, a whole or a half semester will simply be skipped. It is not necessary for you yourself to be the whole future faculty; but your presence and your indubitably *apikoros* [freethinking] personality will give that faculty its character and direction during the process of formation. This can be done only by someone who is wholly free of any deference for the existing university, and who, at the same time, brings to the job the kind of personal reputation which will forbid the university's interfering with him.

As I dictate this it seems more and more plausible to me. As soon as I receive word that you are in general agreement, I'll set the troops marching.

What I wanted to say to you yesterday and could not: those were lovely days.

February 4, 1923, to Rudolf Hallo:
What you say about my relation to European culture I simply fail to understand. When have I ever acted, as you seem to imply, as if I considered it mere air or a fraud? You speak as though you had never read the Star of Redemption. Just remember the introduction to the third part, the Goetheology. Or when have I ever lived as though I believed that? I have allowed myself to combat quite a number of people and tendencies; I think I have conducted

that fight in a very gentlemanly manner; even when I started writing my Hegel book I considered Hegel's philosophy dangerous. My view, which after all is shared by many others, is that European culture today is on the point of collapse and can only be saved if supra-European, suprahuman powers come to its aid. I have no illusion about these powers, among which Judaism is one: they will in turn become secularized and Europeanized, especially if they succeed; indeed, I am aware that the very first gesture of help is also the first gesture toward the new secularization. The ability to secularize themselves again and again proves the eternity of these powers.

I may possibly be wrong here, but many things are possible. He who lives on possibilities is a coward; there's always one you can run to for shelter. A decent person lives not on the ninety-seven and a half possibilities that exist but on the one reality that he has experienced. Since he has experienced it, some provision will have been made for his being sustained by it, and his life will not be fruitless. The "great moment" carries with it an obligation, not of new great moments—that would be frivolous—but that the succeeding small moments shall not gainsay the great ones but substantiate them in their own way, that is, in little. If it were otherwise, man would be taken away from here after his great moment. If this doesn't happen, if he lives on, it is sufficient proof that he is meant to preserve the memory of the great moment through the little ones, and prove the great by the little. There is no other kind of proof, but we need no other.

In the spring of 1923 F. R. dictated an article, "Sermonic Judaism."[12] Next, F. R. wrote the article "Apologetic Think-

[12] See p. 247.

ing," in which he expounded Jewish being as a correspondence between innermost "essences" and external practices and forms. Apologetic thinking, being concerned with "essences," cannot perceive the whole of Jewish being.

In May 1923, Rabbi Leo Baeck, of Berlin, went ahead with the plan which Rabbi Nehemiah Nobel had conceived in the period just before his death, that of conferring on F. R. the rabbinical title *morenu* [our teacher]. May 8, 1923, to Leo Baeck:

I was really moved by your suggestion. But at the same time somewhat disturbed. Nobel meant it quite matter-of-factly; he discussed it with me many times. It was his idea that after a year of study under him I would be ready. He was obviously wrong about the one year. I told him right off that he had no idea how difficult my unlegalistic head would find the *halakhah* [law]. At the time of his death I was still a long way from being able to master independently a *halakhic* piece of the Gemara [Talmud]. Since then —I fell ill shortly afterwards—I have learned little on my own, and what I did learn were, mostly, *aggadic* [non-legal] sections. So I was naturally disturbed by the idea of this unmerited honor. The thought of being treated as *morenu* in the *minyan* [prayer group] that comes to me every Sabbath morning, most of whose members far surpass me in knowledge of Jewish matters, makes me smile. And the fellows to whom I am nothing but a former co-pupil of Nobel's would smile even more. Most of them have no idea that I shall one day really be their teacher and their descendants'.

But then other arguments presented themselves. Of course it is undeserved, but I would certainly have deserved it "had I but time"—therefore "let four captains bear Hamlet to the stage." And I can, after all, keep my *minyan* from taking notice of it. Then, above all, there is my little boy, who will one day be called up to the Torah under this patronymic and there learn that his father, to whom it was not given to be his teacher, may yet, through "ours," be his teacher. If after this explanation the circumstances still seem to warrant it, I would ask you to carry out your proposal. I will receive the gift in deep gratitude.

The title of *morenu* remained a closely guarded secret. It was made public only after F. R's death.

At the end of the summer trimester 1923, Rudolf Hallo resigned as administrator of the Lehrhaus. From the fall of 1923 the Lehrhaus was headed by a group of four men: Martin Buber, Richard Koch, and Eduard Strauss, in addition to F. R. himself. A young lawyer, Rudolf Stahl, became executive secretary. December 1923, to Rudolf Stahl:

Now to the problem of the big lectures. They are the necessary beginning. The eyes and mouth agape which the unsympathetic call "sensation," may also be called *thaumazein* [wondering]; then the thing takes on an entirely different aspect. Of course it must not be the ultimate aim; the way must be opened to questioning and study. It's also natural that those who have just learned to question look with contempt on the mere gapers, just as those who have newly embarked on study do on the enthusiastic questioners. Yet none of the three functions should ever cease entirely. Even he who is deeply engrossed in study must not forget how to question and wonder. The relative measure of these three functions can be argued, but not their necessity.

In the early summer months of 1923, F. R. wrote *The Builders*, an epistle addressed to Martin Buber and dealing with the place of the Law, its study and practice, within Judaism.[13]

---

[13] *See* pp. 234-242 and p. 292.

The progressing paralysis stopped short of the organs most essential for the maintenance of bare life. Thus, complete breakdown and death did not occur. Richard Koch recollects:

While he was still able to speak he asked me once in a letter not to mention again the possibility that he might continue to live for a long time in spite of everything. When I saw him and said to him that he might be wrong and that he should be prepared for such an eventuality, he asked me, with a look of pain I'll never forget, whether I would really wish this upon him. Once he had realized the seriousness of his illness he had expected a rapid, and almost solemn, death.

September 14, 1923, to his mother:
I think it is simply the elementary desire to live and an infinite ability to enjoy that keep me from the thought of suicide, which for most people in my situation would be the normal way out. I do know one thing: I would be willing to shoulder the *sin*, but life remains for me, let's say, the second-highest good. Only the tranquillity with which I regard its end makes me realize that it is not the highest good for me. Yet a year and a half ago, when my condition was still quite tolerable, I felt the same tranquillity.

In the fall of 1923 F. R. wrote an extensive introduction to the *Jüdische Schriften* ("Collected Jewish Writings") of Hermann Cohen. In this introduction he traced the philosophical, and the Jewish, development which led the founder of the Marburg philosophical school to become, in his old age, an interpreter of the Jewish heritage. September 16, 1923, to Martin Buber:
The introduction to Cohen's book gives me tremendous difficulty. I hardly write a single sentence without a guilty conscience. For not only his disciples, but Cohen himself,

would be unable to accept so much as a single sentence. Besides, I don't even manage to understand him. This isn't so serious, for I see that even [Professor Paul] Natorp, in his rather impressive commemorative speech, confesses that he doesn't understand him. But is it proper for the biographer to depart so widely from the autobiography of his hero? I am reminded of a statement Cohen once made about me, I think to my mother: "He has an amazing way of patting and slapping a person in the same phrase." This proves that even then I behaved exactly the same way toward him, so now his shade needn't take offense. But I myself feel scruples about turning him over this way in his grave.

March 28, 1924, to Isaac Breuer:

When I finished the Star of Redemption I thought I would then have decades of learning and living, teaching and learning, before me, and that perhaps toward the end, when I had reached a hoary old age, another book might come out of it, and this would have been a book on the Law.

June 17, 1924, to Martin Buber, on F. R.'s epilogue to the Judah ha-Levi book:

The strange thing, which I knew from the beginning, is that only the epilogue prevents the reader from rejecting the book out of hand. Now practically everyone feels guilty for not having liked the poems. Everybody reads it for the sake of its cheek. Almost every week I hear someone comment on my essay "Sermonic Judaism" but I never hear anything about "Apologetic Thinking," which was, after all, much more substantial, but restrained in tone. The epilogue is the mad delight not only of the fools but of the tolerable readers, too.

August 18, 1924, to Margrit Rosenstock:

Years ago Eugen [Rosenstock] wrote me from Florence
. . . that it takes two to bring up a child, a man and a
woman. This is Rafael's handicap: I can only be a jumping
jack to him, though a marvelous one.

August 22, 1924, to Margarete Susman:

I must thank you for the two letters, which made me very
happy. The Rosenstocks had already told me that you were
planning to write about my Judah ha-Levi book for the
Frankfurter Zeitung. Naturally, I am pleased; the book is
meant, after all, for people who know no Hebrew—which
includes, as I can tell from my own experience, most of
those who "know Hebrew." I myself understand a poem
only after I have translated it; a compromising confession,
but since you have already written your piece, I can safely
make it. Yet parts of them are almost simple, linguistically;
in ten or twelve hours of lessons I would undertake to bring
you far enough along so that you could, if not read "O God,
Thy Name!" at least understand it. Boasting is easy, of
course, but I would undertake it, if you like, even by letter
—an undertaking in the style of the eighteenth century,
which would be fun.

August 25, 1924, to Eugen Rosenstock:

I really didn't expect that The Builders would interest
you. I enclosed it on the spur of the moment. It doesn't constitute a theory of the Law, which I have already given in
the Star of Redemption. I don't call into question again this
universal Jewish—not universally human—imperative. The
problem of The Builders is a much narrower one; it's the
problem of a generation, or possibly of a century: how
"Christian" Jews, national Jews, religious Jews, Jews from
self-defense, sentimentality, loyalty, in short, "hyphenated"

Jews such as the nineteenth century has produced, can once again, without danger to themselves or Judaism, become *Jews*. Thus what is really under discussion here is the ability, while the imperative—metaphysical as well as biographical—is tacitly assumed. . . . It is really addressed only to the "hyphenated" Jews who want to return.

What I have tried to give in The Builders is a hygiene of return. What it warns against is the somersault into the Law, which is tempting because of the biographical crisis preceding it. Despite the existence of the great crisis, the individual should nevertheless wait for smaller events to actualize, through their biographical energy, the new "I can." In this way, the person who returns maintains throughout the process of return his accustomed—un-Jewish—mode of life, and is able to stay alive.

It wasn't that my plan was unnecessary, but that, insofar as I can fathom the good Lord's intentions, I was unnecessary for my plan. This is something quite different.

Back to the plan. Though it is being nipped in the bud, it is nevertheless, in its rudimentary state, the only thing of mine that has had any effect. In all these years no one has taken notice of anything else that has come from me. What *you* see has remained entirely invisible to all Jews, whether or not they have read the Star. For . . . [here five names follow], let alone all the others, I am simply the man who has started observing the Law once more.

Now to the nations. You evidently have no idea *how* different all things Jewish are. Renascences, doctrine, study, Law—everything has a different positional value, even though the number is the same. This goes also for economy, although here the relationship between the Jews and the nations is quite direct, and doubtless revolutionary. The Sabbath *is* a world revolution.

On the Star of Redemption, to Ernst Simon, September 18, 1924:

Once one has written something, one can no longer tell it—at least that's the way it is with me; and whenever, all the same, I've tried to do that I have been punished by having no one listen to me. . . . I am regarded as the "Jewish fanatic," and yet I have written the first unfanatical Jewish book that I know of (that is to say, Jewish and yet unfanatical, unfanatical and yet Jewish). This, if anything, is what will remain of me. I don't take it personally, but consider it part of my destiny.

October 19, 1924, to Victor Ehrenberg:

What you have said about classical antiquity and Germanism seems to me a correct formulation of your problem. But herein lies, also, what drives you toward Judaism. For it is an open secret that the assimilation of classical antiquity in the three stages of national renascence—the Italian of the fifteenth and sixteenth centuries, the Franco-Dutch of the sixteenth and seventeenth, the German of the eighteenth and nineteenth—has played itself out. Why? Because the ship Nationality hasn't sufficient draught to navigate the ocean of world history. It can only acquire this by placing the cargo of Christianity in its hold. Anti-Christianity might also serve, as he who opened the way to the modern epoch has shown. But indifference won't, for it leads of necessity to classicism. So all that remains to us as ballast, if we don't want to become Christian, is our Judaism. Compared with the Christian ballast ours is a little heavy, but the ship doesn't sink; it moves, as I have experienced.

November 5, 1924, to Professor Jonas Cohn:

Your letter has made me very happy. I've never been able to understand why gratitude is considered a virtue; to me it has always seemed a form, and a particularly important one, of Epicurism. I have always remembered—the more vividly the further my road has diverged from yours—with what kindly patience you guided my first steps in the land of philosophy. It was in the winter of 1906-7. You were giving a seminar in the *Critique of Pure Reason;* at first I didn't understand a single word and sat agape while the wizards of the seminar discussed with you. How long ago was this? For me probably even longer than for you.

The "most general religiosity" of which you write I would also call the purest, only I cannot separate it from the historical rock—*I* cannot, the Moment might. You can do it, so I have the courage to ask you to practice this art of separating the most general from the most particular on my Judah ha-Levi, which I am sending you under separate cover.

November 7, 1924, to Max Dienemann, author of *Judentum und Christentum* ("Judaism and Christianity"):

Unmitigated contrast always distorts the truth. Concepts are numbers whose value is determined by their relative positions. It is this positional value which we invariably neglect. We always ask "what?" instead of "what, where?" Only by the addition of *where* does *what* register its correct value. . . . The historical aspect must not be slighted in forming concepts but must be assimilated to the concepts; only when we have pushed the conceptual process to that point will the concept not become bankrupt in front of reality. What's the use of the sharpest antithesis—such as the one between asceticism and non-asceticism—if reality consists on the one hand of dietary laws and on the other of stag hunting. The same is true of such "correct" antitheses as optimism–pessimism, activism–passivism, classicism–romanticism and the like. They become really correct only when we qualify them by stating the nexus in which they are to be used. The mere fact that they are formulable and have been formulated means nothing. Cognition may at times mirror existence, but at other times it hides it, complements it, exaggerates it. Scholarly inquiry aims at existence, and at cognition only insofar as it is related to existence. When our inquiry fastens on the weather vanes of cognition, it may catch a glimpse of the spires, but only of the church's exterior, not of the nave, let alone of the real worshipper who prays inside on his bodily knees.

In October and November of 1924 tho Lohrhaus hold meetings for members of youth organizations. The relevance of Jewish law for the modern Jew, as F. R. treated it in The Builders, was made the subject of extensive discussions. At the end of November, F. R., after reading the reports of the talks, entered the debate with a letter.[14]

The year 1924 was a period of adjustment to life under the conditions created by the paralysis. F. R. himself prescribed in detail the methods for nursing him, for his communicating with those around him, and for his continuing to study and write. He disliked the intervention of doctors, since this was apt to disrupt his day. A doctor was called only in emergencies. From the middle of 1923 a nurse was engaged to assist Mrs. Rosenzweig. Beginning in August 1923, two nurses were brought in, one for the day, one for the night. Several nurses broke down under the strain of the difficult service. The period of trial and adjustment of a new nurse meant discomfort, pain, and loss of precious time. From Dr. Richard Tuteur's notes on F. R.'s daily life:

The patient was taken out of bed at eight o'clock, washed daily down to the hips, the lower part of the body twice or three times a week.

[14] *See* pp. 242-247

At first F. R. was able to walk each morning from his bedroom to the living room, and his chair was pushed after him. But later on he had the strength only to walk three or four yards in his bedroom. In order to have the patient do this, he had to be lifted by the armpits and have first one shoulder raised then the other, thus being swung forward along his vertical axis. It was a great strain, both on him and on the personnel, but he persisted so as to keep up his bodily strength.

Getting him out of bed and dressing him took between two and two and a half hours. This length of time, on account of the many interruptions. The stretching of the legs brought on cramps, which in turn made the legs slip forward, causing him pain; and so the legs had to be bent for him repeatedly.

Eating took up a good deal of time also, breakfast about an hour. From eleven or half past eleven until 1 P.M. F. R. worked; then he had his lunch and nap; from half past four until 8 P.M. he wrote again. Then he had dinner; and afterwards, sitting at his desk, he read until midnight or longer. The nurses were summoned to turn the pages by a clearing of the throat or turning of the head. F. R. was nearsighted and had worn glasses since his eleventh year. In the early stages of the illness he was still able to read in bed and turn the pages himself; later, when it became too hard for him to turn the pages, and before the night nurses had been engaged, he would ask to be given very difficult reading matter, which he could only master very slowly, such as the Talmud, out of consideration for his entourage.

Unless he happened to sleep soundly, he was tormented at night by having to remain long in the same position, and he had to be turned over five or six times a night. He rarely slept either sound enough or long enough. What constitutes relaxation or enjoyment for a well man was for him nearly always accompanied by strain.

Despite the large amount of time that had to be spent

on dressing, undressing, and eating, several hours a day remained for work. When in December 1922 he lost the use of his hand, the patient had to begin dictating to his wife, which he found very hard. But this oral dictation soon came to a stop because of the increasing paralysis of the organ of speech. In the spring of 1923 a typewriter was bought to facilitate communication, a special model manufactured by the General Electric Company; the construction of this machine was such that the person working it had only to move a simple lever over a disk containing all the characters, until the point indicated the desired character, and at the same time one pressed a single key to make the imprint. At first F. R. was able to operate the machine by himself, but later on he had to point out the characters with his left hand. Arm and hand were supported in a sling hanging from a bar next to the sick man. The key was operated by someone else, usually Mrs. Rosenzweig. Eventually his ability to indicate the characters lessened, so that they had to be ascertained by guesswork. Again, Mrs. Rosenzweig was the only person who could do this, for friends who tried to relieve her in the summer of 1923, and who only three months earlier had been able to do so, failed.

In order to facilitate this work it was necessary to use a second disk and lever, attached by means of a connecting rod to the lever manipulated by the patient; the helper then read from the second disk what the patient had indicated on the first. Through years of close association Mrs. Rosenzweig had acquired an instinctive understanding which seemed miraculous to outsiders. Mrs. Rosenzweig also managed every conversation with visitors, by guessing often recurring words after the first or second letter. The patient's extraordinary memory enabled him to dictate and have typed in this fashion, during three or four hours work, the final draft of what he had worked out, down to the smallest detail, during a sleepless night. This method was followed up to the time of his death.

Just as a fairly simple mechanical device proved most successful here in the long run, so it turned out, after trial and error, that the best device for supporting the nerveless head, which tended to roll from side to side, was a massive iron frame of the sort that was used in the early days of photography to hold the subject motionless for a long enough time. This frame stood behind the patient's chair; his neck rested on a cushioned arc, open in front and on top; the front and sides off the neck were fastened with an oblong white-covered cushion to prevent his falling too far forward or sideways. The head was apt to nod. A band around the forehead, supporting the head, was felt by the patient to be painful, and hence was rarely used. The nurse had to tilt the head back against the support again and again, by quickly grasping the patient's forehead; partly through instinctive and partly through conscious movements, the head frequently fell away from the support.

F. R. took an active part in the creation of this supporting apparatus, as well as in the preparation of the typewriter. He was never simply a passive object of medical treatment and feminine nursing, but always the master of the house, whose wish, after the question had been discussed from every side, finally prevailed.

F. R. was the dominant, active center of all domestic affairs—at least to the extent that a man is concerned with such things—as well as of all social contacts. In this regard, too, he planned and organized everything in advance. Visitors were asked to arrive punctually at a specified time. For parties and festivities everything was prepared down to the smallest detail. When the guests arrived the patient was already sitting in his chair; he liked to drink coffee beforehand to make himself alert for conversation. His wife and child ate with the visitors, he by himself later. All conversation was managed through Mrs. Rosenzweig. She was able to answer many questions for him; agreement could be read in his features, or if he disagreed, the typewriter was quickly brought into service so that the conversation never halted but kept moving. On festal days children were invited to amuse themselves as they liked in the attic apartment, with the only son, who, since he had never known his father except as an invalid, looked upon his illness as the most natural thing.

During hours of solitary relaxation a phonograph was found helpful (after March 1924 there was a radio, and the patient could also listen in on the telephone). By writing reviews for a daily paper he acquired a number of very good records. Thus, during breakfast, he would be found listening cheerfully to Fritz Kreisler playing Mendelssohn's violin concerto. He didn't allow his illness to darken his life: just as he never, despite his muteness and extreme difficulty of communication, would renounce such apparently superflous interjections as "For heaven's sake!"—with a little experience one could anticipate them from the mildly shocked expression of his face and mouth— in the same way he insisted on maintaining by every possible means a manner of life consistent with his great gifts and numerous human relationships.

January 6, 1925, to his mother:

The words *pain* and *suffering* which you use seem quite odd to me. A condition into which one has slithered gradually, and consequently got used to, is not suffering but simply a—condition. A condition that leaves room for joy and suffering like any other. A Homeric god might see human life only in terms of pain and suffering. This notion is as false as yours. For instance, I suffer at night if my ear itches and I can't scratch it; but I have only to wait a while and it passes of itself. On such occasions I sometimes become conscious of the abnormality of my condition, which for days at a time I forget. During sleepless nights I often review my life; then the last few years are set off from the rest only as one epoch is set off from another.

What must appear suffering when seen from the outside, is actually only a sum of great difficulties that have to be overcome. Of course there's no telling how things will turn out, once all means of communication fail. And I dare not think how they would be without Edith. The great helper who turns suffering into difficulties, and the little comforter [Rafael], who turns the rest into joy, are what have come of five years ago today [the engagement day]. And despite everything, the three of us, I, Edith, and Rafael, praise the day.

January 16, 1925, to Gertrud Oppenheim:

Why aren't you coming? I rely much more upon visitors than I did last year since writing becomes more and more difficult, and one can't expect letters if one doesn't write any. Here all good intentions are of no avail; it's a psychological law.

January 22, 1925, to Rudolf Ehrenberg:

I think that in these last years we have huddled together more closely than people can or should in the long run. We have lived by twos, fives, and sevens, for two, five, and seven. This kind of thing only works for a while. Then comes a time when one lives first for twenty, fifty, seventy, then later for two hundred, five hundred, seven hundred, etc.—Then one comes to be surrounded by an aura of little understanding and much misunderstanding, and whether one likes it or not, becomes exactly like that aura. Inwardly one struggles against this, and would like to be seen as he really is, that is, as he was years ago when he existed only for two, five, or seven; all to no avail, because eventually there comes the realization that one has actually come to be one's public image. Just as formerly one was the person the two, five, and seven took him to be.

To come down to our own case, I believe that today we have all of us nothing further to share except the past. A gap has come between us, admitting other people, adherents and opponents both.

VI
THE LAST YEARS
1925-1929

The bodily condition deteriorates; the work goes on. The Bible translation is energetically pursued. In his last year, F. R. appears reviewing the major issues that occupied him during his life; he revises, corrects, strives at final forms, at ever purer vision.

In the beginning of 1925, F. R. wrote an article on the Lehrhaus in which he once again expounded his idea of reviving Jewish "learning." During February 1925, in which month F. R. suffered an attack of bronchitis, he wrote "The New Thinking," a more popular presentation of the philosophic background of the Star of Redemption.[1] On the question whether the Star is a "philosophic" or a "Jewish book," F. R. says:

But the "Jewish book" which, after all, it claims to be on the title page? In order to say with absolute truthfulness what I have now to say, I should like to be able to speak in tones as hushed as those of the poet when concluding his mighty fugue on the theme of cosmic beauty with the unforgettable preface: "It appeared to me in the guise of youth, in the shape of a woman." I have received the new thinking in these old words, and so I have passed it on.

[1] *See* pp. 190-208.

I know that instead of these, New Testament words would have risen to a Christian's lips, to a pagan not words from any holy writ of his—for the trajectory of such writ leads away from the original language of mankind, not, like the earthly path of revelation, toward it—but perhaps words entirely his own. But these were the words that came to me. And I really believe that this is a Jewish book; not merely one that treats of "Jewish matters," for then the books of Protestant Old Testament scholars would be Jewish books, but a book to which the old Jewish words have come for the expression of whatever it has to say, and especially of what is new in it. Jewish matters are always past, as is matter generally; but Jewish words, however old, partake of the eternal youth of the word, and once the world is opened to them they will rejuvenate the world.

March 11, 1925, to Hans Ehrenberg, on the same essay, "The New Thinking":

It is really addressed to the Jewish reader. Among the others, it has only found a few scattered ones. It might be feasible to write individual letters to those, but a printed essay can only take into account the six hundred Jews who own the Star of Redemption (there may be a hundred copies among the others). In Jewish circles the book has become downright famous. I could show you the most amazing comments. This prestige really gives me my only platform, for I am writing *against* this prestige. Of course not against the quantity of it, which pleases me well enough, but against its quality. For this reason I deliberately exaggerate in the other direction, the general philosophical.

Precisely the thing I hoped for when I insisted on a Jewish publisher has happened, while the thing that I feared, and that made me hesitate to publish it during my lifetime, has not happened: it has made me famous among the Jews but has not obstructed my influence with the Jews. And the reason for both is that they haven't read it. Again and again I am amazed at how little its readers know it. Everybody thinks it is an admonition to kosher eating. The beautiful phrase of my Catholic name-saint: *tantum quisque intelligit, quantum operatur,* applies also to the passive *intelligitur.* And this is all to the good.

In the early spring of 1925, F. R. wrote a critical essay on classical and modern Hebrew.[2] In April 1925 F. R. suffered a severe attack of grippe. April 21, 1925, to the actress Louise Dumont:

Yesterday Martin Buber was here and mentioned casually that you consider [Carlo] Philips' version of the *Oresteia* impossible to declaim on the stage, and that you prefer Bruesmann's version. I'm not familiar with either one. I only know of Bruesmann's from a review by Stefan Zweig which happened to catch my attention because Bruesmann's *Oresteia* was put out by the publisher of my Judah ha-Levi book. Philips' style of translating I know only from his *Prometheus Bound,* the genesis of which I witnessed years ago in Heidelberg. All the same I'd like to venture a word or two on the subject.

Stefan Zweig's review was meant as praise, but it struck me nevertheless as devastating criticism. I can't recall today exactly what he said, but it was as though one were to praise a translation of Hölderlin's hymns for its easy, playful, frivolous grace, or one of Heine's *Buch der Lieder* for the mysterious grandeur of its language. I have also heard rumors that the philologists reject it as completely inaccurate, but this of course doesn't mean much. Now let's go on to Philips.

[2] *See* pp. 263-271.

Each new poetic language has always seemed to the stage impossible of declamation, even Schiller's blank verse. I seem to remember—you will know exactly—that he had to have the parts of *Wallenstein* written out in prose for the actors in the premier performance at Weimar. And yet this may be the only absolutely stringent duty that the stage has toward dramatic poetry. In everything else the theater may foist its own laws upon the work of art; poetic language alone offers a challenge which the stage must meet without forcing a compromise with its own claims.

For the Aeschylean German which Philips as a translator has created, no traditional declamatory style exists, and for this reason it might be a good idea to call him in, also to help with the training of the chorus. Though he commands practically none of the actor's resources, he has nevertheless a very provocative way of reading. At the time of our personal acquaintance I and my friends had him read plays to us far into the night. The blank-verse rhythm of Goethe's *Natural Daughter* still vibrates in me when I think of it, even after fourteen years, the way the motion of a ship does after one has been ashore for several hours.

May 1925, to Louise Dumont:

The public is always wrong in what it demands, but it is always right *in demanding*. Its demand is always a sign that something isn't right yet, even though it can hardly ever tell what, and so it starts to drivel about the "what." C.M. von Weber said: "Each of them is an ass, and yet together they are the voice of God." After all, the product of a past or foreign theater can only be produced fragmentarily. A Greek tragedy could not be presented, even if one were to reconstruct the Dionysos theater in Athens and begin the play in the morning. We can't substitute for our spectator, who goes to the theater expecting to be amused, though he will perhaps put up with (may possibly even hope for) a slight flavor of church ceremony—we can't substitute for him the Greek audience, who went in the mood of a churchgoer, perhaps hoping to be somewhat amused but willing to take some decorous boredom into the bargain. For this reason, adaptation, quite ruthless and solely intended for effect, is not only permissible but imperative. The word is not sacrosanct; it must endure whatever the stage, which is always only for today—indeed for *tonight*—adds to or subtracts from it. The only thing poetry may defend against the theater is its language, its peculiar rhythm and tone. And provided one makes concessions to the public in every other regard, it will accept the one thing about which one remains intransigent; then it will confound the good with the bad, as ordinarily it does the bad with the good. Upon this alone all our hopes of improvement, as well as the fact that things have improved, rest. The theater of today is not worse but better than it was in Schiller's time.

The *Oresteia* won't be entirely playable until a composer gets hold of the choruses and sets them, not in the Greek manner, but in a wholly contemporary one. In the meantime we can only cut. Or else we must play the *Prometheus,* whose choruses have been cut, either by the poet himself or by the hazards of transmission, to a measure suitable for the modern stage. The *Prometheus* can be cut to make a regular stage play; the *Oresteia,* with its ending that could be plausible only to the Athenian of 457 B.C.E., cannot. And it may not have been considered plausible even at that time. Yet enough that should prove directly effective remains: Agamemnon's entrance, Cassandra, the defiance of the murderers, the recognition scene between brother and sister, the mother's fear, Orestes after the murder, the Furies, Clytemnestra's shade. It would be well worth while to discuss this with the translator, to whom all sorts of ideas must have occurred in over ten years of work. And what of the rhythm? How would we feel about [Stefan] George's poetry without the tradition of its declamation that ultimately goes back to himself?

In the spring of 1925 a young publisher, Lambert Schneider of Berlin, suggested to Buber that he undertake, for publication, a new translation of the Bible. Buber made his acceptance of this large-scale commitment contingent on F. R.'s collaboration. Buber relates:

I had a feeling that my suggestion at once pleased and disturbed him. Later on I came to understand his reaction. Though he no longer expected death within the next few weeks or months, as he had done during the first stage of his illness, he had given up measuring his life in long periods. Here he was being offered, and therefore considered equal to, participation in a project which, as he recognized much sooner than I, would involve several years of intensive work. It meant adopting a different calculus of the future. He said: "Let's try it." "Which chapter?" I asked. He replied: "The first."

Our method of collaborating was the same to the end. I translated, and sent the sheets of the first version, mostly by chapters, to F. R. His replies comprised reservations, references, suggested changes. I immediately incorporated those that struck me at once as being good. We discussed the rest by correspondence, and whatever remained controversial we discussed during my Wednesday visits (I lectured every Wednesday at the University of Frankfort, and spent the rest of the day at the Rosenzweigs.') When we had completed the first draft of a book I would start on the final copy for the printer. Here again we went through the same procedure, and there were new suggestions. The procedure was repeated with the first and second proofs; then, we had the book read to us jointly, and we compared notes, and carried on a discussion for days. With the third proof, we gave our *imprimatur*.

To simplify F. R.'s task I indicated, wherever necessary, my reasons for translating a given passage as I had. Since he had to be spared the lugging of books as much as possible, I appended to each difficult passage the various controversial interpretations, from the oldest commentators to the latest essays in scholarly journals. And yet a single word often became the subject of weeks of correspondence.

May 27, 1925, to Martin Buber, after having been invited by the editors of the *Jüdisches Lexicon* to write the article on Buber:

To parody, and exclaim: Here you may view the holy beast of the Jews, and *no* mystic! is something I can and will do. It is a cry that must be raised for the sake of the good cause, and in such cases I don't take cover behind my soul. But to portray you, to write "about" you, is something I can't do. My illness has removed me to such an extent from my older friends that I could, today, write about them, just because I can no longer, or only to a lesser degree, write to them. But you, who entered on the "seventh day of the feast"[3] are still much too "new (and ever again new) a face" for me to be able to portray you before the public. I must leave it at the fleeting image on my retina, and I hope it will not change while I live.

June 21, 1925, to Hans Ehrenberg:

When a man stands close to a locked gate he sees no more of what is behind it than if he stands far away from

---

[3] A wedding feast lasts seven days; on each day "a new face" among the guests is greeted especially.

it. Besides, since the end of the first year of my illness, I no longer live such an outpost existence. When I realized then that there was a lull, my alerted state somewhat relaxed, and now when the signal comes I shall pack my bag almost as frightened as any normal being.—Incidentally I have repeatedly dealt, in my notes to Judah ha-Levi, with the view of the world from the vantage point near the gate, which is essentially different from the ordinary view in that one can no longer see that world both before and behind, but in only one direction. Therefore: *lege cape*—read and understand.

> In September 1925, Buber and F. R. completed their work on the translation of *Genesis*. F. R. sent the following poem to Buber to celebrate the occasion (September 21, 1925):

I have learned/ That every beginning is an end./ Quit of the task of writing, I wrote, "Into Life"[4]—/After scarcely two years/ The hand ready for work grew lame,/ The tongue ready for speech stood still,/ So only writing was left me.

But this end became a beginning for me:/ What I wrote,/ Has not—thanks to you, dear friend—/ Remained mere writing./ We have written the Word of the Beginning,/ Prime act that pledges the meaning of the end./ And thus the Holy Writ began.

> December 2, 1925, before the end of his thirty-ninth year, to Gertrud Oppenheim:

It is almost as uncanny to me that you should be forty as that I should be turning thirty-nine. My thirty-fifth birthday was the last one I honestly earned by a year of living; since then time has stood still for me, and birthdays fall

[4] The last words of the Star of Redemption.

into my lap like lottery prizes. This also reflects onto the people around me. Only my Rafael is the exception; I read time by him.

In December 1925 F. R. wrote "Scripture and the Spoken Word." At the end of that month the first volume of the new Bible translation appeared. December 30, to Eugen Mayer, who several years earlier had advocated a new translation of the Bible into German (at that time F. R. had maintained that after Luther no new German translation was possible):

I remember very well the conversation you refer to. Indeed, I remember it better than you do. It was on a Saturday afternoon; I had come to see you with my wife. You and I were standing together by the window in the approaching dusk. You told me of your idea that a new Jewish translation of the Bible should be made, so that the community could give each boy, upon his *bar mitzvah,* a copy of the Pentateuch in German, as a remembrance. I opposed the idea of a new translation, but you refused to accept my objections.—When I heard that the Berlin Jewish community was planning a new translation, I even thought of writing a long article against the plan and demanding instead a Jewish revision of Luther's Bible. It would have been a fine article full of thrusts at the German Jews. And now I find myself guilty of the very thing.

It happened exactly the way girls get into trouble—imperceptibly, step by step, until it's done, and then (except that in my case the interval was only six months) the consequences appear. For, whether you believe it or not, this translation began as an attempt to revise the Luther Bible. We departed from Luther's text only step by step, and at first reluctantly (myself), and Buber with a heavy heart. It simply didn't work. You were right that afternoon by the window!

I sometimes fear that the Germans won't stomach this extremely un-Christian Bible, and that our translation will come to stand for the expulsion of the Bible from German culture, as advocated by the "neo-Marcionists," just as Luther's Bible stood for the conquest of Germany through the Bible. But quite possibly, after seventy years a new return will follow this *golus bovel*,[5] and in any case it is only the beginning of the thing and not the final outcome that is within our province.

January 6, 1926, to Nahum Glatzer:
At nineteen I complained to an older friend that I had no ideas of my own whatsoever; at twenty, that I couldn't imagine myself ever writing a book (problems of conviction didn't exist for me at all); in both cases the older man's experienced "wait" helped me to be patient.

February 17, 1926, to Eduard Strauss:
The great thing about your Bible class[6] for me was that it put me for the first time face to face with the naked text, stripped of its traditional trappings. Previously, I had had the experience only with the Psalms and the Song of Songs. I had shied away from reading the Torah and the Prophets except in the context of the Jewish millennia; I had not, here, had the courage to place myself lone, before the lone text.

In June 1926 the translation of *Exodus* was completed. In July 1926 F. R. wrote the extensive essay "Scripture and Luther's Translation."[7] August 1926, to Martin Buber:
We are dealing with two types of readers today: those who know nothing at all, and those who know everything. The former, provided we do our work properly, understand

---

[5] *Galut Bavel*, Babylonian exile, which lasted seventy years.
[6] At the Lehrhaus.
[7] *See* pp. 254-261.

everything; the latter, especially in that case, nothing. The first are those who trust us and themselves because they really believe that what we have written and what they understand is what was meant. The others are the distrustful ones, skeptical toward us and themselves; they always think that what stands on the page and what they understand cannot possibly be what was meant, so they start "comparing." If they compare with the original they'll go over to the other party; since the other party represents one per cent of our readers, our following is thus increased to eleven per cent. The other eighty-nine per cent, who compare us with Luther and Kautzsch,[8] are lost to us; they must be left to die out.

We must write exclusively for the one per cent, with a side glance at the ten per cent. The eighty-nine per cent are no concern of ours. If we had wanted to write for them we would never have started. . . .

The party alignment is only wrong in relation to us; in relation to the work it is right. For the one per cent who know nothing and consequently are able to trust us and their own heads are, viewed as a party, the liberals, while the ten per cent are the orthodox. There are, of course, also the independent individuals, who really give one pleasure.

Beginning of November, 1926, to Martin Buber:

On the subject of the ingratitude of posterity: I don't know if I ever told you my two arch examples of the pedantry of the unnoticeable: the statues on the pediment of the Parthenon, which are as magnificently treated in back as in front, and the choral stanzas of Bach's Passions, especially *O Haupt voll Blut und Wunden,* whose four-part setting with each variation stranger and more beautiful than the one before it, was, in the only performances Bach could

---

[8] Emil Kautzsch, representative of the Wellhausen school of Bible criticism; author of a modern German Bible translation.

foresee, mercilessly drowned out by the church choir. Both these instances impressed me tremendously when I came across them, and had a determining influence on me when I began work myself.

In December 1926 the translation of *Leviticus* and *Numbers* was completed. Also in 1926, publication of a volume of collected essays on religion and philosophy (*Zweistromland*).

December 25, 1926, F. R.'s fortieth birthday. His friends and colleagues presented him with a portfolio of pieces composed for the occasion, and each written in the author's own hand. End of December, to Martin Buber:
I have been reading a great deal in the portfolio. It's fairly bursting with spirit. It is a strange thing to see your own biography unfolding right before your eyes.—The number four, which you are just about to leave behind, is after all a serious number. Three still shows traces of the baby: one still has *carte blanche* for occasional blunders. When one reaches the four—at least that's the way I feel about it now—one is finally and hopelessly grown up.

March 16, 1927, to Hans Trüb:
Up to this week I had no time for anything but the Bible. So I had to delay until now to thank you for your and your wife's kind letter, and for the magnificent azaleas. Then, too, it's also true that I don't find your letter easy to answer. As a rule I shrink from destroying the legend my illness has built up around me. I know too well that without it most people would never find a way to me at all; it is simply the necessary compensation for the revolting sights —the saint's halo must disguise the spittle.[9] But with you I feel that I mustn't let it go at that.

[9] Emitted without control; F.R.'s wife or attendant wiped it away.

Illness, like any other misfortune, improves neither body nor soul. It's a great deal if one is able to maintain one's moral *status quo ante* somewhat! Considered generally, all I do is what is still most bearable to me in my situation. There's in it none of the heroism people imagine. If I weren't working I would simply get terribly bored.

The only remarkable thing in all this is the amount of energy expended. But this almost necessarily involves much brutality—and not only against myself, which would be of no significance. But even the output of energy is only more spectacular, and by no means really as great as when I wrote the Star of Redemption under the most incredible circumstances (the first sections were written down on army postcards, in the midst of conversation with comrades and superiors—"What a whale of a correspondence that fellow Rosenzweig has!").

The one great experience these years have given me is something entirely different. An experience at once very negative and positive. The radical change in my existence has driven away almost all my former friends. . . . Over all human relationships too, invisible and unknown to either party, stands the clause that Frederick the Great wrote in sympathetic ink into all treaties between states: *rebus sic stantibus*. It is only normal that an unforseen radical and permanent change in the condition of either party should make of the relationship a thing of the past. From shipwrecks of this kind decent people try to save as much future as possible; but for the whole past to be transformed into future is a unique miracle. So much for the negative side of the experience.

The positive side is this: just as one's old friendships dissolve, so new ones are formed. The new friends are those who from the beginning have been adjusted to the current state of affairs, and who, while theoretically knowing that things were once different, lack any realistic awareness of this. They can share the new existence, as the former friends could share only the old. Thus life is not impoverished. This has been my most memorable experience. As much as has been taken away is given again. This is no law; it can't be reckoned on in advance, and it doesn't free the heart from fear and hope. But afterwards, once it has been experienced, it is an infinite solace and an inexhaustible source of gratitude. We both greet you most cordially.

In the second half of March, F. R. was ill with bronchial pneumonia accompanied by severe fever. In spring 1927 the translation of *Deuteronomy* was completed. April 19, 1927, to Hans Ehrenberg:

You can get a better understanding of Zionism[10] by considering the significance of socialism for the church. Just as the Social Democrats, even if they are not "religious socialists," even if they are "atheists," are more important for the establishment of the kingdom of God through the church than the church-minded, even the few truly religious ones, and certainly than the vast mass of the semi- or wholly indifferent, so the Zionists are for the synagogue.

Theory is invariably only a line. The roads of life deviate more or less, to right or left, from the beeline of theory. That line indicates only the general direction; anyone who insisted on walking the straight line could not move from the spot. Nevertheless, the beeline is still the right one; the road to the left and the road to the right (to which small-scale maps reduce the network of roads shown by General Staff maps) are in reality as little negotiable as the beeline, and are moreover theoretically false simply because there are two of them.

What I came to an understanding of in 1913, and wrote

[10] *See* pp. 353-358.

down in 1919, in the third part of the Star of Redemption is the beeline. Everything I have done, including the very act of writing down and publishing, as well as all that followed: Academy, Lehrhaus, the founding of a home, the Judah ha-Levi book, the Bible, all this lies to the right of the beeline and can as little be construed in its details from the beeline as what the Zionist does to the left of it. To the right lies the Diaspora, to the left present-day Palestine. It would be a good thing if at least the leaders on both sides could see the beeline. Only a very few do, and rather fewer on the right than on the left. Nevertheless it works; the awareness is not so important as that.

April 21, 1927, to Jacob Rosenheim, leader of separatist orthodox Judaism (Agudath Yisroel), who visited F. R. on that day and discussed the new Bible translation with him:

Where we differ from orthodoxy is in our reluctance to draw from our belief in the holiness or uniqueness of the Torah, and in its character of revelation, any conclusions as to its literary genesis and the philological value of the text as it has come down to us. If all of Wellhausen's theories were correct and the Samaritans really had the better text, our faith would not be shaken in the least. This is the profound difference between you and us—a difference which, it seems to me, may be bridged by mutual esteem but not by understanding. I, at least, fail to understand the religious basis of Hirsch's[11] commentary or [Isaac] Breuer's writings. Still, how does it happen then that our translation is more closely akin to that of Hirsch than to any other?

In May 1927 F. R. exchanged letters with Benno Jacob, a rabbi and one of the representatives of the anti-Zionist

[11] S. R. Hirsch (1808-1888), rabbi and founder of the neo-orthodox movement in Germany.

liberal Jews in Germany. F. R., who was pro-Palestinian but not a Zionist, advocated a revision of the policy of liberal Jewry. May 2, 1927, to Benno Jacob:

The anti-Zionist component of liberalism has become traditional, yet it is in need of revision. The reason being that this element of classical liberalism was not primarily religious but a tribute to the tendency toward political and social emancipation that went hand in hand with it. The survival of Jewish liberalism depends on its being able to disengage itself from these contexts. Just as it was a vital question for political liberalism to disengage itself from the economic ideas of its classical period, the Manchester movement and anti-socialism. Synagogical liberalism is now confronted by the same task that confronted Naumann[12] and his fellow fighters: to break away from a classical alliance and a classical opposition, and to preserve its essential meaning for the future.

May 25, 1927, to August Mühlhausen, who, in return for a copy of the Bible translation, had sent F. R. an offprint of the famous article *Geist* ("Spirit") written by Mühlhausen's teacher, Rudolf Hildebrand, for Grimm's German dictionary:

I was deeply moved by your gift; it came to me, if you'll forgive the silly comparison, like the award of a medal. Throughout the course of this work, which more than anything else I have done moves people to love and hate, nothing so delightful as this wordless gesture has happened to me. Discovering, as I read it page by page, traces of your hand—correcting mostly, but often enough enthusiastically pointing out—became for me not, as it ordinarily might

[12] Friedrich Naumann (1860-1919), co-founder and a leader of the German Democratic Party, German National Assembly, Weimar.

have, merely the height of joy but a confirmation of my first feeling—that this was the way it had to be.

The book itself—I've been reading in it since the day it came, and will probably finish by tonight—I have known hitherto only in libraries, that is to say inadequately. Only now, having before me this separate edition whose existence had escaped me, confined to my room as I have been by my illness for several years—only now do I realize why the essay is so famous, and more than that, why it is not by any means so famous as it deserves to be. For only today has this fight of the philologists for the spirit of the language against the abstract diction of philosophy broadened from a fight between two disciplines and their respective methods into a battle that rages in all intellectual disciplines and walks of life between the old and the new thinking.

This last phrase will tell you how directly your gift went to my heart; I hope the enclosed essay ["The New Thinking"] will make it clear to you. . . .

You will also find in the essay my reason for asking you to accept the Judah ha-Levi book from me. Besides, thanks to the publisher, it has turned out such a beautiful book that through it I can best show you my joy and gratitude.

May 25, 1927, to Gertrud Oppenheim:
The people who wrote the Bible seem to have thought of God much the way Kafka did. I have never read a book that reminded me so much of the Bible as his novel *The Castle*, and that is why reading it certainly cannot be called a pleasure.

July 11, 1927, to Nahum Glatzer, with reference to a conversation on the subject of Goethe:
The other day we really rattled on about him. While his fear of tragedy is in fact a weakness, it is no real defect of character. The only thing that strikes me as odd is

people taking this extraordinarily one-sided man for "universal." He was that really only halfway.

July 29, 1927, to Martin Buber:
On the whole, I am not detached from the Star of Redemption, even though there are many passages in it which I wouldn't write at all today, or would write differently. Which goes to show that man is not a channeled stream but a many-branched one.

In August 1927 the translation of *Joshua* was completed. September 2, 1927, to Martin Buber, on their Bible translation:
Whoever expects a work of art can't possibly understand us. Even though it *is*. But to be seen as one only by people not looking for this. Just as the elegance of a mathematical proof is visible only to those who approach it with a mathematical interest, not to those who are looking for elegance.— I would even go so far as to say that even the pure work of art can only be approached legitimately through a crude interest in its subject matter, and that our aesthetics and our aestheticism block our path to the pure work of art, as well as to the more-than-work-of-art.

September 5, 1927, to Robert Arnold Fritzsche:
Many thanks for your letter and your wife's gift[13] to our Rafael. We haven't given him the picture yet, but are saving it for his fifth birthday, which falls this week; on that day he'll receive it in a small gold frame for hanging. It will be his first glimpse into the Greek world. So far only the two realms of the Bible and Grimm's *Fairy Tales* have been blended in his imagination. Shortly after his birth, when I still expected things to go rapidly with me, I bought him thirteen books for his first thirteen birthdays. This time he

[13] "Aurora" from the Palazzo Rospigigliosi in Rome, copied by Mrs. Fritzsche.

is getting the second volume of Grimm's *Fairy Tales* with Ubbelohde's illustrations, next year the third, and only the following year, and for the next three years, he will receive Schwab's *Myths and Epics of Ancient Greece*.

In September 1927, the translation of *Judges* was completed. To Fritzsche:

Working on the book of Judges has been a joy, the greatest since Genesis. Altogether I am very grateful to Buber for making it possible for me to work and live in the two languages I love.

At the end of 1927 and early in 1928 F. R. edited an anniversary volume for Martin Buber's fiftieth birthday. F. R.'s contribution was a discussion of a passage from Buber's doctor's thesis.

In January 1928 F. R. wrote "The Secret of Form in the Biblical Tales." In February he started to write reviews of recorded music for the *Kasseler Tageblatt*.

February 7, 1928, to Arnold Zweig:

I have always suspected that our common writers' vice of never being satisfied with our readers—instead of marveling anew each time at the miracle that a complete stranger, completely unconcerned with us, should even bother to read what we have written—has its solid foundation in the gross discrepancy between the amount of time the writer spends in writing and the reader in reading. When I once complained of this to Buber he cited, to comfort me, the lasting influence we exert on our readers. This is true enough, but like all drafts on the future, it is only a solace, not a remedy for the present illness.

June 11, 1928, to Hans Trüb:

I don't believe that the patient's personality can be made a factor in the diagnosis. Speaking of my own case: I am convinced that my own metaphysical knowledge and the physical science of my doctor, my layman's instinct and his textbook knowledge that things would come to an end within that very year,[14] were correct. Even though events proved otherwise. The variable that must be added to the diagnosis from textbook and from self-knowledge is not the existing and knowing individual, but the possibility itself of the event. I believe that the reprieve at the end of 1922 was an event absolutely unpredictable from the doctor's most thoroughgoing science or the patient's crystal-clear understanding; it was an event of exactly the same order as the verdict at the end of 1921.

During 1928 and 1929 F. R. was stricken repeatedly with attacks of high fever and disorders of the bronchial organs. A note:
The sufferer alone is permitted to praise God in his works. But all men suffer.

In June 1928 work on the books of *Samuel* was completed. June 12, to August Mühlhausen:
At last I get around to writing again. These days *Samuel* goes into its third—the *imprimatur*—proof, and thus the burden of the last months is lifted from us. It was a tremendous job—Buber says the hardest of his life. There's hardly another book in the Old Testament whose text is so corrupt. The combination of knowing this and wishing to save all that can possibly be saved is what has made our work so difficult.

Also in June 1928 F. R. wrote a review of the first volume of the *Encyclopaedia Judaica,* in which he discussed the Jewish attitude toward biblical scholarship.

[14] *See* p. 110.

September 2, 1928, to Richard Koch:

Things in our life simply don't go according to set decisions. One glides into a new epoch, and the so-called "decision" is as a rule only the final summing up of items long since entered in the ledger by life itself. You remember, last fall I made the biographic diagnosis that your theoretical epoch was beginning. My own autobiographical philosophy of history (after the event, like all philosophy of history) would read like this: After I had suddenly turned philosopher in 1913 (my interest in philosophy had hitherto been purely historical) I conceived, toward the end of 1916, the plan of my chef-d'oeuvre; I must have jotted it down somewhere, probably on the army postcards which at that time I (noncommissioned officer Rosenzweig) sent to Dr. Franz Rosenzweig at Cassel. Of course I was not going to carry out my plan before my seventieth year, because I could not acquire the necessary knowledge before then. The plan envisaged a book *de omnibus rebus et quibusdam aliis,* such as the Star of Redemption did turn out later to be, but in the form of a Bible commentary—hence the need for prolonged study. I think I intended three volumes of commentary: the first on the weekly Torah portions, the second on the respective prophetic readings, the third on the five scrolls. Then ten years ago I wrote, hastily, but as it turned out, fortunately, the commentary, leaving the text aside. Now, strangely enough, I have nevertheless arrived at the text[15] and—as will be clear from what I have said—leaving aside the commentary. In both cases what is left out is of course potentially present.

I have had an experience like Schopenhauer's with regard to my philosophical writings: everything written after the "main work" has turned out to be parerga, paralipomena, and a Second Part that annotates the first. Or rather, since

---

[15] Translation of the Bible.

Schopenhauer's pompous self-importance is distasteful to me, even though my own self-esteem is no whit smaller than his, everything that now comes from my pen is verse written for special occasions. But it does come.

On the other hand, when I consider how little of all I have written has had any effect, or been read, or, indeed, has even been noticed, I find small encouragement toward philosophical writing, even if it were to be done without occasion. I can understand how the Star has met with such little response. But even my notes to Judah ha-Levi, which after all have a tempting hors d'oeuvre format, have remained unread; less than two hundred copies of the second edition, with its some forty additions, have been sold. . . . But the business of being read is a strange one anyway. A critic who knows me as author of the Hegel book writes in a review of Judah ha-Levi, in the *Hamburger Fremdenblatt*: "In a preface, and notes to each poem, he outlines his principles of procedure: this 'commentary' contains a whole philosophy of language! It is to be hoped that Rosenzweig will one day put these ideas in systematic form. So far he has sunk them in aphoristic remarks and historical digressions, thereby inhibiting their full effect." What can you do?[16]

The effect which by rights everything I have written (of course not my early Hegel book and the Schellingianum) should have had—that is, a general, or at least a widespread indignation and concern—has been called forth, strangely enough, only by the Bible translation. Well, it's a kind of proof.

In September 1928, F. R. wrote a review of the second volume of the *Encyclopaedia Judaica*, in which he dis-

---

[16] Philosophy of language had been closely treated by F. R. in his Star of Redemption, which appeared in 1921.

cussed in particular the theological problem of anthropomorphism. Late in 1928, F. R. was invited to prepare a second edition of the Star. He wanted the text to remain unchanged. But the marginal titles prepared in 1922 were to accompany the text. The work on an extensive appendix was supervised by F. R. during January and February 1929. In February 1929 F. R.'s condition grew worse. The pointing on the alphabet tablet became less distinct, and the demands on Mrs. Rosenzweig's ingenuity increased. F. R. refused to stop working or even to reduce his working schedule.

In February the final editorial meetings on the books of Kings took place. F. R. concerned himself with every detail; certain phrases were revised over and over again. He suppressed only his humorous remarks and occasional anecdotes. The work on Isaiah occupied him during the following months.

In April, F. R. wrote the article "On the Significance of the Bible" for the Bible chapter in the *Encyclopaedia Judaica;* the article deals with the role of the Old Testament in Judaism and in Christianity.[17] In May, in an article "Switching Fronts," F. R. reviewed the second edition of *Religion der Vernunft aus den Quellen des Judentums* ("The Religion of Reason from Jewish Sources") by Hermann Cohen. In this article he refers to a controversy between Ernst Cassirer and Martin Heidegger which had recently taken place at a convention in Davos. In June, F. R. received a Hebrew translation of his introduction to the *Jüdische Schriften* ("Collected Jewish Writings") by Hermann Cohen. Friends raised objections to certain phrases in the translation. July 14, 1929, to Julius Guttmann:

It gives me such fiendish pleasure to see myself in the beloved twenty-two [Hebrew] letters, that nothing else seems to matter.

[17] *See* pp. 271-275.

July 5, 1929, to his mother, in connection with this work:

Now something silly. Leo Rosenzweig[18] says that Cohen insisted that in Hebrew translations of his works his first name should be Yehezkel (and Hermann only in brackets). Now I know perfectly well that my name is Levi, which is supposed to correspond to Louis. But this is a ticklish matter, for the whole *am haaratzus* [ignorance] of my early years is bound up with it. Only Levites can properly be called Levi. What happened at my *brit milah* [circumcision] must have been something like what I witnessed thirty years ago in the case of ———. The *mohel* [circumcisor] came to the place where the name had to be pronounced, and hurriedly asked in an interval of the singing, "What's his name?" Uncle ——— turned around in embarassment and someone called out "Reuben!" Greatly relieved, Uncle ——— repeated "Reuben," and the *mohel* sang a trilling cadenza on the chance-born text Reuben. But this isn't the end of this tragi-comedy. Grandfather Louis's name was, of course, not Levi, though I had Levi carved on father's tombstone without bothering to investigate. As I later found out from Uncle Traugott's[19] tombstone, his real name was Yehudah [Judah], which also, of course, corresponds to Louis: the connecting link is the lion Judah of Jacob's blessing. Consequently my correct name should have been Judah ben Samuel, which is exactly the name of the great man whose middle-sized reincarnation upon the road of *ibbur* [transmigration] I am: Judah ha-Levi.

F. R. continued to write his reviews of recorded classical music. Three of the nine essays were written in 1929.

In June 1929 F. R. was occupied in research for an essay on the meaning of God's name in the Bible together

---

[18] The translator of Cohen's writings into Hebrew.
[19] Traugott Rosenzweig, brother of F. R.'s father.

with the various attempts to translate it. July 1929, he wrote "The Eternal (Mendelssohn and the Name of God)." According to F. R., the tetragrammaton implies both the abstract "philosophical" idea of God and the idea of a personal God who is present in the world. The Bible translators had to choose between the "eternal" God of Aristotle and the "omnipresent" God of Abraham. Yet, only the unity of these two God conceptions is the teaching of Judaism. September 30, 1929, to Gertrud Oppenheim:

I couldn't write you a letter yesterday because it was "Buber day."[20] But quite apart from this, I find writing very hard. I could say with Hamlet, "I have of late lost all my mirth." Everything weighs more heavily on me, both public and private matters, my own affairs and those of other people. And the husbandry necessary in reacting to all the tasks and burdens I am constrained to, increases the daily pressure I feel. Odd as it may sound, I have only now come to the point where I would welcome the end—something that most people in my position would have done years ago. Of course this isn't quite true either, as self-analytical generalities never are. I'm still able to enjoy things; it's only that my capacity for suffering has increased more rapidly than my capacity for enjoying.

In October, F. R. wrote a prologue to a Moses Mendelssohn festival. In November F. R. wrote a review of the third and fourth volumes of the *Encyclopaedia Judaica*. Speaking of the purpose of the book review:

In these reviews I avoid on principle any mention of small errors and slips of the kind that give the reviewer of such monumental works an air of superiority in the eyes of naive readers. This kind of glory comes too cheap. One thing is self-evident: where I am well informed I am better in-

[20] Editorial meeting of the translators.

formed than the other man—or at least like to believe so. In all probablity the other man feels the same way about me. But books are not written for those who "know better" but for those who know little or nothing. In other words, not for the reviewer but for the reader. This means that as a reviewer I must not start out from my sporadic superior knowledge but from the ocean of my ignorance. I must not speak from my personal point of view, but represent the interests of the average reader of the group for whom the work is intended. I must praise and blame out of my own experience as a reader and not as one who has once written or intends some day to write on the same subject. It doesn't hurt the reader—that is myself!—if he doesn't go all the way from his one hundred per cent ignorance to one hundred per cent knowledge, but only to eighty or ninety per cent. And if it ever becomes his task to pass on knowledge, he will find it necessary anyway to reduce his faith in what he has read to zero and to aim at one hundred per cent truth, in order that his readers may find in him the eighty or ninety per cent.

> In the body of the article F. R. discusses the section on Bible of the *Encyclopaedia*. The word "Bible," by which the Western world denotes the Old and New Testaments together, in the *Encyclopaedia* denotes only the Old Testament. In his discussion, F. R. reaches back to one of the central motives in the Star of Redemption.

When I ask myself what exactly is the value of a special Jewish treatment of a theme that after all belongs to general scholarship and is even here treated, in all essential features, in that spirit, the answer comes out that the Jewish distillate is something very simple. The word "Bible" is used here in a hundred and thirty-five cross references and countless

"B"-*sigla* for what is commonly called the Old Testament, and only for it. I am sure this has come about quite naturally for most of the contributors, without special editorial pressure, simply through the disposition of the theme and its place in the entire scheme, even though each of the contributors must have noticed it with surprise at one time or another. But this fact, which came about quite simply without being solicited, shows how the old Jewish defiance, the eternal reservation against visible, all-too-visible world history, proclaims itself, in the middle of this most modern Jewish work, in favor of the invisible. And since the last circumstantial speaker of the group[21] found himself on several occasions constrained by world history to say "the Jewish Bible" instead of simply "the Bible," this defiance vindicates itself by denying itself the prerogative of the last word. For while we both should and must insist on our own and cling to it, we should and want to know that our own is not the whole. We should realize that this "own" which we defiantly defend—though it is the secret center of the created world—and this way from which we will not deviate—though it is the secret royal road of·creation—form only part of the created world whose detours are also intended as roads.

These were the last words F. R. wrote for publication.

During the first days of December the Palestinian theater group Habimah gave, in Frankfort, a guest performance of *King David* by the seventeenth-century Spanish dramatist Calderon. Hannah Rovina played the role of Tamar. Visiting the Rosenzweigs, Rovina recited some passages from her part and then, at F. R.'s request, the biblical story, II Samuel 13. This chapter relates how David's son Amnon loved his sister Tamar, and speaks of the "food" which Tamar was to bring to Amnon's chamber in order that

[21] F. R. himself.

170

he "may eat" at her hand. The biblical text uses the word *birya* [food] which implies both refreshment and purification—catharsis. On December 4, F. R. wrote a poem for Hannah Rovina in which he alludes to the catharsis motive:

You have brought into my narrow room
That refreshment, tragic catharsis,
With which you regale thousands outside.
The father was deeply moved and so was the son.
But the latter, his tears streaming, left
The room, protesting angrily,
Thus renewing for you the triumph
Of the most ancient of all tragedies:
Thespis'[22] play, The Fall of Miletus,
So incensed the Athenian citizenry
That it arrested the poet.
Scion of our old race,
Founder of Hebrew tragedy,
Thanks for the refreshment I received at your hand.

Two days later (Friday, December 6), F. R. wrote a letter to Buber, who was then visiting the family home of the Rosenzweigs in Cassel. F. R. enclosed the poem to Rovina, and went on to say:

I enclose the poem so that you may explain to my mother the point, *birya*—catharsis. . . .

On that day F. R. was suffering from a cold. Toward evening his temperature rose to 102.2 degrees. Dr. Richard Koch prescribed for the relief of the cold. The following day (Saturday, December 7), F. R. coughed a great deal but refused to take the prescribed medicine for fear it might affect the heart and breathing. As it happened, Dr. Koch fell ill that day and transferred to care of F. R. to

---

[22] Greek poet of the 6th century B.C.E; reputed founder of the tragic drama.

Dr. Richard Tuteur. In the evening Tuteur phoned the Rosenzweig home and was told that F. R. felt much better and that it would not be necessary to see him before the next day. But during the night (December 7-8), while F. R. was sitting up in a chair before his desk, his condition became worse. The night nurse, who was new to the case and apparently not accustomed to cases of this kind, failed to notify Mrs. Rosenzweig or to call the doctor.

The next morning (Sunday, December 8), the doctor found F. R. very short of breath, his face pale and bluish. He complained of stitches in the left breast. By the alphabet method[23] he indicated: "I am so worn out from forty hours of gasping." Examination led the doctor to suspect a deep-seated broncho-pneumonia on the left side. F. R. was put to bed and given medicine to strengthen the resistance of the heart. Dr. Tuteur relates:

We tried, with a great number of pillows, which had to be arranged and rearranged at the patient's direction, with infinite patience, to settle him comfortably, to dispose his paralyzed limbs, which tended to slip involuntarily from their position, as relaxedly and comfortably for him as possible, and at the same time support his upper body and head in such a way that his gasping for air became tolerable. Minute after minute passed, as the deeply suffering man indicated mutely his constantly changing wishes, while we did our best to help but often failed completely through lack of comprehension. His wife was very exhausted, and hoarse from the continual spelling-out. Then she tried to do something that ordinarily she succeeded in very well, that is, guess the patient's desires and complaints from the general situation of the moment, and from his facial expression. But in the crisis of these hours she was unsuccessful. Again and again she had to resort to the alphabet—especially after he had signified his pain

[23] Whenever neither the special typewriter nor the method described on p. 140 could be used, Mrs. Rosenzweig would spell out the alphabet until a faint signal from F. R. indicated the correct letter.

at this useless guesswork. "I a . . ." was spelled out. Mrs. Rosenzweig guessed "I ask," since she knew from experience that the patient indicated a question in this way. But this time it was not a question that was meant, but the 'a' was followed by 'd'. "I adjure you: spell!" The day nurse, who had known F. R. since 1923, and who because of her absolute and unswerving dedication was in close rapport with him, now tried to relieve his wife. But she recited the alphabet too rapidly, and besides—the patient himself laughed over this the next day—put the 'n' before the 'm.' Things became confused once more. His facial expression, in which a close observer could read approval or rejection, no longer obeyed promptly the impulse of his will, and consequently his "yes" or "no," though intended in time, were expressed too late. It was impossible to relieve Mrs. Rosenzweig in this way. Finally the ceaseless search for a comfortable position came to an end.

Around 4 A.M. F. R. fell asleep and slept until 7 A.M. Upon awakening (Monday, December 9), he asked to have the doctor phoned for permission to be taken out of bed. The doctor wanted to see the patient before making his decision. F. R. felt an insatiable hunger for air and had the windows opened wide. About 10 A.M. the doctor arrived. The pulse could not be felt or counted any more. The broncho-pneumonia had spread to the right lung. The patient continued to gasp for air. The doctor considered using an oxygen tent but gave up the idea, since it would have made it impossible for F. R. to communicate with those around him. Since the bed gave the patient no comfort, because of his difficulty in communicating his wishes, the doctor allowed him to be brought to his chair in the study, after having strengthened his heart with cardiazol and camphor.

The doctor left. The process of transferring F. R. from his bed to his desk took two hours; by 1 P.M. he was in his chair. He fell asleep and slept until 4 P.M.. Then he took some food—the first in several days. After this he asked that his hand be brought into position for a dictation, to be transliterated into the copybook used for the correspondence with Buber. There—written three days earlier—stood the request to explain to his mother "the point, *birya*—catharsis." This was at 6:30 P.M. He pointed to the letter plate of his typewriter, letter by letter, slowly, laboriously, assiduously:

. . . and now it comes, the point of all points, which the Lord has truly revealed to me in my sleep: the point of all points for which there . . .

The writing was interrupted by the entrance of the doctor. He found F. R. sitting quietly up in his chair, leaning his head back against the support. His eyes were clear and rested. He indicated to the doctor that he had slept in the night, but gave the duration of his sleep incorrectly. The nurse corrected his statement. He looked at her much astonished but did not answer. The doctor felt F. R.'s pulse. The pulse barely flickered, like a flame dying for lack of oxygen.

F. R. turned his eyes to his wife to help him "talk." Again she recited the alphabet; letters were combined into words and words into sentences. The words "What does the lodge think of the m . . ." were arrived at. Mrs. Rosenzweig and the doctor tried several combinations, but none fitted. The alphabet was repeated, and they got m-u-s. Mrs. Rosenzweig guessed "music" but this was wrong. Continued recitation of the alphabet brought "Mussolini decree of Baeck." The question referred to Rabbi Leo Baeck's extraordinary demand that the Bne Briss [B'nai B'rith] Lodge (of which Baeck was president) buy 7000 copies of the Buber-Rosenzweig Pentateuch translation. The doctor, an influential member of the lodge, was actually, not at all certain whether this daring project would be approved. However, realizing this might be the last chance to communicate with F. R., he said the lodge would accept.

The answer seemed to please the sick man. He sat relaxed, apparently not suffering. Again he wished to "speak." Mrs. Rosenzweig continued the recitation: "I am improving."

The doctor pointed out that he must not overtax his strength simply because he felt better, but should be sparing of it. F. R. laboriously uttered an inarticulate sound. Mrs. Rosenzweig translated: "Yes, I'll do that." The doctor left about 8 P.M.

F. R. did not wish to continue with the letter whose writing had been interrupted. The sentence remained unfinished.

The day came to an end. Mrs. Rosenzweig retired to rest. The night nurse remained with F. R. in his study. At 2 A.M. she noticed that he had stopped breathing. She gave an emergency injection and ran out to call Mrs. Rosenzweig. When the latter arrived she found F. R. dead.

In keeping with Jewish tradition, the body was placed on the floor and covered with a linen cloth. On a nearby table lay a copy of the Star of Redemption. The mother arrived from Cassel; friends came in. The young son kept saying: You can be sure my father will wake up again.

Mrs. Rosenzweig notified those assembled that it was Franz Rosenzweig's wish to be buried in Frankfort. In the first year of his sickness, he had expressed the desire to be brought to his native Cassel for burial; later, he decided he wanted to remain in Frankfort. His mother then told of a letter he had sent during the war, in which he requested that his body be left wherever it fell should he get killed in the line of duty.

The burial took place December 12, in the new cemetery of the Jewish community. In accordance with Franz Rosenzweig's wish, there was no funeral oration. Martin

Buber read Psalm 73, which contains the inscription Franz Rosenzweig chose for his headstone. As the coffin was lowered into the grave, the sun broke through the clouded skies; a majestic rainbow appeared, the ancient token of the covenant between heaven and earth. Three friends were chosen to recite the Kaddish.

Second Part

The Thought

Selections from Franz Rosenzweig's writings

I

THE NEW THINKING:
PHILOSOPHY AND RELIGION

1.   The Personal Standpoint

I really believe that a philosophy, to be adequate, must
rise out of thinking that is done from the personal standpoint of the thinker. To achieve being objective, the thinker
must proceed boldly from his own subjective situation. The
single condition imposed upon us by objectivity is that
we survey the entire horizon; but we are not obliged to
make this survey from any position other than the one
in which we are, nor are we obliged to make it from no
position at all. Our eyes are, indeed, only our own eyes;
yet it would be folly to imagine we must pluck them out
in order to see straight.
[*Briefe,* p. 597]

2.   The Old and the New Philosophy
From the Star of Redemption[1]

Of Death
All knowledge of the Whole [*das All*] has its source in
death, in the fear of death. Philosophy presumes to cast

---

[1] This first section of the Star of Redemption gives a critical analysis of
the philosophy of German idealism, which F.R. had to overcome before
making his contribution to "New Thinking."

out the fear of the creature, to rob death of its sting, hell of its pestilential breath. All mortal things live in the fear of death; each new birth adds to this fear by a new cause, for it increases the sum of mortality. The womb of the tireless earth incessantly creates new beings, and each is doomed to die, each fearfully anticipates the day when he must make the journey into the dark. But philosophy denies these terrestrial anxieties. It lifts us above the tomb which yawns under our feet at every step. It abandons the body to the abyss, but the free soul soars above. What does philosophy care that the fear of death knows nothing of this division into body and soul, that it bellows "I, I, I," and refuses to acknowledge this relegating of fear to a mere "body"? Though man crawl like a worm into the folds of the naked earth to hide from the whizzing projectiles of blind, inexorable death; though he experience there violently and ineluctably what he has never experienced before: that his *I* would become a mere *It* if he died; and though, with every cry still remaining in his throat, he protest his selfhood against the Inexorable who threatens him with unimaginable extinction—Philosophy smiles her vacant smile on all this anguish, and with outstretched finger indicates to the creature shaking with anxiety for its *here,* a *beyond* of which it is not at all desirous. For what man wants is not at all to escape from any fetters; what he wants is to remain; what he wants is to —live. Philosophy, which warmly recommends to him death as its particular protégé, as the great opportunity of overcoming the narrowness of life, seems only to mock him. Man feels too clearly that while he is condemned to death he is not condemned to suicide. And what philosophy's recommendation really amounts to is a commendation of suicide, not the ordained death of all creatures. Suicide is not natural death, but unnatural death par excellence. The ghastly ability to commit suicide sets man apart from all other beings, known and unknown. It is indeed the index of his stepping out of the natural order. True, it is necessary for every man once in his life to cross the bounds in this fashion. One time he must reverently take down the precious vial; one time he must experience his dreadful poverty, solitude, and estrangement from the rest of the world, and stand facing the naught for a whole night long.[2] But then the earth claims him again. He must not drink the brown juice to the dregs that night. Another way out of the straits of the naught is in store for him than this plunge into the yawning abyss. Man shall not shake off the anguish of earthly life; he shall *remain* in the fear of death.

He shall remain. That is to say, he shall do just what he already desires to do, remain. He shall be relieved of earthly anxiety only when he is relieved of the earth. So long as he remains on earth he shall keep his terrestrial fear. Yet philosophy cheats him of this imperative by weaving the vapor of its idea of the Whole around earthly existence. For it is of course true that a universe would not die, and nothing would ever die in the Whole. Only the single being can die, and everything mortal is lonely. It is this need to dispose of the indivdual, to annihilate the "something," which compels philosophy to embrace "idealism." For idealism, with its denial of everything that sets the individual apart from the Whole, is philosophy's tool for conditioning rebellious matter until it is no longer able to resist being befogged by the notion of the One-and-the Whole. If it could ever happen that all things could be woven into this fog, then death would indeed be swallowed up, if not in an eternal triumph, then in the one universal night of nothingness. And indeed philosophy's final con-

---

[2] An allusion to the first scene in Goethe's *Faust*.

clusion is that death is *nothing*. Actually this is no ultimate conclusion but a first beginning, and death is truly not what it seems, not *nothing* but an inexorable *something* that can't be got rid of. Its harsh cry sounds unabated even out of the fog with which philosophy surrounds it. Philosophy may have succeeded in swallowing it up into nothingness, but it cannot draw its poisonous sting, and man's fear of this sting forever belies cruelly philosophy's compassionate lie.

The Philosophy of the Whole

By denying the dark presupposition of all existence, that is, by refusing to acknowledge death as a something and by dissolving it into nothing, philosophy seems to be working without presuppositions. For henceforth any knowledge of the Whole is based on—nothing. As prior to the one general knowledge of the Whole, only the one, general Nothing is accepted. If philosophy did not want to stop its ears against the cry of anguished humanity it would have to start consciously with this premise: that the nothingness of death is a something; that the nothing of each new death is a new and each time newly terrible something that can neither be talked away nor glossed over in silence. Instead of basing all knowledge on the one and general nothing that hides its head in the sand in order not to hear the anguished death cry, it should have the courage to listen to that cry and not shut its eyes to the ghastly reality. Nothingness is not nothing but something. Thousands of deaths lurk in the dark background of the world as its inexhaustible presupposition; thousands of nothings instead of the one nothing that would really be *nothing;* precisely because they are thousands, these nothings are something. The real multiformity of "nothing" presupposed by philosophy, and the indefeasible reality of death proclaimed by the never-to-be-silenced cry of its victims, belies philosophy's central notion of the one, general knowledge of the Whole, even before that notion has been conceived. Philosophy's three-thousand-five-hundred-year-old secret, which Schopenhauer gave away at her coffin—that Death was her leading muse—is losing its power over us. We don't want a Philosophy that moves in the train of Death and tries to distract us from its perennial dominion by the harmony of her dance. We want no deceptions at all. If death is really something, no philosophy shall any longer turn our gaze from it by claiming to presuppose "nothing." Let us examine this claim a little more closely.

Didn't philosophy, by the very fact of its "sole" presupposition of presupposing nothing, show itself to be full of presuppositions, indeed nothing but presupposition? Throughout the ages thought has been climbing the slope of the same inquiry into the essence of the world; again and again all other questions have agglomerated to this question; and again and again the answer to this question has been looked for in thought. It is as if this presupposition, magnificent in itself, of the thinkable Whole, had obscured the entire field of other possible methods of inquiry. Materialism and idealism, both (not only the former) "as old as philosophy," have an equal share in it. Whatever claimed a degree of independence in the face of it has either been silenced or ignored. Thus was silenced the voice that claimed to be in the possession of knowledge by revelation —revelation as the source of divine knowledge having its spring in a realm beyond thinking. For centuries philosophers have dedicated their work to this dispute between faith and knowledge. The dispute came to an end at the moment when the knowledge of the Whole was consummated. For we may indeed speak of consummation when this knowledge comprises not only its subject—the Whole—but also itself, entirely (at least according to its own claims and in its own genuine way). This came about through Hegel's incorporation of the history of philosophy into his system. Thinking seems unable to go beyond this act of setting itself up visibly as the central fact within its reach, as a part—and of course the concluding one—of the philosophical system. And at the very moment when philosophy has exhausted its formal possibilties and reached its natural limit, the great question forced upon it by the course of world history—that of the relation between knowledge and faith—seems ripe for solution.

Hegel

It is true that more than once in the past a truce has existed between the two hostile powers, based either on a clear separation of their respective claims, or on philosophy's assumption that it had in its own arsenal the keys with which unlock the mysteries of revelation. In both cases philosophy acknowledged the truth of revelation—in the former as a truth that was inaccessible to it, in the latter as a truth that it confirmed. But neither solution sufficed for any lengh of time. Against the first, philosophy's pride soon rebelled, unwilling to admit the existence of a door it couldn't unlock; against the second, faith rebelled, unwilling to be recognized thus casually by philosophy as a truth among other truths. The philosophy of Hegel promised something entirely different. What he proposed was neither separation nor mere concord, but a most intimate relationship. The knowable world is knowable by the same law of thought that, at the apex of Hegel's system, appears as the supreme law of being. And this identical law of thinking and being was first announced in a world-historical event, by revelation; philosophy is thus seen as the consummator, merely, of what was promised by revelation. Nor does philosophy exercise this office only sporadically or at the height of its career; but in every moment, with every breath it draws, it automatically confirms the truth predicated by revelation. Thus the old quarrel seemed to have been composed, heaven and earth reconciled.

Kierkegaard

But both the solution of the problem of faith and the autonomous consummation of knowledge proved illusory. A very colorable illusion, we must admit; for if the above assumption were valid and all knowledge were knowledge of the Whole, contained and at the same time omnipotent in it, then, indeed, the illusion would be the truth rather than an illusion. Whoever wished to raise an objection would have to have an Archimedean fulcrum outside the knowable Whole. From the vantage of such an Archimedean fulcrum Kierkegaard, and not only he, contested Hegel's inclusion of revelation in the Whole. The fulcrum was a personal one: Sören Kierkegaard's—or anyone else's having a first name and a surname—consciousness of his own sin and redemption, which neither needed to be nor was capable of being dissolved in the cosmos. Not capable, because although everything else in him might be translated into general terms, the first name and surname—the *personal* in the strictest sense of the word—remained, and according to those who had this experience, it was precisely this *personal* that mattered.

A New Philosophy

Here two assumptions came face to face. Philosophy was accused of an inability, or rather an incompetence, which it could not admit since it could not see it: for if a subject really existed that was beyond its scope, the vista into this, as into any other beyond, had been shut off by the very fact of the self-containedness it owed to Hegel. The objection disputed the right of philosophy to enter a territory whose existence it denied; philosophy's own territory was not under attack. A different method was needed for that. It was attempted by the philosophical era that began with Schopenhauer and continued through Nietzsche, the end of which is not yet in sight.

Schopenhauer

Schopenhauer was the first among the great thinkers to inquire into the *value* of the world rather than its *essence*. A most unscientific question if it concerned not the world's objective value, its value for a "something," its "meaning" or "purpose"—which would be merely another form of the inquiry as to its essence—but its value for man, possibly even for the individual Arthur Schopenhauer. And it was actually meant in the latter sense. Explicitly, to be sure, the inquiry simply concerned the value of the world for man. And even this question was rendered innocuous when it sought its solution in yet another world system. Any system necessarily implies universal and independent validity. Thus the question put by presystematic man was answered by the saint produced by the system's concluding section. Yet even this was something previously unheard of in philosophy: a type of human being rather than an abstract notion furnishes the keystone of the systematic arch, and truly a keystone, not a mere ethical ornament or appendage. And above all, the tremendous influence of Schopenhauer can only be explained by the fact that people sensed what was actually the case: at the beginning of the system a real man stood, a man who no longer philosophized in the tradition of the history of philosophy, its mandatory as it were, the heir to a current set of problems, but who "had proposed to himself to think about life" because life is "a sorry thing." These proud words of the youth in a conversation with Goethe—the fact that he used the word "life" instead of "world" is significant—are supplemented by the letter in which he offered the completed work to a publisher. Here he describes as the content of philosophy the reaction of an individual mind to the impression made upon it by the world. "An individual mind"—it was after all the human being, Arthur Schopenhauer, who here occupied the position that, according to prevailing notions, should have been occupied by the abstract problem. Man himself, "life," had become the problem, and since he had "proposed to himself" to solve it in philosophical form he had to call into question the value of the world for man—a thoroughly unscientific question, as I have said before, but all the more human for that. Hitherto, philosophical interest had centered exclusively on the knowable Whole; man could only become a subject of philosophy through his relation to that Whole. Now this knowable world was confronted autonomously by something else, by the living human being, and the Whole by that *one* which makes light of everything general, by the "ego and its own." Through the tragedy of Nietzsche's life this new thing was thrust into the stream of the development of the conscious mind.

Nietzsche

For only in this context was it anything new. The poets had all along treated of life and the individual soul. But the philosophers had not. And the saints had all along lived for their own souls. But again the philosophers had not. And here was a man who knew about his life and his soul as poets do, who obeyed their voices as saints do, and who was nevertheless a philosopher. It has become almost a matter of indifference by now what his philosophical findings were. The "Dionysiac," the superman, the blond beast, the eternal recurrence—what has become of them? But he, who in the change of his visions changed himself, whose soul shrank from no height but climbed after the audacious mind up to the sheer peak of insanity, beyond which none can go—he it is whom no one dedicated to philosophy can henceforth pass by. The terrible and challenging image of the absolute fealty of soul to mind can nevermore be obliterated. With the great thinkers of the past the soul was permitted to play the role of wet nurse, possibly of governess, to the mind, but the day came when the grown-up pupil went his own way rejoicing in his freedom and the unlimited view; he would shudder to think back upon the narrow four walls in which he had been reared. Thus the mind enjoyed its independence from the instinctual murkiness in which the mindless spend their days; philosophy was the cool height to which the thinker escaped from the foggy plain. For Nietzsche this division into height and plain within one's own self did not exist; he went his way intact, soul and intellect, man and thinker, an integer to the very last.

The Individual

Thus the individual human being—or rather *an* individual, a very definite individual—gained ascendancy over philosophy—or rather his own philosophy. The philosopher ceased to be a negligible quantity in his philosophy. The compensation in the form of the mind which philosophy promised to whoever sold it his soul was no longer taken seriously. Man—not the one transformed into mind, but the living man for whom his mind was merely the frozen breath of his living soul—had assumed the power of philosophy. Philosophy had to recognize him as something which it couldn't comprehend and yet which, since he had power against it, it could not gainsay. The individual, in the absolute singularity of his proper being, in his private existence defined by his first name and surname, stepped beyond the bounds of the world that knew itself as thinkable, beyond the Whole of philosophy.

The Meta-ethical

Philosophy had thought to grasp man (even as a personality) in ethics. But the effort was doomed to failure, for even as it seized him he dissolved. For while ethics would in principle allow to human action special privileges as against the totality of being, when it came to the test it pulled the human deed back once more into the sphere of the knowable Whole. Nor could it do otherwise, since any ethics necessarily flows back into a conception of the human community as a segment of being. The introduction of a separate category of *action* as against *being* evidently did not furnish sufficient safeguard against this eventual flowing back; it would have been necessary to go back one step farther and anchor action in the ontological ground of a "character" that nevertheless would remain separate from all being: in this way alone could it have been established as a world to itself, apart from the World. Except by Kant this had never been done, and yet it was Kant, of all philosophers, who, through his formulation of the moral law as universally valid act, made the idea of the Whole triumph once more over the human individual. Thus with Kant's followers the "miracle in the phenomenal world"—as Kant defined the concept of freedom—drowned once again, following a certain historical logic, in the miracle of the phenomenal world. It was Kant himself who stood godfather to Hegel's notion of universal history, not only by his work in political philosophy and philosophy of history, but even by his principles of ethics. And while Schopenhauer incorporated Kant's doctrine of intelligible character into his own doctrine of the will, he stripped it of its value, though in a sense directly opposite to that of the great idealists. By making the will the essence of the world Schopenhauer did not, it is true, dissolve the will in the world but instead dissolved the world in the will, and thus he destroyed the distinction, so alive in him, between the being of man and the being of the world.

Thus the new territory that Nietzsche opened to thought must of necessity lie beyond the confines of ethics. Precisely, if we do not wish, in a blind orgy of destruction, to raze the intellectual labor of the past but rather to do full justice to its achievement, we must acknowledge the transcendence of this new question with regard to all that has been traditionally subsumed under ethics, and legitimately so. The conception of the world [*Weltanschauung*] now has for its counterpart the conception of life [*Lebensanschauung*]. Ethics is, and will always remain, part of the conception of the world. The peculiar relationship between the conception of life and of ethics becomes that of an especially intimate opposition, precisely because the two seem to touch, and indeed each claims again and again a share in the solution of the other's problems. In what sense this is actually true will be shown later. But the opposition of the conception of life to the conception of the world becomes sharpened to such a degree into an opposition to the *ethical* aspect of the conception of the world that the problems of the former might very properly be termed meta-ethical.

[*Der Stern der Erlösung*, I, 7-17]

3. The New Thinking   *Feb. 1925*

Philosophy has always inquired into the "essence" of things. This is the concern that marks it off from the unphilosophical thinking of sound common sense, which never bothers to ask what a thing "actually" is. Common sense is content to know that a chair is a chair, and is unconcerned with the possibility that it may, actually, be something quite different. It is just this possibility that philosophy pursues in its inquiry into the essence of things. Philosophy refuses to accept the world as world, God as God, man as man! All these must "actually" be quite different from what they seem, for if they were not, if they were really only what they are, then philosophy—God forbid!—would be utterly superfluous. At least, the species of philosophy that insists on discovering something "entirely different." . . .

In its effort to "reduce" the essence of one thing back to the essence of another, philosophy continues, tirelessly, to work out all possible permutations. From a general point of view, this effort has characterized the three epochs of European philosophy: cosmological antiquity, the theological Middle Ages, and our anthropological modern era—with special emphasis on the pet idea of this modern era: the idea of reducing everything back to *the self*. The method of basing the experience of the world and of God on the experiencing self is still so much a commonplace of the contemporary philosopher that anyone who rejects this method and prefers instead to trace his experience of the world back to the *world*, and his experience of God to God, is simply dismissed. This philosophy regards the reductive method as so self-evident that when it takes the trouble to sentence a heretic it is only because he has been guilty of the wrong variety of reduction. He is burned at the stake, either as a "rank materialist" who claimed that everything is world, or as an "ecstatic mystic" who claimed that everything is God. This philosophy never admits that perhaps someone might not want to say that everything "is" something else. However, precisely the "what is?" question applied to "everything" is responsible for all the wrong answers. If it is worth expressing, then a clause with "is" as its main verb very must contain something new after the "is"—something that has not been said before. And so, if such "is" questions are put concerning God and the world, we must not be surprised when they evoke the "I" as answer. What else remains? For has not everything else, the world and God, already been disposed of before the "is"? And this is true also when the pantheist and his associate the mystic discover that the world and man are of divine "essence," or when the other firm of Messrs. Materialist and Atheist establishes that man is only a sport of "Nature," and God nothing but a reflection of it.

The truth of the matter is that these three first and last subjects of all philosophizing are like onions, and—pare them down to the ultimate shred—you will find nothing but layer on layer, and never anything "entirely different." It is only thinking that is driven into a labyrinth through the alienating power of the little word "is," which replaces one thing by another. But experience, no matter how deeply it probes, will find only the human in man, the worldly in the world, and the godly in God. And it will find the godly only in God, the worldly only in the world, and the human only in man. Is this, then, the *finis philosophiae?* If it were, so much the worse for philosophy! I do not think it is so bad as that. More likely, this very point, where traditional philosophy comes to the end of its way of thinking, is the beginning of philosophy based on experience [*erfahrende Philosophie*]. . . .

The question as to the essence of things can produce nothing but tautological answers. Burrow down and still further down, and God will still be only godly, man only human, and the world only worldly. And this holds equally for all three terms. The concept of God is by no means an exception. God as a *concept* is no more remote than the concepts of man and of the world. On the other hand, the essence of man and the essence of the world are no easier to understand than the essence of God. We know equally much—or equally little—about each of them; we know everything and nothing. If we take each separately, we have exact knowledge, the immediate knowledge of experience, of what God, man, and the world are. If we did not know, how could we talk about it, and—above all—how could we reduce two of these three substances to the third, or deny the possibility of the other two reductions? And we certainly do not know through any knowledge gained from that thinking which maliciously replaces one thing by another, what else may be the nature of God, the world, and man. For if we did so know, how then could immediate knowledge still persist strong enough to impel us to raise this question over and over, and to repeat our attempts at reduction! Ghosts vanish at the cockcrow of knowledge. These ghosts never vanish. Our assumption that one of these essences could be closer, the other remoter from us, rests on a confusion between the *essence* and the *reality* of God, world, and man—a confusion closely related to the misapplication of meaningless words "immanent" and "transcendent." Between God, world, and man there can indeed be nearness and distance, approach and withdrawal, but these do not take shape as permanent qualities in the sense that God, for instance, must be a transcendent being. So far as their essence is concerned, God, the world, and man are all equally transcendent in regard to each other, and as to their reality, we cannot say what they "are," only—but this belongs to a later chapter.

What do we know of them beyond and in between this "everything" and "nothing"? We do at any rate know something, the something we mean by the words godly, human, and worldly. For in using these we mean definite things, one of which cannot be mistaken for the other. Just what do we mean? Where shall we find the three essences as unreal and at the same time as immediate as these three adjectives which keep them thoroughly apart seem to imply?

Where are such forms [*Gestalten*] that have essence yet lack truth, life, or reality, to be found? Where is there a God who is not the true one, and not real, a world not living and not true, and human beings neither real nor alive; forms, each of which does not know and does not want to know anything about the other two? In other words, forms that do not occupy the same space with what we call our reality, our truth, our life, and yet hover over everything that goes on within that space? If the reader will recall his Spengler,[1] he can give his own answer. Spengler's Apollonian culture is concerned with just those gods, worlds, and men that we are speaking of. Spengler's concept of the Euclidean accurately designates the separation in essence, the "transcendence" with relation to one another, which we have here described. Only that Spengler, as always, interprets falsely what he sees correctly.

The mythical Olympus, the plastic cosmos, and the hero of tragedy are not done away with just because they are have-beens. In the strict sense of the word they never "have been" at all. For when the man of ancient Greece prayed, his prayers were certainly not heard by Zeus or Apollo, but obviously by God. Nor did the Greek live in the cosmos. He lived in the created world, whose sun is our sun and shone for Homer as it does for us. And this Greek was, moreover, no hero of Attic tragedy; he was a poor human being, even as you and I. Yet in spite of the fact that these three forms never were real, they are the premise of our

---

[1] The reference is to the definition of culture in *Decline of the West*, by Oswald Spengler, the German philosopher of history.

reality. God is as much alive as the gods of mythology. The created world is as real, and as little mere appearance, as the plastic, finite pales which the Greek thought he was inhabiting, or which as a political being he wished to inhabit, and in his capacity of artist had created around himself. The man to whom God speaks is just as much the true man, just as far from being a mere husk filled with ideals as is the tragic hero stubbornly defying fate. The spiritual forms which, in world history, were isolated only here, only in Spengler's "Apollonian culture," so becoming visible, are present in all life as its secret and invisible premises, regardless of whether it has entered visibly into history, or remained unlimned. That is the character of classical antiquity. . . .

Paganism is not, indeed, the mere bugbear that philosophers of religion make use of to terrorize adults, a role in which the orthodoxy of former centuries cast it. Paganism is no more, no less than truth itself, but truth reduced to its elements, invisible and unrevealed truth. So that whenever paganism sets out to represent the whole instead of an element, the form instead of the invisible, revelation instead of the unrevealed, it becomes a lie. But as an element and the unrevealed contained in the whole, the visible, the revealed, it is everlasting. Just as everlasting as the great objects, the "substances" of thought, in real, unobjective, and unsubstantial experience.

For experience knows nothing of objects. It remembers, it senses, it hopes, and it fears. One might perhaps understand the content of memory by taking it as an object; this would be then a matter of understanding, and no longer the content of memory itself. For I do not remember the content as *my* object. It is only a prejudice of the past three centuries that the "I" must play a part in all consciousness: that a tree cannot be seen by me unless my self sees it.

As a matter of fact, that ego of mine comes to the fore only —when it *comes* to the fore, when, for example, I must emphasize that I for one see the tree because someone else does not see it. In that case, my knowledge shows the tree certainly associated with me, but in any other case, I know only about the tree, and about nothing else. Philosophy's[2] claim that the self is omnipresent in all knowledge distorts the content of this consciousness. . . .

What the new philosophy, the new thinking, actually does is to employ the method of sound common sense as a method of scientific thinking. How is this sound common sense distinguished from the unsound that gets its teeth into something and will not let go until it has gulped the something in its entirety, in the same way as the old philosophy? Common sense waits, goes on living; it has no fixed idea; it knows: all in due time! This is the secret that constitutes the wisdom of the new philosophy, which instructs us to think what Goethe had in mind when he wrote his lines on "understanding in time":

> Why is the truth so woefully
> Removed? To depths of secret banned?
> None understands in time! If we
> But understood betimes, how bland
> The truth would be, how fair to see!
> How near and ready to our hand!

The new thinking, like the age-old thinking of sound common sense, knows that it cannot have cognition independent of time—though heretofore one of philosophy's boasts has been that is able to do this very thing. One cannot begin a conversation with the end, or a war with a

NB

---

[2] F. R. aims at German idealism only, not all philosophy.

peace treaty (as the pacifists would like), or life with death. Willy-nilly, actively or passively, one must await the given time; <u>one cannot skip a single moment</u>. At every moment, cognition is bound to that very moment and cannot make its past not passed, or its future not coming. This holds for everyday matters, and everyone grants it. Everyone knows that the physician, for instance, must consider his treatment bound up with the present, the beginning of his patient's illness with the past, and the death certificate with the future, and that it would be absurd of him to cling so stubbornly to the theory of timeless cognition as to exclude knowledge and experience in making his diagnosis, boldness and individuality in determining his therapy, and fear and hope in giving his prognosis. To cite another example: no one who is making a purchase seriously believes that what he sees, colored by his desire to buy, will look the same to him later when he regrets having bought it. Yet, this is equally true of great, ultimate matters that we think we behold only as something timeless. What God has done, what he does, what he will do; what has happened to the world and what will happen to it; what has happened to man and what he will do—all this cannot be disengaged from its connection with time. One cannot, for instance, perceive the coming kingdom of God as one perceives the created world, and one must not look upon creation as one looks upon the kingdom of the future; no more than one should allow the flash of present experience to char to a past, or wait for the future to bring it; for this lightning flash is always only in the present and to wait for it is the surest way to prevent it from striking. Similarly, a deed is a deed only while it is still in the offing. Once done, it is merely something that has happened, quite indistinguishable from anything else that has happened.

Thus the tenses of reality cannot be interchanged. Just

like every single happening, so reality as a whole has its present, its past, and its future, without which it cannot be, or—at any rate—cannot be *properly* known. Reality too has its past and its future, an everlasting past and an eternal future. To have cognition of God, the world, and man, is to know what they do or what is done to them in these tenses of reality, and to know what they do to one another or what is done to them by one another. And here we presuppose that these three have separate existence, for if they were not separate, they could not act upon one another. If in the "deepest core" the other were identical with myself, as Schopenhauer asserts, I could not love him, for I should be merely loving myself. If God were "within me," or if he were "only my loftier self" then this would be no more than an unnecessarily obscure formulation of an otherwise clear relationship. Above all, this God would hardly have anything to tell me since I know anyhow what my loftier self wishes to tell me. And if there were such a thing as a "godly" man, a theory proclaimed by some German professor fresh from the impact of Rabindranath Tagore's robe, this man would find himself barred from the path to God that is open to every truly human man. Such is the importance of the premise of separate existence, though I shall say no more about it now. For, within reality, and that is all we can experience, the separation is spanned, and what we experience is the experience of the spanning. God veils himself when we try to grasp him; man, our self, withdraws, and the world becomes a visible enigma. God, man, and the world reveal themselves only in their relations to one another, that is, in creation, revelation, and redemption. . . .

In the new thinking, the method of speech replaces the method of thinking maintained in all earlier philosophies.

Thinking is timeless and wants to be timeless. With one
stroke it would establish thousands of connections. It regards the last, the goal, as the first. Speech is bound to
time and nourished by time, and it neither can nor wants
to abandon this element. It does not know in advance just
where it will end. It takes its cues from others. In fact, it
lives by virtue of another's life, whether that other is the
one who listens to a story, answers in the course of a dialogue, or joins in a chorus; while thinking is always a solitary business, even when it is done in common by several
who philosophize together. For even then, the other is only
raising the objections I should raise myself, and this is the
reason why the great majority of philosophic dialogues—
including most of Plato's—are so tedious. In actual conversation, something happens.

I do not know in advance what the other person will say
to me, because I do not even know what I myself am going
to say. I do not even know whether I am going to say anything at all. Perhaps the other person will say the first word,
for in a true conversation this is usually the case; a glance
at the Gospels and the Socratic dialogues will show the
contrast. Usually it is Socrates who sets the conversation
going—going in the direction of philosophical discussion.
For the thinker knows his thoughts in advance, and his ex-
pounding them is merely a concession to what he regards
as the defectiveness of our means of communication. This
defectiveness is not due to our need of speech but to our
need of time. To require time means that we cannot anticipate, that we must wait for everything, that what is ours
depends on what is another's. All this is quite beyond the
comprehension of the thinking thinker, while it is valid for
the "speaking thinker."

I use the term "speaking thinker" for the new thinking.
Speaking thought is, of course, still a form of thinking, just

as the old thinking that depended solely on thinking could not go on without inner speech. The difference between the old and the new, the "logical" and the "grammatical" thinking, does not lie in the fact that one is silent while the other is audible, but in the fact that the latter needs another person, and takes time seriously—actually, these two things are identical. In the old philosophy, "thinking" means thinking for no one else and speaking to no one else (and here, if you prefer, you may substitute "everyone" or the well-known "all the world" for "no one"). But "speaking" means speaking to some one and thinking for some one. And this some one is always a quite definite some one, and he has not merely ears, like "all the world," but also a mouth.

Whatever the Star of Redemption can do to renew our ways of thinking is concentrated in this method. Ludwig Feuerbach was the first to discover it. Hermann Cohen's posthumous work reintroduced it to philosophy, though the author himself was not aware of its iconoclastic power. When I wrote the Star of Redemption, I was already familiar with the pertinent passages in Cohen's book, but their influence was not decisive for the genesis of my own work. The main influence was Eugen Rosenstock; a full year and a half before I began to write I had seen the rough draft of his now published *Angewandte Seelenkunde*. Since then, the new philosophy has been expounded in another work, besides the Star, in the first volume of Hans Ehrenberg's *Fichte*, a study of idealism written in the new form of the true, time-requiring dialogue. Victor von Weizsäcker's *Philosophie des Arztes* will appear shortly. Rudolf Ehrenberg's *Theoretische Biologie* is the first work to subordinate the doctrine of organic nature to the law of real, irreversible time. Martin Buber in his *I and Thou*, and Ferdinand Ebner in *Das Wort und die geistigen Realitäten*, written at exactly the same time as my book, approached the heart of the new thinking (I dealt with that in the middle section of the

Star) independently of the aforementioned books, and of each other. The notes to my Judah ha-Levi give instructive examples of the practical application of the new thinking. The epochal, largely unpublished works of Florens Christian Rang are founded in a precise and profound knowledge of all this.

close to Gutkind + Benjamin

With all these men, theological concerns have assisted the new thinking in coming to the fore. But this does not mean that the new thinking itself is theological, at least not in the sense in which the term has been used up to now, either with respect to the end or the means. The new thinking does not center on the so-called "religious problems," which it treats side by side with, or rather together with, the problems of logic, ethics, and aesthetics; nor has it anything in common with the attitude characteristic of thinking along theological lines, an attitude made up of attack and defense, and never quietly concentrated on the matter in hand. If this is theology, it is, at any rate, no less new as theology than as philosophy. . . . Theology must not debase philosophy to play the part of a handmaid, yet the role of charwoman which philosophy has recently assigned to theology is just as humiliating. The true relationship of these two regenerated sciences is a sisterly one, and this must necessarily lead to the personal union of those who deal with them. Theological problems must be translated into human terms, and human problems brought into the pale of theology. The problem of the name of God, for example, is only part of the problem of the logic of names in general, and an aesthetics that is not concerned with whether artists may attain salvation is an agreeable but incomplete form of scholarly investigation.

God did not, after all, create religion; he created the world. And when he reveals himself, that world not only persists all around us but is more created than ever. For

cf Barth

revelation does not at all destroy true paganism, the paganism of creation; it only accords it the miracle of return and renewal. Revelation is always present, and if it occurred in the past, then it was in that past which is the beginning of the history of mankind: it is the revelation granted to Adam. . . .

We have not yet touched on the two distinct historical manifestations of revelation, on Judaism and its antipodal offspring, Christianity. The new thinking is Jewish or Christian thinking only because and to the extent that these renew the "revelation granted to Adam." On the other hand, because and to the extent that paganism in its historic forms has forgotten or denied this revelation to Adam (who was no more pagan than he was Jewish or Christian), to this extent historic paganism, hardened as it is into a form of its own, is not in the least perennial. Its very independence and rigid form debar it from true reality. It is quite justified that the temples of the gods have crumbled, and their images stand in museums. The part of their service which was governed by prescribed rites may have been nothing but stupendous error, yet the prayers that rose to the gods from a heart in torment, the tears in the eyes of the Carthaginian father offering his son up to Molech— these cannot have remained unheard and unseen. Did God wait for Mount Sinai or, perhaps, Golgotha? No paths that lead from Sinai and Golgotha are guaranteed to lead to him, but neither can he possibly have failed to come to one who sought him on the trails skirting Olympus. There is no temple built so close to him as to give man reassurance in its closeness, and none is so far from him as to make it too difficult for man's hand to reach. There is no direction from which it would not be possible for him to come, and none from which he must come; no block of wood in which he may not once take up his dwelling, and no psalm of David that will always reach his ear.

Judaism and Christianity have a peculiar position in common: even after having become a religion, they find in themselves the impulse to overcome the fixity of a religious institution, and to return to the open field of reality. All historical religions are "founded." Only Judaism and Christianity are not founded religions. Originally they were something quite "unreligious," the one a fact, the other an event. They were surrounded by all kinds of religion, but they themselves would have been dumbfounded to be taken for religions. It is their parody Islam that is a religion from its very start, and never aims to be anything else; it is a deliberately founded religion. . . .

pace
Gutkind

Judaism and Christianity are the two eternal dials for the week- and year-hand of time, time that is constantly being renewed. In them, in their year, the course of world-time, which cannot be imaged forth but only experienced and told, takes shape as an image. In their God, their world and their man, the secret of God, of the world and of man, which can only be experienced but not expressed in the course of life, can be expressed. We do not know what God "is," what the world or what man "is." We only know what they do or what is done to them. But we do know quite accurately what the Jewish or Christian God, the Jewish or Christian world, the Jewish or Christian man, look like. In place of existing substances [*seiende Substanzen*] which are everlasting only in that they are the secret premises of ever renewed reality, we have forms [*Gestalten*] that eternally reflect a reality eternally renewed.[3]

In the Star of Redemption the picture of Judaism and Christianity is determined above all by the quest for an eternity that *exists*, hence by the task of fighting the danger of interpreting the new thinking in the sense (or rather non-sense) of tendencies directed toward a "philosophy of

---

[3] The third book of the Star of Redemption discusses these "forms," Judaism and Christianity.

life" or other irrational goals. In our day and age, all those who are clever enough to avoid the jaws of the Scylla of idealism seem to be drawn into the dark whirlpool of this Charybdis. In both cases, Judaism and Christianity, the picture is not beholden to the ways in which they interpret themselves; in Judaism it does not proceed from the Law, in Christianity it does not proceed from Faith: but in both, from the external, visible forms by whose means they wrest their eternity from time; in Judaism from the fact of the Jewish people, in Christianity from the event on which the Christian community is founded, and only through these do Law and Faith become visible. And so here Judaism and Christianity are set both side by side and in contrast, on a sociological basis. This gives rise to a picture not quite fair to either of them, but which (taking this sacrifice into account) goes beyond the usual apologetics and polemics in the field—probably for the first time. . . .

There still exists the belief that all philosophy should begin with considerations that are part and parcel of a theory of knowledge. Actually, it may end with them. Kant, the originator of the epistemological bias, is—through his criticism—himself such an end, the end of the epoch in history which began with the natural science of the seventeenth century. His criticism is directly applicable only to the philosophy of that epoch. Copernicus pronounced man a mote of dust in the vast universe. Kant's own "Copernican turn of thought," which—to restore the equilibrium—sets man on the throne of that same universe, corresponds to the mote-of-dust idea much more precisely than he himself realized. But his excessive correction of the terrible humiliation Copernicus inflicted on man and his humanity has also been made at the cost of the human quality in man. All criticism follows upon performance. The drama critic will have little to say *before* it, no matter how clever he may be, for his criticism is not supposed to testify to what cleverness he had prior to the performance but to that which the performance evoked in him. Similarly, a theory of knowledge that precedes knowledge has no meaning. For all knowing —whenever anything is really known—is a unique act, and has its own method. Methodological speculation on history in general cannot replace an investigation based on the work of an individual historian any more than the opinion of a professor of literature on some drama will replace the newspaper criticism formulated under the immediate impression of the stage performance. In fact, methodological thought replaces such an investigation to an even slighter degree; for in the case of drama and performance, both are, at least, a matter of the same book, while—fortunately!— there is no "history in general." Now philosophy is governed by the same laws as every piece of scholarly work. Such work must approach its material with methods and instruments never before used in order to discover the secret of just this material, and it is only the student who allows the professor—instead of the material itself—to prescribe the method of approach. . . .

If something is to come out of knowledge, it means that —exactly as in the case of a cake—something has to be put into it. What was put into the Star of Redemption was, first of all, the experience of factuality that precedes all facts of real experience, factuality that forces thinking to employ (instead of its favorite term "actually") the little word "and," the basic word of all experience, the word the philosopher's tongue is not used to. God *and* the world *and* man! This "and" was the beginning of experience and so it must recur in the ultimate aspect of truth. For there must be an "and" within truth itself, within ultimate truth that can only be *one*. Unlike the truth of the philosophers, which is not allowed to know anything but itself, this truth must be truth for some one. If it is to be the one truth, it can be one only for the One, God. And that is why our truth must of necessity become manifold, and why "the" truth must be converted into "our" truth. Thus truth ceases to be what "is" true and becomes a verity that wants to be verified, realized in active life. This becomes the fundamental concept of this new theory of knowledge. This theory replaces the old theories of non-contradiction and objects, and introduces a dynamic for the old static concept of objectivity. Regarded from this new plane, hopelessly static truths like those of mathematics, which the old theory of knowledge took as its point of departure without really ever getting beyond that point, are on the limits (the inferior limits), just as rest is a limit case of motion. The higher and the highest truths can be conceived as truths only via the new thinking, which does not necessitate their being altered to fiction, postulates, or human desiderata. From those most unimportant truths, such as "two times two are four," on which people are apt to agree without making more than a minimum use of their brains (a little less for the multiplication table through ten, a little more for the theory of relativity), the way leads over those truths for which man is willing to pay, on to those that he cannot verify save at the cost of his life, and finally to those that cannot be verified until generations upon generations have given up their lives to that end.

But this messianic theory of knowledge that values truths according to what it has cost to verify them, and according to the bond they create among men, cannot lead beyond the two eternally irreconcilable hopes for the Messiah: the hope for one to come and the hope for one to return; it cannot lead beyond the "and" of these final efforts in behalf of truth. Beyond this, only God can verify the truth, and for him only is there only one truth. Earthly truth still continues to be split, as split as extra-devine factuality, as the original facts: world and man, which—along with the "and"—return in the ultimate facts of Judaism and Christianity, as the world of Law and the Faith of man, as the Law of the world and the man of Faith. . . .

The reader has been denied what he asks and what, after all, he has a right to ask: a slogan under which to bury whatever he has learned about the new thinking in the cemetary of his general education. It was not from ill will that I failed to give him that slogan, but because I really don't know any. It is true that the work in which I have tried to expound the new thinking attacks certain slogans with an animus that goes far beyond any general animus of mine against *isms* of all sorts. But must I, therefore, allow the book to be tagged with the usual opposites of those *isms*? How can I? The designation I would soonest accept would be that of absolute empiricism;[4] this at least covers the attitude of the new thinking in all three areas: the primordial world of the idea, the world of reality, and the transcendental world of truth; the attitude that claims to know nothing more of the divine than what it has experienced— but to know this really, in the teeth of philosophy, which may brand this knowledge as "beyond" the "possible" experience; and nothing more of terrestrial matters than it has experienced—but nothing, although philosophy may laud it as a knowledge "anterior" to all "possible" experience. Such faith in experience might constitute the formulable element in the new thinking, if the aforementioned slogan didn't constitute in itself one of those formulations which, precisely because they come from the author, strike

[4] This term is suggested by the philosophy of Schelling.

the reader as on the one hand not only simple but too simple, and on the other, more difficult than the book itself. Both are inevitable. The greatest of the Jewish poets [Judah ha-Levi] knew the former when he made the sage answer the heathen king [the Kuzari] thus: "My words are too difficult for you, and that is why they seem too simple to you." And the greatest of the German poets knew the latter when he made Mephistopheles answer Faust's eager words, "There many riddles will be solved," with, "But many riddles will also be propounded."

[From *Das neue Denken* ("The New Thinking"), supplementary notes to the Star of Redemption. *Kleinere Schriften*, pp. 377-398]   Feb 1925

4.   Between Philosophy and Theology

From the Star of Redemption

Is it possible, still, to call this new thinking science? Can the term science be applied to a method that surveys each thing by itself, in its countless relations and from its multiple perspectives? Shall a survey whose unity can at best reside within the surveyer—and how dubious is even that! —still be passed off as science? We too must ask this question, as must, with considerable embarrassment, everyone who has been watching either the philosophical or the scientific aspect get the worst of it in current trends in the field of philosophy. Here a need of philosophy becomes manifest which philosophy obviously cannot satisfy alone and unaided. If she is not to sacrifice her new concept (and how can she, since she owes her survival, beyond the critical point of solving her original problem, to this concept and to it alone), then in her very capacity of science she must receive aid from elsewhere. She must cling to her new point of departure, to the subjective, extremely personal, unique self, absorbed in it itself and the standpoint of self, and still attain to the objectivity of science. Where is the bridge to connect extreme subjectivity, one might even say, deaf and blind subjectivity, with the luminous clearness of infinite objectivity?

The answer must anticipate developments and, even so, stop halfway, stop at mere suggestion: the theological concept of revelation must provide the bridge from the most subjective to the most objective. Man, as the recipient of revelation, as one who experiences the content of faith, contains both within himself. And whether the new philosophy admits it or not, such a man is the only thinker fit to deal with it. In order to free herself from aphorism, hence, in order to become scientific, philosophy today wants "theologians" to philosophize, theologians, to be sure, in a new sense of the word. For we shall see that the theologian whom philosophy requires in order to become scientific is a theologian who requires philosophy for the sake of his own honesty. What philosophy demands in the interests of objectivity will—for theology—prove to be a demand in the interests of subjectivity. The two are dependent on each other and thus produce a new type of theologian or philosopher, a type that stands between philosophy and theology. [*Der Stern der Erlösung*, II, 23-24]

5.   Believing Science
A Note[1]

If science and religion attempt to ignore each other while yet having knowledge of each other, then both are on shaky ground. There is only one truth. No honest man can pray to a God whose existence he denies as a scientist. And whoever

[1] This note supplemented a letter to Jacob Rosenheim on the unity of the Bible, in which F.R. had analyzed his attitude to orthodoxy and liberalism.

prays cannot at the same time deny God. This does not mean that the scientist is to discover God in his test tube or historical document. But it does mean that the content of test tube or historical document does not exist without God. The object of science is not God but the world. But God has created the world, and thus the object of science. God is transcendent but also transcendental with regard to science, that is, he makes it possible. Science does not have God for her own, yet could not be without him; he is not a subject of science, but science is subject to him.

This has a number of consequences. Helmholtz[2] has remarked that if an optician were to bring him an optical apparatus like the eye he would undoubtedly reject it. This remark could not have been made by a scientist with faith. Such a scientist, while perhaps not objecting to Helmholtz's criticism of the eye as an inadequate optical apparatus, would yet regard it as something more than a mechanism. To give a different kind of example: in his *History of England*, Ranke discusses Queen Mary's conflict between her filial and her conjugal affections, and remarks: "I believe in the fundamental truthfulness of men in the hours of great inner decisions." Ranke, the founder of the modern critical method, stresses the fact that he believes! What, then, would the attitude of the unbelieving historian be? Simply —unbelieving; just that!

It is not belief that is opposed to science. Believing science stands opposed to unbelieving science, or —since it is the proof of believing science that it includes the unbelieving while, conversely, believing science remains inaccessible to the unbelieving: believing-nonbelieving science is opposed to that which is narrowly unbelieving. And here the word "believing" does not signify a dogmatic tying oneself down, but having a hold which holds one's entire being. In

[2] Hermann Helmholtz (1821-1894), German physicist and physiologist.

this sense heretics can be believing and the ultra-orthodox unbelieving. Graetz's nationalist attitude toward Jewish history, for instance, is a believing one, while Isaac Breuer's juridical view of Jewish history is unbelieving. I use the word "view" deliberately; I think Breuer's actual attitude is more believing than his view.

[*Kleinere Schriften,* pp. 132-133]

6.   Life and Death

The river of life, even when it flows without impediment, flows always away from the sources that gave rise to it, on and on until it reaches the sea. It doesn't return on itself. Life is not eternal. It flows from birth toward death. Day follows day with wearisome monotony. Only the Holidays twine themselves together to form the circle of the year. Only through the Holidays does life experience the eternity of the river that returns to its source. Then life becomes eternal. Then there is no fatigue, no anxiety, no disappointment, for the end becomes the beginning, and the course is marked out. But the working-day is acquainted with weariness, anxiety, disappointment. And even though life is permitted to borrow new strength from the Holiday, from its ever renewed forces, it borrows it only to the end of new weariness, anxiety, and disappointment. The course ahead of it seems endless. Not, like the Holiday, going toward an ever young eternity, but endless toward its ultimate end. Life lives itself toward death.

In this fear of life, this desire to get out of the current, to stand on the bank, hides the wish to elude death. The man who in the full current of life is overcome by torpor has, like the Indian prince, seen Death waiting for him at the goal. So he steps aside from life. He would rather not live, if living means dying. He prefers death in life. He takes refuge from the necessity of death in the torpor of an artificial death. We have led him out of this torpor. But we cannot spare him death; no physician can do this. Indeed, by teaching him to live again we have taught him to go toward death. We have taught him to live his life, even though each step into life brings him closer to death.

Each step is attended by fear. It should not be so. Courage in facing life should silence the fear. Nor is this fear any longer a fear of life. This has been overcome. It is no longer a fear of the next step, for that step has been taken. It is rather anxiety about the step that has been taken. About the lived life which, now that it has been lived, belongs to death. Anxiety turns into disappointment.

This should not exist either. It should be kept down by faith in God. What does success mean to me? But disappointment is not doubt of success. Doubt has lost its force. It is rather disappointment with the event itself. The event should have been life, but instead it is death. Of what use is the knowledge that it will generate life? Disappointment turns into weariness.

This should not happen either. Our cosmic certitude should keep our eyes from closing. Nor do they really close. They keep looking out to see where the hands will grasp next, where the feet will step next. They are not weary of life. Everything still goes forward. They simply refuse to look behind them, for there Death can already be seen doing his work.

It is so difficult to know that all verification lies ahead, to know that only death will verify. That it is the ultimate proving ground of life. And that being able to live means being compelled to die. He who withdraws himself from life may think that he has withdrawn himself from death, but he has actually withdrawn only from life, and death, which he meant to elude, now surrounds him on all sides.

It has crept into his heart, which has been turned to stone. If he is restored to life he must acknowledge the dominion of death. He must no longer wish to live otherwise than deathward. Life becomes simple then, indeed, but only because it does not seek to elude death. And because it is ready at any moment to chant the dirge, yet equally ready to "advance over graves." And ready to know that at the end of the pathway of graves, a grave awaits it.

There is no cure for death. Not even health. But the healthy man has the strength to walk alive to his grave. The sick man invokes Death, and lets himself be carried on his back, half-dead from fear of him. Health experiences even Death only "at the right time." It is good friends with him, and knows that when he comes he will remove the rigid mask and take the flickering torch from the hands of his frightened, weary, disappointed brother, Life. He'll dash it on the ground and extinguish it, and only then under the skies that flame up for the first time when the torch has been extinguished, he'll enfold the swooning one in his arms and only then, when Life has closed its eloquent lips, he'll open his eternally silent mouth and say: "Do you recognize me? I am your brother."

[From *Das Büchlein vom gesunden und kranken Menschenverstand*]

II

RENAISSANCE OF JEWISH LEARNING
AND LIVING

1. On Being a Jewish Person

Introducing the Idea of a Jewish House of Study

The state of the world today may force us to postpone many desirable things, not for a better day but for a better century. It could hardly be asserted that the great urgency of the present moment is to organize the science of Judaism [*Wissenschaft des Judentums*] or to prompt both Jews and non-Jews to the endless writing of books on Jewish subjects. Books are not now the prime need of the day. But what we need more than ever, or at least as much as ever, are human beings—Jewish human beings, to use a catchword that should be cleansed of the partisan associations still clinging to it.

This term should not be taken in its (ostensibly loose) meaning, which is actually a very narrow one—it should not be taken in what I would call the petty-Jewish sense that has been assigned to it by exclusively political or even exclusively cultural Zionism. I mean it in a sense that though certainly including Zionism goes far beyond it. *The Jewish human being*—this does not mean a line drawn to separate us from other kinds of humanity. No dividing walls should rise here. A reality that only sheer stubbornness can deny shows that even within the individual many different spheres can touch or overlap. Yet sheer stubbornness and its counterpart, a cowardly renunciation, seem indeed to be the two main features of our present-day Jewish life.

Just as Jewishness does not know limitations inside the Jewish individual, so does it not limit that individual himself when he faces the outside world. On the contrary, it makes for his humanity. Strange as it may sound to the obtuse ears of the nationalist, being a Jew is no limiting barrier that cuts the Jew off from someone who is limited by being something else. The Jewish human being finds his limitation not in the Frenchman or German but only in another human being as unlimited as himself: the Christian or heathen. Only against them can he measure himself. Only in them does he find individuals who claim to be and are as all-embracing as himself, above and beyond all divisions of nationality and state, ability and character (for these too divide human beings from one another). His Judaism must, to the Jew, be no less comprehensive, no less all-pervasive, no less universal than Christianity is to the Christian human, or heathenism to the heathen humanist.

But how? Does not this mean the revival of that old song, already played to death a hundred years ago, about Judaism as a "religion," as a "creed," the old expedient of a century that tried to analyze the unity of the Jewish individual tidily into a "religion" for several hundred rabbis and a "creed" for several tens of thousands of respectable citizens? God keep us from putting that old cracked record on again— and was it ever intact? No, what we mean by Judaism, the Jewishness of the Jewish human being, is nothing that can be grasped in a "religious literature" or even in a "religious life"; nor can it be "entered" as one's "creed" in the civil registry of births, marriages, and deaths. The point is simply that it is no entity, no subject among other subjects, no one sphere of life among other spheres of life; it is not what the century of emancipation with its cultural mania wanted to reduce it to. It is something inside the individual that makes him a Jew, something infinitesimally small yet immeasurably large, his most impenetrable secret, yet evident in every gesture and every word—especially in the most spontaneous of them. The Jewishness I mean is no "literature." It can be grasped through neither the writing nor reading of books. It is not even—may all the contemporary-minded forgive me!—"undergone." It is only lived—and perhaps not even that. One *is* it.

One is Jewish. But of course Jewishness also exists in itself. And because it exists, because it already is here and was here before me and will remain when I am gone, therefore—but *only* therefore—it is also literature. Only for this reason are there problems of Jewish education. Literature is written for the sake only of those who are in process of development, and of that in each of us which is still developing. Hebrew, knowing no word for "reading" that does not mean "learning" as well, has given this, the secret of all literature, away. For it is a secret, though a quite open one, to these times of ours—obsessed and suffocated as they are by education—that books exist only to transmit that which has been achieved to those who are still developing. While that which is between the achieved and the developing, that which exists today, at this moment—life itself—needs no books. If I myself exist, why ask for something to "educate" me? But children come and ask; and the child in myself awakes—the child that doesn't as yet "exist" and doesn't "live"—and it asks and wants to be educated and to develop --into what? Into something living, into something that exists. But just here is where an end is put to the making of books.

For life stands between two periods of time, in the moment between the past and the future. The living moment itself puts an end to the making of books. Only, right next to it are the realms of book-writing, that is, the two realms of culture. In neither realm does the making of books ever come to an end. No end is ever reached in the exploration of the past, where the moment means nothing until it has been pinned down in the showcase of the past, by those who seek in the future only what can be imagined in terms of the past. And there is no end to the teaching of the coming generation by those who use the moment only for the purpose of opening by their own ardor the unawakened souls of the young, and who take from the past only what is teachable, only that which can find a place in the unlocked souls of the new generation. There is no end to learning, no end to education. Between these two burns the flame of the day, nourished by the limited fuel of the moment; but without its fire the future would remain sealed and without its illumination the past would remain invisible.

Jewish study and teaching, Jewish learning and education —they are dying out among us. This assertion may offend many ears, but in making it I feel myself one with the best among the young, and among the old too—thank goodness for the last, for otherwise I should not feel sure of myself. Since the time of Mendelssohn[1] and Zunz[2] our Jewish learning no longer has the courage to be itself, but instead runs at a respectful distance behind the learning of the "others." At a respectful distance—what others find an old story is so readily marveled at among ourselves as the very latest thing—at least by the small (and rightly so)

---

[1] Moses Mendelssohn (1729-1786), German Jewish philosopher.
[2] Leopold Zunz (1794-1886), founder of the critical study of Judaism.

circle of those who still pay any attention at all to this dance of shadows. What the sparrows chirp from the rooftops of intellectual Germany, still seems terrible heresy to us. Leaving the old ghetto, we have very quickly locked ourselves up in a new one. Only this time we do not want to admit it to ourselves. And this time we occupy ourselves with a learning that is just as little German and just as little Jewish as—well, as, for example, the "German" surnames our grandfathers adopted in the first dizziness of emancipation.

The situation is no better with respect to teaching. . . . The trend toward conversion which every year takes away the best from among us, and not—as is so often and falsely asserted—the worst, can be blamed on our religious instruction. Max Brod's verses on this subject in his great poem "To the Baptized Jews" are as true as prose. Certainly the individual is usually guiltless. Everything is connected with everything else in these matters. We have no teachers because we have no teaching profession; we have no teaching profession because we have no scholars; and we have no scholars because we have no learning. Teaching and study have both deteriorated. And they have done so because we lack that which gives animation to both science and education—life itself.

Life. A void, unfilled for over a century, yawns between the two realms of culture with all the endless making of books that goes on in them. Emancipated Jewry lacks a platform of Jewish life upon which the bookless present can come into its own. Up to the time of emancipation, such a platform was provided by existence within the bounds of old Jewish law and in the Jewish home and synagogal service. Emancipation shattered this platform. True, all three parts exist still, but because they are now only parts, they

218

are no longer what they were when they were joined together—the single platform of a real and contemporaneously lived life, which learning and education had but to serve and from which they drew their greatest strength.

Wherever the Law is still kept among Western Jewry it is no longer a living "Jewishness," one that while largely based on legal paragraphs, was taken naturally and as a matter of course. This sort of Judaism has acquired a polemical point that quite contrary to any original intent—is turned, not against the outsider, but mainly against the large majority of those within Jewry who no longer keep the Law. Today the Law brings out more conspicuously the difference between Jew and Jew than between Jew and Gentile.

Just as the Law, wrenched from its unity with home and worship, is no longer what it once was, so the two other planks of the platform are not what they used to be. And thus the Jewish home, wherever it is still maintained intact, is no longer the heart from which the bloodstream of all Jewish life is pumped, and to which it returns. Slowly but surely the home has lost its dominating position in Jewish existence. Life comes from outside and makes its own demands. The Jewish home can and probably will try to assert itself against the outside world, but the most it can still do is maintain itself. The unity between home and occupation has been destroyed beyond hope; and even the strictest Jewish orthodoxy is forced to initiate its pupils in two different worlds of culture, and to exaggerate the quite new and positive importance of the opposition between Torah and *derekh eretz*,[3] which was of so little significance for the old Judaism. And thus the home has become at best but "one thing" in life, with "another thing" by the side of it, and *outside* it. That "other thing"—one's occupation,

[3] Torah combined with "general culture"; educational principle of neo-orthodoxy in Germany.

one's public activity—is no longer the natural radiation of the home into the outside world; it obeys requirements and laws of its own. The home no longer binds Jewish life into a unity.

And finally there is the synagogue. Thence at least a stream of Jewish life still seems to flow, and though it is pitifully thin it does trickle through the modern Jew even if it does not wash over and around him. The most assimilated assimilationist does as a rule still take some part in its life, be it but for an hour's memorial service, or for his marriage, or at least for his funeral. Those who know and have perhaps experienced personally what forces still slumber in a mere Yom Kippur Jewishness—which many have held on to as the only coin, in an inherited fortune, that still retains its full value—will be careful not to speak disparagingly of the synagogue. But for the same reason that the Jewish home and Law cannot become what they once were, the synagogue cannot become what it once was for our collective existence.

Even if it were possible—and I think it is!—gradually to restore the synagogue's connection with the whole of life out of the small remnant of it which is all that many of us have left, the restored connection would be with a whole that is no longer a whole. For the synagogue no longer acts as a member completing the body of a living life. The beadle no longer knocks at house doors to summon us to *shul*. How many synagogues still have a study room with the heavy folios of the Talmud and its commentaries right next to the room of worship? The synagogue has become, quite in keeping with the spirit of the culture-obsessed, pigeonholing nineteenth century, a "place of religious edification" (or at least it claims to have become this). "Religion," to which life has denied a real place—and rightly, for life rightly rejects such lifeless, partial demands—seeks a safe, and quiet little corner. And it is indeed a little corner: life flows past it unconcerned. Nor can the synagogue, either, do what the Law and the home cannot—give Jewry a platform of Jewish life.

What, then, holds or has held us together since the dawn of emancipation? In what does the community of our contemporary life show itself, that community which alone can lead from the past to a living future? The answer is frightening. Since the beginning of emancipation only one thing has unified the German Jews in a so-called "Jewish life": emancipation itself, the Jewish struggle for equal rights. This alone covers all German Jews, and this alone covers Jews only. From this alone, therefore, those contemporary impulses will have to come which will open up the past to the seeking eyes of the student, and open the future to the capacity for leadership of a determined will. Everyone knows what the true situation is. Here, really, is the final reason why our Jewish scholarship and our Jewish education are in such a bad way. This struggle for equal rights—civil as well as social—has been the only actual "stimulant" our scholarship and our education have got from real life. Which is why neither the one nor the other has been able to free itself from the blinkers of apologetics. Instead of feeling and teaching the enjoyment of that which is ours, and which characterizes us, they have again and again tried but to excuse it. And so we have come to our present pass.

Those who want to work for the moment, for today, without shifting the main burden to an uncertain tomorrow, must take the Jewish individual seriously, here and now, as he is in his wholeness.

But how is this to be done? By beginning modestly—the only way one can begin with very large things that, one feels sure, must be all-inclusive, or else have no existence. What is intended to be of limited scope can be carried out according to a limited, clearly outlined plan—it can be "organized." The unlimited cannot be attained by organization. That which is distant can be reached only through that which is nearest at the moment. Any "plan" is wrong to begin with—simply because it is a plan. The highest things cannot be planned; for them, readiness is everything. Readiness is the one thing we can offer to the Jewish individual within us, the individual we aim at. Only the first gentle push of the will—and "will" is almost too strong a word—that first quite gentle push we give ourselves when in the confusion of the world we once quietly say, "we Jews," and by that expression commit ourselves for the first time to the eternal pledge that, according to an old saying, makes every Jew responsible for every other Jew. Nothing more is assumed than the simple resolve to say once: "Nothing Jewish is alien to me"—and this is in itself hardly a resolve, scarcely anything more than a small impulse to look around oneself and into onself. What each will then see no one can venture to predict.

I will dare to predict only this much: that each will see the whole. For just as it is impossible to attain to the whole without modestly beginning with that which is nearest, so is it impossible for a person not to attain to the whole, the whole that is destined for him, if he has really found the strength to make that first simple and most modest beginning. It is necessary for him to free himself from those stupid claims that would impose Juda-"ism" on him as a canon of definite, circumscribed "Jewish duties" (vulgar orthodoxy), or "Jewish tasks" (vulgar Zionism), or—God forbid—"Jewish ideas" (vulgar liberalism). If he has prepared himself quite simply to have everything that happens to him, inwardly and outwardly, happen to him in a *Jewish way*—his vocation, his nationality, his marriage, and even, if that has to be, his Juda-"ism"—then he may be certain that with the simple assumption of that infinite "pledge" he will become in reality "wholly Jewish."

And there is indeed no other way to become completely Jewish; the Jewish human being arises in no other way. All recipes, whether Zionist, orthodox, or liberal, produce caricatures of men, that become more ridiculous the more closely the recipes are followed. And a caricature of a man is also a caricature of a Jew; for as a Jew one cannot separate the one from the other. There is one recipe alone that can make a person Jewish and hence—because he is a Jew and destined to a Jewish life—a full human being: that recipe is to have no recipe, as I have just tried to show in, I feel, rather inadequate words. Our fathers had a beautiful word for it that says everything: confidence.

Confidence is the word for a state of readiness that does not ask for recipes, and does not mouth perpetually, "What shall I do then?" and "How can I do that?" Confidence is not afraid of the day after tomorrow. It lives in the present, it crosses recklessly the threshold leading from today into tomorrow. Confidence knows only that which is nearest, and therefore it possesses the whole. Confidence walks straight ahead. And yet the street that loses itself in infinity for the fearful, rounds itself imperceptibly into a measurable and yet infinite circle for those who have confidence.

Thus the Jewish individual needs nothing but readiness. Those who would help him can give him nothing but the empty forms of preparedness, which he himself and only he may fill. Who gives him more gives him less. Only the empty vessels in which something can happen may be kept in readiness—"time" and "space." Really nothing more is needed—time to speak in, and space to speak in. This is all that can be "organized" in advance, and it is very little —next to nothing.

Our new Jewish periodicals, which in recent years have taken on more and more of the character of open forums, have sensed this need very subtly. Thus they, and especially Buber's *Der Jude*, which is the best among them, have become real forces in our life, perhaps even the most vital. The "Jewish adult education movement" [*Volkshochschul-Bewegung*]—a bad designation because it suggests an incorrect parallel with the movement for German adult education with its quite different aims—is the latest and perhaps most important movement among contemporary German Jews. But it must make clear to itself what it intends to do. Exploiting the big-city public's insatiable hunger for lectures, it can fill the enormous gaps in Jewish education by supplying what "religious" instruction neglected and what the universities failed to offer. It would probably have to offer as complete a series of courses as possible, a curriculum as encyclopedic as possible—in other words, an education. Given things as they are, however, and despite the best of intentions—which this movement, in contrast to our degenerated system of religious instruction, certainly has—it would become merely a substitute in the long run for something that should normally be offered elsewhere but cannot because the living force, the center and germ cell of a Jewish life, is wanting. Only in such a life the endless book world of education could find its end; here, too, a new, bookless, start could be made.

But the movement in question might try to become this very center of a Jewish life. It might try to become the form for such a life, but certainly only the first, empty, immediate form. It would try to be a beginning. Instead of confronting the seeker of knowledge with a planned whole, to be entered step by step, it would keep itself a mere modest beginning, the mere opportunity to make a beginning. At a university the student is faced with the edifice of a science that is complete in general outline and only needs development in detail; it lies outside the student, and he must enter it and make himself at home in it. This movement, however, would begin with its own bare beginnings, which would be simply a space to speak in and time in which to speak.

Nothing more? Yes, nothing more. Have "confidence" for once. Renounce all plans. Wait. People will appear who prove by the very fact of their coming to the discussion room of a school of Jewish adult education (will someone suggest a better word?) that the Jewish human being is alive in them. Otherwise, they would not come. To begin with, don't offer them anything. Listen. And words will come to the listener, and they will join together and form desires. And desires are the messengers of confidence. Desires that join and men that join together: Jews—and an attempt is made to supply them with what they ask for. This too will be done modestly. For who knows whether desires such as these—real, spontaneous desires, not artificially nurtured by some scheme of education—can be satisfied? But those who know how to listen to real wishes may also know perhaps how to point out the desired way. This will be the hardest task of all. For the teacher able to satisfy such spontaneous desires cannot be a teacher according to a plan; he must be much more and much less, a master and at the same time a pupil. It will not be enough that he himself knows or that he himself can teach. He must be capable of something quite different—he himself must be able to "desire." He who can desire must be the teacher here. The teachers will be discovered in the same discussion room and the same discussion period as the students. And in the same discussion hour the same person may be heard as both master and student. In fact, only when this happens will it become certain that a person is qualified to teach.

It is essential that the discussion place be a single room—without a waiting room. The discussion must be "public." Those who come can wait in the discussion room itself. They can wait until the moment comes for them to join in. The discussion should become a conversation. Anyone who wants to continue the conversation with a single person can make an appointment for some later time. The discussion period should bring everybody together. For it brings people to each other on the basis of what they all have in common—the consciousness, no matter how rudimentary, no matter how obscured or concealed, of being a Jewish human being. That one can meet others on such a basis, that one can desire in common with others—this will be an experience, even if the desire remains unsatisfied. And this should be allowed for. Just as a lecture might not be given for want of an audience, so a desire may go unsatisfied for want of a teacher. This does not matter. The lecture that is announced but never given remains still-born because it remains the intention of but a single person; a common wish, however, that goes unsatisfied stays alive because it unites many.

With the discussion period open to the public, we are assured of this. The public aspect is not propitious to that mortal adversary who dogs the steps of our German Jewry—especially, let it be said, of its non-Zionist elements—the "stuffed shirt." All the "stuffed shirts" and those who aspire to become "stuffed shirts," all these young and old cases of senility, simply won't dare to enter the discussion room. Questions are asked there, but they want proclamations. Doubts are entertained there, but they want programs. Desires are expressed there, but they want demands. It is as unlikely that "stuffed shirts" will stray in among these students—unless they see the light and shed their starched shirt fronts—as it is that the lions of the lecture-platform will be heard among their teachers. There has been enough of speechmaking. The speaker's platform has been perverted into a false pulpit long enough among us—just punishment for a rabbinate that, for the most part, has been able at best to convert the pulpit into a speaker's platform. The voices of those who want these desirous students to desire them as teachers must lose the "true ring" of dead-sure conviction. For those who haven't had more than enough of this ring will hardly find their way to us.

But who else will? I can already hear voices saying: "How vague, how undefined, how cloudy." Let those who talk this way remain in the realm of the certain, the definite, in the bright light of the commonplaceness in which they feel so comfortable. It would be of little use to add to the sobriety they already possess an equally sober and ordinary "Judaism"—which is all they will get if they ask this way.

I can also hear the voices of those who say: "How little." Let those who talk this way remain undisturbed amid the "much" they possess. For it would be of little use to add to their collection of so many different things another little knickknack labeled: "my Jewishness"—which is all they will get if they ask this way.

But perhaps here and there someone will say longingly, "How beautiful," and think hesitantly, "If such a thing only existed—" I grant the doubts of such as *these*. Let them doubt, but let them come. Let them find out whether "such a thing exists." It depends on them and only on them whether it does exist. It depends on their power to wish, their urge to question, their courage to doubt. Among *them* are the students and the masters. Let them come. If they do not come, then Ecclesiastes is right for our generation too: of the making of many books there is no end.

[From *Bildung und kein Ende,* an open letter on education. *Kleinere Schriften,* pp. 79-93]

2. On Jewish Learning

From the Draft of the Address at the Opening of the
Freies Jüdisches Lehrhaus in Frankfort

Today, as the Lehrhaus opens its doors to carry on
the series of Jewish adult education courses which were
held here during the past winter and summer, I shall not
attempt to emulate the revered man[1] whose splendid address launched our last winter's activities by taking a subject
from the vast field of Jewish scholarship. Nor would you
expect it of me, younger and unknown as I am. I intend
only to give you an account of the task we have set ourselves and the goals we have in mind, and I shall try to
formulate these in the simplest of words.

Learning—there are by now, I should say, very few among
you unable to catch the curious note the word sounds, even
today, when it is used in a Jewish context. It is to a book,
the Book, that we owe our survival—that Book which we
use, not by accident, in the very form in which it has
existed for millenia: it is the only book of antiquity that is
still in living use as a scroll.[2] The learning of this book
became an affair of the people, filling the bounds of Jewish
life, completely. Everything was really within this learning
of the Book. There have been "outside books,"[3] but studying
them was looked upon as the first step toward heresy. Occasionally such "outside" elements—Aristotle, for example—
have been successfully naturalized. But in the past few
centuries the strength to do this would seem to have petered
out.

---

[1] Rabbi Nehemiah A. Nobel.
[2] The Torah scrolls that are read in synagogues are written in long-hand
on parchment scrolls.
[3] Apocrypha, "books outside the biblical canon." Here applied to all
"foreign" literature.

Then came the Emancipation. At one blow it vastly enlarged the intellectual horizons of thought and soon, very soon afterwards, of actual living. Jewish "studying" or "learning" has not been able to keep pace with this rapid extension. What is new is not so much the collapse of the outer barriers; even previously, while the ghetto had certainly sheltered the Jew, it had not shut him off. He moved beyond its bounds, and what the ghetto gave him was only peace, home, a home for his spirit. What is new, is not that the Jew's feet could now take him farther than ever before—in the Middle Ages the Jew was not an especially sedentary, but rather a comparatively mobile element of medieval society. The new feature is that the wanderer no longer returns at dusk. The gates of the ghetto no longer close behind him, allowing him to spend the night in solitary learning. To abandon the figure of speech—he finds his spiritual and intellectual home outside the Jewish world.

The old style of learning is helpless before this spiritual emigration. In vain have both Orthodoxy and Liberalism tried to expand into and fill the new domains. No matter how much Jewish Law was stretched, it lacked the power to encompass and assimiliate the life of the intellect and the spirit. The *mezuzah* may have still greeted one at the door, but the bookcase had, at best, a single Jewish corner. And Liberalism fared no better, even though it availed itself of the nimble air squadron of ideas rather than trying to master life by engaging it in hand-to-hand combat with the Law. There was nothing to be done apparently, except dilute the spirit of Judaism (or what passed for it) as much as possible in order to stake off the whole area of intellectual life; to fill it in the true sense was out of the question. High-sounding words were always on tap, words that the Judaism of old had had, but which it was chary of uttering for fear of dulling their edges with too frequent use. High sounding words, like "humanity," "idealism," and so forth, which those who mouthed them thought as encompassing the whole world. But the world resists such superficial embraces. It is impossible to assimiliate to Judaism a field of intellectual and spiritual life through constantly reiterating a catchword and then claiming it to have kinship with some Jewish concept or other. The problems of democracy, for instance, cannot be Judaized merely by referring to the sentence in the Torah: "One law and one ordinance shall be both for you and for the stranger that sojourneth with you" (Num. 15:16), nor those of socialism by citing certain social institutions or social programs in ancient Israel. If we insist on trying, so much the worse for us! For the great, the creative spirits in our midst, have never allowed themselves to be deceived. They have left us. They went everywhere, they found their own spiritual homes, and they created spiritual homes for others. The Book around which we once gathered stands forlorn in this world, and even for those who regard it as a beloved duty to return to it at regular intervals, such a return is nothing but a turning away from life, a turning one's back on life. Their world remains un-Jewish even when they still have a Jewish world to return to. "Learning"—the old form of maintaining the relationship between life and the Book —has failed.

Has it really? No, only in the old form. For down at heel as we are, we should not be a sign and a wonder among the peoples, we should not be the eternal people, if our very illness did not beget its own cure. It is now as it has always been. We draw new strength from the very circumstance that seemed to deal the death blow to "learning," from the desertion of our scholars to the realms of the alien knowledge of the "outside books," from the transformation of our erstwhile *talmide hakhamim*[4] into the instructors and pro-

---

[4] "Disciples of the wise"; religious scholars.

fessors of modern European universities. A new "learning" is about to be born—rather, it has been born.

It is a learning in reverse order. A learning that no longer starts from the Torah and leads into life, but the other way round: from life, from a world that knows nothing of the Law, or pretends to know nothing, back to the Torah. That is the sign of the time.

It is the sign of the time because it is the mark of the men of the time. There is no one today who is not alienated, or who does not contain within himself some small fraction of alienation. All of us to whom Judaism, to whom being a Jew, has again become the pivot of our lives—and I know that in saying this here I am not speaking for myself alone —we all know that in being Jews we must not give up anything, not renounce anything, but lead everything back to Judaism. From the periphery back to the center; from the outside, in.

This is a new sort of learning. A learning for which—in these days—he is the most apt who brings with him the maximum of what is alien. That is to say, *not* the man specializing in Jewish matters; or, if he happens to be such a specialist, he will succeed, not in the capacity of a specialist, but only as one who, too, is alienated, as one who is groping his way home.

It is not a matter of pointing out relations between what is Jewish and what is non-Jewish. There has been enough of that. It is not a matter of apologetics, but rather of finding the way back into the heart of our life. And of being confident that this heart is a Jewish heart. For we are Jews.

That sounds very simple. And so it is. It is really enough to gather together people of all sorts as teachers and students. Just glance at our prospectus. You will find, listed among others, a chemist, a physician, a historian, an artist, a politician. Two-thirds of the teachers are persons who, twenty or thirty years ago, in the only century when Jewish learning had become the monopoly of specialists, would have been denied the right of teaching in a Jewish House of Study. They have come together here as Jews. They have come together in order to "learn"—for Jewish "learning" includes Jewish "teaching." Whoever teaches here—and I believe I may say this in the name of all who are teaching here—knows that in teaching here he need sacrifice nothing of what he is. Whoever gathers—and all of us are "gatherers"—must seize upon that which is to be gathered wherever he finds it. And more than this: he must seize upon himself as well, wherever he may find himself. Were we to do otherwise, we should continue in the errors of a century and perpetuate the failure of that century: the most we could do would be to adorn life with a few "pearls of thought" from the Talmud or some other source, and—for the rest—leave it just as un-Jewish as we found it. But no: we take life as we find it. Our own life and the life of our students; and gradually (or, at times, suddenly) we carry this life from the periphery where we found it to the center. And we ourselves are carried only by a faith which certainly cannot be proved, the faith that this center can be nothing but a Jewish center.

This faith must remain without proof. It carries further than our word. For we hail from the periphery. The oneness of the center is not something that we possess clearly and unambiguously, not something we can be articulate about. Our fathers were better off in that respect. We are not so well off today. We must search for this oneness and have faith that we shall find it. Seen from the periphery, the center does not appear invariably the same. In fact, the center of the circle looks different from each point of the periphery. There are many ways that lead from the outside in. Nevertheless, the inside is oneness and harmony. In the final analysis, everyone here should be speaking about the same thing. And he who speaks as he should, will in the end really have spoken about exactly what everyone else has spoken about. Only the outset, only the point of departure, will be different for everyone.

So, and only so, will you be able to understand the divisions and contrasts in our prospectus.[5] The contrasts are put in solely for the purpose of being bridged. Today what is classical, historical, and modern in Judaism may be placed side by side, but this ought not to be so and in the future will not be so. It is up to us to discover the root-fibers of history in the classical phase, and its harvest in the modern. Whatever is genuinely Jewish must be all three simultaneously. Such has been the case in Judaism in all its productive periods. And we shall leave it to those who stand on the outside to consider contrasts such as that between the Torah and the Prophets, between Halakhah[6] and Haggadah,[7] between world and man, as real contrasts which cannot be reconciled. So far as we are concerned, which one of us is not certain that there could be no Torah without the prophetic powers of Moses, father of all prophets before him and after him? And—on the other hand—that there could be no prophets without the foundation of a Law and an order from which their prophecy derived its rule and measure? As for any contrast between Halakhah and Haggadah—every page of the Talmud shows the student that the two are inseparably intertwined, and every page of Jewish history confirms that the same minds and hearts are preoccupied with both: scholarly inquiry and meditation, legal decision *and* scriptural exegesis. And, finally, the Jewish world! Who could imagine that it would be possible to build it up without man, Jewish man! And what—in the

[5] The courses were divided into three parts: classical, historical, and modern Judaism.
[6] Halakhah refers to sections in the Talmud and rabbinic literature dealing with law.
[7] Haggadah (or Agada) refers to extra-legal, homiletical, ethical, religious, poetic, free interpretation of Scripture; and to legend.

long run—will become of Jewish man if, no matter where he lives, he is not surrounded by an atmosphere Jewish to some degree, by a Jewish world?

So, all of this hangs together. More than that: it is one and the same within itself, and as such it will be presented to you here. You should regard every individual aspect, every individual lecture or seminar you attend, as a part of the whole, which is offered to you only for the sake of the whole.

It is in this sense that now, at the opening of the new term in this hall, I bid you welcome. May the hours you spend here become hours of remembrance, but not in the stale sense of a dead piety that is so frequently the attitude toward Jewish matters. I mean hours of another kind of remembrance, an inner remembering, a turning from externals to that which is within, a turning that, believe me, will and must become for you a returning home. Turn into yourself, return home to your innermost self and to your innermost life.

[*Kleinere Schriften, pp.* 94-99]

3.   Teaching and Law
To Martin Buber

You know the problem I have at heart. Your eight lectures[1] touch on it over and over, and the eighth[2] finally moves it into the foreground. In the earlier lectures, the problem of Jewish law and practice is broached really only

---

[1] Buber, *Reden über des Judentum,* ("Lectures on Judaism"), Frankfort 1923. Buber has advocated a free, unbiased, approach to the classical Jewish teachings (*Lehre*) in their widest sense, not reduced to doctrines and basic concepts. F. R. pleads for a similar formula-free approach to Jewish law (*Gesetz*).

[2] *Herut:* a lecture on youth and religion.

for the sake of completeness. In the final two we feel that it has gained in urgency; if not for yourself, then certainly for your audience. Ultimately it joins with its twin problem, Jewish teachings; and the question: "What shall we do?" attaches to both a very real and immediate interest. But while the problem of teachings has heretofore gone through a visible development which has posed the question fully ripened at the precise moment of the answer, the question of the Law would seem in 1919 to be formulated much as it was in 1909. Because of the contrast, I make bold once again to present for revision the old solution. And even if here and now you can clarify the problem in theory only— that too will be of value. For that matter, what I myself have to say about it is not based on the experience of having reached the goal but on that of seeking and being on the way.

The development that, to my mind, your conception of the teachings has undergone, unfolds in what you call "invisible Judaism." Originally this is treated as a solid concept; something like prophecy versus legalism, or hasidism versus rabbinic opposition. In subsequent lectures, however—or am I mistaken?—it comes to resemble an intricate river system, in which the waters above ground seem everywhere to accompany those in subterranean depths. But in the final lecture, in the blazing light of the question that converts the problem into something actual, the picture changes: the visible streams and those underground are no longer distinguishable from one another, and whether those deeper tides are ever reached depends only on the hand that dips down to take. For you have formulated the goals of our Jewish learning in such a way that nothing Jewish may be excluded as alien. The distinctions between "essential" and "nonessential" which were forced upon us throughout the nineteenth century no longer hold. Now we must learn to recognize the hidden essence in the "nonessential"; and to accept the "essential" as we face it in the realities of Jewish life, where it turns out to be of the same shape as the "nonessential"; indeed, often deriving its shape from the latter.

But now you point to a new principle of selection, through which the vast subject matter of *learning* [*Lernstoff*] you unfurl can again become a *teaching* [*Lehre*], a principle more trustworthy than anyone has attempted to set up. You introduce the concept of inner power. For inner power is what you demand when you ask him who learns to stake his whole being for the learning, to make himself a link in the chain of tradition and thus become a chooser, not through his will but through his ability. We accept as teaching what enters us from out of the accumulated knowledge of the centuries in its apparent and, above all, in its real contradictions. We do not know in advance what is and is not Jewish teaching; when someone tries to tell us, we turn away in unbelief and anger. We discern in the story of Hillel and the heathen,[3] quoted *ad nauseam,* the smiling mockery of the sage, and it is not to his first words that we adhere, but to his final word: go and learn.

But in this wise, the teaching ceases to be something that can be learned, something "knowable" in the sense that it is an already existing "something," some definite subject matter. The subject matter must indeed be learned and known, and in a far wider sense than either the representatives of "Judaism on one foot" or those of traditional erudition and learning ever demanded. For now the outside books,"[4] the books from beyond the pale, and the "women's

[3] A heathen asked Hillel (1st cent.) to explain to him the entire Torah while he was standing on one foot. Hillel answered: "Do not unto your neighbor what you would not have him do unto you; this is the whole Torah; the rest is commentary; go and learn."

[4] Originally pertaining to Apocrypha, which were not to be read by a Jew.

books" that were considered beneath the dignity of that classical form of learning, are both included in the subject matter to be learned, included as equals. But all this that can and should be known is not really knowledge! All this that can and should be taught is not teaching! Teaching begins where the subject matter ceases to be subject matter and changes into inner power. . . .

The *way* to the teaching leads through what is "knowable"; at least that is the high road, the sole road one can in good faith recommend to every questioner; in good faith and even in the well-founded hope that he will find it.

Earlier centuries had already reduced the teachings to a genteel poverty, to a few fundamental concepts; it remained for the nineteenth to pursue this as a consistent method, with the utmost seriousness. You have liberated the teaching from this circumscribed sphere and, in so doing, removed us from the imminent danger of making our spiritual Judaism depend on whether or not it was possible for us to be followers of Kant.

And so it is all the more curious that, after liberating us and pointing the way to a new teaching, your answer to the other side of the question, the question concerning the Law: "What are we to do?"—that your answer should leave this Law in the shackles put upon it—as well as upon the teachings—by the nineteenth century. For is it really Jewish law with which you try to come to terms? and, not succeeding, on which you turn your back only to tell yourself and us who look to you for answer that our sole task must be to take cognizance of the Law with reverence—a reverence which can effect no practical difference in our lives or to our persons? Is that really Jewish law, the law of millennia, studied and lived, analyzed and rhapsodized, the law of everyday and of the day of death, petty and yet sublime, sober and yet woven in legend; a law which knows both the

fire of the Sabbath candle and that of the martyr's stake?
The law Akiba[5] planted and fenced in, and Aher[6] trampled
under, the cradle Spinoza hailed from, the ladder on which
the Baal Shem[7] ascended, the law that always rises beyond
itself, that can never be reached—and yet has always the
possibility of becoming Jewish life, of being expressed in
Jewish faces? Is the Law you speak of not rather the Law
of the Western orthodoxy of the past century?

Here too, to be sure, the limiting process of reducing to
formulas was not initiated in the nineteenth century. Just
as the formulas into which the liberalism of the reformers
wanted to crowd the Jewish spirit can be traced back to a
long line of antecedents, so too can one trace back the
reasons that S. R. Hirsch[8] gives to his *Yisroel-Mensch* for
keeping the Law. But no one before Hirsch and his followers ever seriously attempted to construct Jewish life on the
narrow base of these reasons. For did any Jew prior to this
really think—without having the question put to him—that
he was keeping the Law, and the Law him, only because
God imposed it upon Israel at Sinai? Actually faced by the
question, he might have thought of such an answer; and
the philosophers to whom the question has been put because they were supposedly "professional" thinkers, have
always been fond of giving this very reply.

From Mendelssohn on, our entire people has subjected
itself to the torture of this embarrassing questioning; the
Jewishness of every individual has squirmed on the needle
point of a "why." Certainly, it was high time for an archi-
tect to come and convert this foundation into a wall behind

[5] Talmudic master; 2nd cent.
[6] A heretic; contemporary of Rabbi Akiba.
[7] Founder of hasidism; 18th cent.
[8] Samson Raphael Hirsch (1808-1888), founder of neo-orthodoxy in Germany.

which the people, pressed with questions, could seek shelter. But for those living without questions, this reason for keeping the Law was only one among others and probably not the most cogent. No doubt the Torah, both written and oral was given Moses on Sinai but was it not created before the creation of the world?[9] Written against a background of shining fire in letters of somber flame? And was not the world created for its sake? And did not Adam's son Seth found the first House of Study for the teaching of the Torah? And did not the patriarchs keep the Law for half a millennium before Sinai? And—when it was finally given on Sinai—was it not given in all the seventy languages spoken in the world? It has 613 commandments, a number which, to begin with, mocks all endeavor to count what is countless, but a number which in itself (plus the two commandments heard directly from the lips of the Almighty) represents the numerical value of the word Torah and the sum of the days of the year and the joints in the body of man. Did not these 613 commandments of the Torah include everything that the scrutiny and penetration of later scholars, who "put to shame" our teacher Moses himself, discovered in the crownlets and tips of the letters? And everything that the industrious student could ever hope to discover there, in all future time? The Torah, which God himself learns day after day!

And can we really fancy that Israel kept this Law, this Torah, only because of the one "fact which excluded the possibility of delusion," that the six hundred thousand heard the voice of God on Sinai?[10] This "fact" certainly does play a part, but no greater part than all we have mentioned be-

---

[9] Here and in the following passages, F.R. refers to concepts of Jewish tradition as contained in the Talmud and the Midrash.
[10] A concept of medieval Jewish philosophers.

fore, and all that our ancestors perceived in every "today" of the Torah: that the souls of all generations to come stood on Sinai along with those six hundred thousand, and heard what they heard. For a Jewish consciousness that does not question and is not questioned, all this is as important as that "fact," and that "fact" no whit more important than these other considerations.

The "only" of orthodoxy should no more frighten us away from the Law than the "only" of liberalism, once you had taught us to see, could block our way to the *teaching*. Judaism includes these "onlies," but not in the sense of "on-lies." The problem of the Law cannot be dispatched by merely affirming or denying the pseudo-historical theory of its origin, or the pseudo-juristic theory of its power to obli-gate, theories which Hirsch's orthodoxy made the founda-tion of a rigid and narrow structure, unbeautiful despite its magnificence. Similarly as with teaching which cannot be dispatched by affirming or denying the pseudological theory of the unity of God or the pseudo-ethical theory of the love of one's neighbor, with which Geiger's[11] liberalism painted the façade of the new business or apartment house of eman-cipated Jewry. These are pseudo-historical, pseudo-juristic, pseudo-logical, pseudo-ethical motives: for a miracle does not constitute history, a people is not a juridical fact, martyr-dom is not an arithmetical problem, and love is not social. We can reach both the teachings and the Law only by realizing that we are still on the first lap of the way, and by taking every step upon it, ourselves. But what is this way to the Law?

What was it in the case of the teachings? It was a way that led through the entire realm of the knowable, but

[11] Abraham Geiger (1810-1874), leader of Jewish religious liberalism in Germany.

really *through* it; a way that was not content to touch upon a few heights which yielded a fine view, but struggled along where former eras had not thought it even worth while to blaze a trail and yet would not give him who had traveled its whole length the right to say that he had now arrived at the goal. Even such a one could say no more than that he had gone the whole way but that even for him the goal lay a step beyond—in pathlessness. Then why call it a way—a path? Does a path—any path—lead to pathlessness? What advantage has he who has gone the way over him who right at the outset ventured the leap, which must come in the end in any case? A very small advantage, which most people do not consider worth so much trouble, but which, we believe, justifies the utmost trouble: for only this laborious and aimless detour through knowable Judaism gives us the certainty that the ultimate leap, from that which we know to that which we need to know at any price, the leap to the teachings, leads to *Jewish* teachings.

Other nations do not feel this kind of need. When a member of one of the nations teaches, he is teaching out from amongst his people and toward his people, even if he has learned nothing. All he teaches becomes the possession of his people. For the nations have a face still in the making —each its own. None of them knows at birth just what it is to be; their faces are not molded while they are still in nature's lap.

But our people, the only one that did not originate from the womb of nature that bears nations, but—and this is unheard of!—was led forth "a nation from the midst of another nation" (Deut. 4:34)—our people was decreed a different fate. Its very birth became the great moment of its life, its mere being already harbored its destiny. Even "before it was formed," it was "known," like Jeremiah, its prophet. And so only he who remembers this determining origin can belong to it; while he who no longer can or will utter the new word he has to say "in the name of the original speaker," who refuses to be a link in the golden chain, no longer belongs to his people. And that is why this people must learn what is knowable as a condition for learning what is unknown, for making it his own.

All this holds also for the Law, for doing. Except that what is doable and even what is not doable yet must be done nonetheless, cannot be known like knowledge, but can only be done. But if, for the time being, we set aside this grave difference, the picture is the same. There the way led through all that is knowable; here it leads through all that is doable. . . .[12]

[From *Die Bauleute* ("The Builders"), an epistle on the Jewish law. *Kleinere Schriften*, pp. 107-113]

4. Divine and Human
A Letter[1]

I was startled by Nahum Glatzer's words that only the election of the people of Israel came from God, but that all the details of the Law came from man alone. I should have formulated this—and have actually done so to myself—in very much the same way, but when one hears one's own ideas uttered by someone else, they suddenly become problematic. Can we really draw so rigid a boundary between what is divine and what is human? We must keep in mind the obvious fact that a Law, that the Law as a whole, is

[12] The rest of the epistle discusses the ways by which a Jew can reach acceptance of the Law; this theme recurs in the following essay.

[1] In this letter F.R. reacts to a report on a series of discussions of Judaism at the Freies Jüdisches Lehrhaus. The letter was addressed to the "speakers in the Lehrhaus," Martin Goldner, Nahum Glatzer, Hans Epstein and Lotte Fürth.

the prerequisite for being chosen, the law whereby divine election is turned into human electing, and the passive state of a people being chosen and set apart is changed into the activity on the people's side of doing the deed which sets it apart. The only matter of doubt is whether or to what degree this Law originating in Israel's election coincides with the traditional Jewish law. But here our doubt must be genuine doubt, which willingly listens to reason and is as willing to be swayed to a "yes" as to a "no."

In my thinking about this, another differentiation occurred to me: the differentiation between what can be *stated* about God and what can be *experienced* about God. What can be stated objectively is only the very general formula "God exists." Experience, however, goes much further. What we can thus state—or even prove—about God is related to our possible "experience" in the same way that the empty announcement that two persons have married, or the showing of the marriage certificate, is related to the daily and hourly reality of this marriage. The reality cannot be communicated to a third person; it is no one's concern and yet it is the only thing that counts, and the objective statement of the fact of marriage would be meaningless without this most private, incommunicable reality. And so even the bare fact of marriage does not become real save where it leaves the sphere of what can be objectively stated and enters the secret pale of the festive days and anniversaries of private life.

It is exactly the same with what man experiences about God: it is incommunicable, and he who speaks of it makes himself ridiculous. Modesty must veil this aloneness-together. Yet everyone knows that though unutterable it is not a self-delusion (which a third person might well think it! It is your own fault if you run within striking distance of the psychologist's knife! Why did you blab?). Here, too, it is man's own experience—utterly inexpressible—that is the fulfillment and realization of utterable truth. All that is needed is—to undergo this experience.

And now I suggest that the matter of the details of the Law is analogous to the wealth of experiences, of which only that experience holds which is in the act of being undergone, and holds only for him who is undergoing it. Here too there is no rigid boundary in the relationship between God and man. Here too the only boundary lies between what can and what cannot be expressed. What can be expressed, what can be formulated in terms of theology, so that a Christian too could understand it as an "article of faith," is the connection between election and the Law. But an outsider, no matter how willing and sympathetic, can never be made to accept a single commandment as a "religious" demand. We wholly realize that general theological connection only when we cause it to come alive by fulfilling individual commandments, and transpose it from the objectivity of a theological truth to the "Thou" of the benediction: when he who is called to the reading of the Torah unites, in his benediction before and after the reading, thanks for the "national" election from among all the nations with thanks for the "religious" election to eternal life.

Here too the incomprehensibility from the viewpoint of religion, of the individual commandment does not constitute incomprehensibility per se. Just as a student of William James knows how to put every "religious experience" into the correct cubbyhole of the psychology of religion, and a Freudian student can analyze the experience into its elements of the old yet ever new story, so a student of Wellhausen[2] will trace every commandment back to its human,

---

[2] Julius Wellhausen (1844-1918), German Protestant theologian and Bible critic; he demonstrated an evolution within the original sources of the biblical writings.

folkloristic origin, and a student of Max Weber[3] derive it from the special structure of a people. Psychological analysis finds the solution to all enigmas in self-delusion, and historical sociology finds it in mass delusion. The Law is not understood as a commandment addressed by God to the people but as a soliloquy of the people. We know it differently, not always and not in all things, but again and again. For we know it only when—we *do*.

What do we know when we do? Certainly not that all of these historical and sociological explanations are false. But in the light of the doing, of the right doing in which we experience the reality of the Law, the explanations are of superficial and subsidiary importance. And, in the doing there is even less room for the converse wisdom (which in hours of weakness and emptiness we gladly clutch at for comfort), that these historical and sociological explanations may be true, and that Law is important because it alone guarantees the unity of the people in space and through time. Such timid insight lies behind and beneath the moment of doing, in which we experience just this moment; it is this experience of the theo-human reality of the commandment that permits us to pray: "Blessed art Thou. . . ."

In this immediacy we may not "express" God [*Gott aussprechen*], but rather address God [*Gott ansprechen*] in the individual commandment. For whoever seeks to express him will discover that he who cannot be expressed will become he who cannot be found. Only in the commandment can the voice of him who commands be heard. No matter how well the written word may fit in with our own thoughts, it cannot give us the faith that creation is completed, to the degree that we experience this by keeping the Sabbath, and

---

[3] Max Weber (1864-1920), German sociologist; founder of the so-called "sociology of religion."

inaugurating it with, "And the heaven and the earth were completed." Not that doing necessarily results in hearing and understanding. But one hears differently when one hears in the doing. All the days of the year Balaam's talking ass may be a mere fairy tale, but not on the Sabbath wherein this portion is read in the synagogue, when it speaks to me out of the open Torah. But if not a fairy tale, what then? I cannot say right now; if I should think about it today, when it is past, and try to say what it is, I should probably only utter the platitude that it is a fairy tale. But on that day, in that very hour, it is—well, certainly not a fairy tale, but that which is communicated to me provided I am able to fulfill the command of the hour, namely, to open my ears.

What can be expressed marks the beginning of our way. This is peculiar to our situation, which we must not ignore but see as clearly as possible. The situation of the Jew who never left the fold is different. Jacob Rosenheim once told a young man who confessed to him that he believed in nothing but loved every single commandment: "You need have no misgivings in keeping them all. But, for the time being, do not let yourself be called to the reading of the Torah." So far as we are concerned, just this *mitzvah* which leads from what can to what cannot be expressed is nearest our hearts, while many of the others are alien to us. Our way has led back to the whole, but we are still seeking the individual parts.

Thus, I do not think the boundary between the divine and the human is that between the whole and the parts, but that between something whose origin we recognize with a recognition which can be expressed, communicated, and formulated, and something else whose origin we also recognize and recognize just as clearly, but with a recognition which cannot be expressed and communicated. I should not venture to dub "human" any commandment whatsoever, just because it has not yet been vouchsafed me to say over it: "Blessed art *Thou*." Nor can I imagine the divine nature of the whole (which I, like you, believe in) in any other sense than of Rabbi Nobel's powerful five-minute sermon on God's appearing before Abraham's tent: "And *God* appeared to Abraham . . . and he lifted his eyes . . . and behold: three *men*."

Greeting to all four of you from your old friend who is very happy to see the signs of fresh life in the Lehrhaus.
[*Briefe*, pp. 518-521]

5. Sermonic Judaism
A Review of "Judentum," by E. B. Cohn

"Much preaching wearies the body" (Eccles. 12:12)

A great danger faces the modern rabbi, a danger that threatened his colleagues of yore only rarely and that does not exist to the same degree for the Christian clergyman of today. For the Catholic priest, in whose office the strictly circumscribed liturgical activity occupies by far the most important place, this danger exists hardly at all. But even the Protestant minister usually has in his individual pastoral care a counterbalance against his Sunday sermons, which, at that, are usually short. The rabbi, on the other hand, who was once, when his activities were limited to "learning" and judging, almost completely protected from the dangers of his "spiritual vocation," is now exposed to them more than all others. For he has left behind the sober air of daily learning; with whom, in truth, should he learn? Those who may turn to him are at best seekers, not men ready and prepared for learning in the old sense. And his pastoral activity, unlike that of the Protestant minister, is usually made exceedingly difficult by a certain social isolation in which he finds himself in relation to the most educated and respected circles of his congregation. Thus he is more or less dependent upon preaching, a preaching, incidentally, which he can direct only rarely to the large mass of his congregation, a preaching therefore without echo. And thus the vices of preaching grow in him without restraint. What are these vices?

Preaching is not speaking. The partner in conversation is missing. Consequently motivation and immediacy are lacking. As a result of this, the preacher lacks a criterion for the volume of his sound; in this he resembles the deaf, for he too hears no reply. These dangers now are increased by the lack of subjects. A text does not seem to the preacher to be interesting enough for his public—and in this he may be right. Therefore, he will abandon it as soon as possible and move into the apparently more interesting realms of timeliness. This ardently wooed timeliness, however, has the peculiarity that it seeks to be more truly timely than those who woo it ever imagine. Whoever loves it only for timeliness' sake, it rejects, demanding to be seized in its own timeliness, at its own time, out of the immediacy of an occasion; then and only then will it be conquered. The forced and artificial timeliness of the sermon, therefore, has always a touch of the outlived, of the antiquated. The preacher acts as if he had been asked. But none has asked him. And thus, also from the point of view of the content, all he says seems empty.

This he feels himself. Because of this feeling he yields to the worst temptation. He believes that he must throw himself into the abyss separating him from his audience. But he thereby does not come closer to the audience, he merely hurtles into the depth. His word becomes just then, when it should least be, play-acting. Not that he acts; but he pays the penalty for speaking *for* others after despairing of reaching them. Thus the word comes to a stop in front of the others, and instead of being heard it is looked upon. Thus, that which was to overcome the danger of false notes and superficial speech, itself presents the most terrible of dangers, the danger of the shameless pretense. Under such unlucky stars stands the profession, and we may therefore rightly blame them largely for the fact that this well-meant book did not turn out to be what the author had desired—and what this reviewer would desire along with him. . . .

The book begins with a passage entitled "Confession," which in three pages piles up such indescribably revolting stuff that no one could be blamed for closing the book right there in disgust. Let me hasten to add it would be a mistake, for the book is not so worthless as its beginning. The author himself unintentionally offers the reader an explanation for the horrible shamelessness of this "public confession" by quoting Jeremiah 20:9 as a motto for his book: "And if I say: 'I will not make mention of Him nor speak anymore in His name,' then there is in my heart as it were a burning fire shut up in my bones, and I weary myself to hold it in, but I cannot." That one can still read these words after having read the parody which here follows them testifies to their greatness. I do not mean to say that the "prophetic" is something so extraordinary; the differences between men before God are smaller than a science that has committed itself to the erroneous concept of "the religious genius" would have us believe; the difference between Jeremiah and his parodist lies in something much simpler—in the different situation. Jeremiah really had something to say which might have cost him life and limb; Emil Cohn puts the cloak of these words over his shoulders so as to convey to the reader that he is reading a most significant book; in this there is no other danger than, possibly, ridiculousness. . . .

Then follows the sermon against the wicked "times." Who has not heard it? This reviewer must confess that in face of the wild and repeated attack, he has for some time felt morally compelled to take his stand with the cruelly maltreated underdog; he professes to be a rationalist and materialist. In fear of being unjust, I solicited a friend's opinion and he writes me: "I further believe that Moses Mendelssohn did not live in vain, that railroads and telephones have not been invented in vain. My parents, grandparents, brothers and sisters and friends, all of whom belong to the era which is now unrolling, are as dear to me as my forebears of a thousand years ago and my descendants of a thousand years hence; or I should rather say I'd be glad to know that the forebears were, and the descendants will be, no worse than my contemporaries."

Corresponding to the public confession of the beginning is the public prayer of the end. The *ultima ratio* of the pulpit hero! Content: warm praise of the concluded book and a thrilling announcement of its continuation. Again, as in the case of the confession, let me spare the sensitivity of the reader by not quoting from this laundry list of a prayer. It is horrible.

And yet, this obviously derives from the habit of concluding the sermon with a prayer. As this case demonstrates, an exceedingly risky habit. I have known only one man who could do it, N. A. Nobel. With him it was no habit. Whatever was habit, routine, rabbinate in the bad sense, with him, stayed off the pulpit. When he stood there, the congregation was no ardently and vainly wooed audience: it existed for the sole purpose of carrying him upward. And he stood directly before the Countenance. Thus he could really speak; thus he could pray. We were no onlookers, but, rather, as much of his prayers as the words and letters. So he carried us along. . . .

[*Kleinere Schriften*, pp. 43-49]

III

ON THE SCRIPTURES
AND THEIR LANGUAGE

1. The Language of Faith

The German—and this includes the German within the Jew—can and will read the Bible in German, read it as Luther, Herder, Mendelssohn, read it; the Jew can understand it only in Hebrew. Yet while in the case of the Bible there do obtain certain possible parallelisms, insofar as it is a case of property common to both German and Jew, in the matter of Jewish prayer it is otherwise. Of the language of the Jewish prayer we may state quite categorically that it is untranslatable.

The biblical literature of antiquity is the fountainhead of all living Judaism: the talmudic-rabbinical literature of later ages constitutes its encyclopedia; and in the philosophical writings we see its subtlest sublimation; yet the sum and substance of the whole of historical Judaism, its handbook and memorial tablet, will ever be the Prayer Book: the Daily and the Festival, the Siddur and the Mahzor. He to whom these volumes are not a sealed book has more than grasped the "essence of Judaism." He is informed with it as with life itself; he has within him a "Jewish world."

[From *Zeit ists* ("It Is Time"), a treatise on Jewish education, addressed to Hermann Cohen. *Kleinere Schriften,* pp. 57-58]

2. The Function of Translation

I

The patron saint of the so-called "creative" translators of today is the renowned Professor Ulrich von Wilamowitz-Moellendorff of the University of Berlin. In his much applauded translations of Greek tragedies into the German of popular weeklies, he has revealed the aim he set himself. What he wanted—so he says—was to make Aeschylus more understandable to the reader of today than he was to his Greek contemporaries—a confession we have every reason to be grateful for. The work of our "creative" translators actually seems to aim precisely at this "making more understandable." They are so very anxious to give a helping hand to the poor unfortunate original. Now poetry does not happen to be so easy to understand as prose. This—it is rumored —is due to the poet's inability to be altogether articulate, just as the curious remoteness from life characteristic of Egyptian sculpture is said to have derived from the artist's inability to achieve realism.

There is nothing simpler and more rewarding than to correct these defects and fill out the gaps. This type of translator rejects the idea that what appears alien to us may owe this quality to its style; the very idea of considering the original style is displeasing to him. He focuses his ambition on giving us the masterpieces of the past and of foreign countries in "modern dress." But would the Apollo Belvedere really be improved by a cutaway and a stiff collar?

It is a gross misconception to believe that the translator, in order to fulfill his task, must adapt to German usage whatever is alien. If I were a merchant who had received an order from Turkey, I should send it to a translation bureau and expect that kind of translation. But if the communication from Turkey was a letter from a friend, the translation of such a bureau would no longer be adequate. And why? Because it would not be accurate? It would be just as accurate as the translation of the business letter. But that is not the point. It would be German enough; it would not, however, be sufficiently Turkish! I should not hear the man, his special tone, his cast of mind, his heartbeat. But ought this be expected? Is it not demanding the impossible of a language to ask it to reproduce an alien tone in all its alienness, in other words, not to adapt the foreign tongue to German, but German to the foreign tongue?

No, not the impossible but the indispensable, and not only in the work of translating. The creative aspect of translating can only manifest itself in the region of the creative aspect of speech itself.

The Germanizing of foreign material, such as in the business letter translated by a bureau, is achieved with the German already in existence. That is why this German is understandable, and why the translations of Mueller, Schulze, Cohn, and Wilamowitz are popular—a fact only envy could dispute. They translate into the language of a man—who has nothing to say! And since he has nothing to say, he makes no demands upon language. But a language on which no demands are made by those who speak it stiffens into a mere means of communication that can be supplanted by any kind of Esperanto.

Whoever has something to say, must say it in a new way. He will create his language, and when he has said his say, the face of the language will have changed. The translator makes himself a mouthpiece for the alien voice and transmits it across the chasm of space or time. If this alien voice has something to communicate, the language will be different from what it was before. This is the criterion for conscientious translating. It is certainly unthinkable that a language into which Shakespeare, Isaiah, Dante have been faithfully rendered, could have remained unchanged by this contact. The language will be rejuvenated by the translator as surely as if a genius had arisen in the language itself. Even more so! For the foreign poet does not merely infuse the new language with what he himself has to say. He brings the whole heritage of the spirit of his language to the new language, so that what happens is the renewal of the language not only through an alien person, but through the alien spirit of the original language.

That such a renewal of one language through another—through an alien language—is at all possible presupposes that just as a language has given birth to all who speak it, so all human expression, all alien tongues that ever have been or will be spoken, must be contained in it, at least in the germ. And exactly that is the case. All languages are virtually one. There is no trait in any one language which is not at least latent in every other, though it may appear only in dialects, in the vocabularies of trades and callings, or in the chatter of the nursery. The possibility and the function of translating, its can-be, may-be, and should-be, are based on this essential oneness of all languages, and on the command springing from that oneness that there shall be communication among all men.

We are able to translate because every language has the potentialities of every other; we are permitted to translate provided the translator can convert this possible into the corresponding actual, by cultivating the fallows of his own language; and we must translate, so that the day may come when there shall exist among languages the accord that can grow up out of all individual languages but never out of the empty spaces "between" them.

II

To translate means to serve two masters—something nobody can do. Hence—as is true of all things that in theory no one can do—it becomes, in practice, everyone's job.

Everyone must translate and everyone does translate. Whoever speaks is translating his thoughts for the comprehension he expects from the other, and not for an imaginary general "other" but for this particular other in front of him, whose eyes widen with eagerness or close with boredom, depending on whether or not his interest is aroused. The listener translates the words that strike his ear according to his lights and so—to express it concretely—into the language he himself uses. Everyone has his own language, or rather, everyone would have his own language if there were really such a thing as monologue (such as those logicians, the would-be monologicians, claim for themselves), if all speech were not really dialogue to begin with, and hence translation.

If then all speech is translation, the theoretical impossibility of translating can mean to us only what all such theoretical impossibilities come to mean in life itself: in the course of the "impossible" and necessary compromises which in their sequence make the stuff of life, this theoretical impossibility will give us the courage of a modesty which will then demand of the translation not anything impossible but simply whatever must be done. Thus, in speaking and listening, the "other" need not have my ears or my mouth— this would render unnecessary not only translation but also speaking and listening. And in the speaking and listening between nations, what is needed is neither a translation that is so far from being a translation as to be the original— this would eliminate the listening nation—nor one that is in effect a new original—this would eliminate the speaking nation. These could be desired only by a mad egoism intent on satisfying its own personal or national life and yearning to be in a desert surrounded oasis. Such an attitude is utterly out of harmony in a world created to be not a wilderness but a place to contain every kind of people. . . .

The spoken word may be accompanied by the written

for centuries, without turning into what we designate, rather strangely, as "literary language." The fact that something is written down gives rise to forms of speech adapted to the exigencies of writing; yet beyond that pale of life governed by the printed word speech remains free and creative. So a child may lose the habit of spontaneous speech while he is in the schoolroom, but chatter freely the moment he reaches home. The vitality of his langauge will not be yoked until he falls under the spell of reading, and this is likely to happen, at the very latest, when he begins to read the newspapers. From that time on he will require a special stimulus in order not to speak as he, or rather, as everyone, writes.

In the lives of whole peoples as well, the moment dawns when writing ceases to be a handmaid of language and becomes its mistress. This moment arrives when a body of content comprising the entire life of a people is formulated in writing, when, for the first time, a book appears that "everyone must really have read." From this point on language loses its ability to progress naively. Its path can no longer be determined by whatever it happens to run across. As it advances it must constantly look back to make sure that the point in question is still within the range of vision. But whoever glances back at frequent intervals will certainly walk more slowly than before, and analogously, from the epoch-making moment on, the tempo of development of a language actually slows up. . . .

In a certain sense, every great work in one language can be translated into another language only once. The history of translation shows typical phenomena. First there are a number of interlinear translations, with the modest aim of serving as trots, and free, "creative" renderings that seek to make accessible to the reader the meaning—or what the translator considers the meaning—of the text. . . .

Then, one day, a miracle happens and the spirits of the two languages mate. This does not strike like a bolt out of the blue. The time for such a *hieros gamos,* for such a Holy Wedding, is not ripe until a receptive people reaches out toward the wing-beat of an alien masterpiece with its own yearning and its own utterance, and when its receptiveness is no longer based on curiosity, interest, desire for education, or even aesthetic pleasure, but has become an integral part of the people's historical development. . . .

A good translator will convert the foreign book into something indigenous. This means specifically that the young will experience or be enabled to experience their own spiritual growing pains vicariously in this alien work. And all that is written is written only for the young. Adults have other things to do—better, or worse. . . .

Modern man is neither a believer nor an unbeliever. He believes and he doubts. And so he is nothing, but he is alive. Belief and unbelief "happen" to him and all that he is required to do is not run away from what is happening but make use of it once it has happened. This seems very simple when one has not entered the field of action, but it is actually so difficult that there is probably no one living who has always accomplished it, probably no one who has managed it on more than a very few, rare occasions.

Whoever lives in this way can approach the Bible only with a readiness to believe or not believe, but not with a circumscribed belief that he finds confirmed in it. Yet even this readiness of his must be uncircumscribed and unlimited. Everything, including the unbelievable, can enter the sphere of the believable. For him, the believable does not occur interspersed in not believable and hence unbelievable matter, like veins of metal in rock, nor is the one locked in the other like a kernel embedded in the husk. As a searchlight detaches from darkness now one section of the landscape and now another, and then leaves these again dimmed, so for such a man the days of his own life illumine the Scriptures, and in their quality of humanness permit him to recognize what is more than human, today at one point and tomorrow at another, nor can one day ever vouch for the next to yield a like experience. . . .

This humanness may anywhere become so translucid under the beam of a day of one's life, that it stands suddenly written in his innermost heart; and the divine in human inscription becomes as clear and actual to him for that one pulse beat as if—at that instant—he heard a voice calling to his heart. Not everything in the Scriptures belongs to him—neither today nor ever. But he knows that he belongs to everything in them, and it is only this readiness of his which, when it is directed toward the Scriptures, constitutes belief.

It is not apparent that the Scriptures must be read differently on the basis of such belief, and, therefore, transmitted differently from the way Martin Luther read and transmitted them? Luther reasoned that he must—on occasion—grant Hebrew a place in German, that he must expand his own language to accommodate Hebrew words in those passages that are concerned with the "instruction" and "solace of our conscience." Should not this same kind of reasoning beget new reverence for the word in us who do not know *what* words may, some day, yield instruction and solace, who believe that the hidden sources of instruction and solace may flow from every word in this book? And must not such reverence renew our reading, our understanding, and hence our translating?

Ever since about the middle of the eighteenth century a mass of scholarly controversy has been churning around the aim of emphasizing the literary and human aspect of the Scriptures. But this erudite quarrel oddly confused two questions: what does it mean? and, what did the writer mean to express?—a confusion that these same scholars would otherwise chide emphatically, say in the capacity of reviewers, and with good reason. Nevertheless, this movement has at least attained its critical goal: the Book is no longer surrounded by a golden halo. To conclude from this that it is not holy would be just as naive as attributing to the painters of old the conviction that St. Francis actually walked the earth with a metal ring around his head. What these painters did was to translate into the forms of their art legend's reports on the phenomena of radiance according to the testimony of eyewitnesses. When a contemporary artist paints this aureole of light in another way, or omits it altogether, we need not deduce a lesser faith on his part in the holiness of the saint. The desire to weld faith to the art forms of bygone eras is cheap evasion on the part of those who feel desperately uncomfortable at the mere thought that anyone of "our own time" could have faith at all.

Neither Luther's translation nor the work of any subsequent translator felt an inner obligation to translate out of a regard for the totality of human speech. This is likewise true for another aspect of the language, namely, its elements: the single word. Perhaps Luther did see the problem involved here more clearly than any subsequent translator. He evidences his grasp of it in an introduction to the Psalter,[1] where he comments illuminatingly on the Hebrew words of goodness, truth, and faith; and still more strikingly toward the end of his preface to the *German Psalter* where—disguising a deep seriousness as humor—he promises fifty gulden to any scholar or subtle spirit "who will give a true

---

[1] In the *Third Part of the Old Testament,* 1524-25.

and accurate translation into the German of the single word *heyn* occurring throughout the Scriptures." It is his word, the most intrinsically Lutheran word in the Hebrew lexicon, the word denoting "grace." This in itself, as well as the words cited just previously, proves once again what our investigation has shown throughout: that the dictates of faith determine down to the smallest detail any translation of the Scriptures. The hope springing from the renewal of faith that holds everything profane in the Scriptures (and is there anything not profane?) to be a shell out of which something holy, holy to me, may some day emerge, will also interpret this problem of literalness differently, more comprehensively. Such faith must accept Luther's injunction to "give a true and accurate translation of a given word occurring throughout the Scriptures" as mandatory for each and every word. . . .

I have already stated that all speaking is translating. The Scriptures constitute the first conversation of mankind, a conversation in which gaps of half and whole millennia occur between speech and response. Paul tried to find the answer to the question of the third chapter of Genesis by questioning the words of the twentieth chapter of Exodus. Augustine and Luther repeated his answer, but each added his own answer to it. The former replied with his theory of the *Civitas Dei,* the latter with his *Epistle to the Councilmen,* in which he requested the establishment of Christian schools. In every instance a new phase in this conversation is introduced by translation, translation into the language of tragedy, translation into the language of the *Corpus Juris,* and into that of the *Phenomenology of the Spirit.* No one knows when this conversation will come to an end, but then, no one knew when it began. And so it cannot be terminated by the peevishness, arrogance, or complacent cleverness of any man, but only by the will, the knowledge, and the wisdom of Him who wrought the beginning.

[Part one, from the Epilogue to *Judah ha-Levi*, pp. 153-155, or, *Kleinere Schriften*, pp. 201-203. Part two, from the essay *Die Schrift und Luther* ("Scripture and Luther's Translation"). *Kleinere Schriften*, pp. 141-166]

3. The Style of Medieval Poetry

Medieval Jewish poets in exile all disdain to ignore their being in exile. They might have ignored exile if—as with other poets—their poetry had allowed room to the world. But the world that surrounds them is exile, and so it must remain. The instant they should relinquish their attitude, and open themselves to the influx of the world, that world would become as home to them, would cease to be exile. This exiling of the environment is accomplished through the constant presence of the scriptural word, which places another reality in front of the realities surrounding us and demotes these to the status of mere semblance or, more precisely, parable.

It is not that the Scriptures are used as parable to illustrate the incidents of everyday life, but quite the other way round: these incidents serve to interpret the Scriptures and, in this sense, become parables.

Hence, the relationship is the exact reverse of what we suppose when we hear the expression "mosaic style." The mosaic is characteristic of epochs that produce immature writing. When Einhard[1] describes Charlemagne in words taken from Suetonius'[2] biography of Augustus, it is to project that emperor into the image of Augustus, to explain him with reference to Augustus—not vice versa. When a Jewish poet designates Christianity and Islam by Edom and

---

[1] Einhard (8th-9th cent.), Frankish secretary and biographer of Charlemagne.

[2] Suetonius (1st-2nd cent.), Roman historian; author of *Lives of the Caesars*.

Ishmael, he is not employing Scripture to comment on the present, but the present to comment on Scripture. What prompts this method is not callowness but rather over-ripeness. One is at no loss for a style of one's own; rather, one's style is so wholly one's own that the possibility of dropping into stylelessness never presents itself. Such a relationship to the written word does, of course, presuppose that this word is classical in content as well as in form, and that the classical traits of form and content are inextricably interwoven. The spirit in which Europeans quote provides a rough example. Whoever has listened to Englishmen quoting Shakespeare has certainly noted their inclination to quote the so-called "fine passages." Shakespeare, in the mouth of an Englishman, produces a distinctly "mosaic" effect. For while he quotes, he does not really identify himself with the poet. The modern Englishman's views on the world stem from the century of Cromwell, not of Shakespeare. But when an educated German quotes Goethe and Schiller, he is simultaneously quoting Kant, Fichte, Hegel—in other words, he believes in the essence of that which he is quoting; he is not quoting merely to embellish a social discourse. . . .

The medieval Jew marshals the happy unity of thought and speech in very great degree, and in an exclusiveness dearly paid for. It is not alone lofty thoughts that he casts into chiseled form; any thought that may legitimately call itself a thought moves toward such form. For him, quotation is not a decorative frill but the very wrap to the woof of what he has to say.

[From the Epilogue to *Judah ha-Levi*, pp. 161-162, or, *Kleinere Schriften*, pp. 210-211]

4. Classical and Modern Hebrew

A Review of a Translation Into the Hebrew of Spinoza's Ethics

Jacob Klatzkin, the well-known Zionist, and a disciple of Hermann Cohen, has published, simultaneously with a book in Hebrew on Spinoza, a Hebrew translation of the *Ethics*. The beautifully printed volume before us raises a number of ideas.

It is not the first time the *Ethics* has been translated into Hebrew. This great task was attempted more than fifty years ago by a follower of the Haskalah, the East European Jewish movement of enlightenment, which differed from the West European in that it was directed toward national culture, and hence toward Hebrew. But Klatzkin was the first to bring to the undertaking the prerequisite intellect, scholarship, and language. Klatzkin may therefore justly pride himself on the fact that every future investigator of the meaning of the *Ethics* will have to refer to his translation and to the commentary inherent in it, as in every translation.

Here the translation is a commentary in more than the usual sense. Biographers from the end of the seventeenth century down, and including the most recent one, the Jesuit Von Dunin-Borkowski, have probed for influences that the young Spinoza might have received from the Jewish philosophy of the Middle Ages on the one hand, and from the Kabbalah on the other—received and perhaps exploited for his *Ethics*. Klatzkin, the nationalist, with the ascetic austerity of the scholar, rejects the possiblity of such Jewish influences in the great renegade Jew. In lieu of the influence of ideas, he establishes certain very definite influences in point of language. One of these touches a quite central point, namely, the concept of the "idea"; and in its Spinozistic sense, with its relations to the "ideated," the "ideated things" [the content of the ideas and their objects], and the process of "intellection," it resists adequate translation into the languages of European philosophy. Even in the Latin original it prompts the thinker to bold experiments with neologisms on the one hand, and a renunciation of complete congruence between word and thought on the other. Here we meet with a paradox: in the terminology of Jewish scholasticism, to which Spinoza himself refers, the group of concepts in question has found a formulation both coherent and lucid. So that the Hebrew translation is in the curious position of being more original than the original itself.

Certain speculations then arise. Within Zionist theory, Klatzkin is the leading representative of what he himself calls a "formal nationalism," i.e., a nationalism that denies the Jewish heritage any claim whatsoever on the new generation about to assume it. He does not expect national rebirth to spring from anything but the future—from the miraculous powers of race, soil, and, above all, language. But thus presented, these three factors become so "purely formal," so utterly devoid of substance, that the modern rationalist's belief in miracles must needs surpass that which tradition demanded of the Jews of old.

It is obvious that Klatzkin's extremist theory originated in the experimental laboratories of European nationalism, from which, in the course of the past few decades, not only our own "harmless little merchant people" (as Hermann Cohen once called us in a mood of amiable irony) but most other exotic peoples got their "higher" education; a fact which the champions of the theory do not in the least deny. However, what matters about the theory is not its superficial character but whether it has the strength to shape reality in its own image, or conversely, whether those other repudiated claims, despite the failure of this theory and its maker to grasp their legitimacy, have sufficient force both to reduce the theory *ad absurdum* and compel the theorist to be more sensible than his own theory permits.

This, it seems to me, is precisely what has happened to Klatzkin as translator of Spinoza; and even apart from his special field, it is a sensibility altogether characteristic of this gifted man who stands head and shoulders above his imitators among the Zionist youth. But to return to his translation: Klatzkin tends to deprecate his choice of medieval Jewish terminology, which is solely responsible for bringing these fruits within his reach. He belittles it by defining it as a mere possibility opened up by Spinoza's own terminology, which was still that of the scholastic movement. Yet in his second appendix, equally interesting from the viewpoint of language and of philosophy, he gives the lie to his cool hypothesis.

Neither the naked truth nor the naked untruth has the power to survive. Both must be clothed to be warm. But once they are clothed, they do not appear so very unlike. Look at them from the back and you will almost confuse them, as was true of the black delegates and the white delegates of the League of Nations, at Geneva. The truth that Hebrew is the holy language of the holy people, and the untruth that it is the spoken language of a people like all other peoples, seem irreconcilable. But Jewish reality makes both the truth and the untruth dependent upon each other. This truth rejects utterance by a mouth speaking only in order to shirk any form of action—whether it be an action dictated by the right, or one dictated by the wrong, conception. And in the mouth of one who earnestly transforms it into action, the untruth can imperceptibly change into truth. The great insight of the Midrash: "Even against your own will, I am your God," still stands as epigraph to all that is Jewish—even today. Something holy that wants to turn its back upon everything profane is made profane, and the profane quality of the first day hastens toward the seventh, which will make it holy.

The holiness of the Hebrew language never signified holiness in the original sense of "seclusion," a meaning which has been overcome in classic Judaism. The holy language, the language of God, has always drawn strength for renewal from the spoken language, from the spoken languages of man; and this was so not only in the times of Moses and Isaiah. In other words, holy though it was, Hebrew never stiffened into something rigid and monumental; it always stayed alive. The Hebrew of the Torah and of the Book of Esther, the majesty of the great central prayers, the exquisite proportions of the Mishnah, the baroque of Kalir,[1] the classicism of the great Spanish authors, the pious sobriety of Maimonides, Rashi's[2] serene yet impassioned instruction, the absence of linguistic scruples of the Tibbonides,[3] the crudeness of the Shulhan Arukh, the historicism of the Haskalah in the historical nineteenth century—all this is Hebrew. Numerous tongues contributed to the work on word and phrase, on the fabric of the Hebrew language: the spoken Hebrew of time immemorial, the common Aramaic of the Persian era, the Greek of the times of the Diadochi, then—stronger and more enduring than all—the Aramaic of the Palestinian and Babylonian academies, and, simultaneously, the language of the armies and law courts of Rome and that of the rulers and subjects of the new Persian empire, the Arabic of the physicians and

---

[1] Eleazar Kalir, liturgical poet of the early Middle Ages.

[2] Rashi (Rabbi Solomon Yitzhaki, 11th cent.), Bible and Talmud commentator.

[3] Tibbonides: the Ibn Tibbon family, who translated into Hebrew the Arabic works of Jewish authors.

philosophers of Islam, and the languages of Europe, developing their own structures in the shadow of the widespread tree of the Latin of the universal church.

By the fabric of language so wrought, the Holy of Holies of this sacerdotal people is both veiled from and indicated to the eyes of the peoples of the world. The difference between its vitality and the vitality of a profane language is that nothing once received into it can ever be lost. The holy language grows richer and richer, while the other languages must obey the law of a continual and at times critical self-purification. This act guarantees them the possibility of continuing as spoken language even after they have become written language, even after—as a result of this—a certain historical phase in their development has become classical; and here "classical" denotes a mundane holiness of the language, as it were. But the life of the eternal language unfolds exactly like that of the people. It does not proceed in a sequence of deaths and resurrections, the only expedient whereby everything that lives on earth can prolong its span beyond what nature has allotted. It endures because it cannot, will not, and may not, die. Nothing that has become an integral part of it is ever discarded. Its growth is not that of an organism but of a treasure—the treasure from which the living and dying humanity of peoples may read the coming of the Kingdom. One may read a novel by Thomas Mann without gaining a better understanding of any of the characteristic locutions of the *Simplicissimus*,[4] the *Nibelungenlied*, the *Heliand*, or the Gothic Bible, but one cannot read Klatzkin's Spinoza, or even a Hebrew newspaper, without deriving something that would help to understand Ibn Ezra's[5] com-

---

[4] Important German novel by Hans Jakob von Grimmelshausen (17th cent.).

[5] Abraham ibn Ezra (12th cent.), poet, philologist; his Bible commentaries are distinguished by acute critical observation of textual problems.

mentaries, or talmudic argumentations, or the original text of the Bible. To read Hebrew implies a readiness to assume the total heritage of the language. Reading German, English, or Latin, one merely harvests the crop raised by a single generation on the acre of language.

The holy language in the mouth of the people lacks the true characteristic of a sacred language, that is, separation from the colloquial, and so it never degenerated into anything like the magic sacredness of church Latin or the Arabic of the Koran, which may be, which even *should* be, incomprehensible to the layman—all that is required of him is adherence in spirit and faith. The holy language demands to be understood, word for word. Moreover, the languages spoken by the Jewish people in their everyday life lack the essential characteristic of profane vitality: complete dedication to the present moment. They swarm with quotations. Quotation marks would be their most frequently used form of punctuation—down to the German of the most un-Jewish Jew. If the new Hebrew, the Hebrew spoken in Palestine, should set out to evade this law of Jewish destiny, it might indeed achieve its purpose theoretically, but it would have to bear the consequences. Nor would these consequences be merely what some of our young and old radicals actually desire: that the new Hebrew should no longer be the language of the old Jewish people. More than that, there would probably be no time to realize the hope of a new, "indigenous," "truly national" culture which would automatically solve the problem never yet solved in the entire history of our race, the problem of fusing normality and individuality: for when we are normal, we are exactly like anyone else, and when we are individual, we are a "proverb and a byword" (Deut. 28:37) among nations.

The point is that one cannot simply speak Hebrew as one would like to; one must speak it as it is. And it is tied up with the past. It does have obligations to the rest of the world, even when spoken by the youngest child in the most recently founded settlement. For the center which the new Palestine might at best become in a pre-messianic period would never, in this day and age, be a center in the sense of Ahad Haam, who wished to curb premature messianism only to fall prey to it out of delight in "culture"— it would become a center in the mathematical sense. For, a circle is indeed drawn around its center, but in terms of construction the center does not in the least determine the area the circle will occupy, while the smallest arc of its periphery indicates the location of the center quite unambiguously. Thus a spiritual center such as we have in mind in regard to Palestine can be seen at a great distance and so become representative for all Jewry. But if it is to be a real center, it must depend on the periphery and the laws governing it so long as there is a periphery. To express it plainly and drily to the point of blasphemy: the spirit of this spiritual center cannot grow in the direction of pure, uninhibited nationalism avid for its own development, no matter how much it would like to; just because of its focal character it must constantly keep in sight the periphery which can never be governed by pure nationalism but will always be constrained to regard the national as a function of the religious, and for very simple reasons based on the sociology of minorities. As one probes more deeply into these reasons, they rapidly lead out of the realm of blasphemy, into that of metaphysics: Why have we always been a minority? And why can we not stop being one?

These general observations are especially applicable to language, which is the core of all national life. Language cannot develop as it wants to but as it must. And for the Hebrew language, this "must" does not lie within itself, as in every normal national language but from something beyond its "spokenness," that is, from the heritage of the past, and the connection maintained with those whose Jewishness is essentially that of the heir. But the more apparent the abnormality of this twofold dependency becomes, the more it tends to cast off the shackles of "normalcy." The translator of Spinoza is under no obligation to convert the pseudo-profundity of this great tempter into true insights. His translation must remain a translation, even though the Hebrew moans and groans in the face of a concept such as *natura sive Deus,* which the Latin deals with effortlessly. The lack of the sleek "or" in Hebrew makes it impossible to coax the spirit of the language into combining a term from modern philosophy with a primordial word seething with the storms of creation. Here the eternal language can impose its own peculiar character only in incidental locutions; for example, when it replaces the monotonous tattoo, q.e.d., which recurs throughout the book wherever something has been proved, by the talmudic term, *shema miney,* "Hear [conclude] it from this," in its usual two-letter abbreviation. And this in spite of the fact that Hebrew, like Greek, Latin, and German, is able to express the idea of "demonstration" by a word deriving from the visual sphere. This is a striking instance of how in the very camp of the enemy, at the very heart of the "geometric" method, the spirit of revelation, which is hostile to the image, to "form," manages to break through. "Ye saw no form, only a voice" (Deut. 4:12).

Another example will serve to clarify what I mean by liberation from the shackles of normalcy. I have here in front of me a Zionist picture book with scenes of Palestine and a bilingual text. The preface, originally written in German, describes the Palestinian landscape in all the tints of European and even of Asiatic style—that is, if we accept Rabindranath Tagore as typical of Asia. The author, balancing between a given focus and oscillating contrasts, suddenly pays the following polite call on Revelation: "Is it sheer coincidence that this landscape begot the prophets? That here, as on Mount Sinai, man recognized the exclusive oneness of God, and the one thing he needs: to be moral, that is to say, just?"

In Hebrew, this peroration washed (and washed out!) with all the waters of the idealism of modern German universities, goes like this: "Is it by chance only that this plateau was the birthplace of prophecy? That here, as on Mount Sinai, the One God revealed himself to man, and told him what is good and what the Lord requires of him: to act justly and to love mercy?" The translation has converted educated balderdash into the simplicity of truth, and its success is not due to any degree of ability but to submission to the laws of the language. *Quod erat demonstrandum.* Hear it from this!

[*Kleinere Schriften,* pp. 220-227]

5.   On the Significance of the Bible

It will always be futile to attempt to explain the unique position claimed for the Bible in its very name of Bible, the Book, on the grounds of the quality of its content. For to apply a superlative to a book because of content presupposes dogmatic prejudice. Mohammedanism, for instance, dogmatically states that the Koran is the most beautiful of all books. The only way in which the scholar can grasp and prove the significance of the Bible is by its effect and its destiny: namely, by its effect on, and its destiny in, the course of world history.

Their very first encounters, springing from war or from trade relations, establish certain spiritual contacts among peoples, without however creating between them a world-

271

historical bond. For this, more than a haphazard flow of influences is required; the creation of such a bond demands the conscious transfer into one's sphere of something recognized as alien; in other words, it requires *translation*. The historical moment of the birth of world literature, and hence of supernational consciousness, occurred, in the full light of history, with two events, one of which was only symptomatic while the other had constitutive significance as well. It came when two books, each the very foundation of its national literature, were first translated into another language. At just about the same time, a prisoner of war in Rome translated the Odyssey from Greek into Latin, and Jewish settlers in Alexandria translated the Book of their people into Greek. Whatever unity of spirit and purpose exists on the five continents of this earth today derives from the fusion of these two events, and the consequences thereof, events originally related only because in them the Greeks played the double role of giving and taking.

The origin of the Greek Bible falls between the beginning of the movement that tried to bring Judaism to other peoples and the ebb of that movement before one that was stronger, one that, while accepting the Jewish Bible as its ever present foundation, regarded it merely as the "old" Testament. And from this time on we must distinguish between the direct effects of the Jewish Bible, and the indirect effects springing from its fusion—technical as well as chemical—with the New Testament. Viewed from the standpoint of world history, the former effects are sporadic, no matter how strong they may be at certain junctures, while the latter constitute the indispensable mortar that cements world history into a whole.

Let us first discuss the direct effect. Even that is not direct in the true meaning of the word, for every return to the Jewish Bible occurs with reference to the New Testament, though often in a spirit of opposition. Here we have a more or less deliberate, though rarely fundamental, return to the "Law." Wherever the demands of Christian communal life were not satisfied by the all too primitive model community described in the Acts of the Apostles and in the Epistles, or by the critical attitude toward the world pronounced in the Gospels (critical in both the social and moral aspects), it was—and still is—natural to revert to the Old Testament, to law born of prophecy. The Christian church, the Christian state, Christian economics, and Christian society could not and cannot be established upon the New Testament, which sees the world only in crisis, only face to face with Judgment. In contrast to the pointed paradoxes of the New Testament, the Jewish Bible, sprung from the richness of the life of a whole people, of a whole national literature, offered a solid ground for building the world, and for building in the world, in that its faith in creation was both living and profound—even within the sphere of prophetic criticism and polemics. And so, just because of the manifold origins of the Book, the various edifices could be as different, even opposed to one another, as the various sides and aspects of national life: monarchists and monarchomachists, churches and sects, popes and heretics, reactionaries and revolutionists, protectors of property rights and social reformers, war-enthusiasts and pacifists could and can, did and do, cite the Book as their authority.

But its indirect effect by way of the New Testament is far more important than all these influences and references. The New Testament writings originated in protest against the Jewish Bible, in the belief that salvation had come, that "the time was full," a belief whose burning fervor condensed the long-breathed hope for redemption to a brief span. That Christianity could persist after "this generation" has passed away, while "this world" did not come to an

end; or, to express it in terms of Bible history, that the New
Testament writings became the canonical New Testament—
this Christianity and the New Testament owe to their bond
with Judaism. For the way back to the still persisting Creation
could be found only if the God of Genesis and he "who
has spoken through the prophets" was the same as the one
invoked in the Lord's Prayer and not, as the Gnostics
claimed, an old God dethroned by the God of a new era.
Connection with the created world—this and nothing less
is at stake for Christianity both in the theological identification expressed in the dogma of the Trinity and in the
indentifying of the "word" that "was God" with the Messiah
from David's stem. It is no mere chance that in the struggle
for these identifications, in this struggle against Marcion's
"alien God"—and this "alien" means alien to the Old Covenant—the church created her canon of the New Testament
as a counterpart to the Old Testament. This counterpart was
not, however, intended to supersede the Old Testament,
but only to supplement and outrange it. Whatever cultural
strength Christianity has displayed in the two millennia
since then, and cultural strength here implies strength to
become integrated in the world and to integrate the world
into itself, is due to the effort to retain *its* Old Testament.

And so it is no longer a problem of conscious references
to the Jewish Bible, or of relationships that could be traced
or proved in detail, but of the entire sphere of whatever—
in any degree—might be called a cultural effect of Christianity. What matters here is that Christianity has been
able to synthesize with the world. What matters is the fruit-
ful tension of such syntheses, which has given Christian
Europe her spiritual dominance in the world. Nothing is
altered by the fact that Christianity itself has always regarded this tension as a torment it wished to evade. If
Christianity ever succeeded in its perpetual attempt to
to escape from the limitations and strangeness of the Old

Testament into the wide region of philosophy or the circumscribed pale of nationalism, then Christendom would come to an end, and with it the Bible's, including the Jewish Bible's, participation in world history. For while the course of the one world history that began with this Book may change its protagonists, it cannot lose connection with its origin and each successive step of its development. This connection is precisely what we call world history. No future can undo the past, just as no past can prevent the coming of that which is to come.

It is quite possible that the secularization of religious communities, which began a hundred and fifty years ago, will march on, and that church and synagogue in the old traditional sense will persist only for a small nucleus, while a worldly agent, the "church people," or, in our case, the "Jewish people," will become the general community. If this should take place, the significance of the Holy Scriptures would not lessen but would even grow—as has already been shown both by church and synagogue in the last century and a half. When dogma and Law cease to be the all-embracing frame of the community and serve only as props from within, the Scriptures must not merely fulfil the task of all Scriptures: to establish a connection between generations; they must also assume another which is likewise incumbent on all Scriptures: they must guarantee the connection between the center and the periphery of the community. Thus, even if church and synagogue no longer arched the portal on the road of humanity, the Bible would still continue to be at beck and call, so that humanity could consult it about this very road, "turn its pages again and again," and find "everything in it."[1]

[A section of the article *Bible* in the *Encyclopaedia Judaica. Kleinere Schriften* pp. 124-127]

---

[1] Quoted from the Sayings of the Fathers.

IV

GOD AND MAN

1. The Love of God

A Note on a Poem By Judah ha-Levi

It is difficult to love, even to love God. Indeed, the latter is the most difficult kind of love. For the share of unhappy love that is in all love, even the happiest, and that arises from the tension between wanting to, having to love infinitely, and being able to love only finitely, is here increased *ad infinitum*. To love God always spells happy and unhappy love simultaneously, the very happiest and the very unhappiest. He comes close to man, most close—and then again withdraws to the most distant distance. He is at once the most longed for, and the hardest to bear. His hand protects eternally, but no one can behold his eternal face and remain among the living. Thus the love he returns to his lover, who must entreat it, is always something that must be asked for; in the Hebrew tongue one word denotes both entreating and asking. The solution of these difficulties and antitheses, like the solution of all the difficulties and antitheses of love, lies with the lover, with his strength to face "notwithstandingness," to bear notwithstanding, to let himself be borne notwithstanding. Here it lies with man and the strength he can put into his entreaty that God love him in return.

[*Judah ha-Levi*, pp. 178-179]

2.   The Pantheon of Today

A Note on a Poem By Judah ha-Levi

This hymn[1] and the verse it uses: "For the Lord your God, He is God of gods, and Lord of lords" (Deut. 10:17), are alien to modern man. For here is assumed that gods really *exist,* while today, and this is generally regarded as a "result of religious evolution," mankind has learned to look upon gods as nonexistent. Even the atheist is apt to regard monotheism with gracious tolerance as a necessary step on the road from gods to no god at all. The poet who composed this hymn would have to reject this tolerance. For him the gods are real, yet God is more real. That this is true is hidden from us today solely by the delusion that monotheism is something self-evident. Perhaps "monotheism" is, but the belief in One God is not. The experience of life which tends to make us believe in divers powers resists this belief in one alone. Names change but diversity remains. Culture and civilization, people and state, nation and race, art and science, industry and class, ethos and religion—all these constitute a quite incomplete survey of the pantheon of today. Who will deny the reality of these powers? And never has a "heathen" served his gods more devoutly, more ready to bring sacrifice, than the people of our era serve these. But when we meet with the One, then even today the struggle with the many becomes inevitable, and its issue—only, to be sure, so far as we are concerned—remains uncertain. The Talmud already has it that if God wanted to destroy the

[1] The hymn (Diwan of Judah ha-Levi, ed. H. Brody, III, 75) sings the praise of God as the creator of heaven and earth; of life and the soul; the eternal Lord of passing history and passing gods; he who is glorified by the angels above, and whose redeeming act is awaited by Israel which sanctifies his name in the world.

gods, once and for all, if he wanted to destroy the powers which man is tempted to make idols of, he would have to destroy the world. And yet it is his world, which comes from him and returns to him.

[*Judah ha-Levi*, p. 185]

3. Remote and Near

A Note on a Poem By Judah ha-Levi

A single thought animates this hymn—but it is the ultimate thought the mind of man can grasp and it is the first that Jewish thinking seizes on: that the remote God is none other than the near, the unknown God none other than the revealed, the Creator none other than the Redeemer. The short opening stanza[1] contains it in epigrammatic brevity, and the four following stanzas sound it in hymnic ecstasies streaming from the throne of heaven to the heart of man and soaring back again and again, in giant arcs. This is the thought which was discovered over and over in the sphere of revelation, which inside and outside that sphere was forgotten over and over throughout the centuries, from Paul and Marcion to Harnack[2] and Barth.[3]

Discovered over and over and forgotten over and over! For theologians forget what men discover, and they forget the more readily the better theologians they are. Theology is most dangerous when it is most accurate. Today, after a

---

[1] "Lord, where shall I find Thee?
High and hidden is Thy place;
And where shall I not find Thee?
The world is full of Thy glory."
    (Translated by Nina Salaman.)

[2] Adolf von Harnack (1851-1930), German Protestant theologian.

[3] Karl Barth (1886-   ), Swiss Protestant representative of dialectic theology.

long period of drought, we have a theology—largely Protestant—that leaves nothing to be desired with regard to accuracy. Now we know it! We understand that God is "wholly Other"; that to talk of him is to talk him away, that all we can tell is what his effect is on us. The result of this stupendous accuracy is that, just because we are accurate, we now stand in a circle like children: one says something quite accurate; his neighbor snubs him with the still more accurate statement that his utterance was false because it was accurate, and so we make the rounds until we get back to the first. The whole procedure is called theology.

The point is that we theologians cannot stop converting our knowledge into rules and regulations for the conduct of God. We know that God can be perceived only through his presence, and instantly make this into the rule that he must not let himself be perceived in his absence. As a matter of fact, it would be quite safe to leave it to him just when and how and to what extent he wishes to be perceived. All we need do is simply to say what we know, and to say it calmly or vehemently (but whether calmly or vehemently is not up to us either), and as accurately as possible, and this accuracy *is* up to us!

When God comes near to us we do, indeed, perceive only the unutterable. But that is not our duty and—as we call it in our heart of hearts—our merit, because we are such very excellent modern theologians. We just cannot do otherwise, for he is so very close to us. We have no reason whatsover to snub one another for uttering the unutterable. So long as it is and wants to be unutterable, it will see to it that we cannot utter it. So when we do begin to utter it, this probably happens because it itself makes possible our utterance, inadequate though that be, by its—or rather his, God's—withdrawal from us. In making himself remote he lets us perceive him as one who is remote, and when he is very remote, that is, when he has withdrawn from us completely, we can even—inquisitors of the new theology, hand me over to temporal justice!—we can even *prove* him!

The possibility of proving the existence of God is the very natural result of the fact that certain theologians never weary of repeating that God is the "wholly Other." Or not even the result. This otherness is, in itself, the modern proof of God's existence, for it is the residue of all other proofs rarefied to the utmost remoteness of abstraction. But before this extreme point of remoteness is reached, each earlier proof has its proper place—governed by the degree of man's remoteness—and constitutes the precise expression of what is still visible from there. And so it is not at all a sign of being hopelessly lost to know that God is perfect being, or the primordial cause, or even that he is the ideal of ethics. When such statements are proffered as honest knowledge, it is only a sign that at the moment such knowledge was gained God was really very far away from the one gaining it. But what do we mean by the phrase "honest knowledge"? Nothing but what it actually means, to wit, nothing that does not concern us and that we do not concern. Without such concern, even an investigation of agriculture in fifteenth-century Germany is worthless, while with it, dicta such as "God is holy," or even just "God is," are as true as our modern approximations.

For nearness and remoteness in themselves do not reveal whether this mutual concern, whether this sole condition that renders knowledge true, really prevails, whether here man concerns God, and God man. Even when God is terribly near, man can turn away his eyes, and then he has not the smallest glimpse of what has happened to him. And even at a very great distance, the burning gaze of God and man can fuse in such a way that the coldest abstractions grow warm in the mouth of Maimonides or Hermann Cohen—warmer than all our agonized drivel. It is not nearness or remoteness that matters. What matters is that, near or remote, whatever is uttered, is uttered before God with the "Thou" of the refrain of our poem, a "Thou" that never turns away.

[*Judah ha-Levi*, pp. 188-190]

4. The Name

A Note on a Poem By Judah ha-Levi

The paradox of God's being simultaneously near and remote is essentially expressed in the fact that he has a name. Whatever has a name can be talked about, can be talked to, according to whether it is absent or present. God is never absent. Hence there is no theoretical concept of God; there is of the false gods, but not of the one, the true. God alone has a name that is also a concept; his concept is also his name. . . .

Remoteness and nearness also serves to help the poet solve the problem of the purpose of the world, which was a subject of prime importance in the philosophy of religion of that era. Everything created has a double function: first, it is simply there, it has being, its own being, and its own purpose. But it is also there for the sake of *something* else, in the final analysis, for the sake of *everything* else. Insofar as it is itself and its own purpose, it experiences the near God; insofar as it is related to something else, it experiences the remote God. For the remote God is the God of the world, which is always a whole, a whole made up of totally different parts, while the near God is the God of the heart, the heart which is never as much itself, and nothing but itself, as when it suffers.

It is striking that the second couplet,[1] which gives the content of the poem very simply and briefly, uses the concrete word "dwell" in speaking of the being of God that is high above the world and far away from the world. This "dwell" usually indicates the dwelling of God's glory on earth, among God's people, and in his house. But the word used in the poem to designate God's dwelling in the crushed heart is the most abstract word one can think of, a word which even deviates from that in the verse of the Bible (Isa. 57:15) on which the passage is based. It is the word "is," a typical philosopher's term, which Occidental scholasticism rendered as "exist." This contradiction reveals the ultimate depths of Jewish thought and faith. Here *bore olam*, the Creator of the world, does not mean something remote, as the content of the words seems to indicate. On the contrary: in popular speech the words are fraught with emotion, they are something near, and in the case of the God of the heart, the heart never for a moment forgets that he is the one—who *is*. So here the spark does not merely oscillate between the two poles of nearness and remoteness, but each pole itself has a positive and negative charge, only in different pattern. The Creator who is above the world takes up his "habitation," and the abstract God of philosophy has his "being" in the crushed heart. When Hermann Cohen was in Marburg, he once expounded the God-idea of his *Ethics* to an old Jew of that city. The Jew listened with reverent attention, but when Cohen was through, he asked: "And where is the *bore olam?*"[2] Cohen had no answer to this, and tears rose in his eyes.

[*Judah ha-Levi*, pp. 190-191]

[1] "God whose dwelling is high above the world; yet he, too, exists in the crushed heart and with suffering man."

[2] "Creator of the universe," a pious Jew's intimate appellation for God.

5.   On the Tempting of God
From the Star of Redemption

That God can be tempted is perhaps the most absurd of
the many absurd claims which faith has launched in the
world. Is it possible that God, the Creator, in whose sight—
so says faith—peoples are like drops in a bucket, can really
be tempted by man, the maggot—once more to quote the
words of this faith—and by man's son, the worm! And even
though the reference here is probably to the giver of revelation rather than to the almighty Creator, yet how unthinkable that he, if he really is the God of love, could be
tempted by man! Would this not mean that God is curbed
in his love, that he is bound by the deeds of man instead
of—as faith itself believes—following only the urge of his
own love in untrammeled freedom? Or could man tempt
the Redeemer? That is the more possible, for—according to
the precepts of faith—man actually has a certain degree of
freedom in relation to the Redeemer which he does not
have as the creature and child of God: the freedom to act,
or, at the very least, the freedom to make a decision, to
pray. But it is in this prayer that Jews and Christians both
repeat always, "Lead us not into temptation." This would
seem to charge God with a twofold denial, of his provi-
dence, and of his fatherly love. It supposes that he himself
indulges in the impious sport of "tempting" his creature,
his child. Thus if prayer really gave an occasion to tempt
God to him who uttered the prayer, still, he would be in-
hibited by his continual fear that it was he who was being
tempted at the very moment he thought himself to be doing the tempting. Or can it be that the possibility of tempting God rests on the fact that God tempts man? But what

if this possibility—and mark that I say "possibility"—should indicate the freedom man has at least before God, the Redeemer, if not before God, the Creator and Revealer (for man was created without his volition, and receives revelation through no merit of his own, yet God does not wish to redeem him "without his participation"). What if this freedom of prayer, then, indicates the possibility of tempting God! Would this not mean that the tempting of man by God is the necessary premise for this very freedom of man?

This is, indeed, the truth of the matter. A rabbinical legend tells of a river in a far-off country, a river so devout that it does not flow on the Sabbath. If, instead of the Main, it were this river that flowed through Frankfort, all the Frankfort Jews would doubtless practice the strictest observance of the Sabbath. God does not give signs like these. Apparently, he fears the inevitable result: the most enslaved, the timid, and the meager of soul would then be the most devout. It appears that God desires for his own only the free. But the mere invisibility of his reign is not enough to divide the free from the enslaved; for when in doubt the timid are timid enough to join that side which it cannot "in any event" hurt to belong to, and which possibly—say with fifty per cent of probability—may even entail profit. So, in order to segregate souls God must not merely not foster but even injure. He therefore has no choice in the matter: he must tempt man. He must not merely hide his reign, he must deceive man about it. He must make it difficult, even impossible for man to see it, so that man may have the opportunity to believe in God truly, that is, to believe in him in freedom, and to trust in him. And man, in his turn, must take into account the possibility that God is only "tempting" him so that he may have a stimulus to preserve his trust in the face of all evil promptings, and turn a deaf ear to the eternal voice of Job's wife which urges him to curse God and die!

Man must know that he is tempted at times for the sake of his freedom. He must learn to believe in this freedom of his. He must believe that whereas it may be bounded in all other spheres, it is boundless in his relation to God. To him God's own command, graven in tablets of stone, must be "freedom upon the tablets"—an untranslatable pun of the forefathers.[1] Everything, so these say, lies in the hand of God, except one thing: the fear of God. And in what can this freedom manifest itself more boldly than in the certainty of being able to tempt God? Thus, in prayer, the possibility of tempting comes from the two sides, of God and of man; prayer is yoked between these two possibilities. And while it fears the tempting by God, it feels its own power to tempt him in turn.

[*Der Stern der Erlösung*, III, 7-9]

6.   The Content of Revelation
A Note on a Poem By Judah ha-Levi

All that God ever reveals in revelation is—revelation. Or, to express it differently, he reveals nothing but himself to man. The relation of this accusative and dative to each other is the one and only content of revelation. Whatever does not follow directly from this covenant between God and man, whatever cannot prove its direct bearing on this covenant, cannot be a part of it. The problem has not been *solved* for the visionary who beheld the vision; it has been *dissolved*.

[*Judah ha-Levi*, p. 174]

---

[1] "And the writing was the writing of God, graven [*harut*] upon the tablets" (Exod. 32:16), is interpreted by the Talmud as "freedom [*herut*] upon the tablets."

see version in 92 Poems w. R A Cohen p. 29

7. On the Day of Atonement

A Note on a Poem By Judah ha-Levi

Does God take the first step, or does man? Is it possible for man to take it? This is a real question and not, as the Protestant theologians of today would like to believe, a preliminary question that has already been answered. But neither is it "the distinction between Judaism and Christianity," as Jewish theologians in their understandable desire for harmless "criteria of distinction" would like to believe. It is the true question of the true heart of man. For, to revert to the neo-Protestant theologians, it makes a decided difference whether the paradox of "the servile will" is proclaimed by a rebel in world history, or by a peaceful professor and writer. In the first case, life supplements the theory and stamps it with truth; in the second, life raises it to the nth degree and hence to an exaggerated theory, false to the nth degree. Had Luther died on the thirtieth of October, 1517,[1] all the audacities of his commentary on the *Epistle to the Romans* would have been nothing but the extravaganzas of a late scholastic.

The question is real because man, whenever he stands before God, is sensible of his own weakness and therefore forced to expect and implore God to take the first step. Yet at the same time he hears what he cannot help but hear: God demanding this first step from him, from man. No manner of theory can ignore this, neither the one that tries to discredit the demand of God as heard by man, nor the theory that interprets the powerlessness felt by man as a delusion of Satan. Nor, of course, any theory that seeks to evade so crude an alternative by some sophistical distribu-

---

[1] I.e., one day before he nailed to the church door at Wittenberg his revolutionary 95 theses.

tion, some meticulous apportioning of roles. The whole matter continues in the form of an unending dialogue in which, as in every dialogue, he who happens to have been the last to speak is "right," and so God must be right because in the end it is he who has the last word; in the ultimate end!

That is how the Midrash interprets this problem. It presents man and God, the congregation of Israel and their Lord, as engaged in a dialogue. Going back to the close of Lamentations (5:21) and the prophecy in Malachi (3:7), it has them express to each other the longing for the first step as the condition for the second, which each then pledges himself to take. And it is on this Midrash that Judah ha-Levi built up his great dialogue between man and God[2] which is intended for the noon hours of the great Day of Atonement.

In Judah ha-Levi's other dialogues between God and man, the characters talk to each other face to face. In this one under consideration, one feels an awful distance. Through remonstrance and desire, profound despair, humility and resolve, passion and pleading, the voice of man remains a cry from the depths, while the voice of God, whether it demands, warns, or promises, is a call from on high. Just on this day of days, which is devoted to atonement and reconciliation, the tension between God and man seems irreconcilable.

And the very element that ordinarily serves to lessen this tension here increases it. Though usually the ways of God are remote from the ways of man, the way of Israel's God and the way of his people meet on Mount Sinai which is ever aflame. On this day too, when the Jew is nothing but man and God nothing but the judge of the world, the bridge is still not blotted from consciousness. Both sides even set foot on it, but it does not lead to the opposite bank. When (in this poem) man addresses God as the giver of his Jewish law and his Jewish sufferings, God replies with the most

---

[2] *Diwan of Judah ha-Levi*, ed. H. Brody, III, 298.

exigent demand upon man, upon man only. And when man stammers out his words from the depths of his crushed humanness, and humanness only, God reminds him of his Jewish life in the sonship of God, of miracle and the Law. On this day of awe even nearness becomes an element of remoteness. The dialogue continues with the same infinite distance as at the start between the two voices.

But here it is man who has the last word. In the closing stanza[3] God is silent. What does this silence mean? . . . The poem was written for the noon hours of the Day of Atonement. . . . But the last word is possible only at the last moment of the day. And if it is man who utters it, though God should, then this last word—of the day, of life, of history—can only be the word that comes after God has finished speaking. It must be uttered in the only way in which man can pronounce the "I" of God: in professing him. Only in this profession, which occurs in the last minutes of the day, does our poem, as well as the entire day, find its solution. It is man who, in the sight of God, gives to himself the answer granting him the fulfillment of his prayer of return, of homecoming, for this one moment, which anticipates the last. In this moment, he is as close to God, as near to his throne, as it is ever accorded man to be. In the ecstasy of this nearness, the "Thou" is silent, it does not answer him, neither the "Thou" to which he cried out in despair, nor the "Thou" he longs for and loves. . . . But he is permitted to anticipate this highest, this ultimate moment only because a few minutes later, when the sounding of the ram's horn proclaims the close of the holiday, he will recite the evening prayer of his everyday life, which has recommenced, and say: "Forgive us, our Father, for we have sinned."

[*Judah ha-Levi,* pp. 180-182]

[3] The closing stanza concerns Israel: "You have rejected the people which is near to you. . . . Can it find help if you will not pity it and raise it from the depths—a people which awaits the day of promise."

8.   On Miracles

A Note on a Poem By Judah ha-Levi

In Hebrew, the original meaning of the word "holy" is "set apart." At the outset, God's working is the quiet, almost inaudible work of first beginnings; and there, for the time being, everything remains just as it is. Creation seems so age-old that it may almost be considered "eternal," and the voice of conscience so absolute that it may almost be called "autonomous." Hence orthodox disciples of Kant might well conceive that it would not really change anything to yield to the religious position that God made both starry sky and conscience. But the position cannot be so lightly taken. God is not merely he who was. He is not merely the fundament, the support of the world and of man. Unless such belief is backed by the experience of the live present, unless it springs from this present, it is empty, a mere "yielding." Without this God who with mighty actions intervenes in this day of our present life, the quiet, inaudible God who maintains the world and our heart that he created dims to a fairy tale— worse, to a dogma. He is the Holy One who sets himself apart, and everywhere he sets something apart, effecting something unheard of, election, holiness. Without the revealed miracles of this day, the hidden miracles of everyday would be invisible, invisible at least as miracles. Only from the revelation of what is set apart do we learn to revere the Creator in what is "natural." Only the tremors of holiness sanctify even the realm of the profane.

It is, therefore, essential to miracle that it be drawn into the living presence of holiness. The question as to why miracles do not come to pass "today" as they used to "once upon a time," is simply stupid. Miracles never "came to pass" anyway. The atmosphere of the past blights all miracle. The Bible itself explains the miracle of the Red Sea *post eventum* as something "natural." Every miracle can be explained—after the event. Not because the miracle is no miracle, but because explanation is explanation. Miracle always occurs in the present and, at most, in the future. One can implore and experience it, and while the experience is still present, one can feel gratitude. When it no longer seems a thing of the present, all there is left to do is explain. Every miracle is possible, even the most absurd, even that an ax floats.[1] After it has happened, there will be no trouble in finding an explanation for it. The sole precondition for its coming to pass is that one can seek it in prayer. But with true prayer, and that means prayer apart from the will; not with willed prayer, which is the magic practiced by the medicine man. But when true prayer is possible, then the most impossible becomes possible, and if true prayer is impossible, then the most possible becomes impossible. Thus it may be possible that the dead awaken, and impossible that the sick be healed. There is nothing that is impossible in itself, but there is much we consider so impossible that we cannot bring ourselves to pray for it, and much else we consider entirely possible and which yet we do not pray for, because for some reason or other we have not the strength to do so.

In fact nothing is miraculous about a miracle except that it comes when it does. The east wind has probably swept bare the ford in the Red Sea hundreds of times, and will do so again hundreds of times. But that it did this at a moment when the people in their distress set foot in the sea—that is the miracle. What only a moment before was coveted future, becomes present and actual. This enriching of a present moment with the past, with its own past, gives it the power to continue as a present and not a past moment, and thus raises it from the stream of all the other moments, whose com-

[1] Reference to the miracle performed by Elisha (II Kings 6:1-7).

panion it remains nonetheless. Thus the miracle becomes the germ-cell of holiness which is alive so long as it retains connection with this its origin, so long as it continues to be miraculous. The Creator, who created the *one* creation, laughs at the dividing lines man tries to draw, and washes them away again and again with the deluge of primordial chaos. But the dividing lines God himself draws reach over all creation, and in growing oneness and universality manifest the silent mystery of the one creation.

[*Judah ha-Levi*, pp. 193-194]

9.   Freedom

A Note on a Poem By Judah ha-Levi

God gives man the freedom to make the most significant decision, he gives freedom for just that—only for that. But giving it, he yet retains the powers of realization in his own treasure-trove. Out of that treasure, he dispenses only to him who has made the decision, and only on a request which must be repeated over and over. For in giving freedom, God does not want to make himself superfluous; on the contrary, he wants to make himself indispensable. He grants man the fief of today, and so makes himself Lord of tomorrow. That is why man must tremble for his today so long as there can be a tomorrow. Just as compulsion sent by God was the beginning of realization, so at the end, close to the goal, there is the driving force of the fear roused by God, the fear that perhaps this day will not be followed by a tomorrow. And through this fear the deed is born at last, the deed that transports today across into the eternal tomorrow.

[*Judah ha-Levi*, p. 257]

V

THE JEWISH PEOPLE

1. Living History

The fact that we do not live within the laws of world
history, or, to state it positively, the fact of our everlastingness, renders all the phases of our history simultaneous. In
the history of other peoples, reaching back for what has been
left behind is only necessary from time to time; for us, it is
a constant, vital necessity. And we must not forget that it is
a *vital* necessity, for we must be able to *live* within our
everlastingness.

[From *Die Bauleute* ("The Builders"). *Kleinere Schriften,* p. 119]

2.   The Eternal People
From the Star of Redemption

The Promise of Eternity
"Blessed art Thou . . . who hast planted eternal life in our
midst."[1] The fire burns at the core of the star.[2] The rays go
forth only from this fire; and flow unresisted to the outside.
The fire of the core must burn incessantly. Its flame must
eternally feed upon itself. It requires no fuel from without.

---

[1] Benediction after the reading of a section of the Torah.
[2] F. R. regards Judaism as "the eternal fire," and Christianity as "the
eternal rays" issuing forth from the "star" of redemption.

Time has no power over it and must roll past. It must produce its own time and reproduce itself forever. It must make its life everlasting in the succession of generations, each producing the generation to come, and bearing witness to those gone by. Bearing witness takes place in bearing—two meanings but one act, in which eternal life is realized. Elsewhere, past and future are divorced, the one sinking back, the other coming on; here they grow into one. The bearing of the future is a direct bearing witness to the past. The son is born so that he may bear witness to his father's father. The grandson renews the name of the forebear. The patriarchs of old call upon their last descendant by his name—which is theirs. Above the darkness of the future burns the star-strewn heaven of the promise: "So shall thy seed be."[3]

The Eternal People: Jewish Fate

There is only one community in which such a linked sequence of everlasting life goes from grandfather to grandson, only one which cannot utter the "we" of its unity without hearing deep within a voice that adds: "are eternal." It must be a blood-community, because only blood gives present warrant to the hope for a future. If some other community, one that does not propagate itself from its own blood, desires to claim eternity for its "we," the only way open to it is to secure a place in the future. All eternity not based on blood must be based on the will and on hope. Only a community based on common blood feels the warrant of eternity warm in its veins even now. For such a community only, time is not a foe that must be tamed, a foe it may or may not defeat—though it hopes it may!—but its child and the child of its child. It alone regards as the present what, for other communities, is the future, or, at any rate, something outside the present. For it alone the future is not something alien but

[3] Gen. 15:5.

something of its own, something it carries in its womb and which might be born any day. While every other community that lays claim to eternity must take measures to pass the torch of the present on to the future, the blood-community does not have to resort to such measures. It does not have to hire the services of the spirit; the natural propagation of the body guarantees it eternity.

The Peoples and Their Native Soil

What holds generally for peoples as groups united through blood relationship over against communities of the spirit, holds for our people in particular. Among the peoples of the earth, the Jewish people is "the one people,"[4] as it calls itself on the high rung of its life, which it ascends Sabbath after Sabbath. The peoples of the world are not content with the bonds of blood. They sink their roots into the night of earth, lifeless in itself but the spender of life, and from the lastingness of earth they conclude that they themselves will last. Their will to eternity clings to the soil and to the reign over the soil, to the land. The earth of their homeland is watered by the blood of their sons, for they do not trust in the life of a community of blood, in a community that can dispense with anchorage in solid earth. We were the only ones who trusted in blood and abandoned the land; and so we preserved the priceless sap of life which pledged us that it would be eternal. Among the peoples of the world, we were the only ones who separated what lived within us from all community with what is dead. For while the earth nourishes, it also binds. Whenever a people loves the soil of its native land more than its own life, it is in danger—as all the peoples of the world are—that, though nine times out of ten this love will save the native soil from the foe and, along with it, the

4 Prayer; cf. II Sam. 7:23.

life of the people, in the end the soil will persist as that which was loved more strongly, and the people will leave their lifeblood upon it. In the final analysis, the people belong to him who conquers the land. It cannot be otherwise, because people cling to the soil more than to their life as a people. Thus the earth betrays a people that entrusted its permanence to earth. The soil endures, but the peoples who live on it pass.

The Holy Land

And so, in contrast to the history of other peoples, the earliest legends about the tribe of the eternal people are not based on indigenousness. Only the father of mankind sprang from the earth itself, and even he only in a physical sense. But the father of Israel came from the outside. His story, as it is told in the holy books, begins with God's command to leave the land of his birth and go to a land God will point out to him. Thus in the dawn of its earliest beginnings, as well as later in the bright light of history, this people is a people in exile, in the Egyptian exile and subsequently in that of Babylonia. To the eternal people, home never is home in the sense of land, as it is to the peoples of the world who plough the land and live and thrive on it, until they have all but forgotten that being a people means something besides being rooted in a land. The eternal people has not been permitted to while away time in any home. It never loses the untrammeled freedom of a wanderer who is more faithful a knight to his country when he roams abroad, craving adventure and yearning for the land he has left behind, than when he lives in that land. In the most profound sense possible, this people has a land of its own only in that it has a land it yearns for—a holy land. And so even when it has a home, this people, in recurrent contrast to all other peoples on earth, is not allowed full possession of that home. It is only "a stranger and a sojourner."[5] God tells it: "The land is mine."[6] The holiness of the land removed it from the people's spontaneous reach while it could still reach out for it. This holiness increases the longing for what is lost, to infinity, and so the people can never be entirely at home in any other land. This longing compels it to concentrate the full force of its will on a thing which, for other peoples, is only one among others yet which to it is essential and vital: the community of blood. In doing this, the will to be a people dares not cling to any mechanical means; the will can realize its end only through the people itself.

The Peoples and Their Languages

But is a native land the only thing aside from blood on which a people's community can rest? Does not a people have a living sign of solidarity, no matter where its children may go? Has not every people its own language? It would seem that the language of the peoples of the world is not bound to something lifeless, something external. It lives together with man, with the whole of man, with the unity of his bodily and spiritual life, which cannot be broken as long as he lives. So language is not bound to anything external. But is it really less transitory because of this? If it is closely bound up with the life of the people, what happens to it when that life dies? The same that happens to it so long as that life lives: the language participates in the ultimate experience of this life: it also dies. Down to the most subtle detail, the languages of the peoples follow the live changes in their destinies, but this very dependence forces them to share the fate of all things alive: the fate of dying. Language is alive because it too can die. Eternity would be an unwelcome gift to it. Only because it is not eternal, only because

[5] Gen. 23:4.
[6] Lev. 25:23.

it is a faithful reflection of the destiny of a people among other peoples, of a people passing through the various phases of its life, does it deserve to be called the most vital possession of a people, yes, its very life. And so every people of the world is doubtless right in fighting for its own language. But the peoples should know that it is not their eternity they are fighting for, that whatever is gained in the struggle is something quite other than eternity; it is time.

The Holy Language

That is why the eternal people has lost its own language and, all over the world, speaks a language dictated by external destiny, the language of the nation whose guest it happens to be. And if it is not claiming hospitality but living in a settlement of its own, it speaks the language of the people from whose country it emigrated, of the people that gave it the strength to found a new settlement. In foreign lands it never draws this strength from itself alone, from its own community of blood, but always from something that was added elsewhere; the "Spaniol"[7] in the Balkan countries, the Yiddish in Eastern Europe, are the best-known instances of this. While every other people is one with its own language, while that language withers in its mouth the moment it ceases to be a people, the Jewish people never quite grows one with the languages it speaks. Even when it speaks the language of its host, a special vocabulary, or, at least, a special selection from the general vocabulary, a special word order, its own feeling for what is beautiful or ugly in the language, betray that it is not its own.

Since time immemorial, the Jewish people's own language has ceased to be the language of daily life and yet—as its constant influence on the language of daily life shows—it is

[7] Spaniol: Judaeo-Spanish, spoken by the Sephardic Jews in the Balkans, Greece, and Asia Minor.

anything but a dead language. It is not dead but, as the people themselves call it, a holy language. The holiness of the people's own language has an effect similar to that of the holiness of its own land: it does not allow all their feeling to be lavished on everyday life. It prevents the eternal people from ever being quite in harmony with the times. By encompassing prayer, the ultimate, loftiest region of life, with a holy region of that language, it even prevents this people from ever living in complete freedom and spontaneity. For the freedom and spontaneity of life rest on the fact that man can express in words all he thinks, and that he feels he can do this. When he loses this ability, when he thinks he must be silent in his anguish because it is given only to the "poet to say what he suffers," not alone is the strength of a people's language broken, but its spontaneity too is hopelessly destroyed.

Precisely this ultimate and most fundamental spontaneity is denied the Jew because he addresses God in a language different from the one he uses to speak to his brother. As a result he cannot speak to his brother at all. He communicates with him by a glance rather than in words, and nothing is more essentially Jewish in the deepest sense than a profound distrust of the power of the word and a fervent belief in the power of silence. The holiness of the holy language which the Jew employs only for prayer does not permit his life to put out roots into the soil of a language of its own. So far as his language is concerned, the Jew feels always he is in a foreign land, and knows that the home of his language is in the region of the holy language, a region everyday speech can never invade. The proof of this lies in the peculiar circumstance that, a least in the silent symbols of writing, the language of everyday tries to maintain contact with the old holy language which everyday speech lost long ago. This is altogether different from the situation of the peoples of the world; for with them, the case is that the spoken language survives a written language that is lost, rather than that the written language survives a language no longer spoken on everyday occasions. In his very silence, and in the silent symbols of speech, the Jew feels a connection between his everyday language and the holy language of his holiday.

The Peoples and Their Law

For the peoples of the world, language is the carrier and messenger of time-bound, flowing, changing, and, therefore, transitory life. But the language of the eternal people drives it back to its own life which is beyond external life, which courses through the veins of its living body and is, therefore, eternal. And if the Jew is thus barred from his own soil and his own language, how much more is he deprived of the outwardly visible life the nations live in accordance with their own customs and laws. For a people lives out its day in these two: in custom and law, in what has been handed down from yesterday through force of habit, and in what has been laid down for the morrow. Every day stands between a yesterday and a tomorrow, and all that lives proves it is alive by not standing still one certain day but making of that day a yesterday, and setting in its place a tomorrow. Peoples, too, stay alive by constantly transforming their today into new customs, into new eternal yesterdays, while at the same time they lay down new laws structured out of their today, for the service of their tomorrow. Thus, in the life of the nations, today is a moment which passes fleet as an arrow. And so long as this arrow is in flight, so long as new custom is added to the old, new law outstrips the old, the river of a people's life is in flux, alive. For so long do peoples live within time; for so long is time their heritage and their acre. In addition to their own soil and their own language, the increase in custom and the renewal of law give them the final and strongest guarantee of their own life: a time of their own. So long as a people computes a time of its own—and it computes this time according to its still living store of customs and memories, and the continuous renewal of its lawgiving powers, its leaders and kings—just so long has it power over time, just so long is it not dead.

The Holy Law

And here again the eternal people buys its eternity at the cost of its temporal life. Time is not its time, nor its acre and heritage. For this people, the moment petrifies and stands between unincreased past and immovable future, and so the moment is not fleeting. Custom and law, past and future, become two changeless masses; in this process they cease to be past and future and, in their very rigidity, they too are transmuted into a changeless present. Custom and law, not to be increased or changed, flow into the common basin of what is valid now and forever. A single form of life welding custom and law into one fills the moment and renders it eternal. But because of this, the moment is lifted out of the flux of time; and life, sanctified, no longer has the quality of temporal life. While the myth of peoples changes incessantly—parts of the past are continually being forgotten while others are remembered as myth—here the myth becomes eternal and is not subject to change. And while the peoples of the world live in a cycle of revolutions in which their law sheds its old skin over and over, here the Law is supreme, a law that can be forsaken but never changed.

The holy teaching of the Law—for the name Torah designates both teaching and law as one—raises the people from the temporality and historicity of life, and deprives it of the power over time. The Jewish people does not count years according to a system of its own. For it, neither the memory of its history nor the years of office of its lawgivers can become a measure of time. That is because the memory of its history does not form a point fixed in the past, a point which, year after year, becomes increasingly past. It is a memory which is really not past at all, but eternally present. Every single member of this community is bound to regard the exodus from Egypt as if he himself had been one of those to go.[8] Here there are no lawgivers who renew the law according to the living flux of time. Even what might, for all practical purposes, be considered an innovation must be presented as if it were part of the everlasting Law and had been revealed in the revelation of that Law. And so the chronology of this people cannot be a reckoning of its own time, for the people is timeless; it has no time of its own. It must count years according to the years the world exists. And so again, and for the third time, we see here, in the relation to its own history, what we saw before in its relation to language and land, that this people is denied a life in time for the sake of life in eternity. It cannot experience the history of the nations creatively, and fully. Its position is always somewhere between the temporal and the holy, always separated from the one by the other. And so, in the final analysis, it is not alive in the sense the nations are alive: in a national life manifest on this earth, in a national language giving voice to the soul of the people, in national territory, solidly based and staked out on the soil. It is alive only in that which guarantees it will endure beyond time, in that which pledges it everlastingness, in drawing its own eternity from the sources of the blood.

Fate and Eternity

But just because this people trusts only in the eternity it creates and in nothing else in the world, it really *believes*

---

[8] Quoted from the Passover Haggadah (cf. Mishnah Pesahim X. 5).

in its eternity, while all the peoples of the world believe in common with individual man that death, even although it be at a very distant juncture, must come eventually. The love they bear their own group is grave and sweet with this premonition of death. Love is wholly sweet only when it is love for what is mortal. The secret of ultimate sweetness is bound up with the bitterness of death. The peoples of the world, then, foresee a time when their land with its mountains and rivers will lie beneath the sky even as now, but be inhabited by others, a time when their language will be buried in books and their customs and laws stripped of living force. We alone cannot imagine such a time. For we have long ago been robbed of all the things in which the peoples of the world are rooted. For us, land and language, custom and law, have long left the circle of the living and have been raised to the rung of holiness. But we are still living, and live in eternity. Our life is no longer meshed with anything outside ourselves. We have struck root in ourselves. We do not root in earth and so we are eternal wanderers, but deeply rooted in our own body and blood. And it is this rooting in ourselves, and in nothing but ourselves, that vouchsafes eternity.

The One People: Jewish Individuality

What does this mean: to root in one's self? What does it mean that here one individual people does not seek the warrant of its existence in the external, and reaches out for eternity in its very lack of relations with the outside world? It means no more and no less than that one people, though it is only *one* people, claims to containing the Whole. For whatever is individual is not eternal because the Whole is outside it. It can maintain its individuality only by becoming somehow a part of that Whole. An individual entity which, in spite of its individuality, strove for eternity, would have to take the Whole into itself. With reference to the Jewish people this means that it would have to collect within itself the elements of God, world, and man, of which the Whole consists. God, man, and world of a people are the God, man, and world of that people only because they are just as different and differentiated from other gods, men, and worlds as the people itself from other peoples. The very difference of an individual people from other peoples establishes its connection with them. There are two sides to every boundary. By setting separating borders for ourselves, we border on something else. By being an *individual* people, a nation becomes a people among others. To close oneself off is to come close to another. But this does not hold when a people refuses to be merely an individual people and wants to be "the one people." Under these circumstances it must not close itself off within borders, but include within itself such borders as would, through their double function, tend to make it one individual people among others. And the same is true of its God, man, and world. These three must likewise not be distinguished from those of others; their distinction must be included within its own borders. Since this people wants to be the one people, the God, man, and world must contain the distinguishing characteristics that make them God, man, and world of the one people. In order that each be something very definite and particular, one God, one man, one world, and yet at the same time the Whole: God, man, and world, they must contain opposite poles within themselves.

Polarity

God within himself separates into the God who creates and the God who reveals, the God of omnipotent justice, and the God of love and mercy.[9] Man within himself separates

[9] According to the Talmud, the divine name Elohim indicates the attribute of justice, YHWH the attribute of mercy.

into the soul beloved by God and the lover who loves his neighbor. The world separates into the existence of the creature that longs for God's creation, and life that grows toward and into the kingdom of God. Up to now, we regarded all these separations not as separations but as a sequence of voices taking up the theme in the great fugue of God's day. Up to now, we regarded as essential not separation but union, the union into one harmony. Now, for the first time, now that we are preparing to see eternity as something present at every hour instead of as the twelfth stroke of the world clock, these synthesizing voices appear as antitheses. For in the sheer present which renews itself hour by hour, it is no longer possible for them to pass one another, to interweave in contrapuntal motion; they oppose one another with inflexible rigidity.

The Jewish God

To his people, God the Lord is simultaneously the God of retribution and the God of love. In the same breath, they call on him as "our God" and as "King of the universe," or—to indicate the same contrast in a more intimate sphere—as "our Father" and "our King." He wants to be served with "trembling"[10] and yet rejoices when his children overcome their fear at his wondrous signs. Whenever the Scriptures mention his majesty the next verses are sure to speak of his meekness.[11] He demands the visible signs of offering and prayer brought to his name, and of "the affliction of our soul" in his sight. And almost in the same breath he scorns both and wants to be honored only with the secret fervor of the heart, in the love of one's neighbor, and in anonymous works of justice which no one may recognize as having been done for the sake of his name. He has elected his people, but

[10] Ps. 2:11.
[11] A talmudic tenet (Megillah 31a).

elected it to visit upon them all their iniquities. He wants every knee to bend to him and yet he is enthroned above Israel's songs of praise.[12] Israel intercedes with him in behalf of the sinning peoples of the world and he afflicts Israel with disease so that those other peoples may be healed.[13] Both stand before God: Israel, his servant, and the kings of the peoples; and the strands of suffering and guilt, of love and judgment, of sin and atonement, are so inextricably twined that human hands cannot untangle them.

The Jewish Man

And man, who is created in the image of God, Jewish man as he faces his God, is a veritable repository of contradictions. As the beloved of God, as Israel, he knows that God has elected him and may well forget that he is not alone with God, that God knows others whom he himself may or may not know, that to Egypt and Assyria too, God says: "my people."[14] He knows he is loved—so why concern himself with the world! In his blissful togetherness-alone with God, he may consider himself man, and man alone, and look up in surprise when the world tries to remind him that not every man harbors the same certainty of being God's child as he himself. Yet no one knows better than he that being dear to God is only a beginning, and that man remains unredeemed so long as nothing but this beginning has been realized. Over against Israel, eternally loved by God and faithful and perfect in eternity, stands he who is eternally to come, he who waits, and wanders, and grows eternally— the Messiah. Over against the man of earliest beginnings, against Adam the son of man, stands the man of endings, the son of David the king. Over against him who was created

[12] Ps. 22:4.
[13] Isa. 53.
[14] Isa. 19:25.

305

from the stuff of earth and the breath of the mouth of God, is the descendant from the stem of anointed kings; over against the patriarch, the latest offspring; over against the first, who draws about him the mantle of divine love, the last, from whom salvation issues forth to the ends of the earth; over against the first miracles, the last, which—so it is said—will be greater than the first.

The Jewish World

Finally, the Jewish world: it has been dematerialized and permeated with spirit through the power of blessings which are said over everything and branch everywhere. But this world, also, is twofold and teeming with contradictions in every single thing. Everything that happens in it is ambivalent since it is related both to this and the coming world. The fact that the two worlds, this world and the coming, stand side by side, is all-important. Even the object that receives a soul by a benediction spoken over it has a twofold function: in "this" world it serves everyday purposes, almost as though it had never been blessed, but at the same time it has been rendered one of the stones of which the "coming" world will be built. Benediction splits this world in order to make it whole and one again for what is to come, but for the present all that is visible is the split. As the contrast between holy and profane, Sabbath and workaday, "Torah and the way of earth," spiritual life and the earning of a livelihood, this split goes through all of life. As it divides the life of Israel into holy and profane, so it divides the whole earth into Israel and the peoples. But the division is not simple in the sense that the holy shuts out the profane. The contrast penetrates to the innermost core, and just as the benediction touches everything that is profane and makes it holy, so, quite suddenly, the devout and the wise among all the peoples will participate in the eternal life of the coming world, which but a short time ago seemed reserved for Israel alone. Those who were blessed will themselves become a blessing.

This maze of paradoxes appears when one tries to consider the elements of Jewish life as static elements. The question as to what is the essence can only be answered by exposing paradoxes, and thus cannot really be answered at all. But life that is alive does not ask about essence. It just lives, and insofar as it lives, it answers all questions even before it asks them. What in the investigation of essence seemed a maze of paradoxes falls into an orderly pattern in the yearly rings of life.

[*Der Stern der Erlösung*, III, 48-61]

3. The Jewish Year

From the Star of Redemption[1]

The Holy People: The Jewish Year

In eternity the spoken word fades away into the silence of perfect togetherness—for union occurs in silence only; the word unites, but those who are united fall silent. And so liturgy, the reflector which focuses the sunbeams of eternity in the small circle of the year, must introduce man to this silence. But even in liturgy, shared silence can come only at the end, and all that goes before is a preparation for this end. In the stage of preparation the word still dominates the scene. The word itself must take man to the point of learning how to share silence. His preparation begins with learning to hear.

---

[1] In this section F. R. interprets the fabric of the Jewish calendar in the light of his concept of Creation-Revelation-Redemption, the formulation of which is the substance of the work.

Sociology of the Multitude: The Listening

Nothing would seem easier than this. But here we are concerned with a kind of hearing quite different from that required in dialogue. For in the course of a dialogue he who happens to be listening also speaks, and he does not speak merely when he is actually uttering words, not even mainly when he is uttering words, but just as much when through his eager attention, through the assent or dissent expressed in his glances, he conjures words to the lips of the current speaker. Here it is not this hearing of the eye which is meant, but the true hearing of the ear. What must be learned here is not the kind of hearing that stimulates the speaker to speak but hearing that has nothing to do with a possible reply. Many shall hear. And so the one who speaks must not be the speaker of his own words, for from where could he take his "own" words save from the eloquent glances of his hearers? Provided he is a true speaker, even he who speaks before many is actually carrying on a conversation. The listening crowd, this many-headed monster, is constantly giving the public orator his cue by agreement and displeasure, by interjections and general restlessness, and by the conflicting moods it forces him to parry at every moment. If the orator wants to make himself independent of his audience, he must "deliver" a speech he has memorized instead of speaking impromptu, and so run the risk of having his listeners fall asleep. The more impromptu the impromptu speech is, the more certainly it will give rise to two factions in the audience, and so to something diametrically opposed to unanimous attention on the part of all the hearers. The very essence of the "programmatic speech" is that it is "delivered" and not given. Its purpose is to create an atmosphere of complete unanimity in a gathering—at any cost whatsoever—and so the speaker must necessarily recite a well-prepared program. The unanimity in hearing that is nothing but hearing, the hearing in which a multitude is "all ears," is not due to the person of the speaker, but to the fact that the living, speaking person recedes behind the reader of words, and not even behind the reader, but behind the words he reads. This is why a sermon must be on a "text." It is only this connection with a text that secures it fervent attention on the part of the entire audience. Spontaneous words from the lips of the preacher would not even be spoken with the aim of arousing fervor. Such words would only serve to dissolve the common attention of the hearers. But the text that the assembled congregation values as the word of God secures him who reads it the unanimous attention of all who have come together to hear it. And insofar as everything he says professes to be an interpretation of that text, he holds this unanimous attention throughout his sermon. For a sermon that evoked interjections, or made it hard for the audience to refrain from them, a sermon in which the silence of the hearers could be discharged otherwise than by singing in unison, would be a poor sermon though it might be a good political speech. A political speech, on the other hand, would be a failure if it were not interrupted by "hear, hear" and applause, if the audience were not gay and excited. The sermon as well as the reading of the text is supposed to beget unanimous silence on the part of the assembled congregation. And the nature of the sermon is determined by the fact that it is not a speech but exegesis; the most important part of it is the reading of the text from the Scriptures, for in that reading the unanimity of hearing, and hence the firm foundation for entire unanimity among the congregation, is established.

The Sabbath

Only established, only founded. But as such a foundation, the reading of the Torah becomes the liturgical focus of the holiday on which the spiritual year is founded, of the Sabbath. In the circle of weekly portions which, in the course of one year, cover all of the Torah, the spiritual year is paced out, and the paces of this course are the Sabbaths. By and large, every Sabbath is just like any other, but the difference in the portions from the Scriptures distinguishes each from each, and this difference shows that they are not final in themselves but only parts of a higher order, of the year. For only in the year do the differentiating elements of the individual parts again fuse into a whole. The Sabbath lends reality to the year. This reality must be re-created week by week. One might say that the spiritual year knows only what is dealt with in this portion, but it becomes a year because every week is nothing but a fleeting moment. It is only in the sequence of Sabbaths that the year rounds to a garland. The very regularity in the sequence of Sabbaths, the very fact that, aside from the variation in the Scripture portions, one Sabbath is just like the other, makes them the cornerstones of the year. The year as a spiritual year is created only through them. They precede everything that may still come, and imperturbably go side by side with all else, following their even course amid the splendors of feast days. Through all the surge of joy and sorrow, of anguish and bliss that the feasts bring with them, the even flow of the Sabbaths goes on, the even flow which makes possible those whirlpools of the soul. In the Sabbath the year is created, and thus the main significance of the Sabbath lies in the symbolic meaning of its liturgy: it is a holiday that commemorates Creation.

The Feast of Creation

For God created heaven and earth in six days, and on the seventh he rested. And so the seventh day became the "day of rest," the "Sabbath," to celebrate the "memorial

of the work of creation,"[2] or, more accurately, the completion
of that work—"and the heaven and the earth were finished,
and all the host of them."[3] The Sabbath reflects the creation
of the world in the year. Just as the world is always there,
and wholly there before anything at all happens in it, so
the order of the Sabbaths precedes all the festivals which
commemorate events, and completes its course in the year,
undisturbed by other feasts. And just as creation is not contained in the fact that the world was created once, but requires for its fulfillment renewal at every dawn, so the Sabbath, as the festival of creation, must not be one that is
celebrated only once a year, but one that is renewed throughout the year, week after week the same, and yet week after
week different, because of the difference in the weekly portions. And just as creation is wholly complete, for revelation
adds to it nothing that was not already latent in it as presage,
so the festival of creation must also contain the entire content of the festivals of revelation; in its own inner course
from evening to evening it must be all presage.

Friday Evening

On the Sabbath—in contrast to weekdays—the great prayer
of benedictions, repeated thrice daily, is enriched by inserts
of poetry which convert the simple repetition into an organized and rounded whole. The addition to the prayer on the
eve of the Sabbath refers to the institution of the Sabbath
in the creation of the world. Here the words that conclude
the story of creation occur: " . . . and the heaven and the
earth were finished." On returning from the service in the
House of Prayer, this is repeated in the home, by the holy
light of the candles, before—in the blessing over bread and

---

[2] A passage from the Sabbath home liturgy.
[3] Gen. 2:1.

311

wine as the divine gifts of the earth—the divine nature of what is earthly is attested in the glow of the Sabbath lights and the entire day thus consecrated as a festival commemorating creation. For bread and wine are the most perfect works of man, works that cannot be surpassed. They cannot, however, be compared to his other works in which his inventive mind artfully combines the gifts of nature, and in the act of combining goads itself on to greater and greater artfulness. Bread and wine are nothing but the ennobled gifts of earth; one is the basis of all the strength of life, the other of all its joy. Both were perfected in the youth of the world and of the people thereon, and neither can ever grow old. Every mouthful of bread and every sip of wine tastes just as wonderful as the first we ever savored, and certainly no less wonderful than in time immemorial they tasted to those who for the first time harvested the grain for bread and gathered the fruits of the vine.

Sabbath Morning

While the eve of the Sabbath is primarily a festival in honor of creation, the morning celebrates Revelation. Here the poetic insert in the great prayer of benedictions proclaims the joy of Moses at God's gift of the Sabbath. And the joy of the great receiver of revelation, to whom God "spoke face to face as a man speaketh unto his friend,"[4] and to whom he gave greater recognition than to any later prophet of Israel, is followed, in the order of the day, with the reading of the weekly portion to the congregation by its representatives. On the eve of the Sabbath, expression is given to the knowledge that the earth is a creation; in the morning, we find utterance of the people's awareness of being elect through the gift of the Torah which signifies that eternal life

[4] Exod. 33:11.

has been planted in their midst. The man called forth to the Torah from the congregation approaches the book of revelation in the knowledge of being elect. When he leaves the book and again merges with the congregation, he does so in the knowledge of eternal life. But within the Sabbath, too, this knowledge of eternal life carries him over the threshold separating both revelation and creation from redemption. The Afternoon Prayer becomes the prayer of Redemption.

Sabbath Afternoon

In the insert in this prayer, Israel is more than the chosen people, it is the "one and only" people, the people of the One and Only God. Here all the fervor which the praying Jew breathes into the holy word "One," the fervor which compels the coming of the Kingdom, is at its greatest intensity. Twice daily, in the morning and in the evening profession,[5] after the community of Israel has been created through the injunction to "hear," and the immediate presence of God has been acknowledged by the invocation of God as "our God," God's "unity" is proclaimed as his eternal name beyond all name, beyond all presence. And we know that this proclamation is more than a fleeting word; we know that within it the eternal union of God with his people and of his people with mankind occurs through every individual "taking upon himself the yoke of the kingdom of God."[6] All this vibrates in the Afternoon Prayer of the Sabbath, in the hymn on the one people of the One and Only God. And the songs of the "third meal," at which old men and children gather around the long table in the light of the waning day, reel with the transport of certainty that the Messiah will come and will come soon.

[5] "Hear, O Israel: the Lord our God, the Lord is one."
[6] This is done, according to the Talmud (Mishnah Berakhot II. 2), by reciting this profession.

The Close of the Sabbath

But this entire course of the day of God is included in the circuit of the individual Sabbath like a preview that can only be realized to the full in other festivals yet to come. The realization does not occur in the Sabbath itself. The Sabbath is and remains a festival of rest, of reflection. It is the static foundation of the year which—aside from the sequence of weekly portions—is informed with motion only by the cycle of other festivals. As ornaments carved on a frame are the hints of the contents of revelation that make the actual pictures to be set within that frame, each at its own given time. The Sabbath itself is not merely a festival, but also just another day in the week, and very much so. It does not stand out in the year like the actual festivals, even though the structure of the year is based upon it; it stands out in the week. And so it also merges with the week again. When the congregation enters the House of God it acclaims the Sabbath with joy, as the bridegroom does the bride, but later the Sabbath vanishes into quotidian life like a dream. The smallest circuit set for man, the workday week, begins again. A child holds the light that an older man lit while, with closed eyes, he drinks a cup of wine, waking from the dream of perfection spun by the festival of the seventh day. A way must be found from the sanctuary back into the workaday world. The year, all of life, is built up on the shift from the holy to the profane, from the seventh to the first day, from perfection to outset, from old age to early youth. The Sabbath is the dream of perfection, but it is only a dream. Only in its being both does it become the cornerstone of life; only as the festival of perfection does it become the constant renewal of creation.

Rest

For this is the ultimate significance of the Sabbath: it was instituted primarily to commemorate the work of the beginning and thus forms the solid and lasting basis of the spiritual year. On the other hand, its institution was the first sign of revelation within the act of creation itself; though veiled, the revealed name of God appears in the Scriptures for the first time in the words instituting the Sabbath. So, through being at once the sign of creation and the first revelation, it is also, and even mainly, the anticipation of redemption. For what is redemption if not the concord between revelation and creation? And what is the first ineluctable premise for such concord, save man's rest after he has done the work of this earth! Six days he has worked and attended to all his affairs; now, on the seventh, he rests. Six days he has uttered the many useful and useless things the workday demanded of him, but on the seventh he obeys the command of the prophet: he lets his tongue rest from the talk of everyday, and learns to be silent, to *listen*. And this sanctifying of the day of rest by *listening* to God's voice in silence must be shared by all members of his house. It must not be fretted by the noise of giving orders. The man-servant and the maid-servant must also rest; and it is even said that just for the sake of their rest the day of rest was instituted, for when rest has penetrated to them, then all the house is, indeed, freed from the noise and chatter of the weekday, and redeemed to rest.

Perfection

The rest is intended to signify redemption and not a period of collecting oneself for more work. Work is an ever new beginning. The first day of work is the first day of the week, but the day of rest is the seventh. The feast of creation is the feast of perfection. In celebrating it we go, in the midst of creation, beyond creation and revelation. The great Sabbath prayer of benedictions involves none of those requests that are concerned with the needs of the individual. There are not merely none of the weekday requests for creature comforts, such as a good year, a good harvest, health, intelligence, and good management, but also none of the requests of every child of God for forgiveness of sins, and ultimate redemption. Besides the requests for peace and the coming of the Kingdom—individual as well as community requests—there is only praise and thanks. For on the Sabbath the congregation feels as if it were already redeemed—to the degree such a feeling is at all possible in anticipation. The Sabbath is the feast of creation, but of a creation wrought for the sake of redemption. This feast instituted at the close of creation is creation's meaning and goal. That is why we do not celebrate the festival of the primordial work of creation on the first day of creation, but on its last, on the seventh day.

Sociology of the Community: The Meal

Silent listening was only the beginning of community. It instituted community; and, as always, here too there had to be continual return to the original institution, so that by this summoning to concentration new strength could again and again be drawn from the depths of the beginning. But the inner life of the community does not begin and end with this initial silent listening. This life is born only in an act which is essentially a renewal. Not in a mere repetition of a beginning once created, but in the re-creating of what has grown effete. The re-creating of bodily life, the transforming of matter grown old, occurs in the course of a meal. Even for the individual, eating and drinking constitute rebirth for the body. For the community, the meal taken in common is the action through which it is reborn to conscious life.

The silent *community of hearing* and heeding establishes even the smallest community, that of the household. The household is based on the circumstance that the word of the father of the family is heard and heeded. Still, the *common life* of the household does not become manifest in the common heeding but in the meal at which all the members of the house gather round the table. Here each is the equal of every other; each lives for himself and yet is joined with all the others. It is not table talk that establishes this community, for in many rural districts it is not customary to speak during the meal, it is even contrary to custom. Talking at table does not, at any rate, establish community; at most it expresses it. One can talk in the street and in the square wherever people meet haphazardly. The common meal with its silent community represents actual community alive in the midst of life.

Wherever a meal is held in common, there is such community, whether it be in the house, in monasteries, lodges, clubs, or in fraternities. And wherever such community is absent, as, for instance, in schoolrooms or at lectures, or even at the meetings of seminars, it is lacking even though the basis of community, listening in common, is most certainly in evidence. It takes social occasions, such as school excursions, or informal evenings for the members of the seminar, to achieve true community life on that basis which, in itself, is nothing but a basis. The shame of primitive peoples at the mere thought of eating together, and the opprobrious practice—in restaurants—of eating alone and especially of reading one's paper while eating, are signs of a civilization that is either unripe and sour, or overripe and touched with rot. The sweet, fully ripened fruit of humanity craves the community of man with man in the very act of renewing the life of the body. Even without this community the discipline of common obedience may, of course, persist. The suspicious savage, for instance, who takes his meal in solitude, is not trying to make himself independent of the laws of his tribe any more than the confirmed bachelor dining alone in his restaurant is deliberately falling short of the requirements of his particular duties. Common obedience may persist, but what is missing is the feeling of freedom which alone can conjure up the life of the community against the unfailing background of a common discipline. The common life as represented by the common meal is, of course, not the ultimate experience; it is no more ultimate than common listening. But on the road of education to the ultimate experience of common silence this is the second station, just as common listening is the first. The common meal is an integral part of the Sabbath as well as of all other feasts. But as the actual focus of the feast we find it in the first of those festivals which together, in their sequence within the solid frame of the year, reflect the people's eternal course in changing images.

The Feasts of Revelation

The three pilgrimage festivals, that of the deliverance from Egypt, that of the revelation of the Ten Commandments, and the Feast of Booths in the wilderness, feasts to which everyone in the land once journeyed to the common sanctuary, give an image of the people as the carrier of revelation. Creation and redemption, too, are revealed in revelation, creation because it was done for the sake of redemption and thus, in a narrower sense, is actually the creation of revelation; redemption because revelation bids us wait for it. And so, in the course of the destiny of the people chosen for revelation, the periods of the feasts in which this people grows aware of its vocation to be the recipient of revelation are grouped around the day and the moment on which revelation is actually received. This vocation is shown in three stages: the people are created into *a people;* this people is endowed with the words of revelation; and with the Torah it has received this people wanders through the wilderness of the world. The eight-day periods of the Passover and of the Feast of Booths are grouped around the two-day Feast of Weeks. In these three festivals, the steps of eternal history pace the ground of the year with its cycle of Sabbaths, a ground which is, as it were, eternal in nature. For these feasts only *seem* to be feasts of commemoration. In reality, the historical element in them is living and present, and what is said to every participant at the first festival holds for them all: that he must celebrate the feast as though he himself had been delivered from Egypt. The beginning, the middle, and the end of this national history, the founding, the zenith, and the eternity of the people, are reborn with every new generation.

The Feast of Deliverance

The welding of people into a people takes place in its deliverance. And so the feast that comes at the beginning of its national history is a feast of deliverance. Because of this, the Sabbath can legitimately be interpreted as a reminder of the exodus from Egypt. For the freedom of the man-servant and the maid-servant which it proclaims is conditioned by the deliverance of the people as a people from the servitude of Egypt. And in every command to respect the freedom of even the man-servant, of even the alien among the people, the law of God renews the awareness of the connection holding between the freedom within the people, a freedom decreed by God, and the freeing of the people from Egyptian servitude, a liberation enacted by God. Like the creation of the world, the creation of the people contains the final goal, the final purpose for which it was effected. So it is that the people have come to feel this feast as the most vivid of the three, including the meaning of the two others.

Among the many meals of the spiritual year, the evening meal of the Passover at which the father of the household gathers together all his family is the meal of meals. It is the only one that from first to last has the character of worship; hence the Seder ("Order") is, from first to last, liturgically regulated. From the very start the word "freedom" sheds its light upon it. The freedom of this meal at which all are equally free is expressed in a number of rites which "distinguish this night from all nights," among them the reclining of the participants on cushions. And even more vividly than in this reminiscence of the reclining of the guests in the symposia of antiquity, this particular freedom expresses itself in the fact that the youngest child is the one to speak, and that what the father says at table is adapted to this child's personality and his degree of maturity. In contrast to all instruction, which is necessarily autocratic and never on a basis of equality, the sign of a true and free social intercourse is this, that the one who stands—relatively speaking—nearest the periphery of the circle, gives the cue for the level on which the conversation is to be conducted. For this conversation must include him. No one who is there in the flesh shall be excluded in the spirit. The freedom of a society is always the freedom of everyone who belongs to it. Thus this meal is a symbol of the people's vocation for freedom. That this vocation is only a beginning, only the *initial* creation of the people, is shown in another aspect of this prominence of the youngest child. Since this youngest was permitted to speak for himself, the entire ceremony has, after all, to assume the form of instruction. The father of the family speaks, the household listens, and only in the further course of the evening is there more and more common independence until, in the songs of praise and the table songs of the second part of the meal, songs which float between divine mystery and the jesting mood begot by wine, the last shred of autocracy in the order of the meal dissolves into community.

The founding of the people affords a glimpse of its future destinies, but no more than a glimpse. All its further destinies are prefigured in its origin. It is not only today that enemies rise to destroy us; they rose to destroy us in every generation, back to the first, which went out of Egypt, and in every generation God saved us![7] And we should have been content with what he did for us when he delivered us from the servitude of Egypt, but he to whom he alone suffices did not consider it sufficient. He led us to Mount Sinai and on to the place of rest in his sanctuary.[7] The texts read from the Scriptures on the last days of the feast give a survey from the origin on to what is latent in this origin, in this creation of the people: on to revelation and ultimate redemption. The reading of the Song of Songs[8] points to revelation. A distant view of redemption is afforded by Isaiah's prophecy[9] of the shoot that shall come forth out of the stock of Jesse and smite the land with the rod of his mouth, of the day when the wolf shall dwell with the lamb and the world shall be as full of the knowledge of the Lord as the sea is of water. But the stock shall stand, an ensign for the peoples, and the heathen shall seek it. And this is the deepest meaning of the farewell which those who participate in the evening meal bid one another: Next year in Jerusalem! In every house where the meal is celebrated a cup filled with wine stands ready for the prophet Elijah, the precursor of the shoot from the stock of Jesse, who is forever "turning the hearts of the fathers to their children and the hearts of the children to their fathers,"[10] so that the flow of blood may not cease during the long night of time, and stream on toward a morning to come.

[7] A paraphrase of a passage in the Passover Haggadah.
[8] Customarily done after the conclusion of the Passover Seder.
[9] Isa. 11:1-10, a part of the portion of the Prophets read on the eighth day of Passover.
[10] Mal. 3:24.

The Feast of Revelation

Among the three feasts of the people of the revelation, the feast of the revelation in a narrower sense lasts only two brief days. As a momentary present, revelation stands between the long, the everlasting has-been of the past and the eternal to-come of the future. And just as revelation is intimately linked with creation, so that it is contained in it, while creation in turn points to revelation, presaging revelation as a fulfilment of creation, so the feast of revelation to the people is closely connected with that which commemorates the founding of the people. From the second day of the feast of deliverance on, a counting of days to the feast of the revelation begins both in the House of God and in the home. The festival itself is concentrated exclusively on the twofold miracle of Sinai: God's descent to his people and the proclaiming of the Ten Commandments. In contrast to the feast in memory of the origin of the people, which contains everything else in the germ, this feast knows of nothing save of Him. The before and after of revelation remain in shadow. The people is wholly immersed in its togetherness with God. Even the passages read from the Prophets do not open backward or forward vistas, but guide the eye already turned inward still more wholly inward: Ezekiel's enigmatic vision of the celestial chariot which carries the throne of God, and Habakkuk's stormy song of God's tempestuous entry into the world, the first pointing to the secrets of God's essence, the second a picturing of his almighty manifestation, but both within the scope of the greatest moment of revelation. Neither do the festival hymns composed at a later date ever tire of inventing new poetic paraphrases for the one great content of revelation, for the Ten Commandments.

The Feast of Booths

But the people is not allowed to linger in the sheltering shade of Sinai, in which God sheathed it so that it might be alone with him. It must leave the hidden togetherness with God and issue forth into the world. It must start upon its wanderings through the wilderness, the wanderings whose end the generation that stood under Sinai shall not live to see. It will be a later-born generation that will find rest in the divine sanctuary of home, when the wanderings through the wilderness are over. The Feast of Booths is the feast of both wanderings and rest. In memory of those long wanderings of the past which finally led to rest, the members of the family do not have their merry meal in the familiar rooms of the house but under a roof which is quickly constructed, a makeshift roof with heaven shining through the gaps. This serves to remind the people that no matter how solid the house of today may seem, no matter how temptingly it beckons to rest and unimperiled living, it is but a tent which permits only a pause in the long wanderings through the wilderness of centuries. For rest, the rest of which the builder of the first Temple spoke, does not come until all these wanderings are at an end, and his words are read at this feast: "Blessed be He that has given rest unto his people."[11]

The passages from the Prophets read on the occasion of this festival again prove—if there is still need of such proof —that this double meaning is the meaning of the feast, that it is a feast of redemption only within the circle of the three festivals of revelation. Because of this, redemption is celebrated here only as the hope and certainty of future redemption; and while this feast is celebrated in the same month

[11] I Kings 8:56, a part of the portion from the Prophets read on the eighth day of the feast.

as the Days of Awe, which are the feasts of a redemption present and eternal, and borders on these Days in neighborly fashion, it does not coincide with them. On the first day of the Feast of Booths the majestic closing chapter from Zechariah is read, the chapter concerning the day of the Lord with the prediction that concludes the daily service: "And the Lord shall be King over all the earth; in that day shall the Lord be One, and His name: One."

This ultimate word of hope concludes the daily service of the assembled congregation, and also comes at the conclusion of the spiritual year. On the other days of the festival, these words are paralleled by the ones Solomon spoke at the dedication of the Temple, when the wandering ark at last found the rest the people had already found under Joshua. Solomon's concluding words wonderfully connect the hope for future recognition "that all the peoples of the earth may know that the Lord, He is God; there is none else,"[12] with a warning to the one people: "Let your heart, therefore, be whole with the Lord."[13] And in the chapter from Ezekiel read at this festival, classical expression is given to this merging into each other of unity of the heart, unity of God, and unity of peoples which, in the concept of the sanctification of God's name through *the* people for all the peoples, forms the inmost basis of Judaism. This chapter is also the biblical source of the prayer which is primarily the prayer of this threefold sanctification, the Kaddish: "Thus will I magnify Myself and sanctify Myself, and I will make Myself known in the eyes of many nations; and they shall know that I am the Lord."[14]

Thus the Feast of Booths is not only a festival of rest for the people, but also the festival of the ultimate hope. It is a

[12] I Kings 8:60.
[13] I Kings 8:61.
[14] Ezek. 38:23.

festival of rest only in that it breathes hope. In this festival of redemption there is no present redemption. Redemption is only a hope, only something expected in the course of wanderings. And so this feast cannot be the last word, since it does not include redemption in its own domains but only glimpses it and lets it be glimpsed from the mountain of revelation. As the Sabbath flows back into the weekday, so this close of the spiritual year is not permitted to be an actual close but must flow back into the beginning. On the festival of Rejoicing in the Law, the last word in the Torah gives rise to the first. And the old man who, in the name of the congregation, is in charge of this transition, is not called "husband of the Torah," but through all time goes by the name of "bridegroom of the Torah." It is not without good cause that the book full of corroding doubt, Ecclesiastes, is assigned to be read at the Feast of Booths. The disenchantment which follows upon the Sabbath the moment its fragrance has been breathed for the last time and the weekday asserts itself in all its old unbroken strength is, as it were, included in the festival itself through the reading of Ecclesiastes. Although the Feast of Booths celebrates redemption and rest, it is nevertheless the festival of wandering through the wilderness. Neither in the feasts that unite people at a common meal, nor in those that unite them in common listening, does man have the experience of community begot by ultimate silence. Beyond the mere founding of the community in the common word, beyond the expression of the community in a common life, there must be something higher, even if this something lies at the farthest border of community life and constitutes community beyond common life.

Sociology of the Whole: The Greeting

The institution of listening in common became the premise of living in common. The community was called by a common name and as it responded, it began to exist. Now they could sit down at the table of life together. But the common meal united the community only at the hours in which it was eaten. And this meal constituted a community only of those whom it actually united. Only invited guests come to a meal. But anyone at all who hears the word can obey it. Only he who is invited can come to the meal, and that means he who has heard the word. Before he comes to the meal, he does not know the other guests. He himself did indeed hear the invitation, but then each one heard only himself being invited. Not before the meal does he become acquainted with the others. The common silence of those who heard the word is still a silence of the individual. Only at table do the guests become acquainted, in the talk which springs from sitting at table together. And so, when the guests leave, they are no longer strangers to one another. They greet one another when they meet again. Such greeting is the loftiest symbol of silence. They are silent because they know one another. If all men, all contemporaries, all the dead and all the still unborn, were to greet one another, they would have had to eat a pound of salt with one another—as the saying goes. But this premise cannot be established. And yet it is this greeting, alone, of all to all that would constitute the utmost community, the silence that can never again be broken. The voices of all who have not heard the call disturb the devoutness of listening. The quiet of the family table is not respected by the noise of those who have not been invited and pass unsuspectingly beneath the lit window. The silence would be perfect, and the community common to all, only if there were no one who was not silent. The precondition for the greeting of all to all, wherein this common silence expresses itself, would have to be listening in common and eating in common, just as every ordinary greeting has for its premise at least an introduction and the exchange of a few words. But how is this greeting of all to all to take place?

How can it take place? How is it brought about where it does take place—say in the army? Certainly not in the salute of two soldiers who meet! If this greeting, this salute, is from a private to an officer, it is only a token of listening in common, and by no means of listening on the part of one alone. If it is given to a comrade, it constitutes a reminder of working and suffering together, being hungry and being on guard together, of the common march and the dangers common to both. The stiff salute is intended for the discipline reigning everywhere and at every instant, which is the basis of the whole structure; the comradely greeting is given for the sake of a common life, which is not by any means always and everywhere but exists at certain moments while remaining in abeyance at others. Both together, unrelenting discipline and the easily awakened sense of comradeship, the first lasting, the second transitory, support and renew the morale of the army. Both are the sources of this common spirit, but not all of this spirit becomes visible in these two forms of greeting. This greeting is never anything more than one of the elements constituting the whole.

The whole, and the knowledge that one belongs to it, can only be experienced in a parade, in saluting a flag, in review before the commander-in-chief. Here, where the salute is directed to one who need salute no one at all, or who, like the flag, is not even in a position to salute, it does not merely express obedience common to soldier and officer alike, but the spirit common to all the members of this army, always. For the soldier feels that the stuff of the flag and the stem of his kings is older than anything living, and will survive it.

And what is meant here is not community of living, for neither flag nor king can die, but destiny, insofar as it is common to all those who salute here, now, and forever. Thus we know the sole way in which this greeting of all to all can take place, independent of how many of the living are prepared for such greeting by a common word and a common meal that has gone before; independent of the obvious fact that such a community of all through all can never be realized. The greeting takes place in this, that those who are prepared by such twofold community prostrate themselves in common before the Lord of all time. Kneeling in common before the Lord of all in the world, and "of the spirits in all flesh,"[15] opens the way for the community, and only for this community and the individual within it, the way to the all-embracing common unity where everyone knows everyone else and greets him wordlessly—face to face.

The Feasts of Redemption

The Days of Awe are festivals of a special character, celebrated in the month of that feast which, among the feasts of the community, has as its content: arriving at rest. What distinguishes the Days of Awe from all other festivals is that here and only here does the Jew kneel. Here he does what he refused to do before the king of Persia, what no power on earth can compel him to do, and what he need not do before God on any other day of the year, or in any other situation he may face during his lifetime. And he does not kneel to confess a fault or to pray for forgiveness of sins, acts to which this festival is primarily dedicated. He kneels only in beholding the immediate nearness of God, hence on an occasion which transcends the earthly needs of today. For the same reason, the Prayer of Benedictions said on every Sabbath omits the request for forgiveness of sins.

[15] Num. 16:22.

The Day of Atonement, which climaxes the ten-day period of redemption, is quite properly called the Sabbath of Sabbaths. The congregation now rises to the feeling of God's nearness as it sees in memory the Temple service of old, and visualizes especially the moment when the priest, this once in all the year, pronounced the ineffable name of God that was expressed by a circumlocution on all other occasions, and the assembled people fell on their knees. And the congregation participates directly in the feeling of God's nearness when it says the prayer that is bound up with the promise of a future time, "when every knee shall bow before God, when the idols will be utterly cut off, when the world will be perfected under the kingdom of the Almighty, and all the children of flesh will call upon his name, when he will turn unto himself all the wicked of the earth, and all will accept the yoke of his kingdom." On the Days of Awe, this prayer mounts beyond the version of the Concluding Prayer of the everyday service. On these Days of Awe the plea for bringing about such a future is already part of the Central Prayer, which—in solemn words—calls for the day when all creatures will prostrate themselves that "they may all form a single band to do God's will with a whole heart." But the Concluding Prayer, which utters this cry day after day, silences it on the Days of Awe, and, in complete awareness that this congregation is not yet the "single band" of all that is created, anticipates the moment of eternal redemption by seizing on it now, in the present. And what the congregation merely expresses in words in the course of the year, it here expresses in action: it prostrates itself before the King of Kings.

The Judgment

Thus the Days of Awe, New Year's Day, and the Day of Atonement place the eternity of redemption into time. The horn blown on New Year's Day at the peak of the festival stamps the day as a "day of judgment." The judgment usually thought of as at the end of time is here placed in the immediate present. And so it cannot be the world that is being judged—for where could the world be at this very present! It is the individual who faces judgment. Every individual is meted out his destiny according to his actions. The verdict for the past and the coming year is written on New Year's Day, and it is sealed on the Day of Atonement, when the last reprieve constituted by these ten days of penitence and turning to God is over. The year becomes representative of eternity, in complete representation. In the annual return of this day of judgment, eternity is stripped of every trace of the beyond, of every vestige of remoteness; it is actually there, within the grasp of every individual and holding every individual close in its strong grasp. He is no longer part of the eternal history of the eternal people, nor is he part of the eternally changing history of the world. There is no more waiting, no more hiding behind history. The individual confronts judgment without any intermediary factor. He stands in the congregation. He says "We." But the "We" of this day are not the "We" of the people in history; the sin for which we crave forgiveness is not the sin of transgression of laws which separates this people from the other peoples of the world. On these days, the individual in all his naked individuality stands immediately before God. Only his human sin is named in the moving recital of the sins "which we have sinned," a recital which is far more than mere recital. It shines into the most hidden corners of being and calls forth the confession of the One sin in the unchanging human heart.

Sin

And so "We" in whose community the individual recognizes his sin, can be nothing less than the congregation of mankind itself. Just as the year, on these days, represents eternity, so Israel represents mankind. Israel is aware of praying "with the sinners." And—no matter what the origin of the obscure phrase may be—this means praying, in the capacity of all of mankind, "with" everyone. For everyone is a sinner. Though the soul is pure when God gives it to man, it is immediately snatched into the struggle between the two urges of his heart divided against itself. And though he may concentrate his will over and over, though he renew his purpose and vow and begin the work of unifying and purifying his divided heart over and over, still at that boundary between two years which signifies eternity, all purpose becomes vain, and all consecration desecration. . . .

Death and Life

Throughout these days, a wholly visible sign expresses the underlying motif, namely, that for the individual, eternity is here shifted into time. For on these days the worshipper wears his shroud. It is true that even on ordinary days, the moment when the prayer shawl—chlamys and toga of antiquity— is donned, that moment directs the mind to the shroud, and to eternal life when God will sheathe the soul in his mantle. Thus the weekday and the weekly Sabbath, as well as creation itself, illumine death as the crown and goal of creation. But the entire shroud, comprising not only the shawl but also the under-robe—chiton and tunic of antiquity—is not the costume of everyday. Death is the ultimate, the boundary of creation. Creation cannot encompass death as such. Only revelation has the knowledge—and it is the primary knowledge of revelation—that love is as strong as death. And so in some parts, a man wears, on his wedding day under the bridal canopy, his complete shroud which he has received from the hands of the bride. Not until he is married does he become a true member of his

people. It is significant that at a boy's birth the father prays
that it may be vouchsafed him to bring up his son to the
Torah, to the bridal canopy, and to good works. To learn the
Torah and to keep the commandments is the omnipresent
basis of Jewish life. Marriage brings with it the full realization of this life, for only then do the "good works" become
possible. Only the man needs to be aware that the Torah is
the basis of his life. When a daughter is born, the father
simply prays that he may lead her to the bridal canopy and
to good works. For a woman has this basis of Jewish life
for her own without having to learn it deliberately over and
over, as the man who is less securely rooted in the depths
of nature is compelled to do. According to ancient law, it
is the woman who propagates Jewish blood. The child of
a Jewish mother is Jewish by birth, just as the child of parents who are both Jewish.

Thus, in the individual life, it is marriage that fills mere
Jewish existence with soul. The household is the chamber
of the Jewish heart. Revelation wakens something in creation that is as strong as death and sets it up against death
and against all of creation. The new creation of revelation is
the soul, which is unearthly in earthly life. Similarly, the
bridegroom wears his death attire as his wedding attire, and
at the very moment he becomes a true member of the eternal people he challenges death and becomes as strong as
death. But that which is a moment in the life of the individual is also a moment, but an eternal moment, in the
spiritual year. Here too, the father of the family wears his
shroud, not as the attire of death but as wedding attire, on
one single occasion: at the first of the feasts of revelation,
at the Passover Seder, the evening meal of the electing of
the people to freedom. Here too, the garments worn in
death indicate the transition from mere creation to revelation. The shroud is worn at the first of the three feasts, and

here too, in drinking and eating, in gay, childlike jests and merry songs, it is a challenge to death.

Atonement

But on the Days of Awe it is worn in a very different spirit. Here it is not a wedding attire but the true attire of death. Man is utterly alone on the day of his death, when he is clothed in his shroud, and in the prayers of these days he is also alone. They too set him, lonely and naked, straight before the throne of God. In time to come, God will judge him solely by his own deeds and the thoughts of his own heart. God will not ask about those around him and what they have done to help him or to corrupt him. He will be judged solely according to what he himself has done and thought. On the Days of Awe, too, he confronts the eyes of his judge in utter loneliness, as if he were dead in the midst of life, a member of the community of man which, like himself, has placed itself beyond the grave in the very fullness of living. Everything lies behind him. At the commencement of the last day, the Day of Atonement, for which the preceding nine Days of Awe were only a preparation, he had prayed that all his vows, his self-consecration, and his good resolves might be annulled, and in that prayer he had attained to that pure humility which asks to be nothing but the erring child of Him and before Him, whom he implores to forgive him just as He forgave "all the congregation of the children of Israel, and the stranger that sojourneth among them, for in respect of all the people it was done in error." Now he is ready to confess, and to repeat the confession of his own sin in the sight of God. He is no longer guilty before man. If he were oppressed by guilt against man, he would have to have it remitted in confessing it, man to man. The Day of Atonement does not remit such guilt and has nothing to do with it. On the Day of Atonement, all sins, even those committed against and pardoned by man, are sins before God, the sins of the solitary individual, the sins of the soul. And God lifts up his countenance to this united and lonely pleading of men in their shrouds, men beyond the grave, of a community of souls, God who loves man both before and after he has sinned, God whom man, in his need, may challenge, asking why he has forsaken him, God who is "merciful and gracious, long-suffering and abundant in goodness and truth, who keeps his mercy unto the thousandth generation, who forgives iniquity and transgression and sin, and has mercy on him who returns." And so man to whom the divine countenance is lifted bursts out into the exultant profession:[16] "The Lord is God:" this God of love, he alone is God!

The Way Back into the Year

Everything earthly lies so far behind the transport of eternity in this profession, that it is difficult to imagine that a way can lead back from here into the circuit of the year. That is why it is most significant for the structure of the spiritual year that the festivals of immediate redemption do not conclude the feast month of redemption which closes the annual cycle of Sabbaths. For after them comes the Feast of Booths, which is a feast of redemption founded on the base of an unredeemed era and of a people yet within the pale of history. In the common unity of man, the soul was alone with God. To neutralize this foretaste of eternity, the Feast of Booths reinstates the reality of time. Thus the circuit of the year can recommence, for only within this circuit are we allowed to conjure eternity up into time.

It was the circuit of a people. In it, a people was at its goal and knew it was at the goal. The people had solved for

---

[16] The very last sentence in the service of the Day of Atonement.

itself the contradiction between creation and revelation. It lived in its own redemption. It had anticipated eternity. The future is the driving power in the circuit of its year. The present passes not because the past prods it on but because the future snatches it toward itself. Somehow, even the festivals of creation and revelation flow into redemption. What gives the year strength to begin anew and link its ring, which is without beginning and end, into the chain of time, is this, that the feeling that redemption is still unattained breaks through again, and thereby the thought of eternity, which seemed contained in the cup of the moment, brims up and surges over the rim. But the people remains the eternal people. The meaning of its life in time is that the years come and go, one after the other as a sequence of waiting, or perhaps wandering, but not of growth. For growth would imply that perfection in time is still unattained, and so it would be a denial of the people's eternity. Eternity is just this: that time no longer has a right to a place between the present moment and perfection and that the whole future is to be grasped today.

[*Der Stern der Erlösung*, III, 61-87]

4. Outcast and Elect

A Note to a Poem By Judah ha-Levi

This people has a unique characteristic which, when one tries to dismiss it through the front door of reason, forces an entrance through the back door of feeling. It is evident in the paroxysms of an anti-Semitism that never found madder expression than in the hundred and twenty years during which everyone tried to prove that Jews were no different from other people. The unique characteristic of the people is this: that it looks at itself in about the same way as the outside world looks at it. A whole world asserts that the

Jewish people is outcast and elect, both; and the Jewish people does not itself, in some assertion of its own, refute this dictum, but instead merely confirms it. Except that seen from the outside, the characterization assumes the form of external connectedness, while from within it represents an inseparable whole, and the vessels of curse and blessing communicate so closely that the latter can overflow only when the former too is full to the brim.

[*Judah ha-Levi*, p. 223]

5. The Nations and their States

From the Star of Redemption[1]

And so the eternal people must forget the world's growth, must cease to think thereon. It must look upon the world, its own world, as complete, though the soul may yet be on the way: the soul can indeed overtake the final goal in one single leap. And if not, it must needs wait and wander on —to quote the wise Spanish proverb, "Patience, and a new shuffle of the cards." Waiting and wandering is the business of the soul, growth that of the world. It is this very growth that the eternal people denies itself. As nationality, it has reached the point to which the nations of the world still aspire. Its world has reached the goal. The Jew finds in his people the perfect fusion with a world of his own, and to achieve this fusion himself, he need not sacrifice a jot of his peculiar existence. The nations have been in a state of inner conflict ever since Christianity with its supernational power came upon them. Ever since then, and everywhere, a Siegfried is at strife with that stranger, the man of the cross, in his very appearance so antagonizing a character.

---

[1] In F. R.'s text, this and the succeeding chapter follow immediately after the discussion of the Jewish year.

A Siegfried who, depending on the nation he comes from, may be blond and blue-eyed, or dark and small-boned, or brown and dark-eyed, wrestles again and again with this stranger who resists the continued attempts to assimilate him to that nation's own longing and vision. The Jew alone suffers no conflict between the supreme vision which is placed before his soul and the people among whom his life has placed him. He alone possesses the unity of myth which the nations lost through the influx of Christianity, which they were bound to lose, for their own myth was pagan, and, by leading them into this myth, led them away from God and their neighbor. The Jew's myth, leading him into his people, brings him face to face with God who is also the God of all nations. The Jewish people feels no conflict between what is its very own and what is supreme; the love it has for itself inevitably becomes love for its neighbor.

Because the Jewish people is beyond the contradiction that constitutes the vital drive in the life of the nations—the contradiction between national characteristics and world history, home and faith, earth and heaven—it knows nothing of war. For the peoples of antiquity, war was after all only one among other natural expressions of life: it held no fundamental contradiction. To the nations war means staking life in order to live. A nation that fares forth to war accepts the possibility of dying. This is not significant so long as nations regard themselves as mortal. While this conviction lasts, it is of no importance that of the two legitimate reasons for waging war as given by the great Roman orator—that of *salus* and that of *fides*, self-preservation and the keeping of the pledged word—the second may sometimes be in contradiction to the first. There is, after all, no good reason why Saguntum and its people shall not perish from the earth. But what it means becomes clear when Augustine, who is responsible for the clever refutation of

Cicero, declares: the church cannot fall into such conflict between its own welfare and the faith pledged to a higher being; for the church, *salus* and *fides* are one and the same thing. What Augustine here says of the church holds in a narrower sense also for worldly communities, for nations and states which have begun to regard their own existence from the highest point of view. . . .

As against the life of the nations of the world, constantly involved in a war of faith, the Jewish people has left its war of faith far behind in its mythical antiquity. Hence, whatever wars it experiences are purely political wars. But since the concept of a war of faith is ingrained in it, it cannot take these wars as seriously as the peoples of antiquity to whom such a concept was alien. In the whole Christian world, the Jew is practically the only human being who cannot take war seriously, and this makes him the only genuine pacifist. For that reason, and because he experiences perfect community in his spiritual year, he remains remote from the chronology of the rest of the world, even though this has long ceased to be a chronology peculiar to individual peoples and, as Christian chronology, is accepted as a principle common to the world at large. He does not have to wait for world history to unroll its long course to let him gain what he feels he already possesses in the circuit of every year: the experience of the immediacy of each single individual to God, realized in the perfect community of all with God.

The Jewish people has already reached the goal toward which the nations are still moving. It has that inner unity of faith and life which, while Augustine may ascribe it to the church in the form of the unity between *fides* and *salus*, is still no more than a dream to the nations within the church. But just because it has that unity, the Jewish people is bound to be outside the world that does not yet have it. Through living in a state of eternal peace it is outside of time agitated by wars. Insofar as it has reached the goal which it anticipates in hope, it cannot belong to the procession of those who approach this goal through the work of centuries. Its soul, replete with the vistas afforded by hope, grows numb to the concerns, the doing and the struggling of the world. The consecration poured over it as over a priestly people renders its life "unproductive." Its holiness hinders it from devoting its soul to a still unhallowed world, no matter how much the body may be bound up with it. This people must deny itself active and full participation in the life of this world with its daily, apparently conclusive, solving of all contradictions. It is not permitted to recognize this daily solving of contradictions, for that would render it disloyal to the hope of a final solution. In order to keep unharmed the vision of the ultimate community it must deny itself the satisfaction the peoples of the world constantly enjoy in the functioning of their state. For the state is the ever changing guise under which time moves step by step toward eternity. So far as God's people is concerned, eternity has already come—even in the midst of time! For the nations of the world there is only the current era. But the state symbolizes the attempt to give nations eternity within the confines of time, an attempt which must of necessity be repeated again and again. The very fact that the state does try it, and *must* try it, makes it the imitator and rival of the people which is in itself eternal, a people which would cease to have a claim to its own eternity if the state were able to attain what it is striving for.

[*Der Stern der Erlösung*, III, 87-92]

6.   History and the Kingdom of God

From the Star of Redemption

The true eternity of the eternal people must always be alien and vexing to the state, and to the history of the world. In the epochs of world history the state wields its sharp sword and carves hours of eternity into the bark of the growing tree of life, while the eternal people, untroubled and untouched, year after year adds ring upon ring to the stem of its eternal life. The power of world history breaks against this quiet life which looks neither right nor left. Again and again world history may claim that its newest eternity is the true eternity. Over and against all such claims we set the calm and· silent image of our existence, which forces both him who wants to see and him who does not, to realize that eternity is nothing of the startlingly newest. Force may coerce the "newest" into an identification with the "final," to make it appear the very newest eternity indeed. But that is not like the bond which obtains between the latest grandson and the earliest forebear. Over and over, our existence sets before the eyes of the nations this true eternity of life, this turning of the hearts of the fathers to their children: wordless evidence which gives the lie to the worldly and all-too-worldly sham eternity of the historical moments of the nations, moments expressed in the destiny of their states. So long as the kingdom of God is still to come, the course of world history will always only reconcile creation within itself, only the moment which is about to come with that which has just passed.

Only the eternal people, which is not encompassed by world history, can—at every moment—bind creation as a whole to redemption while redemption is still to come. The life of this people, alone, burns with a fire that feeds on itself, and hence needs no sword to supply the flame with fuel from the forests of the world. The fire burns through and in itself, and sends forth rays which shine out into the world and illumine it; the fire is not aware of the rays, nor does it have need of their light for itself. It burns silently and eternally. The seed of eternal life has been planted, and can wait for the budding. The seed knows nothing of the tree that grows from it, not even when it flings its shadow over the whole world. In time to come, a seed that is like the first will fall from the fruits of that tree. "Blessed art Thou . . . who hast planted eternal life in our midst."

[*Der Stern der Erlösung*, III, 95-96]

7. The Church and the Synagogue
From a Letter[1]

Christianity acknowledges the God of the Jews, not as God but as "the Father of Jesus Christ." Christianity itself cleaves to the "Lord" because it knows that the Father can be reached only through him. With his church, he remains as the "Lord" for all time, until the end of the world, but then he will cease to be the Lord, and he too will be subject to the Father who will, on this day, be all in all. We are wholly agreed as to what Christ and his church mean to the world: no one can reach the Father save through him.

No one can reach the Father! But the situation is quite different for one who does not have to reach the Father because he is already with him. And this is true of the people of Israel (though not of individual Jews). Chosen by

[1] Written to Rudolf Ehrenberg after F. R. reached the decision to remain a Jew.

its Father, the people of Israel gazes fixedly across the world and history, over to that last, most distant time when the Father, the One and Only, will be "all in all." Then, when Christ ceases to be the Lord, Israel will cease to be the chosen people. On this day, God will lose the name by which only Israel calls him; God will then no longer be "its" God. But until that day dawns, the lifework of Israel is to anticipate the eternal day, in profession and in action, to be its living presage, to hallow the name of God through its, Israel's, own holiness and with its Law as a people of priests. How this people of God stands in the world, what anguish inflicted from the outside (persecutions) and from the inside (inflexibility) it assumes by setting itself apart from the world—on this too we are wholly agreed.

But the synagogue bows to this anguish of denying the world for the sake of the same ultimate hope that impels the church to bow to the anguish of affirming the world; and this is not merely an accidental meeting in eternity— as, for instance, a meeting of believers in God with humane pacifists. Since the roots of this hope, the God of all time, here and beyond, spring from common ground, and the revelation of the Old Testament is common to both church and synagogue, these depend on each other.

The synagogue, which is immortal but stands with broken staff and bound eyes, must renounce all work in this world, and muster all her strength to preserve her life and keep herself untainted by life. And so she leaves the work in the world to the church and recognizes the church as the salvation for all heathens in all time. The synagogue knows that what the works of its ritual do for Israel, the works of love do for the world outside of Israel. But the synagogue refuses to admit that the strength with which the church performs her works of love is more than "divine," that this strength is in itself a power of God. Herein the synagogue gazes fixedly into the future.

And the church, with unbreakable staff and eyes open to the world, this champion certain of victory, always faces the danger of having the vanquished draw up laws for her. Sent to all men, she must nevertheless not lose herself in what is common to all men. Her word is always to be "foolishness and a stumbling block." Greeks of then and today and all time see to it that it remains foolishness. Again and again they will ask: why is just *this* word supposed to be the power of God, and not that other, and not a third word as well? Why just Jesus and not (or at least, not also) Goethe? And such talk will go on until doomsday, only that it will grow less and less vociferous, less and less audible with every external or internal victory of the church, for wisdom which deems itself wise falls silent before visible demonstration. And when the last Greek has been silenced through the work which the church performed in time, the word of the cross—at the end of time but still included in time—will no longer be foolishness to anyone.

But always, even then, it will be a stumbling block. No one with the Greek point of view saw a stumbling block in the demand to admit the existence of a power of God in the world, for to a Greek the world was full of gods. The only thing he could not understand was why he should revere just the one savior and his cross; and it is the same today, and so it will always be.

But the eyes of the synagogue were covered by a band; she saw no world—so how could she have seen gods in it? She could see only by dint of her prophetic inner eye, and she saw nothing but the ultimate, the most remote. Thus, the demand to see what was close at hand and present, in the same way as she saw only the most remote, vexed her. So it is today and so it will always be. That is why, whenever the church forgets she is a stumbling block and desires to become reconciled with what is "common to all men" (a procedure which would be welcome to the Greeks, who, like a certain emperor, would like to erect a statue to Christ in the temple of their gods), the synagogue confronts the church as a silent warner who is not seduced by what is common to all men and knows only of the stumbling block. Then the church again turns to affirmation and utters the word of the cross. The church knows that Israel will be spared until the day when the last Greek has died, when the work of love is completed, when the Day of Judgment, the day wherein hope reaps its harvest, dawns. But what the church admits for Israel in general she denies the individual Jew. So far as he is concerned, the church shall and will test her strength in the attempt to convert him. For gazing into the future is not a source of strength for the faith of the church as it is for the synagogue, but only a vision of the goal of hope. The strength of her faith bids her look about and do the works of her love in the Here and Now.

[*Briefe,* pp. 73-75]

8. The Jew and the Christian
From the Exchange of Letters With Eugen Rosenstock

Yes, the stubbornness of the Jews is a Christian dogma; so much so that, after the church had developed her actual dogma in the first century—the substantial part dealing with God and man—she spent the entire second century, and not only the second century, in establishing the "second dogma" (the formal part of her dogma: her historical self-consciousness). Thereby she became the church of the Scriptures, or, rather, of tradition, instead of the church of spirit; became, in short, the *church plain,* the church that has gone down in history. The afterpains of this idea extended into the third and fourth centuries and even later, for Augustine made it his affair long after the church had done with it. Paul's theory of the relation of the Gospels to the Law might have remained a "personal theory"; the Hellenizing church (Gospel of John) of the first century, which defended the doctrine of the pneuma with magnificent naivety, hardly concerned herself with it. But then came gnosis, pointed to Paul, tried to eliminate the personal and theoretical element from his doctrine and develop objective aspects over and against his personal ideas. (Paul said: The Jews are rejected, but Christ arose from them. Marcion said: Consequently the Jews belong to the devil and Christ to God.) Then the church which, up to this point, had been quite naive in her own gnosis (we read in St. John that all salvation hails from the Jews) suddenly became seeing, set the tradition before the pneuma and, through a great *ritornar al segno,* fixed this tradition at its cardinal point, at Paul who had founded it, by deliberately stabilizing his personal theory as dogma. The church established the identity of the Creator (and thus of Him who revealed himself on Sinai) with the Father of Jesus Christ on the one hand, and the humanity of Christ on the other, as reciprocal shibboleths against every form of heresy: and thereby made herself a power in history. The rest you know better than I.

But could not this dogma of the stubbornness of the Jews be likewise a Jewish dogma? It not only could be; it is. But the awareness of being rejected has an entirely different place in Jewish dogmatics and is the very counterpart of the Christian awareness of being elected to rulership, an awareness which exists beyond the vestige of a doubt. Jewish religious evaluation of the destruction of the Temple in the year 70 is tuned to this concept. But the parallel you are looking for is another, nonetheless: a Jewish dogma concerning the relationship of Judaism to Christianity must correspond to the dogma of the church concerning her relation to Judaism. And you recognize this Jewish dogma only in the modern liberal-Jewish theory of the "daughter religion," which gradually educates the world for Judaism. Now this theory actually hails from Judaism's classical period of dogma building, from the peak of Jewish scholasticism which falls between Arabic and Christian scholasticism (al-Ghazali, Maimonides, Thomas Aquinas). Our period of formulating the dogma according to the difference between your concept of faith and ours did not come until then. At a time when you were developing your dogma, we were formulating our *jus canonicum*, and later it was vice versa. This peculiar relation holds down to the smallest detail. When you were systematizing your dogma, for example, we were systematizing our Law. You mysticized your dogma after you had set it up, we did so before, etc., etc., and this relation is conditioned by the difference in the deepest roots of Judaism and Christianity.

Judah ha-Levi, one of the two scholastics, has it that Christianity is the tree that grows from the seed of Judaism. It flings its shadow across the earth, and its fruit will again harbor the seed which no one who saw that tree ever recognized. Thus Christianity as a universal power is Jewish dogma, just as Judaism as the stubborn source and the last convert is Christian dogma. . . .

The "pride of the Jew" is the Jewish expression of the concept of Christianity as the "forerunner." This pride is difficult to explain to an outsider. What you see of it seems foolish and petty, just as it is almost impossible for a Jew to judge anti-Semitism by anything but its vulgar manifestations. The metaphysical reason for this pride can be formulated thus: (1) that we know the truth; (2) that we have reached the goal; (3) that at the bottom of his heart any Jew will consider the Christian's relationship to God, and hence his religion, a meager and roundabout affair. For to

the Jew it is incomprehensible that one should need a teacher, be he who he may, to learn what is obvious and matter
of course to him, namely to call God our Father. Why
should a third person have to be between me and my Father
in heaven? This is no invention of modern apologists but
simply Jewish instinct. . . .

You recall the passage in the Gospel of John where Christ
tells his disciples that they are not to leave the world, but
to remain within it. The people of Israel, which might well
be the speaker of all that is said in this Gospel, could tell
its members exactly the same thing, and it does really, for
"to sanctify the Name of God in the world," is a frequently
used phrase. This is the source of all the ambiguity in Jewish life, as well as that of all the impetus in Christian life.
Insofar as the Jew is "in the world," he is subordinate to
this law and no one can tell him that he may go just so
far and no further, that this or that is the borderline he
dare not cross. For a simple "as little as possible" would
constitute a poor standard, because if I set up as a standard
for all my actions the slogan "as little as possible outside
Jewish bounds," this might—under certain conditions—result
in the lowering of achievement inside Jewish bounds. And
so on general principles I tell myself "as much as possible
inside Jewish bounds," yet I know that in individual instances I cannot timidly fend off a certain amount of action
outside these bounds. And I also know that, from your point
of view, this makes me guilty of the crime of callousness.
But I can be responsible for my actions only at their source
and focus; they elude me at the peripheries. Shall I, then,
let the castle itself fall to ruins in order to strengthen the
endangered outer bulwarks? Shall I become converted, I
who was born "chosen"? Does the alternative of conversion
even exist for me? Have I boarded a galley haphazardly?
Is it not actually *my ship?* You became acquainted with me

on land, and hardly noticed that my ship was in port. In those days I loafed around in sailors' bars more than was necessary, and so you may well ask what business I have on the ship. And you will not really believe that it is my ship and I belong there (*pour faire quoi? y vivre et y mourir*)—you will not and cannot believe until the passage is clear again and I fare forth to sea.

Or even not until we meet out there on the high seas? With you, everything is possible!

[*Briefe*, pp. 667-673]

9.   The Love of One's Enemies
A Note to a Poem By Judah ha-Levi

If we regard the dictum "love your enemy" (in the Sermon on the Mount) as an ethical postulate, that is, from the standpoint of unreality, we cannot do justice to it any more than to other great realities. The Christian love of one's enemy is a reality—wherever it can be nothing else. It becomes reality and can be nothing else the moment the church or the individual follows the original command of Christianity to proselytize. Then the love of one's enemy becomes the strongest weapon with which to conquer the world, for the enemy is loved as one who will become a brother.

And so, if there is to be a Jewish love of one's enemy, it must be something quite different. For here the reality is not that of a community graced with the mercies of conquest, but with those of being defeated. . . . The Jew loves his enemy as the executor of divine judgment which, because he accepts it, becomes his own. And he, in contrast to all the other human beings, must accept it, for he is the only one who does not have Jews at his disposal for playing

348

the role of scapegoat. The love with which man loves God becomes the supreme law of all love with which he can love man, even love to extremes—but does love recognize extremes?—even to the love of one's enemy.

[*Judah ha-Levi*, p. 233]

10. "Survival"

A Note to a Poem By Judah ha-Levi

The question as to how the Jewish people has survived all its sufferings has often been put, and there have been many more or less clever, which means more or less stupid, answers. The true reason, for which the plural "reasons" does not exist, emerges in this poem. It begins with a cry from an abyss of suffering, an abyss so terribly deep that He whom the cry is destined to reach is at first merely a target for outcry, doubt, and blasphemy. And in the very act of crying out doubt and blasphemy which exceed all biblical models because they are fed on the poisonous juices of a philosophy of doubt and blasphemy, the eye still recognizes that He to whom the cry mounts is circled with stars. The unburdened mouth professes the power of Him who commands the hosts of heaven, the heart drowns in the ecstasy of beholding the glory of God—and all suffering is forgotten.

[*Judah ha-Levi*, pp. 227-228]

ZION AND THE REMNANT OF ISRAEL

1. The True and the False Messiah

A Note to a Poem By Judah ha Levi

The expectation of the coming of the Messiah, by which and because of which Judaism lives, would be a meaningless theologumenon, a mere "idea" in the philosophical sense, empty babble, if the appearance again and again of a "false Messiah" did not render it reality and unreality, illusion and disillusion. The false Messiah is as old as the hope for the true Messiah. He is the changing form of this changeless hope. He separates every Jewish generation into those whose faith is strong enough to give themselves up to an illusion, and those whose hope is so strong that they do not allow themselves to be deluded. The former are the better, the latter the stronger. The former bleed as victims on the altar of the eternity of the people, the latter are the priests who perform the service at this altar. And this goes on until the day when all will be reversed, when the belief of the believers will become truth, and the hope of the hoping a lie. Then—and no one knows whether this "then" will not be this very day—the task of the hoping will come to an end and, when the morning of that day breaks, everyone who still belongs among those who hope and not among those who believe will run the risk of being rejected. This danger hovers over the apparently less endangered life of the hopeful.

Hermann Cohen once said to me—he was over seventy at the time: "I am still hoping to see the dawn of the messianic era." What Cohen, who believed in the false Messiah of the nineteenth century, meant by that was the conversion of Christians to the "pure monotheism" of his Judaism, a conversion which he thought the liberal Protestant theology of his day was initiating. I was startled by the vigor of his belief that it would happen "speedily in our days," and did not dare tell him that I did not think these indications were true signs. All I said was that I did not believe I should live to see it. At that he asked: "But when do *you* think it will be?" I did not have the heart not to mention any date at all, and so I answered: "Perhaps in hundreds of years." But he understood me to say: "Perhaps in a hundred years," and cried: "Oh, please say in fifty!"

[*Judah ha-Levi*, p. 239]

2. Prayer for Sacrifices

A Note to a Poem By Judah ha-Levi

A dream transported Judah the Levite among his brothers serving in the Temple.[1] He reveled in the spectacle of the sacrifices. To him they represented the re-established immediacy of the presence of God. In the same century, Maimonides accurately enumerated in his Code[2] the laws governing sacrifice, as they would go into force after the rebuilding of the Temple. But in his philosophical work,[3] taking Leviticus 17:7 as his point of departure, he dealt

---

[1] Reference to a phrase in the poem.
[2] Mishneh Torah, code of Jewish law.
[3] Moreh Nevukhim (*Guide to the Perplexed*).

351

with the institution of sacrifice as a mere pedagogical concession on the part of Moses. Today this institution and the prayers to have it re-established have become an embarrassing question, a fact the reformists admit and the orthodoxy tries to gloss over.

The reasons usually given for rejection of sacrifices are so weak that they obviously cannot be the true ones. For the horror at the "slaughter of innocent animals" is comical rather than serious on the lips of confirmed non-vegetarians. Whatever is said beyond this, however, holds for every other visible and established ritual just as much as for sacrifice, which manifests the relationship between the natural necessity of taking food on the one hand and Him who gives food on the other.

Still, there is a difference even for one who sees this motivation quite clearly. He too finds it difficult to utter the prayer for the reinstitution of sacrifice. And that is as it should be. The difference between prescribed prayer and spontaneous prayer is that the latter is born out of the need of the moment, while the former teaches him who prays to feel a need he might otherwise not feel. This is particularly true of the prayers for the messianic age, insofar as they are not merely tuned to the desire for liberation from the pressure of the present. Man is sufficiently rooted in all life, even the most difficult, so that, although he may have good reason to long for a partial change, he fears a radical one. And such a radical change, *the* radical change, is the messianic age, which will indeed set an end to the hell of world history, but also to its ambiguities and seeming lack of responsibilities. In the messianic age everything will become clearly visible, yet man shies away from this perfect clarity and the unequivocal responsibility it entails, just as he shies away from God's nearness in death, a nearness he may earnestly covet without, however, bringing himself to relinquish his love of life, even of an imperfect and sinful life. For such change is much too radical! Yet he must learn to pray for this radical change even though that prayer may be difficult for him until the change actually occurs.

What Judah ha-Levi discovered when he woke from his dream and returned to the world was that God is with man even in our present world with its inadequacy and confusion, its half-measures and mirages; or, rather, that man is with him, or can find a way to him. If yearning were to forget what it already possesses it would be a lie, but if possession forgot to yearn—that would be death.

[*Judah ha-Levi*, pp. 241-242]

3. Zionism
From Four Letters[1]

I

The first great messianic movement in Judaism (if I exclude the return from the Babylonian exile), the Bar Kokhba movement under Hadrian, which in its outer manifestations was the greatest of all, was purely political, even purely military so far as the person of its leader was concerned. And yet Rabbi Akiba, the greatest *homo religiosus* of the Judaism of the Pharisaic centuries, joined it, declared Bar Kokhba to be the Messiah, and suffered martyrdom for his faith.

From this alone you must realize that we cannot work with concepts exclusively. We must look at the person, at persons. Today the great majority of Jews in the Diaspora deny both in theory and practice what you regard as holy,

[1] The first letter is addressed to the Christian theologian Hans Ehrenberg; the second, third and fourth, to the reform rabbi Benno Jacob.

and would like to be like the nations, like the others. Only Zionism confirms and lives what you regard as holy. The great majority of its adherents confirm it in practice, a strong minority also confirm it in theory. I think that for your purposes the Central-Verein[2] journal published by anti-Zionist Jews would perhaps be the most important literature on Zionism. There you would find out where the "going in the ways of Europe" is really being done.

The prophets observed an objective critical attitude toward their own state, the Pharisees toward the states of the Diaspora. In both cases it was really objectivity, not negation; it was an attitude of non-identification. The nineteenth century destroyed both these forms of objectivity (the Pharisean in practice and the prophets' in theory) by falsifying into cosmopolitanism what, in reality, was a revolutionary criticism of their own state. It is a matter of course that Zionism finds itself impelled to restore the attitude of prophetic criticism of its own community. That is certain. But it is not certain whether, and to what extent, Pharisean critical objectivity can be re-established for the Diaspora which persists even in Palestine.

II

Jerusalem as a messianic symbol? If a symbol is to be more than an arbitrary appendage, then it must somewhere and somehow exist as an entirely asymbolical reality. My own experience does not convince me that the air of Palestine renders men wise.[2a] But I do believe that my Frankfort wisdom could not exist without the land of Israel, and not only without that which was but also not without that which will be, that which has a future: hence, not without

[2] Central-Verein Deutscher Staatsbürger jüdischen Glaubens (Central Organization of German Citizens of Jewish Faith), founded in Berlin in 1893.
[2a] A talmudic proverb.

the Palestine of today which—within itself—links the past
to the future. Warmth is not only to be found where there
is sunlight—that is a Zionist superstition—but wherever I
have a good stove. But the coal and the wood which warm
me today could not have grown and would not warm me
if there were no sun, if the sun had not existed and did
not exist. The real sun! Not merely a painted symbol, no
matter how attractive the painting!

III

Philo? Yes, we say it just about like that to this day,
especially when we write "in Flaccum."[3] But what is left
of all the Alexandrine glory of the Jews? Philo's own nephew
was a Roman general who conducted pogroms! And you
and I, at any rate, do not owe the fact of our existence
and our being Jews to those self-satisfied citizens of the
Diaspora but to the contemporary and later Tannaim of
Palestine. I find myself unable to formulate just exactly
how I think the messianic future will be. But that is no
proof against it! When the time comes, the details will fall
into place. I am not naive enough to fancy that peace among
peoples and groups can come about without a radical change
in human nature, a change which, contemplated from the
present, must appear in the light of a miracle. That I do
have faith in that future I owe to our Prayer Book. I cannot
exclude Zion from this faith. Just how great, how Jewish,
how "modern" a Palestine will be grouped around it, I do
not know. But when the time comes I am sure I shall not

[3] "Against Flaccus," by Philo, an account of anti-Jewish excesses in Alexandria. B. Jacob had quoted Philo: "Because of their great number, the
Jews cannot all live in one country, and so they occupy many of the most
fertile lands and islands of Europe and Asia. They regard Jerusalem, the
site of the holy temple of the highest God, as their mother city, but give
the name of fatherland to whatever country they are born and reared in,
and where their fathers, grandfathers and great-grandfathers, etc. have
lived."

be disturbed by the fact that this Zion—not a heavenly but a messianic and hence earthly Zion—will be surrounded by, in all likelihood, what is "modern" in the sense of the time; no more than I am disturbed by the paraphernalia of the "history of civilization" which is grouped around my mental image of biblical antiquity; but also no more than I begrudge the Palestine of today its factories and automobile roads. It belongs!

Belongs to what? To men, and these men are what I can see even today. And, if my impressions are reliable, there are better Jews among the Zionists than among us—regardless of theory. You will probably agree to this. . . .

IV

Can Zionism as a political movement do more than it does for religion in Palestine? We shouldn't expect it to exert pressure on conscience! All that we can demand of it is to allow freedom of conscience and, beyond that, to respect religion wherever it might come into conflict with it officially. Zionism, both here and in Palestine, satisfies both of these demands at least as much as the Central-Verein. I consider a definite religious program just as inappropriate for Zionism as for the Central-Verein. Religion, too, has every reason to reject the clumsy service of politicians. What religion needs is spontaneity! And when I consider what has spontaneously arisen in Palestine, I must admit that nowhere in the world have the demands of Jewish religious liberalism been met, even today, as fully as there. I shall not go into the question of the observance of circumcision, although you yourself know how this matter stands in present-day Germany, and particularly in those circles from which the German Halutzim are recruited. But take the observance of the Sabbath! The orthodox may consider smoking, writing letters, or the holding of sports festivals on the part of the settlers as *hillul shabbat* [desecration of the Sabbath]. But we cannot feel that way about it, least of all I myself! Originally I made it my principle to refrain from all business correspondence on the Sabbath, but saw no harm in writing letters to friends. Nor did I give up this liberal interpretation of keeping the Sabbath until once, when Henry Rothschild and I were discussing some matter concerning the Lehrhaus, he tried to make me jot down notes, since—so he said—I did not mind writing on the Sabbath. That experience, which taught me how unfeasible it is to draw such fine distinctions unless everyone else draws them too, finally drove me to accept the orthodox practice on this point, though to come to the decision was not easy for me. Therefore, how can I regard as less good Jews all those who observe the Sabbath in the liberal way which seems adequate for us today, and which I myself gave up only under duress! As for Tel Aviv, the "town of speculators," which most Zionists view as a questionable Zionist achievement—I cannot help being impressed by the fact that all stores there close from *kiddush* to *havdalah*,[4] and that thus, at any rate, the mold into which the content of the Sabbath can flow is provided. Where could we find that here! Where could you, or one of your liberal colleagues, find so excellent an opportunity for crowded pews? And when I hear how the pupils read the Bible in the Biram School,[5] a typically nationalistic institution, I shudder at the mere thought of the religious instruction we offer our children.

All this has originated under the aegis of nationalistic Zionism. But I do not believe that a movement should be judged by the standards of its extreme theoreticians. What

[4] I.e., from Friday evening to Saturday evening.
[5] Beth Sefer Reali Ivri (Hebrew secondary school) in Haifa, founded by Dr. Arthur Biram.

I mean is that Zionism must not be judged by the theories of Klatzkin,[6] nor the standpoint of the Central-Verein by the work of Naumann.[7] We always find the characteristic feature of a movement at that juncture where the movement veers away from the theoretical conclusions and gravitates back to earth. The constant, which must be introduced into the formula before we can use it to calculate reality, is not made up of the little inconsistencies of current politics but of this one great inconsistency that is decisive for the effect, of this angle of refraction which is characteristic of the movement.

I can well imagine that the phrase: "You are not yet the right one," can be hurled at every current era. But I do not see how this species of thinking could be used as a pattern for the future or, which is worse, for all future time, without thereby ruining the future. I cannot understand how one can pray for something one considers impossible from the very outset. I cannot pray that two and two may add up to five. What the prophets had in mind was a future Zion on earth. The eternity we Jews speak of is not located in infinity, but "in a time soon to come, in our days." Do read my comment on the poem "The Happy Tidings" in my Judah ha-Levi volume.[8] I should like you to because of the story I tell there about Hermann Cohen. According to the words of a philosopher whom I regard as an authority even greater than Hermann Cohen, what is not to come save in eternity will not come in all eternity.

[*Briefe,* pp. 585-586; 588; 591-594]

---

[6] *See* the essay "Classical and Modern Hebrew" in this volume.

[7] Max Naumann, spokesman of the Verband Nationaldeutscher Juden, an association of Jews who could not "feel and think otherwise than German."

[8] *See* "The True and the False Messiah" in this volume.

4.   The Poet's Reply

A Note to a Poem By Judah ha-Levi

The poet's decision [to go to the land of Israel] became known and he was warned to give it up by an epistle in verse; its content we can guess at only through his reply, but in any case it indicates how stupendous his decision must have appeared at the time.

We do not know the author of the epistle, and yet he seems so familiar to us that we could identify him with a hundred persons we do know. The assimilationist, too, has a place among the eternal figures of Judaism. And his arguments have not changed through the ages. They are the same—shall we say alarmingly the same? He contends that Jerusalem no longer concerns us because now, just as in the time before David conquered it, it is inhabited by the "blind and the lame" [II Sam. 5:6 and 8], by alien nations. And then, just as today, this unhistorical historic argument is connected with an unphilosophical philosophical argument; only the unpolitical political argument is not stressed, but that would after all be quite inappropriate in the case of an individual. And then, just as today, the philosophy that must serve as a foil for national forgetfulness is derived from the Greeks, who knew only of eternity without beginning and without end, and not of the One, the Eternal who establishes the beginning and the end.

The poet's reply with its quotation from Psalm 122:8 f. [1] sounds the undying double chord of the love of Zion: God and the people. Because of the Temple and because of our brothers, Jerusalem remains to us what it was. The

---

[1] "For my brethren and companions' sakes, I will now say: 'Peace be within thee.' For the sake of the house of the Lord our God I will seek thy good."

details of the argument deal at great length with the "historical" objection of the "no longer" concept, and refute it by citing a situation corresponding to our own, the "not yet" situation of the patriarchs, who regarded the land which was no more theirs than it is ours, nevertheless, as holy. In the course of his reply, Judah ha-Levi points to the orgies piety celebrates in honor of the dead, orgies by means of which it redeems itself from any concern with visualizing the living present as pregnant with future; his reply acclaims the land as the only safe refuge: the site of historical memories as well as of eschatological hopes. And this reply is quite aware that it represents the great highway compared with which all shifts and objections in the words of the opponent are nothing but devious side paths.

The words of one opponent have been forgotten; the reply has endured.

[*Judah ha-Levi,* pp. 244-245]

5.   The Remnant of Israel
From the Star of Redemption

From Israel to the Messiah, from the people that stood on Sinai to the day when the Temple in Jerusalem "shall be called a house of prayer for all peoples,"[1] a concept can be traced that originated with the prophets and has been governing our inner history ever since: the concept of the remnant. The remnant of Israel, of those who remained faithful, of the true people within the people, guarantees at every moment that there is a bridge between the two poles. Though in all other instances Jewish consciousness may fluctuate wildly between the two poles of life estab-

[1] Isa. 56:7.

lished in the first inner turning of the pagan man into man open to and resolved upon revelation, the pole of the innermost experience of divine love and that of a devoted activation of love in holy living, the idea of the remnant represents both together: acceptance of the "yoke of the commandments" and acceptance of the "yoke of the kingdom of God."[2]

If the Messiah came today, the remnant would be ready to receive him. In defiance of all temporal history, Jewish history is the history of this remnant, of whom the words of the prophet that it "will remain,"[3] hold now and forever. Temporal history deals invariably with expansion. Might is the fundamental concept of history because, with the rise of Christianity, revelation began to spread over the world, and thus all will to expansion, even that which is consciously nothing but worldly, has unconsciously become the servant of this great movement of expansion. But Judaism, and only Judaism, maintains itself by subtraction, by a narrowing down, by the formation of ever new remnants. This holds already for the external aspect, the continual desertion. But it also holds within Judaism itself. It is constantly sloughing off whatever is un-Jewish in order to rebuild itself by shaping over and over the new remnants of what is primordially Jewish. It keeps on adjusting to the outside world so that again and again it may withdraw into its own inner world. There is no group, no trend, scarcely an individual in Jewry that does not regard his manner of sacrificing what is unimportant in order to stabilize the rest as the only right manner; and who, therefore, does not consider himself the true "remnant of Israel." This he actually is.

[2] Mishnah Berakhot II. 2.
[3] Isa. 11:11.

In Judaism, man is always a remnant—somehow or other. Somehow or other, he is always something left over, an inner being whose husk has been seized upon and swept away by the current of the world, while he himself, that is to say what remained of him, stands on the shore. Something within him is waiting. And he has something within himself. He may give very different names to what he is waiting for, and to what is inside himself. Often he will not be able to find any name for it at all. But he has the feeling that both this having and this waiting are intimately bound up with each other. And just that is the feeling of the "remnant" which has been accorded revelation and is waiting for salvation.

The strange questions which—according to tradition[4]—the supreme Judge will at some time put to the Jew, indicate the two sides of this feeling. The one: "Have you taught yourself to deduce one thing from another?" means: Were you fully aware that everything that can possibly happen to you was given you in the gift of revelation at a time long before you were born? And the other: "Have you waited for salvation?" refers to that direction toward the future coming of the kingdom which we have in our blood the moment we are born, and which never leaves us. Thus, in this feeling which unites two tendencies, man narrows down to Jewish man. . . . Jewish man is wholly with himself. Here the future, which is usually a tremendous weight on man's soul, has come to rest. His heart is wholly at one with itself in the feeling of being the remnant. Here the Jew is nothing but a Jew. The revelation he has been accorded, the redemption to which he has been called, have both flooded the narrow space which opens between his self and his people.

[*Der Stern der Erlösung*, III, 185-187]

4 Talmud (Shabbat 31a).

ACKNOWLEDGEMENTS

In the course of gathering material for this book, the editor had the gracious and untiring assistance of Mrs. Edith Rosenzweig-Scheinmann, and the good advice of Mrs. Gertrud Oppenheim. Hitherto unpublished letters and diaries, besides those in the editor's own possession, were put at his disposal by Dr. Richard Tuteur, Professors Martin Buber, Gershom G. Scholem and Richard Koch. A rare manuscript copy of "Das Büchlein vom gesunden und kranken Menschenverstand" (a part of which is here published for the first time) was given to the editor by Dr. Ernst Baumann of Johannesburg.

For the selection from and arrangement of Rosenzweig's writings, the editor consulted Professor Ernst Simon and gratefully accepted his suggestions. Warm thanks are due to Professors Emil Fackenheim, Abraham J. Heschel, Fritz Kaufmann, Eugen Rosenstock-Huessy, Shalom Spiegel, Mrs. Sherry Abel, Dr. F. Bamberger and Mr. Arthur A. Cohen, with whom the editor discussed a number of questions. The major part of Rosenzweig's German texts has been translated by Dr. Francis C. Golffing. The essay, "On Being a Jewish Person" was translated by Clement Greenberg; and "Sermonic Judaism" by Steven S. Schwarzschild.

BIOGRAPHICAL DATES

December 25, 1886	Born in Cassel, Germany.
I. Summer 1905 to autumn 1907	Study of medicine at the Universities of Göttingen, Munich, Freiburg. Preliminary medical examinations
Winter 1907 to summer 1912	Study of modern history and philosophy at the Universities of Berlin and Freiburg
January 1910	Beginning of research in Hegel's political doctrines
Summer 1912	Ph.D. degree
October to December 1912	Military training in Darmstadt.
II. First part of 1913	At the University of Leipzig; courses in Jurisprudence
Night of July 7, 1913	Discussion on religion with Eugen Rosenstock. Intention of conversion to Christianity
October 11, 1913	Atonement Day service in Berlin. Decision to remain a Jew
Fall 1913 to fall 1914	Jewish studies in Berlin; meets Hermann Cohen
April 1914	Writes *Atheistic Theology* ("Atheistische Theologie"), his first essay in Jewish religious thinking
March to May 1914	Discovery of a Schelling philosophical program.
III. September 1914	Enters the Red Cross service
Beginning 1915	A volunteer for the regular army
January-February 1916	At the Distance Measuring School La Fère in France
March 12, 1916	With an anti-aircraft gun unit to the Balkan battle front

May 1916	Starts an exchange of letters on Jewish and Christian theology with Eugen Rosenstock
September 1916	Beginning interest in the problem of Jewish religious instruction in Germany
1916-1917	Writes articles on political and strategical questions, and draws up a Central European educational program
March 1917	Writes *It Is Time* ("Zeit ists"), an open letter on Jewish education in Germany
Spring 1917	First contact with Sephardic Jews in Üsküb, [Yugoslavia]
October 1917	Writing the "germ cell" of the later work, Star of Redemption
March 19, 1918	Death of his father
May-June 1918	Attending an officers' training course in Rembertow near Warsaw. First contact with East European Jews
July 11 - August 1, 1918	Influenza and pneumonia; military hospital in Leipzig
August 22, 1918	Starts to write the *Star of Redemption,* upon returning to the Balkan front
End of September 1918	Retreat of the Balkan troops; attack of malaria
December 1918	Release from the army; return to Cassel
February 16, 1919	Concludes *Star of Redemption.*
IV. April 1919	Meets Rabbi Nehemiah A. Nobel in Frankfort
1919	Opening of Academy for the Science of Judaism, a research institute
January 6, 1920	Engagement to Edith Hahn
January 1920	Writes *On Education* ("Bildung und kein Ende")
March 29, 1920	Marriage

August 1, 1920	Appointed head of the Freies Jüdisches Lehrhaus in Frankfort
1920	Publication of *Hegel and the State* ("Hegel und der Staat")
December 1920	Establishes a home in an attic of Schumannstrasse 10
1921	Publication of *Star of Redemption* ("Der Stern der Erlösung")
November or December 1921	Notices first symptoms of a serious disease.
V. February 8, 1922	Medical checkup reveals amyotrophic lateral sclerosis with progressive paralysis of the bulba
June-July 1922	Prepares second edition of *Star of Redemption*
August 1922	Writing becomes difficult; speech less articulate
September 8, 1922	Birth of son, Rafael
1922	Works on translation of poems by Judah ha-Levi
December 1922	Ability to write ceases entirely. Letters and writings being dictated
Spring 1923	Ability to speak ceases entirely
Summer 1923	Rabbinical title conferred by Rabbi Leo Baeck
Fall 1923	Paralysis finally stops all movements of limbs. Disintegration halts before the organs essential for maintenance of bare life are involved
1923	Works on Epilogue and Notes to *Judah ha-Levi*, writes *The Builders* ("Die Bauleute"), an Introduction to *Collected Jewish Writings* by Hermann Cohen and several articles
Spring 1924	Publication of *Judah ha-Levi*
1924	Adjustment for an indefinite period of life under conditions of the paralysis. Works on translation of additional Judah ha-Levi poems.

VI.	Spring 1925	Beginning of work on the Bible translation, with Martin Buber
	September 1925	Completion of the translation of *Genesis*
	1925	Article *The New Thinking* ("Das neue Denken"), articles on translating and on the Lehrhaus
	June 1926	Completion of the translation of *Exodus*
	December 1926	Completion of the translation of *Leviticus* and *Numbers*
	1926	Publication of *Zweistromland,* collected essays
	December 25, 1926	40th birthday
	March 1927	Broncho-pneumonia and severe fever
	Spring 1927	Completion of the translation of *Deuteronomy*
	August-September 1927	Completion of the translation of *Joshua* and *Judges*
	1927	Publication of second, expanded edition of *Judah ha-Levi*
	June 1928	Completion of the translation of the books of *Samuel*
	1928	Repeated attacks of high fever. Articles on biblical problems, reviews
	February 1929	Deterioration of general health condition. Completion of the translation of the books of *Kings*
	1929	Articles on biblical, philosophical, religious, and historical problems
	November 1929	Completion of the translation of *Isaiah*
	December 6, 1929	A cold leading to broncho-pneumonia
	December 10, 1929	Death.

LIST OF FRANZ ROSENZWEIG'S WRITINGS

Der Stern der Erlösung (Star of Redemption). First edition, Frankfort on the Main 1921. Second edition, Frankfort 1930.

Die Schrift (Translation of the Bible; F. R. together with Martin Buber). Volumes I to X, (Genesis to Isaiah). Berlin 1925 seq. Originally issued by Verlag Lambert Schneider. (Volumes XI to XV, Jeremiah to Proverbs, translated by Martin Buber only). Definitive edition published by the Schocken Verlag.

Jehuda Halevi (92 poems of Judah ha-Levi; translation and commentary). Berlin 1927.

Briefe (Letters). Edited by Edith Rosenzweig with the cooperation of Ernst Simon. Schocken Verlag, Berlin 1935.

Die Schrift und ihre Verdeutschung (Essays on the Bible translation and interpretation, by Martin Buber and F. R.), Schocken Verlag, Berlin 1936.

Kleinere Schriften (Collected Writings). Schocken Verlag, Berlin 1937.

The following list of writings, arranged in the order of their composition, records first the English rendition of the titles as used in this book and, in parenthesis, the original German title. Essays included in *Kleinere Schriften* are marked K.S.; those included in *Die Schrift und ihre Verdeutschung* are marked S.V. (Only writings mentioned in the present volume are listed.)

The Hero (Der Held). Sketch. Not published.

Hegel and the State (Hegel und der Staat). 2 vols. München und Berlin 1920.

Atheistic Theology (Atheistische Theologie). K.S.

A Prolegomenon to German Idealistic Philosophy (Das älteste Systemprogramm des deutschen Idealismus. "Schellingianum"). Sitzungsberichte der Heidelberger Akademie der Wissenschaften; philosophisch-historische Klasse, 1917. K.S.

Judaism and Germanism (Judentum und Deutschtum. Bemerkungen zu der Hermann Cohenschen Schrift). K.S., under the title "Über das jüdische Volkstum."

People's School and State School (Volksschule und Reichsschule). K.S.

Oekumene (Ökumene. Zur Geschichte der geschichtlichen Welt). Not published.

It Is Time (Zeit ists. Gedanken über das jüdische Bildungsproblem des Augenblicks). Berlin-München 1917. 2nd ed., 1918. K.S.

"Germ Cell" of the Star of Redemption (Urzelle des Stern der Erlösung). K.S.

Star of Redemption (Der Stern der Erlösung). Frankfort on the Main 1921. 2nd ed., 1930.

On Education (Bildung und kein Ende). Frankfort on the Main 1920. K.S.

Grace after Meals (Tischdank). Jüdische Bücherei, vol. XXII. Berlin 1920.

A New Approach to the Study of Jewish Sources (Neues Lernen). Almanach des Schocken Verlags auf das Jahr 5695. Berlin 1934. K.S.

A Treatise on Healthy and Unhealthy Thinking (Das Büchlein vom gesunden und kranken Menschenverstand). A section published for the first time in this volume.

Home Service for Sabbath and Holidays. Kaddish Derabbanan. (Häusliche Feier, Lernkaddisch.) In "Gabe Herrn Rabbiner Dr. Nobel zum 50. Geburtstag dargebracht." Frankfort on the Main 1921.

Friday Evening Service (Der Freitagabend). Not published.

Judah ha-Levi (or, Sixty Hymns and Poems of Judah ha-Levi, in German) (Sechzig Hymnen und Gedichte des Jehuda Halevi. Deutsch. Mit einem Nachwort und mit Anmerkungen). Konstanz 1924. 2nd ed., "Jehuda Halevi 92 Hymnen und Gedichte." Berlin 1927. The Epilogue, in K.S.

Sermonic Judaism (Ein Rabbinerbuch). Der Jude, Vol. VII. 1923. K.S.

Apologetic Thinking (Apologetisches Denken). Der Jude, Vol. VII. 1923. K.S.

The Builders (Die Bauleute). Der Jude, Vol. VIII. 1924. As a pamphlet, Berlin 1925. K.S.

Introduction to the Collected Jewish Writings of Hermann Cohen (Einleitung zu Hermann Cohens jüdischen Schriften). Berlin 1924, Vol. I. pp. XII ff. K.S.

On the Lehrhaus (Das Freie Jüdische Lehrhaus). K.S.

The New Thinking (Das neue Denken. Einige nachträgliche Bemerkungen zum Stern der Erlösung). Der Morgen, Vol. I. February 1925. K.S.

On Classical and Modern Hebrew (Neuhebräisch?) Der Morgen, Vol. II. April 1926. K.S.

Translation of the Bible (Die Schrift. Zu verdeutschen unternommen von Martin Buber gemeinsam mit F. R.). Berlin 1925-1929.

Martin Buber. In "Jüdisches Lexikon," Vol. I. Berlin 1927.

Scripture and the Spoken Word (Die Schrift und das Wort). Die Kreatur, Vol. I. Berlin 1926. K.S.; S.V.

Scripture and Luther's Translation (Die Schrift und Luther). Berlin 1926. K.S.; S.V.

Collected Essays in Religion and Philosophy (Zweistromland). Berlin 1926.

Anniversary Volume for Martin Buber's 50 Birthday (Aus unbekannten Schriften). Edited by F. R. Berlin 1928.

A Passage from Buber's Doctor's Thesis (Aus Bubers Dissertation). In "Aus unbekannten Schriften."

The Secret of Form in the Biblical Tales (Das Formgeheimnis der biblischen Erzählungen). Kunstwart, February 1928. K.S.;S.V.

Reviews of Recorded Music (Der Konzertsaal auf der Schallplatte). Nine articles in the *Kasseler Tageblatt,* starting May 13, 1928. K.S.

Review of the First Volume of the Encyclopaedia Judaica (Zum ersten Band der Encyclopaedia Judaica. Mit einer Anmerkung über jüdische Bibelwissenschaft). Der Morgen, Vol. IV. August 1928. K.S.

Review of the Second Volume of the Encyclopaedia Judaica (Zum zweiten Band der Encyclopaedia Judaica. Mit einer Anmerkung über Anthropomorphismus). Der Morgen, Vol. IV. December 1928. K.S.

The Significance of the Bible in World History (Weltgeschicht-

liche Bedeutung der Bibel). Encyclopaedia Judaica, Vol.
IV. Berlin 1929. K.S.
Switching Fronts (Vertauschte Fronten). Der Morgen, Vol. VI.
1930. K.S.
The Eternal ("Der Ewige." Mendelssohn und der Gottesname).
Gedenkbuch für Moses Mendelssohn. Berlin 1929. K.S.; S.V.
Prologue to a Moses Mendelssohn Festival (Vorspruch zu einer
Mendelssohnfeier). Der Morgen, Vol. V. 1929. K.S.
Review of the Third and Fourth Volumes of the Encyclopaedia
Judaica (Zum dritten und vierten Band der Encyclopaedia
Judaica). Der Morgen, Vol. V. December 1929. K.S.

Understanding the Sick and the Healthy: A View of World, Man,
and God [English translation from the manuscript of Das
Büchlein vom gesunden und kranken Menschenverstand].
Edited with an introduction by N. N. Glatzer. New York
1953.
On Jewish Learning [English translation of the three epistles,
Zeit ist's, Bildung und kein Ende, Die Bauleute, and addi-
tional material]. Edited by N. N. Glatzer. New York 1955.
Der Stern der Erlösung [Third edition, prepared by Edith
Scheinmann-Rosenzweig]. Heidelberg 1954.
Naharayim [Selected essays in a Hebrew translation by Jehoshua
Amir; introduction by Sh. H. Bergmann]. Jerusalem 1960.

REFERENCES

First Part: The Life

References to the numerous passages from the printed volume of Rosenzweig's letters (Briefe, Berlin 1935) are omitted; the reader can find the original text under the date of the particular letter. This list provides references to letters quoted without a date and to material outside the letters and outside the diaries of Rosenzweig which are published here for the first time.

p. 23 One day: Franz Rosenzweig—Buch des Gedenkens, Berlin 1930, p. 40

23 During our conversation: Briefe, p. 71

25 New Year's and Atonement Day: Information given by F. R.'s mother to the editor

29 I had the surprise: Kleinere Schriften, pp. 291 f.

29 From a notebook: *Ibid.*, p. 337

33 A nation: Kleinere Schriften, pp. 27 f.

57 What concern of mine: From the editor's collection

88 Nobel made: Briefe, p. 448

89 I'll never forget: Franz Rosenzweig—Buch des Gedenkens, pp. 41 f.

92 Letter to Ilse Hahn: Almanach des Schocken Verlags auf das Jahr 5698, pp. 79 f.

93 At the end: Briefe, p. 456

94 Letter to Meinecke: Original in the possession of Edith Rosenzweig-Scheinmann

100 Letter to G. Scholem: Original in the possession of Prof. Scholem

105 We reached Heppenheim: Briefe, p. 461 f.

108 Koch tells: Der Morgen, V (1930), pp. 571 ff.

113 Speaking to: From the editor's collection

114 Speaking to: From the editor's collection

115 Our lodgings: Briefe, p. 435

115 For the second: Briefe, p. 438

117 By August: Information given by Dr. Richard Tuteur

119 Joseph Prager: Franz Rosenzweig—Buch des Gedenkens, p. 42

121 To Joseph Prager: Briefe, p. 447

122 To Margarete Susman: Briefe, p. 513

123 At the end: From Dr. Tuteur's diary

125 To Martin Buber: Original in the possession of Prof. Buber

132 Richard Koch: Der Morgen, V (1930), p. 577

144 But the Jewish book: Kleinere Schriften, p. 391

149 Buber relates: Die Schrift und ihre Verdeutschung, Berlin 1936, pp. 318 ff.

160 Subject of Goethe: From the editor's collection

163 The sufferer: Judah ha-Levi, p. 187

166 To Julius Guttmann: From the editor's collection

168 In these reviews: Kleinere Schriften, p. 534

169 When I ask: Ibid., p. 537

171 On that day: From Dr. Tuteur's diary

174 And now it comes: Briefe, p. 633.

Second Part: The Thought

Passages and sections from the following writings by Rosenzweig appear in translation (the numerals refer to the pages in the present volume):

LIST OF PERSONS

(Relatives, friends, acquaintances, mentioned in the biographical part of the book. The bracketed information pertains to the time after Rosenzweig's death)

Agnon, S. Y., Hebrew novelist and short story writer [Jerusalem]

Alsberg, Adele, *see* Rosenzweig, Adele

Alsberg, Amschel, 1833-1914, maternal grandfather

Badt, Dr. Hermann, early friend; later ministerial director in Berlin [died in 1945, in Israel]

Baeck, Dr. Leo, theologian; rabbi in Berlin [died in 1956, in London, England]

Breuer, Dr. Isaac, lawyer and novelist, spokesman of orthodox separatist Judaism [died in 1946, in Israel]

Brod, Dr. Max, novelist in Prague [Tel Aviv]

Buber Dr. Martin, Jewish philosopher; later professor at the University of Frankfort [professor emeritus, Hebrew University, Jerusalem]

Cohen, Dr. Hermann, 1842-1918, professor of philosophy at the University in Marburg; later professor at the Hochschule für die Wissenschaft des Judentums in Berlin

Cohn, Dr. Jonas, professor of philosophy at the University in Freiburg [died]

Dienemann, Dr. Max, rabbi in Offenbach, Germany [died in 1939, in Tel Aviv]

Dumont, Louise, German actress [died in 1931]

Ehrenberg, Dr. Hans, cousin, Christian theologian; later professor of philosophy at the University in Heidelberg [died in 1958]

Ehrenberg, Julie, 1827-1922, grand aunt

Ehrenberg, Dr. Richard, 1857-1921, professor of economics, University of Rostock, Germany; uncle

Ehrenberg, Dr. Rudolf, cousin, physiologist and Christian theological writer; later professor at the University in Göttingen, Germany [Göttingen]

374

Ehrenberg, Samuel Meir, 1773-1853, great-grand uncle

Ehrenberg, Dr. Victor, cousin, historian; later professor of history at the Universities in Frankfort and Prague [reader in ancient history, University of London]

Frank, Gertrud, *see* Oppenheim, Gertrud

Fritzsche, Dr. Robert Arnold, librarian in Giessen, Germany [died in 1939]

Fromm, Dr. Erich, young scholar in Frankfort [psychoanalyst in New York]

Glatzer, Dr. Nahum N., lecturer at the Lehrhaus, later at the University in Frankfort [professor of Jewish history, Brandeis University]

Goitein, Dr. Fritz Shlomoh D., young semitist in Frankfort [professor of Semitics, Hebrew University, Jerusalem]

Goldner, Dr. Martin, physician; secretary of the Lehrhaus [professor, State University of New York]

Guttmann, Dr. Julius, professor of Jewish philosophy at the Hochschule in Berlin [professor, Hebrew University, Jerusalem; died in 1950]

Hahn, Edith, *see* Rosenzweig, Edith

Hahn, Ilse, sister-in-law [Jerusalem]

Hahn, Rudolf, jurist, father-in-law [died in 1932]

Hallo, Dr. Rudolf, egyptologist; successor of F. R. in the Lehrhaus leadership [died in 1933]

Jacob, Dr. Benno, rabbi in Dortmund, Germany [died in 1945, in London, England]

Kähler, Siegfried, student of Professor Meinecke; later professor of history at the University in Breslau [Göttingen, Germany]

Koch, Dr. Richard, physician and professor of history of medicine at the University in Frankfort [died in 1949 in the Caucasus]

Mayer, Dr. Eugen, Jewish community administrator in Frankfort [editor in Jerusalem]

Meinecke, Dr. Friedrich, professor of history at the University in Freiburg [Berlin]

Mühlhausen, August, Germanic scholar [died]

Nobel, Dr. Nehemiah A., 1871-1922, rabbi in Frankfort

Oppenheim, Gertrud, nee Frank, cousin and early friend [Johannesburg, S.A.]

Prager, Dr. Joseph, early friend; later neurologist [Haifa, Israel]

Rickert, Dr. Heinrich, professor of philosophy at the University in Freiburg, later in Heidelberg [died in 1936]

Rosenheim, Jacob, leader of the orthodox separatist Jewry in Germany [Tel Aviv]

Rosenstock-Huessy, Dr. Eugen, early friend, later professor of law and sociology at the Universities in Leipzig and Breslau [professor of social philosophy, Dartmouth College]

Rosenstock-Huessy, Margrit, early friend; wife of Eugen Rosenstock [died in 1959]

Rosenzweig, Adam, 1826-1908, grand uncle

Rosenzweig, Adele, nee Alsberg, 1867-1933, mother

Rosenzweig, Edith, née Hahn, wife [Mrs. Scheinmann, Berlin]

Rosenzweig, Georg, 1857-1918, father

Rosenzweig, Rafael, son [farmer and educator in Israel]

Rothschild, Henry, merchant, landlord in Frankfort [died]

Rovina, Hannah, actress [Habimah, Tel Aviv]

Schocken, Salman, industrialist and publisher [Jerusalem and New York; died in 1959]

Scholem, Dr. Gershom Gerhard, Jewish scholar [professor of Jewish mysticism, Hebrew University, Jerusalem]

Simon, Dr. Ernst, historian and educator; lecturer at the Lehrhaus [professor of education, Hebrew University, Jerusalem]

Stahl, Dr. Rudolf, lawyer; executive secretary of the Lehrhaus [New York]

Strauss, Dr. Eduard, chemist; co-director and lecturer at the Lehrhaus [died in 1952, in New York]

Susman, Margarete von Bendemann, writer, [Zurich, Switzerland]

Trüb, Dr. Hans, psychiatrist in Zurich, Switzerland [died in 1949]

Tuteur, Dr. Richard, physician in Frankfort [Denver, Col.]

Weizsäcker, Dr. Victor von, professor of medicine at the University in Heidelberg [Heidelberg]

Wolfskehl, Karl, poet [died in 1948, in New Zealand]

SELECTED BIBLIOGRAPHY

English

Jacob B. Agus, "The Life and Influence of Franz Rosenzweig." *Modern Philosophies of Judaism.* New York, 1941.

––––––, *Guideposts in Modern Judaism.* New York, 1954, pp. 116-120.

Alexander Altmann, "F. R. and Eugen Rosenstock-Huessey: An Introduction to their 'Letters on Judaism and Christianity.'" *The Journal of Religion,* XXIV. Chicago, 1944.

––––––, "Theology in Twentieth-Century German Jewry," *Year Book I,* Leo Baeck Institute. London, 1956, pp. 205-208.

––––––, "F. R. on History." *Between East and West.* London, 1958.

Leo Baeck, "Types of Jewish Self-Understanding." *Judaism,* IX. 2. New York, 1960 [English translation of "F. R." in *Von Moses Mendelssohn zu F. R.*]

S. H. Bergman, "F. R.: Beyond Liberalism and Orthodoxy." *Faith and Reason.* Edited by A. Jospe. Washington, 1961.

Bertha Badt-Strauss, "F. R. and Jewish Religious Usage." *Reconstructionist,* VII. New York, 1942.

Samuel S. Cohon, "The Existentialist Trend in Theology." *Yearbook LXIII,* The Central Conference of American Rabbis. Cincinnati, 1953.

Israel Efros, "Rosenzweig's Star of Redemption." *Jewish Quarterly Review,* XXVII. Philadelphia, 1936.

Dorothy M. Emmet, "The Letters of F. R. and Eugen Rosenstock-Huessy." *The Journal of Religion,* XXV. Chicago, 1945.

Emil L. Fackenheim, "F. R.: His Life and Thought" (A Review). *Judaism,* II. New York, 1953.

––––––, "On Jewish Learning" (A Review), *Judaism,* V. New York, 1956.

Nahum N. Glatzer, "F. R." *Yivo Annual of Jewish Social Science*, I. New York, 1946.

————, "F. R.: The Story of a Conversion." *Judaism*, I. New York, 1952.

————, "F. R.: Toward a New Jewish Learning." *Commentary*, XIII. New York, 1952.

————, "F. R.: Discovery of the East European Jews." *Commentary*, XV. New York, 1953.

————, "Theory and Practice: A Note on F. R." *Journal*, Central Conference of American Rabbis, XI. New York, 1955.

————, "The Frankfort Lehrhaus." *Year Book I*, Leo Baeck Institute. London, 1956.

————, "F. R." Modern Jewish Thinkers. Washington, 1961.

————, "F. R. in his Student Years." *Paul Lazarus Memorial Volume*. Haifa, 1961.

Will Herberg, "Rosenzweig's Judaism of Personal Existence." *Commentary*, X. New York, 1950.

Daniel L. Leifer, "Buber and Rosenzweig: Two Types of Revelation." *Mosaic*. Harvard-Radcliffe Hillel Societies. II, 1. Cambridge, Mass., 1961.

Ludwig Lewisohn, "God's Law and Man's Need" (A Review). *Herald Tribune Book Review* (March 8). New York, 1953.

————, "Guide and Example for Our Times" (A Review). *Congress Weekly* (March 9). New York, 1953.

A. Lichtigfeld, "F. R." *Philosophy and Revelation*. London, 1937.

Hans Liebeschütz, "Jewish Thought in Its German Background" *Year Book I*, Leo Baeck Institute. London, 1956, pp. 212-236.

Karl Löwith, "M. Heidegger and F. R. or Temporality and Eternity." *Philosophy and Phenomenological Research*, III. Buffalo, 1942.

Ignaz Maybaum, "F. R.'s Life and Work." *The Chief Rabbi's Festival Volume*. London, 1944.

Eugen Mayer, "F. R.'s Legacy" (A Review). *The Jerusalem Post* (December 10). Jerusalem, 1954.

Kenneth D. Miller, "Faith of a Jew" (A Review). *Saturday Review* (February 21). New York, 1953.

Reinhold Niebuhr, "Rosenzweig's Message" (A Review). *Commentary*, XV. New York, 1953.

Jakob J. Petuchowski, "The Concept of Revelation in Reform Judaism." *Yearbook LXIX*, Central Conference of American Rabbis. Cincinnati, 1959.

Joachim Prinz, "Example of a Human Life" (A Review). *The Jewish News* (May 1). Newark, 1953.

S. Rappaport, "The Legacy of German Jewry" *Jewish Affairs* I. Johannesburg, 1946.

Harold V. Ribalov, "A German Jewish Leader" (A Review). *Saturday Review* (March 6). New York, 1954.

Philip Rieff, "Understanding the Sick and the Healthy" (A Review). *The Journal of Religion*, XXXV. Chicago, 1955.

Joseph Rivlin, "F. R.: A Portrait." *Jewish Heritage*, I. Washington, 1958.

Richard L. Rubenstein, "F. R. on Jewish Education and Jewish Law" (A Review). *The Reconstructionist*, XXII. New York, 1956.

Howard M. Sachar, *The Course of Modern Jewish History*, Cleveland-New York, 1958, pp. 413ff.

Steven S. Schwarzschild, "F. R. and Existentialism." *Yearbook LXII*, The Central Conference of American Rabbis. Cincinnati, 1952.

————, "R. on Judaism and Christianity." *Conservative Judaism*, XI. New York, 1956.

————, *F. R. (1886-1929)*, *Guide of Reversioners*. Makers of Modern Jewish History, No. 3. Hillel Foundation. London, s.a. [1960].

David W. Silverman, "Understanding the Sick and the Healthy" (A Review). *Judaism*, IV. New York, 1955.

Herbert Stroop, "F. R.: His Life and Thought" (A Review). *The Baptist Leader*. Philadelphia, 1953.

Jacob Taubes, "The Issue Between Judaism and Christianity." *Commentary*, XVI. New York, 1953.

Hebrew and Yiddish

Shmuel Hugo Bergman, "R. ve-sifro kokhav ha-geulah." *Hogey ha-dor*. Tel Aviv, 1935.

――――, "Hayahadut be-mikhtavav shel F. R." *Keneset* II. Jerusalem, 1932.

――――, "Mada maamin." *Moznayim*. Tel Aviv, 1944.

――――, "Hitgalut, tefilah u-geulah be-mishnato shel F. R." *Al F. R.* (*Diyyune Beth Hillel*). Jerusalem, 1956.

――――, "Sefer bilti yadua shel F. R." *Moznayim* III. Tel Aviv, 1956.

Simon Bernstein, "Ha-hozeh mi-Frankfurt." *Sefer ha-Shanah liyhudey Amerika,* New York, 1938.

Jacob Fleischmann, "Shene ha-netzahim." *Iyyun,* V. Jerusalem, 1954.

――――, "F. R. kemevaker ha-tziyonut." *Al F. R.* (*Diyyune Beth Hillel*). Jerusalem, 1956.

Nahum N. Glatzer, "F. R., zain leben un zaine idees." *Yivo Library.* New York, 1945.

――――, "F. R. ishiyuto ve-torato," *Hatekufah*, XXX-XXXI. New York, 1946.

――――, "Ha-hinukh ha-yotzer ve-hamada ha-maamin shel F. R." *Sefer ha-Shanah liyhudey Amerika,* VIII-IX. New York, 1946.

――――, "Shnato ha-aharonah shel F. R." *Schocken Jubilee Volume.* Tel Aviv, 1952.

――――, "Haleshonot . . . be-mishnato shel R." *Yuval Shay.* Ramat Gan, 1958.

――――, "F. R." *Hokhmat Yisrael be-maarav Europa.* New York, 1958.

――――, *F. R.: Hayyav u-massav.* Tel Aviv, 1959.

Yitzhak Julius Guttmann, *Ha-filosofia shel ha-yahadut.* Jerusalem, 1951, pp. 329-355.

Yitzhak Heinemann, "F. R.," *Taame ha-Mitzvot* II, 7. Jerusalem, 1956.

Nathan Rothenstreich, *Ha-mahshavah ha-yehudit ba-et ha-hadashah.* Tel Aviv, 1951. II, 164-251.

――――, "Basis ha-filosofia shel F. R." *Al F. R.* (*Diyyune Beth Hillel*). Jerusalem, 1956.

Gershom Scholem, *F. R. ve-sifro kokhav ha-geulah.* Jerusalem, 1930.

Yitzhak Shenhar, "Demut ehad." *Am Vasefer.* Tel Aviv, 1957.

Ernst Simon, "Mekomo shel F. R. ba-hinukh ha-yehudi." *Al F. R.* (*Diyyune Beth Hillel*). Jerusalem, 1956.

German, Dutch, Italian, and French

Franz Rosenzweig, eine Gedenkschrift. Frankfurt a.M., 1930. [Collection of memorial articles, bibliography, etc.].

Franz Rosenzweig, ein Buch des Gedenkens. Berlin, 1930. [Collection of memorial articles].

"Franz Rosenzweig zum 70. Geburtstage." *Mitteilungsblatt,* Tel Aviv, December, 1956.

Leo Baeck, "F. R." *Wege im Judentum.* Berlin, 1933.

————, "F. R." *Von Moses Mendelssohn zu F. R.* Stuttgart, 1958.

Schalom Ben-Chorin, "*F. R. als Erzieher.*" *Judaica,* XI. Zürich, 1955.

S. H. Bergmann, "F. R." *La Rassegna Mensile di Israel,* XVI, 3-4. Rome, 1950.

Martin Buber, "F. R." *Kampf um Israel.* Berlin, 1933.

Joseph Carlebach, "Die religionsphilosophische Stellung F. R.'s." *Jeschurun,* XVII. Berlin, 1930.

Hans Ehrenberg, "Neue Philosophie." *Frankfurter Zeitung,* December 29, 1922.

Else Freund, *Die Philosophie F. R.'s. Ein Beitrag zur Analyse seines Werkes: "Der Stern der Erlösung."* [Dissertation]. Breslau, 1933.

————, *Die Existenzphilosophie F. R.'s.* Berlin, 1933. [A second, revised, edition, appeared in Hamburg, 1959].

Nahum N. Glatzer, "F. R., Religionsphilosoph." *Lebensbilder aus Kurhessen und Waldeck,* VI. Marburg, 1958.

Martin G. Goldner, "F. R. in seiner Krankheit." *Bulletin,* No. 4, Leo Baeck Institute, Tel Aviv, 1958.

Hermann Levin Goldschmidt, *Das Vermächtnis des deutschen Judentums.* Frankfurt a.M., 1957, pp. 104-112; 125-127.

Otto Gruendler, "Eine jüdische Offenbarungsphilosophie." *Hochland,* XIX. Munich, 1922.

M. Grünewald, "Wege zu einer jüdischen Theologie." *Frankfurter Jüdisches Gemeindeblatt,* September, 1933.

Julius Guttmann, "F. R." *Korrespondenzblatt der Akademie für die Wissenschaft des Judentums,* X. Berlin, 1929.

Richard Koch, "F. R. und seine Krankheit." *Der Morgen,* V. Berlin, 1930.

————, "Das Freie Jüdische Lehrhaus." *Der Jude,* VII. Berlin, 1933.

Fritz Kuiper, "F. R." *Nederlands Theologisch Tijdschrift*, XII. Wageningen, 1957.

Hans Lamm, "F. R.'s Leben und Werk." *Allgemeine Zeitung der Juden Deutschlands*, XIV (December 18) Duesseldorf, 1959.

Eugen Mayer, "Zehn Briefe F. R.'s" *Bulletin*, No. 9, Leo Baeck Institute. Tel Aviv, 1960.

K. H. Miskotte, "F. R." *Het Wezen der joodsche Religie*. Amsterdam, 1932.

Claus Götz Müller, "F. R. und das Christentum." *Die Zeitwende*, XXII. Hamburg, 1951.

André Neher, *Une approche théologique et sociologique de la relation judéo-chrétienne: le dialogue Franz Rosenzweig-Eugen Rosenstock*. Cahiers de l'Institute de Science économique appliquée. Paris, 1959.

Jacob Rosenheim, "F. R. und die Orthodoxie." *Ohale Yaakov*, Frankfurt a.M., 1930.

Eugen Rosenstock-Huessy, "Rueckblick auf die Kreatur." *Deutsche Beitrage*, Chicago, 1946.

Arie Sborovitz, "Offenbarung und Offenbarungsreligion in F. R.'s Stern der Erlösung." Jerusalem, 1942.

Gerhard Scholem, "Der Stern der Erlösung," *Bayerische Israelitische Gemeindezeitung*, Munich, 1931, No. 11, pp. 167-169.

Hans-Joachim Schoeps, "F. R. und seine Stellung zum jüdischen Gesetz." *Jüdisches Gemeindeblatt für die britische Zone*, II. June 11, 1947.

Ernst Simon, "R. und das jüdische Bildungsproblem." *Korrespondenzblatt der Akademie für die Wissenschaft des Judentums*, XI. Berlin, 1930.

————, "F. R." *Jüdische Rundschau* (January 17), Marburg, 1930.

Eduard Strauss, "F. R.: Der Denker; das Werk; die Briefe." *Aufsätze und Anmerkungen*. New York, 1946.

Margarete Susman, "F. R." *Der Morgen*, V. Berlin, 1930.

————, "F. R." *Gestalten und Kreise*. Stuttgart-Konstanz, 1954.

Karl Thieme, "F. R.: Zum Gespräch zwischen Judenheit und Christentum." *Hochland*. Munich, 1957.

Victor von Weizsäcker, "F. R." *Begegnungen und Entscheidungen*. Stuttgart, 1949.

INDEX

An asterisk after a page numeral indicates a letter of F.R. to the person listed. F.R. in parentheses indicates a reference to the personal life or to the writings of Rosenzweig.

Goethe, xxxvi, 3, 5, 7, 13, 16, 20, 44-45, 50, 59, 62, 65, 96, 103, 107, 117, 123, 126, 128, 160, 187, 196, 208, 262, 343
Goitein, F.S.D., 121
Goldner, Martin, 242
Gospel of John, 345, 347
Gothic Bible, 267
Grace after Meals (F.R.), 93, 100
Graetz, Heinrich, 115, 211
Grammatical thinking, 200
Greek, Greek culture, xvi, 7, 63, 142, 147-148, 161, 194-195, 252, 266, 270, 272, 343, 359
Grimm's *German Dictionary*, 159
Guttmann, Julius, xxvii, 166*

Haas, Ludwig, 76-77
Habakkuk, 322
Habimah, 170
Hadrian, 353
Haeckel, Ernst, 4
Hahn, Edith, see Rosenzweig, Edith
Hahn, Ilse, 92
Hain (Riesengebirge), 17
Halakhah, see Jewish Law
Hallo, Rudolf, 93, 100, 105*, 112*, 117-118, 124*, 128*, 131
Happiness, 46, 67, 82-83, 114
Harnack, Adolf von, 8, 278
Hasidism, hasidic, 75, 105, 128, 235
Haskalah, 263, 266
Havdalah, 314, 357
Heathen, see Pagan
Hebrew language, xxxii, 40-41, 54, 62, 90, 93, 101-102, 116, 118, 134, 146, 162, 166, 251, 258, 263-271, 297-299, 302
Heder, 75-78
Hegel, G.W.F., xi, xiii, xv, xvi, xxxiv, 17, 20-21, 31, 81, 93, 184-185, 189, 262
Hegel and the State (Hegel und der Staat; F.R.), x, 21-23, 33, 93-94, 96, 129, 165
Heidegger, Martin, xxvi, 166
Heidelberg, 78, 99, 105, 146; H. Academy of Sciences, 31

La Fère (France), 34
Lamentations, 287
Land of Israel, 294-296, 302, 359
Language, xxvi, 147-148, 160, 165, 253-257, 263-264, 296-299
Latin, 63, 88, 264, 267-268, 270, 272
Lehranstalt für die Wissenschaft des Judentums, 29, 34, 68
Lehrhaus, see Freies Jüdisches Lehrhaus
Leipzig, 25, 27, 80, 111
Lessing, Gotthold Ephraim, 21, 89
Letters (Briefe; F.R.), xxxv
Levetzow, Ulrike von, 117
Lewandowski, Louis, 123
Liberalism, political, 159
Library (F.R.), 119-120
Life, 67, 72-73, 79, 91-92, 114-115, 129, 132, 151, 164, 186-187, 211-213, 307, 331-332
Listening, 308-309, 315-316, 326-327
Living Thoughts of Freud (Waelder), x
Logic (Cohen), 74
Love, xxiii, xiv, xxv, 31, 83, 90, 240, 276, 302, 305, 331, 344, 348-349
Luther, Martin, 56, 101, 152-154, 251, 258-260, 286

Macedonia, Macedonian front, ix, xxii, 47, 49, 65
Magic, 290
Mahomet (Goethe), 13
Mahzor, 61, 251
Maimon, Solomon, 37
Maimonides, 266, 281, 346, 351
Malachi, 287
Manchester movement, 159
Mann, Thomas, 267
Marburg school, 29, 132
Marcion, 153, 274, 278, 345
Marriage, married life, 10, 88, 243, 332
Martyrdom, 240, 353
Mary, Queen, 210
Materialism, 183, 191, 250
Mathematics, 12, 15